YIDDISH THEATRE

THE LITTMAN LIBRARY OF
JEWISH CIVILIZATION

Dedicated to the memory of
LOUIS THOMAS SIDNEY LITTMAN
*who founded the Littman Library for the love of God
and as an act of charity in memory of his father*
JOSEPH AARON LITTMAN
and to the memory of
ROBERT JOSEPH LITTMAN
who continued what his father Louis had begun
יהא זכרם ברוך

'*Get wisdom, get understanding:
Forsake her not and she shall preserve thee*'
PROV. 4:5

*The Littman Library of Jewish Civilization is a registered UK charity
Registered charity no. 1000784*

Yiddish Theatre

◆

New Approaches

◆

Edited by

JOEL BERKOWITZ

London

The Littman Library of Jewish Civilization
in association with Liverpool University Press

The Littman Library of Jewish Civilization
Registered office: 4th floor, 7–10 Chandos Street, London WIG 9DQ

in association with Liverpool University Press
4 Cambridge Street, Liverpool L69 7ZU, UK
www.liverpooluniversitypress.co.uk/littman

Managing Editor: Connie Webber

Distributed in North America by
Oxford University Press Inc., 198 Madison Avenue,
New York, NY 10016, USA

First published 2003
First published in paperback 2008

Catalogue records for this book are available from the
British Library and the Library of Congress

ISBN 978-1-904113-77-5

Publishing co-ordinator: Janet Moth
Copy-editing: Laurien Berkeley
Indexing: Sarah Ereira
Designed by Pete Russell, Faringdon, Oxon.
Typeset by Footnote Graphics, Warminster, Wilts.

Printed and bound in Great Britain by
CPI Group (UK) Ltd., Croydon, CR0 4YY

for
Dov-Ber Kerler

and in memory of
John Klier
1944–2007

Acknowledgements

ɴ

THIS volume, like a theatrical production, has been a joint effort, and different sorts of contributions have helped it come together. The road to publication began with a long telephone conversation with Connie Webber, Managing Editor of the Littman Library, who began by asking tough questions about the project's rationale, and ultimately became its eloquent champion. The book has benefited immeasurably from the hard work and insights of Connie and her staff, and I am particularly grateful to Janet Moth, Laurien Berkeley, and Ludo Craddock for all their assistance.

Earlier versions of the chapters collected in this volume were presented at the first International Workshop on Yiddish Theatre, Drama, and Performance, held at Yarnton Manor in Oxford in July 1999. A substantial subsidy from the European Science Foundation made the workshop possible, and additional funding from the Faculty of Medieval and Modern Languages of the University of Oxford enhanced the conference activities. The publication of this book has been greatly enhanced by a generous Faculty Research Award from the University of Albany.

A standing ovation to the performers and scholars—in addition to the contributors to this volume—who helped make the workshop a success: Dror Abend-David, Jean Baumgarten, Helen Beer, Mendy Cahan, Jeremy Dauber, Jerold Frakes, Ben Furnish, Raphael Goldwasser, Itzik Gottesman, Avraham Greenbaum, Nina Hein, Shifra Lerer, Bernard Mendelovich, Laura Mincer, Edna Nahshon, Yitskhok Niborski, Alyssa Quint, Ronald Robboy, Vassili Schedrin, Joseph Schein, Leah Shlanger, Jutta Strauss, Jeffrey Veidlinger, and Moshe Yassur. Special thanks as well to Brad Sabin Hill for his many helpful suggestions for compiling the bibliography, and to Barbara Henry for her assistance with the transcription of Russian.

The workshop—and therefore this collection—would not have been possible without the vision and initiative of my friend and colleague Dov-Ber Kerler, and would not have been nearly as much fun without his unfailing good humour. This book is dedicated to him.

J.B.

Contents

Note on Transliteration and Orthography   xi

List of Plates   xii

List of Tables   xiii

Introduction: Writing the History of the Yiddish Theatre   I
JOEL BERKOWITZ

I. PURIMSHPIL

1. The 'Low' Culture of the *Purimshpil*   29
AHUVA BELKIN

II. REPERTOIRE

2. Romanticism and the Yiddish Theatre   47
NAHMA SANDROW

3. Jewish Plays on the Russian Stage: St Petersburg,
1905–1917   61
BARBARA HENRY

4. The Text of Goldfaden's *Di kishefmakherin* and the
Operetta Tradition   77
PAOLA BERTOLONE

5. *Shulamis* and *Bar kokhba*: Renewed Jewish Role Models
in Goldfaden and Halkin   87
SETH L. WOLITZ

III. REGIONAL CENTRES

6. Yiddish Theatre in Vienna, 1880–1938   107
BRIGITTE DALINGER

7. Stories in Song: The *Melo-deklamatsyes* of
   Joseph Markovitsh   119
   DAVID MAZOWER

8. From Goldfaden to Goldfaden in Cracow's Jewish
   Theatres   139
   MIROSŁAWA M. BUŁAT

IV. CENSORSHIP

9. 'Exit, Pursued by a Bear': Russian Administrators and
   the Ban on Yiddish Theatre in Imperial Russia   159
   JOHN KLIER

10. The Censorship of Sholem Asch's *Got fun nekome*,
    London, 1946   175
    LEONARD PRAGER

V. CRITICISM

11. The Child Who Wouldn't Grow Up: Yiddish Theatre
    and its Critics   201
    NINA WARNKE

Notes on Contributors   217

Bibliography   221

Index   257

Note on Transliteration and Orthography

Yiddish

The transliteration of Yiddish words into the Latin alphabet generally follows the YIVO system of orthography throughout this book, providing a direct correspondence between Latin letters and the sounds of standard literary Yiddish. The sounds made by the letters in the left-hand column are pronounced as follows:

a	'a' as a 'father'	*oy*	'oy' as in 'boy'
ay	'i' as in 'wine'	*u*	similar to 'oo' in 'book'
e	'e' as in 'bed'	*dzh*	'j' as in 'jury'
ey	'a' as in 'gate'	*kh*	'ch' as in 'Bach' or 'chutzpah'
i	'i' as in 'sit'	*tsh*	'ch' as in 'cheer'
o	'o' as in 'gold'	*zh*	'j' as in the French 'je'

I have made three exceptions to this rule:

1. No attempt has been made to standardize non-standard Yiddish orthography.
2. When Yiddish names or words have a commonly accepted Latin transcription, I have used that: for example, 'Thomashefsky' rather than 'Tomashevski', *chutzpah* rather than *khutspe*.
3. I have tried to strike a balance between consistency of transcription and usefulness to researchers. When I think it more likely that one will find an individual referred to in library catalogues, books, etc. by a specific English spelling, I have followed that: for example, 'Zylbercweig' rather than 'Zilbertsvayg'.

Russian

Russian text throughout this volume is rendered in a modified version of the British system. In proper names that include a 'soft sign' (*myagkii znak*), the soft sign is omitted in transliteration (so Kugel, not Kugel'; Gogol, not Gogol'). For Russian terms, however, such as *pravo zhitel'stva* (residence permit), the soft sign is retained in transliteration. When it comes to transliteration of the names of Yiddish actors who performed in Russia, and titles of Yiddish plays performed in Russia, this book uses Yiddish rather than Slavonic transliteration (hence 'Tsezeyt un tseshpreyt', not 'Tsezeit un tseshpreit').

List of Plates

☙

between pages 118 and 119

1. Seventeenth-century sketch of a *purimshpil*

2. Frontispiece of one of several published texts of Goldfaden's *Di kishefmakherin*

3. Actress Clara Young, darling of theatre critics in St Petersburg in the early 1900s, in a photo taken in the 1920s

4. The theatre critic seating *shund* (popular plays; literally 'trash') on the back of 'Moyshe', the Yiddish audience

5. Actor/manager Jacob P. Adler breast-feeding 'Moyshe' (the Yiddish audience) as his competitors look on in dismay

6. Ludwig Satz and Lilly Feinman in Joseph Markovitsh's *Farshidene glikn* (London, 1913)

7. Maurice Schwartz as Uriel Mazik in Jacob Gordin's *Got, mentsh un tayvl* (Yiddish Art Theatre, New York, 1919)

8. Alexander Stein and Miriam Orleska as Khonen and Leah in the Vilna Troupe's production of Ansky's *Der dibek* (Warsaw, 1920)

9. Egon Brecher, Paul (Benzvi) Baratoff, and Isaac Deutsch, the leading figures behind Vienna's Freie Jüdische Volksbühne (1919–23)

10. Maurice Schwartz as Bobe Yakhne in Goldfaden's *Di kishefmakherin* (Yiddish Art Theatre, New York, 1925)

11. A scene from H. Leivick's *Der goylem* (Lublin, *c.*1925)

12. Marketplace scene in a stylized revival of Goldfaden's *Di kishefmakherin* (Yiddish Art Theatre, New York, 1925)

13. Corpses rising from the dead in the Vilna Troupe's production of I. L. Peretz's *Baynakht afn altn mark* (Warsaw, 1928)

14. Unidentified production at the Jüdische Künstlerspiele or Jüdische Bühne, Vienna, early 1930s

15. Sleeping shepherds in the desert in Goldfaden's *Shulamis* (Varshever Yidisher Kunst Teater, Warsaw, 1938)

16. Postcard advertising Joseph Kessler's production of Lateiner's *Di seyder nakht* (Pavilion Theatre, London, 1928)

17. Zygmunt Turkow in the title role of Sholem Aleykhem's *Tevye der milkhiker*

18. Abish Meisels in his London office, *c.*1945

19. Michal Szwejlich as Hotsmakh in Yankev Rotboym's *A goldfaden kholem* (Warsaw, 1970s)

List of Tables

❧

9.1. Performances of Yiddish theatre groups in the Russian empire (actual and proposed) under the ban of 1883   168

10.1. Applications to the Lord Chamberlain's Office, London, for licences to perform Yiddish plays: alphabetical listing by author   188

10.2. Applications to the Lord Chamberlain's Office, London, for licences to perform Yiddish plays: chronological listing by date of licence   193

Writing the History of the Yiddish Theatre

☙

JOEL BERKOWITZ

A difficult task awaits the future historian [of the Yiddish theatre] not in the sense of determining facts and dates, not in the sense of disentangling the 'apocryphal' elements in the memoirs, but in the sense of figuring out the relationship between the Yiddish stage and Jewish life . . .

NOKHEM BUKHVALD, Teater (1943)

YIDDISH THEATRE: A THUMBNAIL SKETCH

THE very idea of a collection of essays on the Yiddish theatre published by a press devoted to the study of Jewish civilization may strike the reader as something of a novelty. The extent of a non-specialist's knowledge of the Yiddish theatre rarely goes beyond amusing anecdotes, the melodies of a few popular songs, or perhaps distant memories of performances on New York's Lower East Side or in London's East End. That the Yiddish theatre is not only worthy of academic study, but has a long and a complex history that can contribute to our understanding of Jewish civilization, may come as a surprise to many readers. Scholars who study the subject, however—either as the focus of their research or in conjunction with related fields such as Yiddish literature, theatre history, Jewish folklore, or European history—appreciate what a rich story the Yiddish theatre has to tell. This book seeks not only to contribute to the telling of that story from a variety of perspectives, but, in doing so, to make readers aware of some of the methodological possibilities that can be brought to bear on this scholarship.

Every step in the development of the Yiddish theatre over its centuries of existence went hand in hand with broader historical and cultural developments, both within and beyond the Jewish world. Entertainments in Yiddish originated in the Middle Ages, and like the roots of the modern European theatre as a whole, Yiddish performance initially grew out of religious rituals and festivals. The *batkhn*, or wedding jester, enlivened proceedings with his witty, often improvised jokes and songs, though, as the musicologist Abraham Idelsohn notes, 'the field of the *badchonim* [or *batkhonim*, plural of *batkhn*] was not limited to merry-making only. The songs reflected all phases and vicissitudes of Jewish life.'[1] More narrative-driven entertainments were presented on Purim, a holiday celebrating the Jewish victory over enemies in ancient Persia, though the *purimshpil* also contained generous helpings of ad lib performance. Both of these traditions would evolve over the centuries, providing fertile sources of inspiration for professional playwrights, and continuing to exist in limited circles today, particularly in Orthodox or hasidic communities.[2]

While the *purimshpiler* and the *batkhn* helped to establish a largely seasonal or occasional performance tradition in Yiddish culture, the Jewish Enlightenment movement, or Haskalah, which began in Germany in the late eighteenth century, paved the way for a stable, professional Yiddish theatre while inspiring much of its early repertoire. The enlighteners—maskilim, as they were known in Hebrew and Yiddish—used an array of materials in the service of their underlying goal of persuading and aiding the Jewish people to embrace the intellectual and cultural achievements of the secular world. Thus, Moses Mendelssohn (1729–86) and his followers translated the Bible into German, and also set a precedent for later maskilim by publishing polemical essays, popular science articles, chrestomathies (selections of passages for study), satirical novels and poems, and occasionally dramas. While there was no professional venue for presenting these plays, some were intended for amateur production and others for private readings. A number of these works circulated in manuscript, and in a few cases in published form. We may draw a loose analogy between the Haskalah plays and those performed in English universities in the 1520s and 1530s. Both forms represent a movement away from religion-based drama and towards the development of a growing secular tradition. Both tended to follow models from other cultures: the early Tudor

[1] Abraham Z. Idelsohn, *Jewish Music: Its Historical Development* (New York: Henry Holt, 1929; repr. New York: Dover, 1992), 440. For further information on the figure of the *batkhn*, see Y. Lifshits, 'Batkhonim un leytsim bay yidn' [Jewish Wedding Entertainers and Jesters], in Jacob Shatzky (ed.), *Arkhiv far der geshikhte fun yidishn teater un drame* [Archive for the History of Yiddish Theatre and Drama] (New York: YIVO, 1930), 38–74; Ariela Krasney, *Habadhan* [The Wedding Jester] (Ramat Gan: Bar-Ilan University Press, 1998).

[2] The seminal study of the *purimshpil* is Khone Shmeruk's critical anthology *Maḥazot mikra'im beyidish, 1697–1750* [Yiddish Biblical Plays, 1697–1750] (Jerusalem: Israel Academy of Sciences and Humanities, 1979). For an authoritative overview of various forms of Yiddish performance from the Middle Ages to the mid-eighteenth century, see Yitskhok Shiper, *Geshikhte fun yidisher teater-kunst un drame* [The History of Yiddish Theatre Art and Drama], 3 vols. (Warsaw: Kulturlige, 1923–8). For an annotated play text of a contemporary *purimshpil*, see Shifra Epstein, 'Danielshpil' baḥasidut bobov [The 'Daniel' Play of the Bobover Hasidim] (Jerusalem: Magnes Press, 1998).

dramatists drew upon the techniques of Roman comedy, while the maskilim borrowed situations from French and German plays, as Mendelssohn's protégé Aaron Halle Wolfssohn (1754–1835) did when he wrote *Laykhtzin und fremelay* (Frivolity and False Piety, *c*.1794), a Judaized version of Molière's *Tartuffe*.

Wolfssohn proved to be remarkably adept, especially considering that he had no professional framework for developing his playwriting skills. Not all the maskilic dramatists wrote plays as tightly structured as Wolfssohn's, but however tenuous the connection between their dramaturgy and actual stage practice, the ideas they put forward would have a profound effect on the development of the professional Yiddish theatre. The nineteenth century would bring an ever-widening search on the part of Europe's Jews for alternative means of religious and national identification, and thus a greater openness to social practices that had traditionally been treated as anathema. In its assertion that the Jewish people should not only learn from the cultural expression of their non-Jewish neighbours, but also produce secular literature, art, and music of their own, the Haskalah helped to open the door to the possibility of a professional theatre created by and for Yiddish speakers.[3]

There still remained, however, formidable barriers to putting such an idea into practice. With no professional Jewish theatre tradition, who would write and perform the plays? Who would compose and perform the music? Where would such entertainments take place? How would anyone know how to find, produce, and use all the necessary supporting materials—costumes, make-up, sets, and so on? And, just as important, could one actually obtain permission to perform from Jewish communal authorities and municipal or state officials? Records show companies trying to tackle these very issues in the early and mid-nineteenth century. One troupe attempted to stage a Yiddish performance in Warsaw during Purim in the mid-1830s, and later that decade one David Hellin applied to present fifteen performances in Yiddish. Both requests were denied after the local synagogue council appealed to the city's police commissioner. Those who wrote the appeal, which was preserved in municipal archives, asked the commissioner to consider that the performance of such material would be an 'indecent mockery that leads to demoralization and is strictly forbidden by religious laws'.[4] The official ruled that Hellin

---

[3] Important studies of Haskalah drama include Max Erik, *Etyudn tsu der geshikhte fun der haskole* [Studies on the History of the Haskalah] (Minsk: Melukhe-farlag far vayruslendisher Kultur, 1934); Zalmen Reyzen, *Fun mendelson biz mendele* [From Mendelssohn to Mendele] (Warsaw: Farlag Kultur-lige, 1923); and Meir Viner, *Tsu der geshikhte fun der yidisher literature in 19-tn yorhundert* [Towards the History of Yiddish Literature in the Nineteenth Century], 2 vols. (New York: YKUF, 1945), vol. i.

[4] B. Gorin, *Di geshikhte fun idishn teater* [The History of the Yiddish Theatre], 2 vols. (New York: Literarisher Farlag, 1918), i. 133.

would not be given permission to perform unless he gained the approval of the Jewish community.

Despite such resistance, professional performances did take place in Warsaw in 1838:

Warsaw has a theatre where plays of national history are performed in the Judaeo-German dialect. . . . The director of that theatre in Warsaw is Isaac Shoyshpiler (he took that name a couple of years ago). He is also the writer of several unpublished works for the stage in the Judaeo-German dialect. His play *Moses*, in the style of Schiller, is filled with the loftiest ideas.[5]

A newspaper review later that year tells us more about the play and its reception:

It has been several years since the members of the Jewish community in our capital (Warsaw) received government permission to build a theatre where plays are performed in the Hebrew-German dialect . . . That theatre, after countless difficulties, finally opened last Monday (5 November 1838) with a drama in five acts, partly in rhyme, partly in prose, with the title *Moses*. This is the first attempt at drama by a very talented young actor and playwright, Herr Isaac Shertsshpiler of Vienna. He himself performed the title role . . . Everyone agrees that the play contains well-delineated characters, several situations at the highest level of drama, and language that at times recalls the elevated simplicity of biblical style. The play was received with great warmth. The audience called the playwright out three times, and greeted him with unanimous applause.[6]

More information about Isaac Shoyshpiler (Isaac the Actor) eludes us, but these reports provide some tantalizing information. For one thing, the performances took place nowhere near Purim, so even as other companies were trying in vain to stage productions during the Jewish month of Adar, Shoyshpiler's apparently professional company managed to put on their play in a season unconnected with traditional Yiddish performance. What became of the troupe after *Moses*, however, is unclear, as is the issue of whether they had any competition or immediate successors, either in Warsaw or elsewhere.

Most students of the Yiddish theatre have settled on a firmer date, some four decades later, for the birth of the professional Yiddish stage, and have seen Avrom Goldfaden (1840–1908) as its 'father'. While such an epithet implicitly erases the centuries of Yiddish performance tradition that pre-dated Goldfaden, there is no doubt about the pivotal role he played in setting in motion the developments that would establish a lasting, professional

---

[5] *Algemeiner Zeitung des Judentums*, 26 July 1838; quoted in Sholem Perlmuter, *Yidishe dramaturgn un teater-kompozitors* [Yiddish Playwrights and Theatre Composers] (New York: YKUF, 1952), 27.

[6] *Journal de Frankfurt*, 4 Dec. 1838, quoted in Perlmuter, *Yidishe dramaturgn un teatr-kompozitors*, 27–8.

Yiddish theatre. Although the details surrounding his first ventures are less than clear—indeed, Goldfaden himself played no small part in creating the legend of those early performances—we do know that he formed a small company in Jassy, Romania, in 1876, and immediately began writing sketches, vaudevilles, and full-length plays for them.[7]

Many of these early works were clearly in the spirit of the Haskalah, but changing theatrical, social, and political conditions would have a marked impact on the development of Yiddish drama and theatre. After the assassination of Tsar Alexander II and the repressive measures taken by his son Alexander III, Yiddish drama tended to turn away from the battles it had been waging within the Jewish community in order to present a more heroic picture of Jewish life, both ancient and contemporary. This was true of Goldfaden as well as of his fellow playwrights such as Joseph Lateiner (1853–1935) and Moyshe Hurwitz (1844–1910), his main rivals during the infancy of the professional Yiddish theatre. Their troupes competed with each other throughout the Pale of Settlement—the regions of the Russian empire where Jews were allowed to live—and drew enough of an audience to support spin-off companies such as the one led by Goldfaden's brother Naftule.

Such support would not last long, however, for the Jews of eastern Europe had more pressing issues than theatre on their mind. A wave of pogroms threatened the lives and property of Russian Jews in the early 1880s. Migrations of Jews from rural areas to major cities overwhelmed urban Jewish communities, and taxed the efforts of relief organizations. A steady stream of Jews, which soon swelled to a flood, headed for safe havens elsewhere: western Europe, the Americas, South Africa, and Palestine. And wherever Yiddish-speaking Jews travelled, they took their performance traditions with them. Within a mere decade the Yiddish theatre was thriving on New York's Bowery, with companies that failed in that market setting up shop in Philadelphia, Chicago, and other cities. Eventually, a worldwide network of Yiddish theatre would be established. Moscow, Warsaw, and New York were arguably the most important centres, with dozens of other sites of significant activity, from London to Johannesburg to Buenos Aires, and countless additional points between major hubs. The worldwide Yiddish theatre was enriched by a perpetual interchange between local innovations and the international movement of Yiddish theatre personnel, critics, and audiences.

[7] For Goldfaden's own accounts of the early years of his theatrical activity, see 'Goldfadens oytobiografishe materyaln' [Goldfaden's Autobiographical Materials], in Jacob Shatzky (ed.), *Goldfaden-bukh* [Goldfaden Book] (New York: Idisher Teater Muzey, 1926), 40–68, and 'Fun shmendrik biz ben ami' (1907), repr. in Jacob Shatzky (ed.), *Arkhiv far der geshikhte fun yidishn teater un drame*, 265–70.

Because the Yiddish theatre tacitly said to its audiences 'Whither thou goest, I will go', it provides a running commentary on the lives of central and eastern European Jews and their descendants. Everything they experienced was played out, in one way or another, on the stage. Ideological differences within the Jewish community, persecution from without, mass migration across Europe and on to other continents, the quest for a Jewish homeland, the tension between accommodating to changing social conditions and adhering to one's own religious traditions—all the central themes in the modern Jewish experience were dramatized in the Yiddish theatre. Performers brought these issues to life in wine gardens, taverns, homes, salons, and permanent theatre buildings, where audiences flocked for more than mere entertainment. Even when seemingly most escapist, the Yiddish theatre speaks eloquently—if we know how to listen—about what those audiences were experiencing, not just in the auditorium but in other facets of their lives as well.

PRACTICAL AND INTERPRETATIVE CHALLENGES

If the Yiddish theatre has so much to tell us about the Jewish experience, why is so little known about it outside the circle of a handful of specialists? There are many reasons for this, some of them mirroring the history of the Yiddish theatre itself. Yiddish performers and playwrights were often itinerant not just as entertainers seeking out new audiences, but also as Jews fleeing persecution and economic hardship. Many of them made their careers in a variety of countries, and not infrequently in two or more languages. Their movements can be difficult to retrace, their manuscripts difficult or impossible to recover. Countless performers and writers were murdered in ghettos, concentration camps, and gulags—a tragic fact commemorated by the fifth volume of Zalmen Zylbercweig's *Leksikon fun yidishn teater* (Lexicon of the Yiddish Theatre), in which an eerie refrain echoes through the biographies of the nearly 500 artists and scholars whose careers it chronicles: 'murdered by the Nazis', with the occasional variation 'murdered by fascists'.[8] In short, the usual barriers to historical scholarship are magnified in the case of the Yiddish theatre by the violent upheavals of much of its modern existence.

Of course, there are less dramatic obstacles to gathering the materials needed to document theatrical productions of bygone eras. Much has undoubtedly disappeared simply because no one thought it was worth preserving. In the pages that follow Ahuva Belkin (Chapter 1) notes that the

---

[8] Zalmen Zylbercweig, *Leksikon fun yidishn teater*, 6 vols. (New York: Elisheva, 1931–70), vol. v (1967).

purimshpiln dating back to the Middle Ages sometimes proved so controversial that Jews threw the texts on the bonfire. What happened, then, to all the
purimshpil texts—the vast majority—that faced no such threat? Most people
who performed and wrote them undoubtedly never entertained the idea that
these seasonal entertainments might in any sense be historically important.
Traditional Jews look after their canonical texts with great care, and when
such works fall into an irretrievable state of disrepair they are buried with
much the same care as people are: in a *geniza*, a holy repository for 'deceased'
books. Few Jews would have lavished such care on the text of a Yiddish farce
performed in a spirit of drunken revelry; they might have been more inclined
to use the pages of last season's *purimshpil* for wrapping fish.

The specific conditions that gave rise to the Yiddish theatre, then—and
those that all but destroyed it—continue to make themselves felt in concrete
ways to the scholar seeking to undertake historical research. More general
challenges to the writing of theatre history constantly intervene as well. The
same sort of contempt heaped upon the Yiddish theatre by many religious and
community leaders finds parallels in theatrical cultures throughout history
and around the world; the 'anti-theatrical prejudice', as Jonas Barish has
demonstrated, has had a formidable history.[9] Other sorts of prejudice have
led critics to look down their noses at Yiddish drama and performance as
'lowbrow' phenomena not worthy of serious consideration. Such critics have
tended to view Yiddish drama in Manichaean terms, setting up dichotomies
of *kunst* (art) versus *shund* (trash), or 'better' versus 'worse' plays (and, as
Nina Warnke has wryly observed, it was not by chance that the critics called
the plays 'better' rather than 'good'[10]). Here is a typical assessment by the
critic Zishe Kornblith:

For the intelligent person with a more or less developed aesthetic feeling, the great,
huge difference between the creation of a poet and the cobbled-together work of a
shund-writer—even the best of them—is so clear that it stares him in the face. It
emanates from every . . . situation, from every character, and from the entire structure of the plot. To say that there is no sharp line between artistic literature and
shund work is to say that an intelligent person will not see the difference between a
truth and a clumsy lie, that a person with an aesthetic sense will not see the difference between beauty and ugliness.[11]

United States Supreme Court Justice Potter Stewart, declining to define the
term 'pornography', famously but not very helpfully declared, 'I know it
when I see it.' Kornblith, like many of his colleagues among Yiddish critics,

[9] Jonas Barish, *The Anti-Theatrical Prejudice* (Berkeley: University of California Press, 1981).
[10] See p. 211 below.
[11] Z. Kornblith, *Di dramatishe kunst* [The Dramatic Art] (New York: Itshe Biderman, 1928), 150.

suggests that *you* know it when *you* see it—if you are sufficiently intelligent
and cultivated, that is. Fellow critic Nokhem Bukhvald made a more concerted effort to create a taxonomy of *shund*, calling it 'the sort of vulgar
theatrical entertainment that is suited to the taste of a naive, barely cultivated
audience. . . . It includes banal plays with two-dimensional situations and
characters, and both cobbled-together elements of entertainment—songs,
rhymes, jokes, tricks, and freak shows—and moments of coarseness, obscenity,
and pornography.'[12]

   Such views were of course not restricted to Yiddish drama, but since the
Second World War the Yiddish theatre has been a pale shadow of its former
self, and has not lived to enjoy the new appreciation ushered in by the recent
growth in studies of popular culture. The cultural historian Lawrence Levine
neatly sums up what can get lost when aesthetic lines are drawn so rigidly,
and on the basis of such stern value judgements:

Obviously we need to make distinctions within culture as within every other realm
of human endeavor, although I do spend a fair amount of time wondering if by
making those distinctions as rigidly hierarchical as we tend to, we are not limiting
the dimensions of our understanding of culture, which could be furthered by
having a more open and fluid set of divisions more conducive to facilitating truly
complex comparisons we presently lack.[13]

Approaching Yiddish drama very much in the spirit Levine describes, Nahma
Sandrow once made the following attempt to clarify just what constitutes the
popular entertainment the critics denigrated as 'trash':

Shund is the sort of art that most cultures and most people like best. It is not by any
means the sum of the culture. It is art for the masses. It's neither the string quartet
nor the piously preserved folk song, but the commercial, mass-produced jukebox
song. Songs on a jukebox may seem all alike; yet there's always a new one which is
the rage. Jukeboxes used to offer not just music, but a whole spectacle of changing
records and colored lights; that, too, could be called *shund*. Calendar pictures of
puppies, pin-ups, and sad-eyed children are *shund*. So are soap operas, the Grand
Ole Opry, a lot of Broadway shows, *I Love Lucy* and *Hee Haw*, John Wayne cowboy
movies, and Charlton Heston Biblical epics.[14]

When tackling a subject as unabashedly populist as the Yiddish theatre
tended to be, one can hardly do worse than stubbornly cling to aesthetic criteria deriving strictly from Aristotle's *Poetics*; doing so will almost surely blind
us to what made the Yiddish theatre such compelling entertainment to its

   [12] Bukhvald, *Teater* (New York: Farlag-Komitet Teater, 1943), 305.
   [13] Lawrence W. Levine, *Highbrow/Lowbrow: The Emergence of Cultural Hierarchy in America*
(Cambridge, Mass.: Harvard University Press, 1988), 7–8.
   [14] Nahma Sandrow, *Vagabond Stars: A World History of Yiddish Theatre* (Syracuse, NY: Syracuse
University Press, 1999), 110.

legions of audiences around the world. To quote Nahma Sandrow again: although *shund* is 'meant mainly to provide actors with good roles and audiences with laughs and thrills, that does not necessarily mean that it's bad theater. It can have energy, theatricality, flair, flashes of art and wit; in Yiddish theater, as in other popular art forms, what people call *shund* can be very good stuff indeed.'[15]

Even when the critic or historian approaches the material in a spirit of discovery rather than judgementally, considerable obstacles stand in the way of the task of documenting theatrical performances. How to convey the fleeting impressions of a evening in the theatre—the raising of an actor's eyebrow, the colour of a shawl, the tilt of a platform, the stir or languor of an audience—once the performance is over? Nothing like an exact record of such performances can possibly exist, but those of us who want to preserve and better understand the history of the Yiddish theatre have a variety of resources at our disposal. Yet the gathering of such sources as extant play scripts, newspaper reviews and articles, memoirs, programmes, and other evidence is just the beginning. To interpret these materials, the researcher faces daunting challenges—perhaps most obviously, the language barrier. Collectively, the scholars who have contributed to this volume draw upon sources written in Yiddish, Hebrew, Russian, Polish, German, French, and English. We can easily add Spanish, Ukrainian, and Romanian to the list of languages in which commentators have added significantly to our knowledge of Yiddish performances, with further evidence contributed by speakers of Dutch, Portuguese, and other tongues.

As arduous as it may be to ascend this Tower of Babel, even more daunting is the unending task of striving to understand enough of the many strands of knowledge related to the Yiddish theatre to make any sense of it. A well-known figure in Jewish folklore is that of the *goylem* (or *golem*), a clay creature shaped in human form and given life. Were I to be given the power to create a *goylem* and train it to work on the history of Yiddish theatre—and thereby to endow the creature with any relevant background knowledge—I would start with the following: a grounding in the canonical Jewish religious texts, particularly the Torah and Talmud; the ability to read many of the languages named above, particularly Yiddish, Hebrew, Russian, Polish, German, and English; a solid and broad literary education; training in theatre history, dramatic literature, and theatrical theory and criticism; an overall familiarity with Jewish history, as well as with the histories of the countries in which the Yiddish theatre was most active; and musical training, with a focus on opera and operettas, in order to be able to evaluate the substantial musical

---

[15] Ibid. 111.

component of the Yiddish theatre. One could go on to other disciplines that
would add to the theatre historian's intellectual toolbox, but that should give
our clay scholar a running start.

The complexity of the Yiddish theatre's development, combined with the
fact that until now it has been researched by mere mortals, helps to account
for some of the gaps in its historiography up to this point. In order to understand what the essays in this volume contribute to the field—and, just as
important, what remains to be done to tell the full story of the Yiddish
theatre—a survey of central issues in the historical study of the Yiddish
theatre is in order.

YIDDISH THEATRE HISTORIOGRAPHY

Whatever their collective shortcomings as theatre history, one striking theme
runs through many accounts of the Yiddish stage: the writers' fascination with
the very idea of chronicling the Yiddish theatre. One theatregoer describes performances he saw in Odessa as a 10-year-old boy in 1877, just one year after
Goldfaden formed his first company:

> The entrance to the Marienteater was very large. There was also a large courtyard
> there, where the entrance to the gallery was located. The main entrance to the court-
> yard was always packed with people, young and old alike, who were called *teater-
> lyubetilyes* [theatre-lovers]. They used to tell all sorts of stories and legends about the
> Yiddish theatre, the plays, and the actors and actresses.[16]

'All sorts of stories and legends' after a mere year of activity! Yiddish theatre
audiences wasted no time in weaving legends around the actors they idolized.
And Yiddish critics wasted little time in providing a 'history' for the modern
Yiddish theatre that has been based far too often on 'all sorts of stories and
legends'.

The first attempt to write such a history, two decades after Goldfaden
formed his first company, appeared in the 1897 collection *Di idishe bine* (The
Yiddish Stage), which billed itself as a 'jubilee volume' celebrating twenty
years of Yiddish theatre. The first volume of the anthology, compiled by the
New York-based editor Khonen Minikes, contained historical essays, satirical
and autobiographical articles, and other writings about the Yiddish theatre;
the second volume was filled with the lyrics of popular theatre songs. Minikes
claimed an educational purpose for the collection that other intellectual leaders on the Lower East Side would increasingly subscribe to in coming years:

[16] B. Vaynshteyn, 'Di ershte yorn fun yidishn teater in odes un in nyu-york' [The First Years of
the Yiddish Theatre in Odessa and New York], in Shatzky (ed.), *Arkhiv far der geshikhte fun yidishn
teater un drame*, 247.

'The time has finally come for us to regard the Yiddish theatre as an educational force, as the Christians regard their theatres.' Lest readers be distracted by the sheer entertainment value of the contents, Minikes warned them, 'Do not read these articles as you read a story. These are serious articles to which their writers have devoted their time and thought. Every point has been worked out with care, and it is therefore worth while for you to read [them] over and over. Read them! Study them!'[17] Minikes' words may have reminded at least some readers of the rabbis and teachers who exhorted them to pay the same sort of attention when studying Torah.

After a preface by the linguist Alexander Harkavy in praise of the centuries of progress made since the ancient theatre of China and India, and of Greece and Rome, *Di idishe bine* settles into its first and longest article: a sixty-page essay by the playwright Moyshe Zeifert, himself a prolific journalist and novelist, entitled 'The History of the Yiddish Theatre'. Zeifert created a tripartite periodization: (1) Goldfaden and his companies' activities up to the enactment of the ban on Yiddish theatre in Russia in 1883; (2) the first years in New York, leading up to what Zeifert saw as a golden age around 1883–5; and (3) the current period of the early and mid-1890s, which the author perceived as a period of decline.

Zeifert's specific complaints about the condition of American Yiddish theatre are of less concern to us than his approach to the writing of theatre history—an approach that would greatly influence later journalists, critics, and even academic writers. His positivist outlook, exemplified by his uncritical acceptance of prevailing truisms and his division of theatre history into tidy historical periods, has been replicated time and again. Countless critics and historians, for example, have continued to call Goldfaden the father of the Yiddish theatre as if it were a God-given fact rather than a man-made construct, or have accepted wholesale actor Boris Thomashefsky's account of the first professional Yiddish performance in New York City. To question such commonplaces is not necessarily to reject them out of hand, but too many commentators have followed the intellectual short cuts created by their predecessors rather than seeking fresh insights along less well-marked paths.[18] The contributors to this volume have not been afraid to stray from the main road in search of innovative discoveries of their own, sometimes challenging accepted notions head on, at other points refining previously held ideas.

[17] Khonen Y. Minikes, 'Hakdomes hame'asef' [Introduction to the Collection], in id. (ed.), *Di idishe bine* [The Yiddish Stage] (New York: Katzenelenbogen, 1897), unpaginated.
[18] Aaron Seidman offers a lesson in myth-making in his dissection of Boris Thomashefsky's description of the birth of the American Yiddish theatre. See 'The First Performance of Yiddish Theatre in America', *Jewish Social Studies*, 10 (1948), 67–70.

Ever since Zeifert, numerous amateur and professional students of the Yiddish theatre have undertaken the task of documenting some facet of its history—so much so that, quantitatively speaking, it might seem that much of what needs to be said has already been published. Beyond general, popular histories by Bernard Gorin (in Yiddish) and Nahma Sandrow (in English), a wealth of more specific studies can also be found. A great deal of information, however, remains undiscovered, for several reasons. Much of what has been written about the subject has tended to recycle half-truths, unconfirmed anecdotes, misconceptions, and perhaps even outright lies. The result is a kind of modern mythology, many of whose tenets are implicitly or explicitly challenged by the scholars whose work is represented here.

Furthermore, artistic and ideological agendas have driven much of the research on the subject. Soviet writers, for example, viewed the development of Yiddish theatre and drama from the vantage point of their political commitment. Critics and historians such as Yekhezkel Dobrushin, Meir Viner, Nokhem Oyslender, and Uri Finkel produced some of the most penetrating studies of the Yiddish theatre to date, but their ideology sometimes markedly encroaches on their interpretations—at times even leading them to take liberties in creating ostensibly authoritative versions of dramatic texts. Yet even when scholars approach their material from less overtly political positions, they are not necessarily immune to agenda-driven scholarship. David Lifson, for example, whose *Yiddish Theatre in America*[19] has often been treated as a definitive overview, tends to browbeat readers for some 600 pages with the idea that the Yiddish theatre produced nothing of value before the Yiddish Art Theatre emerged in New York in 1918. The merits of that specific troupe aside, Lifson's thesis perpetuates the tyranny of 'high' culture, leading him to overlook the vitality of much of popular Yiddish performance.

Other sorts of agendas colour the writing of theatrical autobiographies. For many chroniclers of the Yiddish theatre, the writing of 'history' has often flowed seamlessly into autobiography: to a considerable extent, the actors and playwrights who formed the first professional companies *were* the history of the modern Yiddish theatre. And indeed, much of what we know—or, more problematically, what we think we know—about the history of the Yiddish theatre comes from reading the many memoirs written by those who worked in Yiddish theatre, as well as tributes written by their sons and daughters. At their worst, like any show business autobiography, such works can be as insufferable as their authors must have been at parties, spewing out reams of self-congratulation and jealous gossip of little interest to the historian except perhaps to reveal the personal alliances and animosities that fuelled

---

[19] New York: Thomas Yoseloff, 1965.

and broke theatrical partnerships. Many of these memoirs, however, provide the invaluable understanding of the insider, and can thus enable the researcher to see into corners of the subject that other commentators could not reach.

It is true that one must use such sources with care, regardless of the language in which they were written. As the theatre historian Thomas Postlewait reminds us:

Though possibly derived from diaries, appointment books, or scrapbooks of press cuttings, theatre autobiographies are often notable more for their well-rehearsed anecdotes than for their accuracy on productions, people, and places. Typically, they are episodic, chatty, and, of course, self-aggrandizing. Their defining character, and often their charm, depends upon the self-serving performance of the autobiographer, a masquerade moved from stage to page. This characteristic trait of playing to the audience is hardly a fault . . . but it does present special problems for the theatre historian and biographer.[20]

Postlewait goes on to elaborate on these 'special problems'—distortions introduced by narrative conventions, rhetorical devices, intended audiences, and so on—but notes that autobiographies 'require interpretation, not just neat dissection into true and false categories'.[21] With these caveats in mind, however, we can still find valuable material in the autobiographies of actors such as Celia (Tsili) Adler, Peysekhke Burshteyn, Avrom Morevski, Bessie Thomashefsky, Boris Thomashefsky, the brothers Jonas and Zygmunt Turkow, Herman Yablokoff, and Boaz Young; the playwrights Osip Dimov, Peretz Hirschbein, and Leon Kobrin; the director Mikhl Weichert; and the composer Joseph Rumshinsky.[22]

[20] Thomas Postlewait, 'Autobiography and Theatre History', in Thomas Postlewait and Bruce A. McConachie (eds.), *Interpreting the Theatrical Past* (Iowa City: University of Iowa Press, 1989), 252.   [21] Ibid. 259.

[22] For actors' memoirs printed in book form in Yiddish, see, *inter alia*, Jacob Adler, *A Life on the Stage*, ed. and trans. Lulla Rosenfeld (New York: Knopf, 1999); Tsili Adler with Yakov Tikman, *Tsili adler dertseylt* [Celia Adler Relates], 2 vols. (New York: Tsili Adler Foundation un Bukh-Komitet, 1959); Peysekhke Burshteyn, *Geshpilt a lebn* [A Life Performed] (Tel Aviv: no publisher given, 1980); Luba Kadison and Joseph Buloff, *On Stage, Off Stage* (Cambridge, Mass.: Harvard University Press, 1992); Ida Kaminska, *My Life, My Theater*, trans. Curt Leviant (New York: Macmillan, 1973); Avrom Morevski, *Ahin un tsurik* [There and Back], 4 vols. (Warsaw: Farlag Yidish Bukh, 1960), trans. and abridged as *There and Back* by Joseph Leftwich (St Louis: Warren H. Green, 1967); Zygmunt Turkow, *Di ibergerisene tkufe* [The Interrupted Era] (Buenos Aires: Tsentral-farband far Poylishe Yidn in Argentine, 1961) and *Teater-zikhroynes fun a shturmisher tsayt* [Theatre Memoirs of a Tempestuous Time] (Buenos Aires: Tsentral-farband far Poylishe Yidn in Argentine, 1956); Bessie Thomashefsky, *Mayn lebns-geshikhte* [My Life Story] (New York: Varhayt, 1916); Boris Thomashefsky, *Mayn lebns-geshikhte* (New York: Trio Press, 1937); Herman Yablokoff, *Arum der velt mit yidish teater* [Around the World with Yiddish Theatre], 2 vols. (New York: no publisher given, 1968–9), trans. and abridged as *Der payats* by Bella Mysell Yablokoff (Silver Spring, Md.: Bartleby Press, 1995); Boaz Young, *Mayn lebn in teater* [My Life in the Theatre] (New York: YKUF, 1950). Playwrights' memoirs include Osip Dimov, *Vos ikh gedenk* [What I Remember], 2 vols. (New York: CYCO, 1943); Khone Gotesfeld, *Vos ikh gedenk fun mayn lebn* [What I Remember

While all of the aforementioned works are available in book form, countless others were serialized in Yiddish newspapers without ever appearing as books. Since anyone working with Yiddish newspapers lacks a database or directory of articles akin to the *New York Times Index*, the main tool for finding such memoirs—and, for that matter, much of what one finds in Yiddish periodicals—is serendipity, an exciting but unreliable instrument for carrying out historical research. One has little way of knowing whether any specific actor's reminiscences were ever serialized, except perhaps by asking colleagues and hoping that in such cases Lady Luck has been kinder to them. The historian Jacob Shatzky has sagely remarked that writing the history of the Yiddish theatre is 'a task that should not be done by an individual. We need to rouse the interest of many individuals.'[23] Perhaps one of the most valuable resources that the small but growing international community of students of Yiddish theatre could collectively assemble is a bibliography or database of the memoirs of those who worked in the theatre that appeared in periodicals but were never published in book form. The same could be said of theatre reviews, which filled countless column inches in Yiddish periodicals around the world, but have rarely been collected in book form.[24]

Creators of Yiddish theatre often led lives at least as dramatic as those of the characters on stage, with economic need, persecution, wars, and the search for new audiences scattering them throughout the Jewish Diaspora—and, for that matter, to Israel as well. The drama—and, for the theatre historian, the historical significance—of their lives and careers have, however, barely been exploited. So far, only a few of these figures have been the subject of biographies, and these works have often contained more anecdote than analysis. Still, readers can benefit from studies of playwrights such as Avrom

from My Life] (New York: Fareynikte Galitsyaner in Amerike, 1960); Peretz Hirschbein, *Mayne kinder-yorn* [My Childhood Years] (Warsaw: Literarishe Bleter, 1932); Leon Kobrin, *Erinerungen fun a yidishn dramaturg* [Recollections of a Yiddish Playwright], 2 vols. (New York: Komitet far Kobrins Shriftn, 1925); and Mikhl Weichert, *Zikhroynes* [Memoirs] (Tel Aviv: Hamenorah, 1960). Autobiographies by other sorts of Yiddish theatre personnel are less plentiful, but note director Alexander Granovsky, *Ot geyt a mentsh* [There Goes a Man], trans. Jacob Mestel (New York: YKUF, 1948), and composer Joseph Rumshinsky's *Klangen fun mayn lebn* [Echoes of My Life] (New York: Itshe Biderman, 1944). Excerpts in English translation from the memoirs of the actors David Kessler, Celia Adler, Herman Yablokoff, and Peysekhke Burshteyn and the composer Sholem Secunda are collected in Joseph C. Landis (ed.), *Memoirs of the Yiddish Stage* (Flushing, NY: Queens College Press, 1984).

[23] Jacob Shatzky, Introduction to id. (ed.), *Arkhiv far der geshikhte fun yidishn teater un drame*, p. v.

[24] Notable exceptions to the dearth of theatre reviews in book form are A. Mukdoyni [Alexander Kapel], *Teater* (New York: A. Mukdoiny Yubiley-Komitet, 1927); Moyshe Nadir, *Mayne hent hobn fargosn dos dozige blut* [My Hands Spilled that Blood] (New York: Farlag Verbe, 1919); Noah Prilutski, *Yidish teater*, 2 vols. (Białystok: A. Albek, 1921); and Mikhl Weichert, *Teater un drame*, 2 vols. (Warsaw: Farlag Yiddish, B. Kletskin, 1922–6).

Goldfaden, Jacob Gordin, and Y. L. Peretz; the writer and performer Moyshe Broderzon; and the actors Jacob P. Adler, David Kessler, Esther-Rokhl Kaminska, Shloyme Mikhoels, Sigmund Mogulesco, and Maurice Schwartz.[25] The lives and careers of a few figures, such as Goldfaden, Gordin, and Mikhoels, have been documented in numerous books and articles, while many other significant personalities have as yet received little or no coverage. Far more attention needs to be paid to the many other individuals who played an important role in the development of the Yiddish theatre, but whose activity has yet to be discussed at any length by biographers or theatre historians.

A similar trend can be found in the historiography of Yiddish theatre companies, where a few troupes have attracted the lion's share of scholarly attention; these include the Yiddish Art Theatre, the Artef (Arbeter Teater

---

[25] Goldfaden has been written about far more than any other Yiddish theatre figure. Major critical and/or biographical studies include Nokhem Oyslender and Uri Finkel, *A. goldfadn: materyaln far a biografye* [A. Goldfaden: Materials towards a Biography] (Minsk: Institut far Vayruslendisher Kultur, 1926); Shatzky (ed.), *Goldfaden-bukh*; and Jacob Shatzky (ed.), *Hundert yor goldfadn* [A Hundred Years of Goldfaden] (New York: YIVO, 1940). Yitskhok Turkow-Grudberg compares the lives and work of the two playwrights in *Goldfaden un gordin* (Tel Aviv: S. Grinhoyz, 1969). Gordin's career is documented at greater length in Kalmen Marmor, *Yankev gordin* [Jacob Gordin] (New York: YKUF, 1953) and Zalmen Zylbercweig, *Di velt fun yankev gordin* [The World of Jacob Gordin] (Tel Aviv: Elisheva, 1964). Of the many studies of Y. L. Peretz, two books are devoted specifically to his theatrical activity: A. Mukdoyni, *Yitskhok leybush perets un dos yidishe teater* [Yitskhok Leybush Peretz and the Yiddish Theatre] (New York: YKUF, 1949) and Khone Shmeruk, *Peretses yiesh-viziye* [Peretz's Vision of Despair] (New York: YIVO, 1971), a critical edition of the writer's apocalyptic symbolist drama *Baynakht afn altn mark* (A Night in the Old Marketplace, 1907). While Polish Yiddish artist Moyshe Broderzon performed and directed as well as wrote, Gilles Rozier's *Moyshe Broderzon: Un écrivain yiddish d'avant-garde* (Saint-Denis: Presses Universitaires de Vincennes, 1999) focuses on his written output as a poet and playwright. The dramatic life and violent death of Soviet Yiddish actor–director Shloyme (or Solomon) Mikhoels have fascinated biographers; see Mikhail Goldenberg, *Zhizn i sudba Solomona Mikhoelsa* [The Life and Fate of Solomon Mikhoels] (Baltimore: Vestnik, 1995); Y. Lyubomirski, *Mikoels* (Moscow: Izdat. Iskusstvo, 1938); Natalia Vovsi-Mikhoels, *Avi shelomo mikhoels* [My Father Shloyme Mikhoels] (Tel Aviv: Hakibbutz Hameuchad, 1982). For biographies of other Yiddish performers, see, *inter alia*, Jack Bernardi, *My Father the Actor* (New York: W. W. Norton, 1971); Dovid Denk, *Shvarts of vays* [Black (or 'Schwartz') on White] (New York: no publisher given, 1963); Jerome Lawrence, *Actor: The Life and Times of Paul Muni* (New York: Putnam, 1974); M. Osherovitsh, *Dovid kesler un muni vayzenfraynd* [David Kessler and Muni Weisenfreund (Paul Muni)] (New York: no publisher given, 1930); Lulla Adler Rosenfeld, *Bright Star of Exile: Jacob Adler and the Yiddish Theatre* (New York: Thomas Y. Crowell, 1977); Joseph Schildkraut, *My Father and I* (New York: Viking, 1959); Yitskhok Turkow-Grudberg, *Di mame ester rokhl* [My Mother, Esther Rokhl]. (Warsaw: Yidish Bukh, 1951); and Zalmen Zylbercweig, *Di velt fun ester-rokhl kaminska* [The World of Esther-Rokhl Kaminska] (Mexico: no publisher given, 1969). The most extensive—though far from exhaustive—collection of biographical sketches of Yiddish theatre personnel is Zylbercweig, *Leksikon fun yidishn teater*, discussed in greater detail below. Sholem Perlmuter, *Yidishe dramaturgn un teater-kompozitors* also contains profiles of fifty-two dramatists and twenty-two composers. Countless additional recollections of the careers of Yiddish performers, often written by the colleagues with whom they worked most closely, are scattered in the pages of Yiddish newspapers.

Farband, or Workers' Theatre Collective), and the Moscow State Yiddish Theatre (Gosudarstvennyi evreiskii teatr, internationally famous under its Russian acronym GOSET).[26] One of the bright spots in recent scholarship is the appearance of well-researched scholarly studies of the latter two troupes: Edna Nahshon's *Yiddish Proletarian Theatre* and Jeffrey Veidlinger's *The Moscow State Yiddish Theater*.[27] One can only hope that such publications represent a trend towards greater coverage of historically important companies, for many others deserve similar treatment.

Complementing the studies of specific ensembles are monographs on theatrical activity in specific cities or even neighbourhoods. Two distinct phases of activity in New York, the early period on the Bowery and the post-First World War era on Second Avenue, are chronicled by Marvin Seiger and Diane Cypkin respectively.[28] Both pull together extensive research on companies, theatre buildings, and repertoire. Most of the research that has been done on the American Yiddish theatre focuses on New York; besides the works already mentioned here, this is true of my own study of American Yiddish Shakespeare productions,[29] and of chapters on Yiddish theatre in Sandrow's *Vagabond Stars* and two classic studies of the Lower East Side, Irving Howe's *World of our Fathers* and Hutchins Hapgood's *Spirit of the Ghetto*.[30] That is not to say that the subject has been exhausted; indeed, all of the areas requiring further research that Seiger identified in his pioneering 1960 study still apply:

[26] In addition to the biographies of Schwartz mentioned above, two other studies profile his company, the Yiddish Art Theatre: A. H. Bialin, *Moris shvarts un der yidisher kunst teater* [Maurice Schwartz and the Yiddish Art Theatre] (New York: Itshe Biderman, 1934) and Lifson, *The Yiddish Theatre in America*. For accounts of the Moscow State Yiddish Theatre, see Moyshe Litvakov, *Finf yor melukhisher idisher kamer-teater* [Five Years of the State Yiddish Chamber Theatre] (Moscow: Farlag Shul un Bukh, 1924); Y. Lyubomirski, *Af di lebnsvegn* [On Life's Journey] (Moscow: Farlag Sovetski Pisatel, 1976); Béatrice Picon-Vallin, *Le Théâtre juif soviétique pendant les années vingt* (Lausanne: La Cité-L'Âge d'Homme, 1973); Yosef Shayn, *Arum moskver yidishn teater* [Around the Moscow Yiddish Theatre] (Paris: Éditions Polyglottes, 1964); and id., 'Yidisher teater in sovetn-farband' [Yiddish Theatre in the Soviet Union], in Itsik Manger, Jonas Turkow, and Moyshe Perenson (eds.), *Yidisher teater in eyrope tsvishn beyde velt-milkhomes: sovetn-farband, mayrev-eyrope, baltishe lender* [Yiddish Theatre in Europe between the World Wars: The Soviet Union, Western Europe, and the Baltic Countries], 2 vols. (New York: Congress for Jewish Culture, 1968–71).
[27] See Edna Nahshon, *Yiddish Proletarian Theatre: The Art and Politics of the Artef 1925–1940* (Westport, Conn.: Greenwood Press, 1998), and Jeffrey Veidlinger, *The Moscow State Yiddish Theater* (Bloomington: Indiana University Press, 2000).
[28] Marvin Seiger, 'A History of the Yiddish Theatre in New York City to 1892', Ph.D. diss., Indiana University, 1960; Diane Cypkin, 'Second Avenue: The Yiddish Broadway', Ph.D. thesis, New York University, 1986.
[29] *Shakespeare on the American Yiddish Stage* (Iowa City: University of Iowa Press, 2002).
[30] Irving Howe, *World of our Fathers* (New York: Harcourt Brace Jovanovich, 1976); Hutchins Hapgood, *The Spirit of the Ghetto* (1902; repr. Cambridge, Mass.: Harvard University Press, 1967).

Much detailed information is still needed concerning such topics as: the Golubok company, Pinkhes Thomashefsky's troupe, the Karp–Silberman troupe, the Mogulesko–Finkel troupe, and the Adler troupe. Individual biographies of the first important stars (Heine, Karp, Silberman, Golubok, etc.) would also be valuable, as would biographies of the first dramatists in New York (Barski, Lateiner, Hurwitz, Weissman, Seiffert, Paley, etc.). There is also a vast area for research concerning the written drama used in production.[31]

Nina Warnke (Chapter 11) examines an additional avenue of investigation in this study, which in a sense builds upon Seiger's close scrutiny of contemporary newspaper reviews and ephemera. Rather than read as received truths the opinions of early twentieth-century critics, Warnke scrutinizes the ideological stances that led them to view Yiddish theatregoers in New York as a pack of unruly children, and in the process sheds light on a critical stance that has had a profound impact on both the history and historiography of the Yiddish stage. As far as other areas of the United States are concerned, Philadelphia and Detroit have received a modicum of scholarly attention, but other local or regional histories would make excellent subjects for monographs.[32] Elsewhere in North and South America writers in Yiddish, French, and Spanish have discussed activity in Canada and South America, though much more needs to be done to provide the full picture of Yiddish performance in the Americas.[33]

Just as New York looms large over American-based studies, Moscow has dominated the attention of scholars writing about the Yiddish theatre in Europe. GOSET in particular has been a darling of critics and historians; its work has been chronicled by eyewitnesses such as Moyshe Litvakov and Joseph Schein, and by later writers such as Béatrice Picon-Vallin and Jeffrey Veidlinger. Mordechai Altshuler, a noted historian of Soviet Jewry, has

[31] Seiger, 'A History of the Yiddish Theatre in New York City to 1892', p. xiii.

[32] For studies of the Yiddish theatre in American cities outside New York, see Moses Freeman, *Fuftsik yor geshikhte fun idishn lebn in filadelfye* [fifty Years of the History of Jewish Life in Philadelphia], 2 vols. (Philadelphia: Kultur, 1934), ii. 189–229; Dovid Ber Tirkel, *Di yugntlekhe bine: geshikhte fun di idish-hebreyishe dramatishe gezelshaftn* [The Juvenile Stage: The History of Yiddish–Hebrew Dramatic Societies] (Philadelphia: Hebrew Literature Society, 1940); and James Miller, *The Detroit Yiddish Theater, 1920 to 1937* (Detroit: Wayne State University Press, 1967).

[33] The Yiddish theatre in Buenos Aires, arguably the most vibrant in the Americas outside New York, has been the subject of several books. See A. Mide, *Epizodn fun yidishn teater* [Episodes from the Yiddish Theatre] (Buenos Aires: Asociación judeo argentina de estúdios históricos, 1954); Bentsion Palepade, *Zikhroynes fun a halbn yorhundert idish teater* [Memoirs of a Half-Century of Yiddish Theatre] (Buenos Aires: no publisher given, 1946); Shmuel Rozhansky, *Gedrukte vort un teater in argentine* [The Printed Word and Theatre in Argentina] (Buenos Aires: no publisher given, 1941); and Nekhemye Tsuker (ed.), *Zeks yor beser idish teater* [Six Years of Better Yiddish Theatre] (Buenos Aires: no publisher given, 1951). On the Yiddish theatre in Montreal, see Jean-Marc Larrue, *Le Théâtre yiddish à Montréal* (Montreal: Éditions Jeu, 1996).

opened up the field by widening the focus to important Soviet centres such as Ukraine and Belarus.[34] The pre-Soviet period of activity in the Russian empire has been chronicled in admirable detail by Nokhem Oyslender,[35] but two of the chapters in this volume examine questions that have tended to be either uncritically reported or completely overlooked by earlier scholars. John Klier, a prolific historian of nineteenth-century Russia, has unearthed archival documentation of the tsarist ban on Yiddish theatre, technically in force from 1883 to 1905 (Chapter 9). Like many other events in the history of the Yiddish theatre, the ban has entered the realm of legend more than fact; students of the Yiddish theatre are aware of its existence, but not of the nuances behind it. Klier establishes exactly when the ban was enforced and lifted, and the departures from official policy both during and after the period of state censure. Far less familiar is the fact that Yiddish plays were often produced in Russian translation in the period between the Russian revolutions. Barbara Henry's documentation of this trend, and of the reception of the plays in Moscow and St Petersburg, opens up a new vista through which to explore the relationship between the Yiddish theatre and neighbouring cultures (Chapter 3).

Other areas of eastern Europe have generally received less extensive coverage than Russia and the Soviet Union, although the early professional theatre in Romania and various phases of the Yiddish theatre in Poland have each been the subject of several studies, a number of these having been produced by Polish theatre historians in recent years.[36] One of these scholars, Mirosława Bułat, gives us a taste of this scholarship with her chapter on Goldfaden

[34] Mordechai Altshuler (ed.), *Hate'atron hayehudi bevrit hamo'atsot* [The Jewish Theatre in the Soviet Union] (Jerusalem: Hebrew University, 1996). See also Anna Gershtein, 'Notes on the Jewish State Theater of Belorussia', *Jews in Eastern Europe*, 27 (1995), 27–42, and Y. Lyubomirski, *Melukhisher yidisher teater in ukrayne* [State Theatre in Ukraine] (Kharkov: Literatur un Kunst, 1931).

[35] N. Oyslender, *Yidisher teater, 1887–1917* [Yiddish Theatre, 1887–1917] (Moscow: Melukhe-farlag, 1940).

[36] On Romania, see *Akhtsik yor yidish teater in rumenye, 1876–1956* [Eighty Years of Yiddish Theatre in Romania, 1876–1956] (Bucharest: no publisher given, 1956); and Yisroel Berkovitsh, *Hundert yor yidish teater in rumenye* [A Hundred Years of Yiddish Theatre in Romania] (Bucharest: Criterion, 1976). For sources on Poland, see, *inter alia*, Manger, Turkow, and Perenson (eds.), *Yidisher teater in eyrope tsvishn beyde velt-milkhomes*, vol. i; Yitskhok Turkow-Grudberg, *Varshe: dos vigele fun yidishn teater* [Warsaw: The Cradle of Yiddish Theatre] (Warsaw: Yidish Bukh, 1956) and id., *Yidish teater in poyln* [Yiddish Theatre in Poland] (Warsaw: Yidish Bukh, 1951). For a concise and informative overview of writings on the Yiddish theatre in Poland, see Michael Steinlauf, 'Sources for the History of Jewish Theatre in Poland', *Gal-Ed: On the History of the Jews in Poland*, 15–16 (1997), 83–103. Recent scholarship includes a special issue of the Polish theatre journal *Pamiętnik Teatralny* devoted to Jewish theatre in Poland to 1939: *Pamiętnik Teatralny*, 41 (1992), with additional material in vol. 44 (1995), 255–303; and Jan Michalik and Eugenia Prokop-Janiec (eds.), *Teatr żydowski w Krakowie: Studia i materiały* [Yiddish Theatre in Cracow: Studies and Materials] (Cracow: Uniwersytet Jagielloński, 1995).

in Cracow, showing the city to be a secondary but significant player on the rich Polish Yiddish theatrical scene (Chapter 8). Nearby Vienna fulfilled a similar function, as Brigitte Dalinger, author of a book on the Yiddish theatre in Vienna, illustrates (Chapter 6); in the home of Freud, Mahler, and Schnitzler, the Ostjuden created a modest but vibrant forum for dramatizing their hopes, dreams, and fears in Yiddish.

David Mazower and Leonard Prager move the story further westward in their explorations of the Yiddish theatre in London (Chapters 7 and 10). Mazower describes and illustrates *melo-deklamatsyes*, or 'stories in song', by the prolific London playwright Joseph Markovitsh. Besides contributing to our knowledge of an important centre of Yiddish theatre in its day, Mazower's chapter raises the question of genres and sub-genres aside from those that usually receive attention.[37] The censorship of Sholem Asch's controversial drama *Got fun nekome* (God of Vengeance, 1907), the subject of Leonard Prager's investigations here, is well known, but usually via the obscenity trial of a company that performed the play in New York in 1923. Prager takes a different instance of the censorship of the play, in 1940s London, and explores the repercussions for the Jewish community's relationship with the British authorities.[38]

Other contributors to this volume help to fill gaps in the study of Yiddish drama, which David Schneider has called 'the Cinderella of Yiddish literature, neglected both by the theatre critic and the literary critic'.[39] Schneider rightly called scholars' attention to this dual oversight, and his synopsis of what remains to be done regarding scholarship in this area remains pertinent:

[37] Studies of Yiddish performance forms besides traditional plays are rare. Two exceptions are Edward Portnoy, 'Modicut Puppet Theatre: Modernism, Satire, and Yiddish Culture', *TDR* 43 (Fall 1999), 115–34; and Nahma Sandrow, '"A Little Letter to Mama": Traditions in Yiddish Vaudeville', in Myron Matlaw and Ray B. Browne (eds.), *American Popular Entertainment* (Westport, Conn.: Greenwood Press, 1979), 87–95.

[38] The second volume of Manger *et al.* (eds.), *Yidisher teater in eyrope tsvishn beyde velt-milkhomes* contains articles on the Soviet Union, the Baltic states, Romania, England, Austria, Czechoslovakia, Hungary, Germany, Yugoslavia, Belgium, and France. For further reading on Yiddish theatre in central and western Europe, see David A. Brenner, 'Making Jargon Respectable: Leo Winz, Ost und West and the Reception of Yiddish Theatre in Pre-Hitler Germany', *Leo Baeck Institute Year Book* (1997), 51–66; Brigitte Dalinger, *'Verloschene Sterne': Geschichte des jüdischen Theaters in Vienna* ['Extinguished Stars': The History of the Jewish Theatre in Vienna] (Vienna: Picus Verlag, 1998); Herbert Freeden, *Jüdisches Theater in Nazideutschland* [Jewish Theatre in Nazi Gerrmany] (Tübingen: Mohr, 1964); David Mazower, *Yiddish Theatre in London*, 2nd edn. (London: Jewish Museum, 1996); Leonard Prager, *Yiddish Culture in Britain: A Guide* (Frankfurt am Main: Peter Lang, 1990); and Peter Sprengel, *Scheunenviertel-Theater. Jüdische Schauspeiltruppen und jiddische Dramatik in Berlin (1900–1918)* (Berlin: Fannei & Walz, 1995).

[39] David Schneider, 'Critical Approaches to Modern Yiddish Drama', in Dov-Ber Kerler (ed.), *History of Yiddish Studies*, vol. iii of *Winter Studies in Yiddish* (Chur: Harwood Academic Publishers, 1991), 103. Schneider provides a valuable overview and bibliography of the significant studies of Yiddish drama.

It is for the contemporary critic to try and discover whether . . . there are forms, styles and contents which characterize the Yiddish drama as opposed to other dramatic literature; whether these elements are 'Jewish' or 'Yiddish,' i.e. whether Yiddish drama shares certain characteristics with Hebrew drama, at least with Hebrew drama of the same period. finally, research must be started into the as yet untouched question of whether Yiddish dramaturgy differs in any way from other Yiddish genres (e.g. in the themes it prefers, its style, language). These tasks can only be carried out with success if . . . the drama is finally examined as a self-contained and distinctive genre within Yiddish literature.[40]

A number of these questions are taken up by the chapters in this book. Ahuva Belkin describes the earthy, carnivalesque quality of early Yiddish drama (Chapter 1). Moving to a later era, Nahma Sandrow sets modern Yiddish drama in the thematic context of Romantic drama, particularly in the theories and practice of French and German Romantics such as Hugo, Goethe, and Schiller (Chapter 2). Paola Bertolone examines Goldfaden's enormously popular operetta *Di kishefmakherin* (The Sorceress, 1877) through the lens of broader questions relating to operetta (Chapter 4), while Seth Wolitz provides a different perspective on two other popular Goldfaden operettas (Chapter 5). Wolitz treats us to a remarkable instance of dramaturgical development in two distinct sociopolitial contexts, discussing the texts of *Shulamis* (1881) and *Bar kokhba* (1883) both as Goldfaden conceived them for his audience and in the adaptations of both works in the 1930s by the Soviet Yiddish poet and playwright Shmuel Halkin.

With the many gaps that exist in the scholarship on the Yiddish theatre, it is unsurprising that the field lacks authoritative reference works. There is no scholarly history of the full lifespan of the Yiddish theatre to date; nothing approaching a complete guide to Yiddish drama exists. Nevertheless, reference materials of various kinds can serve as springboards to further research. The first port of call for most historians of Yiddish theatre is Zalmen Zylbercweig's six-volume *Leksikon fun yidishn teater*,[41] which contains entries on thousands of theatre personnel, with additional articles on, for example, *purimshpiln* and *batkhonim*. Zylbercweig culled material from newspaper reviews, memoirs, and letters from the subjects and their colleagues, providing contemporary and posthumous assessments as well as bibliographic information for each entry. Readers, however, should beware of the *Leksikon*'s many inaccuracies; wherever possible, information such as dates should be

[40] Schneider, 'Critical Approaches to Modern Yiddish Drama', 111.

[41] A seventh, as yet unpublished, volume of Zylbercweig's *Leksikon*—apparently consisting of galley proofs all but ready for publication—is housed in the archives of the YIVO Institute in New York. The publication of this typescript would be a great boon to theatre researchers.

confirmed independently. The bibliographies are sporadic at best, although they often include sources difficult to locate elsewhere. Finally, Zylbercweig's editing methods inevitably left many enormous gaps. He compiled the volumes one at a time, over a thirty-year period, and many of the early entries were written when their subjects were still young, thus giving an incomplete picture of their careers. Nevertheless, for all its faults, the *Leksikon* remains an important source of information; when used skilfully in conjunction with other materials, it can prove a valuable tool.

More accurate, both factually and in terms of alphabetization, is the eight-volume *Leksikon far der nayer yidisher literatur* (Lexicon of New Yiddish Literature), which contains reliable articles on playwrights as well as on Yiddish writers of every other stripe. This scope can be illuminating in itself, for it allows the researcher to learn not only about writers known primarily as dramatists, but also about writers better known for their achievements in other genres, but who made sorties into playwriting as well.[42] Complementing this committee-written lexicon are other, more individualistic ones: the literary historian Zalmen Reyzen's *Leksikon fun der yidisher literatur, prese un filologye* (Lexicon of Yiddish Literature Press, and Philology), and the multi-faceted writer and critic Melekh Ravitsh's *Mayn leksikon* (My Lexicon), both four-volume works.[43] Like the *Leksikon far der nayer yidisher literatur*—itself a more encyclopaedic follow-up to Reyzen—both Reyzen's and Ravitsh's works deal with writers in various genres. Ravitsh's title is apt, for he shaped his lexicon according to the cultural arenas he knew best, starting with writers and performers in his native Poland and travelling, as he did, to Israel and New York.

Three sections of the present volume provide further bibliographic information. John Klier's list of plays (Table 9.1) produced while the ban on Yiddish theatre in Russia was officially in effect fills in a missing piece of a historical puzzle, and may lay the groundwork for future researchers to enquire further into those productions. A different sort of theatrical censorship lies behind Leonard Prager's appendix of Yiddish plays in the collection of the Lord Chamberlain's Office in London (Tables 10.1 and 10.2). The Licensing Act of 1737, which remained in effect until 1968, prohibited the

---

[42] *Leksikon far der nayer yidisher literatur*, 8 vols. (New York: CYCO, 1956–81). See also Berl Kagan, *Leksikon fun yidish-shraybers* [Lexicon of Yiddish Writers] (New York: R. Ilman-Kohen, 1986), which adds over 600 names to the list of writers compiled in the eight-volume *Leksikon*, and provides supplementary information about many other writers and an appendix listing the pseudonyms and assumed names of many Yiddish authors.

[43] Zalmen Reyzen, *Leksikon fun der yidisher literatur, prese un filologye*, 4 vols. (Vilna: B. Kletskin, 1926–9); Melekh Ravitsh, *Mayn leksikon*, 4 vols. (vols. i–iii Montreal; vol. iv Tel Aviv, 1945–82).

performance for 'gain, hire, or reward' of any play not previously licensed by the Lord Chamberlain. All copies of scripts sent for licensing have been preserved, providing a rich record of the performed repertoire in London, including the Yiddish repertoire. Censorship may make life difficult for the artist, but it often proves to be a godsend to the historian.

The bibliography to this volume is conceived as a companion piece to this introduction: a more detailed survey, in bibliographic rather than narrative form, of the state of Yiddish theatre studies so far. Even serious students of the subject may be surprised by the range of materials cited here, which includes not only the major resources mentioned above, but memoirs written by lesser-known actors, writers, and even theatregoers; published and unpublished studies of Yiddish drama and performance; and monographs on theatrical activity on six continents (no record of Yiddish performances in Antarctica having yet come to light).

One resource as yet in its infancy, but offering the promise of opening up new ways of teaching and studying cultural history, is the internet. So far, the quality of websites with information on Yiddish theatre is extremely uneven, and most are probably best avoided. A few worthwhile sites are worth mentioning, however. The Library of Congress in Washington runs a handsomely produced website called 'American Variety Stage: Vaudeville and Popular Entertainment, 1870–1920'. Along with sections on the magician Harry Houdini, theatre playbills and programmes, sound recordings, motion pictures, and English play scripts is a section featuring the complete manuscripts of seventy-seven Yiddish plays out of some 1,200 housed in the Hebraic section of the African and Middle Eastern division of the library. '2nd Avenue Online' also displays some archival material, such as sound recordings of songs by the beloved composer Sholem Secunda, as well as information on the history of the Yiddish theatre and resources for studying that history. An 'Encyclopedia' section, for example, features brief articles on the people who worked in Yiddish theatre as well as on plays, songs, and theatres, while another area of the site contains useful descriptions of the holdings of such archives and libraries as the Harvard Theatre Collection and the YIVO Institute for Jewish Research. Two other worthwhile websites provide information on the European Yiddish theatre. From the home page of the Jewish Museum of London one can visit a brief illustrated history of the Yiddish theatre in the East End. And the Jewish Heritage Society's site contains articles and bibliographies in Russian on the Yiddish theatre in Russia. Of course, inaccuracies can surface in web-based resources just as easily as in printed texts, so, as with any secondary material, the researcher should take care to check information from even the most useful pages on the internet against other sources.[44]

THE YIDDISH THEATRE AND JEWISH CIVILIZATION

Having discussed how the chapters that follow contribute to the historiography of the Yiddish theatre, we can return to the question of what they add to our understanding of broader questions of Jewish civilization. Although the contributors approach their material from a variety of perspectives, they share the impulse to set their investigations in social and/or aesthetic contexts, thereby forging connections between Yiddish and other European drama, Jewish and Christian arts and society, and the relationship between theatrical performance and the various institutions and individuals with a stake in the theatrical event: audiences, critics, communities, and government authorities.

All of those entities make frequent appearances, in different guises, throughout the book. The *purimshpiln* were often sufficiently subversive to make Jewish as well as Christian authorities nervous, and at times to cause the plays to be banned or their texts to be burned in public, or both. At a later period of substantial political turmoil the tsarist authorities prohibited Yiddish performances in the Russian empire, but, as John Klier shows us, the implementation of the ban depended on local officials, who did not always enforce the decree to the letter, if at all. We might be more surprised to find British officials stepping in to stop the performance of a controversial Yiddish play in London just a year after the Second World War ended, and even more surprised that they did so only at the behest of Jewish officials. All three of these studies reveal the seriousness with which various governments and communities have regarded the Yiddish theatre as a social force, and the delicate balance of power between various individuals and institutions in regulating Yiddish performances, both de jure and de facto.

Non-Jews often approached the Yiddish theatre not only in an official capacity but as spectators and critics as well. Brigitte Dalinger describes non-Jewish critics attending the Yiddish theatre in Vienna—where the German lingua franca lowered the language barrier between Jew and non-Jew—and playwright Abish Meisels staging one of his works as a direct response to the rise of antisemitism during a wave of Jewish immigration from eastern Europe during the First World War. A similar impulse, under even more

---

[44] The address for the 'American Variety Stage' is < http://lcweb2.loc.gov/ammem/vshtml/vshome. html >. 2nd Avenue Online can be found at < http://www.yap.cat.nyu.edu >. For the Jewish Museum of London's online theatre exhibition, see < http://jewmusm.ort.org/yiddish >. The Jewish Heritage Society's website is located at < http://www.jewish-heritage.org >.

ominous circumstances, led the Polish Yiddish director Zygmunt Turkow to stage adaptations of Goldfaden's *Shulamis* and *Bar kokhba* in Warsaw and Cracow in the late 1930s, as Mirosława Bułat documents. Turkow's decision echoed that of his colleagues in Moscow just a few years earlier, when the poet Shmuel Halkin's adaptations of the same Goldfaden plays were mounted to display a heroic vision of the Jewish past to the Soviet authorities. Seth Wolitz discusses how Goldfaden's and Halkin's versions were products of their times, and also of the sensibilities of their authors. Examples such as these illustrate how acutely aware Yiddish playwrights, performers, and theatre managers have been of events and attitudes beyond the walls of the theatre, and how that awareness has affected the content and presentation of the Yiddish repertoire.

Yiddish playwrights often had calmer moments to absorb influences from their predecessors and contemporaries working in other languages. The form of the *purimshpil* was based on that of the German *Fastnachtspiel*, and the bawdy spirit of Yiddish Purim plays, illustrated with numerous piquant examples by Ahuva Belkin, mirrored that of many medieval plays in other cultures. Taking more recent examples, Nahma Sandrow describes how Romantic ideals of drama permeated Yiddish playwriting, thus injecting such themes as emotionalism, nationalism, and rebellion into many of the most popular works in the Yiddish repertoire. Certainly Goldfaden was aware of Romantic literature and drew upon its motifs, as he did on a variety of both Jewish and European sources, including the operetta tradition. As Paola Bertolone shows, that tradition influenced the conception, publishing history, and production of one of Goldfaden's most beloved works, *The Sorceress*. Like Goldfaden, the London Yiddish playwright Joseph Markovitsh sometimes set his own words to music, and Markovitsh too created a blend of Western artistic conventions with Jewish subject matter that endeared him to his audiences.

Critics were often just as sensitive to intellectual trends as playwrights were. The critics working on New York's Lower East Side at the beginning of the twentieth century tended to model themselves on Russian intellectuals, a stance that fed directly into their campaign to reform the Yiddish stage, and in the process to view Yiddish audiences as children who 'wouldn't grow up', as Nina Warnke puts it. Yet the intellectual traffic moved on a two-way street, even if it was perhaps heavier in one direction than the other. Barbara Henry's research shows many plays from the Yiddish repertoire enjoying great success in the Russian language in the period leading up to the October Revolution.

The eleven chapters that follow offer a taste of the state of current research—and of the possibilities for future enquiry. I am not so cautiously optimistic that research into Yiddish theatre will blossom in coming years, widely expanding our knowledge of the subject and introducing vastly increased possibilities for intellectual cross-fertilization. In a 1971 survey of the historiography of Yiddish theatre Yekhiel Hirshhoyt observed that the history of non-Jewish theatre in the West had been chronicled largely by academics, while the Yiddish theatre had to rely on 'volunteers'—playwrights, critics, or simply passionate amateurs.[45] The situation has changed dramatically since then. With the increased acceptance in universities of the study and teaching of both popular culture and ethnic literature and culture, research on the Yiddish theatre has gained increasing academic respectability. Scholars in the field hold positions in departments of theatre, Jewish studies, history, English, and other disciplines. They present their findings at academic conferences around the world, and publish in journals devoted to a wide range of specialities. In short, after decades of intermittent bursts of activity, the study of Yiddish theatre is beginning to come into its own as a scholarly endeavour, in the process enhancing our understanding not only of plays and productions, but of the larger social context in which they were performed.

---

[45] Y. Hirshhoyt, 'Di historiker funem yidishn teater' [The Historians of the Yiddish Theatre], in Manger, Turkow, and Perenson (eds.), *Yidisher teater in eyrope tsvishn beyde velt-milkhomes*, 8.

I. PURIMSHPIL

The 'Low' Culture of the Purimshpil

ॐ

A H U V A   B E L K I N

T HE nineteenth-century critic of Jewish literature Elazar Shulman (1837–
1904) spoke for both the maskilim and the Orthodox in his unflattering
view of the theatrical genre of *purimshpil*: 'the gory show known as *Akhashveyresh-shpil* [Ahasuerus Play] . . . [was] obviously conceived by some name-
less devil, whose bloodthirsty language evokes horror and pain; [these are]
words from a foul mouth, which the paper can barely tolerate . . . The creator
was a Polish vagabond living in Germany, the scum of the earth, the subject
of incessant complaints.'[1] Indeed, reading the surviving texts today, in an
industrial world that long ago abandoned unrestrained revelry, can be bewil-
dering. The plays seem to be unstructured: many of the monologues do not
belong to the main plot, the entrances are unmotivated, and the mythical
characters are made into fools. Absorbed into popular humour, the language
is totally unrestrained, containing indecencies and obscenities, insults, curses,
and blasphemies.

Mordkhe, the pious man of the Megillah (the book of Esther), frequently
uses vulgar expressions in the *purimshpiln*. In *Eyn sheyn purimshpil* (A Lovely
Purim Play, 1697) he completes his long mock prayer with:

Yoyne fishlvitsh	Jonah Fishlvitsh
Brengt eyn zak floymen,	Brings in a sack of plums.
Ikh shtek den finger in arsh.	I stick my finger in my arse.
Homen lekt den doymen.[2]	Homen licks the dung.

(ll. 796–9)

---

[1] Elazar Shulman, *Sefat-yehudit ashkenazit vesifrutah: mikets hame'ah ha-15 ad kets shenot hame'ah
ha-18* [The Jewish Ashkenazi Language and its Literature: From the End of the Fifteenth Century
to the End of the Eighteenth Century] (Riga: Eli Levin Press, 1913).

[2] *Eyn sheyn purimshpil* (1697), Municipal Library, Leipzig, no. 35. See Khone Shmeruk, *Mahazot
mikra'im beyidish, 1697–1750* [Yiddish Biblical Plays, 1697–1750] (Jerusalem: Israel Academy of Sciences
ahd Humanities, 1979).

In a later version of the *Akhashveyresh-shpil* (1708) Mordkhe abuses the king:

> Leshone toyve, shtinkndige beytsim.
> Den meylekh zoln geshveln zayne beytsim.
>
> (ll. 172–3)
>
> Happy New Year, stinking eggs.
> May the king's balls grow and swell.

And no less vulgar:

> Adoyni hameylekh ikh bin in eyn vald gezesn.
> Un, hob ayer geflitst hob ikh gehert. . . .
>
> (ll. 203–4)
>
> My lord and king, once I was sitting in the woods.
> And I heard you fart.[3]

When Mordkhe weaves sections from various prayers into his supplication on behalf of the Jewish people, he deliberately jumbles up the liturgy.

The translation of the Bible into German by the maskilim offered further opportunities for parody, with the insertion of curses and other blasphemous statements. *Dus pirimspiel. Du spielt die Rolle Humen in Mordche* (The *Purimshpil*: Here Hamen and Mordkhe Play a Role) distorts the Hebrew of Jacob's blessing in Genesis 48: 16: 'The Angel who redeemed me from all evil, may he bless the boys; and let my name be named in them, and the name of my fathers Abraham and Isaac; and let them grow into a multitude in the midst of the earth.' The passage concerned, which imitates the traditional method of rote learning of biblical passages, is replete with puns and inside jokes:

Hamalakh—der gesaltsener,	The angel—salted,
Hagoyel—der imgesipter,	Which redeemed—dirty,
Oysi—mir,	Me—for me,
A make dir,	A blow—to you,
Mikol—der shtekn,	From all—the stick,
Ra—der beyzer stren,	Evil—a star,
Yevoyrekh—er zol makhn knien,	Bless—knelt down,
Es—in,	The—inside,
Haneorim—di yunge lompn,	Lads—young rascals,
Veyikorey bahem—un es zol vern oysgerisn,	Read—tore,
Shemi—dayn nomen,	My name—your name,
Yemakh shemoy—in zayn nomen,	His name will perish,
Avrom—der shinder,	Abraham the skinner,
	Isaac—the blind,

---

[3] See Johann J. Schudt, *Jüdische Merckwürdigkeiten vorstellende was sich Curieuses und Denckwürdiges in den neuen Zeiten* [Jewish Oddities: Presenting that which is Curious and Memorable in Recent Times], 4 vols. (Frankfurt: no publisher given, 1714–18), iii. 202–25.

Yitskhok—der blinder,
Yankev—hot ongemakht a ful zekele
    mit kinder,
Veyigdu—un falst onleygn,
Bekeyrev—mitn kepele,
Haorets—in der erd arayn. Omeyn!⁴

Jacob—who filled his sack with
    offspring,
Grow into a multitude—pull him,
In the midst—with the head,
Of the land—May the earth devour
    you. Amen!

(ll. 222–39)

The complexity and bilingualism of the puns and double entendres that run through this passage defy any but the most literal translation. In essence, however, everything sacred about the original biblical passage is referred to irreverently here. Not only does the speaker profane the biblical patriarchs, but he liberally curses his addressee, concluding, 'May the Earth devour you. Amen!'

Mordkhe indulges in numerous instances of scatological humour, from comic gesticulations and sexual allusions to blunt talk of sex and genitalia. Even in the relatively dignified edition of *Akta ester mit akhashveyresh* (The Story of Esther and Ahasuerus) issued in Prague in 1720 under Rabbi David Oppenheim, Mordkhe's obscenities are still in evidence.⁵ Asked about his status at court, he answers, 'Di malke iz mayn shayster kind' (l. 772), deliberately distorting the word 'shvester' (sister) to read 'shayster', which sounds like 'shayse' (shit), so that the expected response, 'The queen is my cousin', becomes 'The queen is my shit-child'. The courtiers reprimand him for his response, and ask what language he is using; Mordkhe answers, 'Af lek dayn arsh' (l. 778), which sounds very similar to 'Af lataynish' (Latin), but is in fact a command to lick his arse. In reply to their repeated question 'Vos iz den dos far eyn shprakh?' ('What language is that?'), Mordkhe uses a further play on words: 'Ikh bin in tukhes' ('I am up your arse'; l. 779), substituting *tukhes* (arse) for *toes* (mistake).

Further adding to the riotous spirit of the plays, Mordkhe and Homen behave like quarrelling fools, exchanging insults such as 'Villain!', 'Thief!', 'Idiot!', 'Stupid!' Where the stage directions call for an improvised vocal response, such as 'kumt Mordkhe un zogt vos er zogt' ('Mordkhe enters and says whatever he says'; l. 610) or 'Entfert Mordkhe vos ert entfert' ('Mordkhe answers whatever he answers'; l. 1090), we may assume that the players used

---

⁴ *Dus Pirimspiel. Du spielt die Rolle Humen in Mordche*, ed. Samuel Weissenberg, in 'Das Purimspiel von Ahasverus und Esther' [The Purim Play of Ahasuerus and Esther], *Mitteilungen der Gesellschaft für jüdische Volkskunde*, 13 (1904), 1–27. Weissenberg (1867–1928), a Jewish ethnographer and anthropologist from Yelisvetgrad (Kherson, Russia), compiled the verbal traditional *purimshpil* of his home town to save it from oblivion. He wrote in Latin transcription based on popular Yiddish. See Weissenberg's introduction to the play under the title 'Das Purimspiel von Ahasverus und Esther', *Mitteilungen der Gesellschaft für jüdische Volkskunde*, 13 (1904), 1–3.

⁵ See Shmeruk, *Mahazot*, 405–532.

the latitude they were given to improvise to go even further than the written text allowed.

The licence and indiscipline that were so pronounced in the *purimshpil* drew the wrath of the community elders. The strong objections the rabbinical establishment had always held towards the very institution of the theatre were now vindicated by this challenge to Jewish asceticism. And once the improvised text of a play had been put in writing and become subject to closer scrutiny, it was doomed. Johann Schudt (1664–1772), who published the play in his four-volume work on the Jews and their customs, records that the Jewish authorities were ashamed of what they had written and, indeed, the elders of Frankfurt burned the entire edition.[6]

Until the twentieth century academic researchers ignored most forms of popular culture, including folk theatre. Owing to the traditional link between theatre research and written dramatic texts, theatrical genres not based on written texts have been either neglected or treated as inferior—to quote Brecht, as 'a mixture of earthy humour and sentimentality, homespun morality and cheap sex'.[7] Researchers have concentrated on literary drama produced by well-known playwrights whose work is staged by established theatres or read by an educated readership. It was not until the late twentieth century, with increased recognition of the 'other' through the rise of postmodernism, that folk culture emerged as a subject considered worthy of literary study.

Modern scholars addressing the history of Jewish literature have dismissed the *purimshpil* texts as examples of literary degradation. Emphasizing the lascivious language and indecencies, they have treated the genre as marginal and trivial, and its writers as no more than drunken clowns. It has been assumed that some learned primary dramatic text existed, which the folk players, 'those tasteless, ill-bred, barbarous boors', 'debased with coarse humour and plain language'.[8] Suspecting that the plays were corrupted texts, critics have gone so far as to accuse the anonymous authors of plagiarism.[9] Throughout most of the twentieth century the literary criteria of 'high

[6] Schudt, *Jüdische Merckwürdigkeiten*, ii. 316. On the antagonism of the religious Jewish authorities in Germany towards the *purimshpil*, see Dov Weinryb, 'Gormim kalkalim vesotsialim bahaskalah hayehudit begermaniyah' [Economic and Social Factors in the Jewish Enlightenment in Germany], in *Keneset lezekher haim nahman bialik* [Conference in Memory of Chaim Nachman Bialik] (Tel Aviv: Dvir, 1938).

[7] Bertolt Brecht, 'Notes on the Folk Play' (1957), in id., *Brecht on Theatre*, ed. and trans. John Willett (New York: Hill & Wang, 1964), 153–6.

[8] Yisroel Tsinberg, *Di geshikhte fun der literatur bay yidn* [The History of Jewish Literature], 10 vols. (Vilna: Tamar, 1929–66), vol. vi; Max Erik, who discusses the literary Yiddish genre, refers to the *purimshpil* as 'primitive'. See *Di geshikhte fun der yidisher literatur fun di eltste tsaytn biz der haskole tkufe* [The History of Yiddish Literature from Olden Times to the Haskalah Period] (Warsaw: Kultur-lige, 1928).   [9] See, *inter alia*, Tsinberg, *Di geshikhte fun der literatur bay yidn*.

culture' were applied to them, while their theatrical realization in the productions themselves was largely ignored.[10]

In my view the parody, grotesque humour, crude physicality, obscenities,
swearing, and cursing in the *purimshpil* were part of the folk festive culture and
a sign of normality in the life of the Jewish people. Whether the *purimshpil* has a
literary prototype or not, the popular theatre of the feast of Purim should not
be considered degenerate; it should be judged as a folk play, rather than by
literary criteria. The players, themes, motifs, and style come out of the folk
genre, in which a traditional show based upon a well-known myth is put on at
festival time in small communities whose members are also the performers.

The *purimshpil*, moreover, may be regarded as a liminoid manifestation, if
we embrace Victor Turner's term for the new collective creation of liminal
phenomena in complex societies.[11] In identifying the liminal phase, characterized by a digression from social norms, Turner follows the anthropologist
Arnold Van Gennep, who has described the three phases of the rites of
passage of the individual from one stage in life to the next: separation, transition, and incorporation. During the intervening phase of transition, which
Van Gennep calls *limen* (threshold), the individual finds himself in a period
and area of ambiguity—in the words of Van Gennep, 'betwixt and between'.[12]
Anthropologists have taken this tripartite structure and applied it to communal activities and seasonal festivals, which they regard as liminal events.

The *purimshpil* preserved as conspicuously as any other folk drama the
liminal traits of the ritual, which became explicit in the Jewish carnival feast.
The customs of the feast—including its liturgical conventions, such as the
official reading of the Megillah and the abuse of Homen which provide the
plot of the play—retain the primary liminal features of reversal.[13] The privilege of parodying their cultural heritage was met with antagonism in the
Jewish society where these liminal traits were still sacrosanct.

Nevertheless, as a liminoid phenomenon, the *purimshpil* combines a festive
theatre that affirms the hegemony of Jewish culture with an expression of
popular culture in which the canonical sources are harnessed in order to parody

[10] In their seminal works on the *purimshpil* Noyekh Prilutski and Khone Shmeruk managed to
save some texts from oblivion, but they did not consider them within the context of the popular
culture. See Prilutski, *Zamlbikher far yidishn folklor, filologye un kulturgeshikhte* [Anthologies
of Yiddish Folklore, Philology, and Cultural History] (Warsaw: Nayer Farlag, 1912); Shmeruk,
Maḥazot.

[11] Victor Turner, *From Ritual to Theatre: The Human Seriousness of Play* (New York: PAJ Publications, 1982), 20–60.

[12] Arnold Van Gennep, *The Rites of Passage*, trans. M. Vizedom and G. Caffee (Chicago: University of Chicago Press, 1960).

[13] See Ahuva Belkin, 'Citing Scripture for a Purpose: The Jewish *Purimspiel* as a Parody', *Assaph*,
C12 (1997), 45–59.

the authorities. The feast of Purim became dramatized only when it began acquiring elements from the 'other culture', as Bakhtin terms the carnival culture: parody, echoes of ready-made motifs and folk sketches, bawdy jokes, self-deprecation, obscenities of sex and violence, preoccupation with the body, and scatology and ribald dialogue.[14] Through the influence of carnival revelry in Europe and the annual festive-dramatic revival of its liminal narrative through symbols and masks, transgressing every boundary, the seeds of the Jewish folk theatre germinated.

While it is true that the *Akhashveyresh-shpil*, as a meta-text, parodies the biblical original, perhaps more than any other genre it plays to an audience familiar with that original. In acting out the ancient myth, the players enhanced the ritual through the fictional world, drawing their audience back 2,000 years to the palace of Ahasuerus in Persia. And although the show evolved—or degenerated, as the Orthodox authorities would have it—into clownish manipulation, portraying the mythical heroes as a parody of the contemporary rabbi, matchmaker, cantor, and other familiar community members, in whom the spectators saw themselves, the liminal symbols were intensified. Though the mythical events were represented by amateur actors in a burlesque that evolved into parody, those watching identified with the plot and the message of the *purimshpil*, which they perceived as analogous to their situation as Jews in the Diaspora, still suffering persecution and winning redemption.

The festive theatrical genre links carnival culture and 'official' culture through the texts it is based on as well as through the messages it conveys. The Megillah was read in Hebrew, the language of religious literature, liturgy, and scriptural commentary, while the carnival show required an everyday, informal language that everyone could understand. The vernacular Yiddish eased the transition from non-dramatic parody to theatre, deflating the solemnity of the ritual and of the biblical schema, replacing it with parody and adding oral material such as sketches, jokes, satires, and folk songs.

The study of Jewish popular theatre raises questions regarding the interaction between folk and high culture. Contemporary folklore research questions whether it is possible to draw polarized distinctions such as 'high–low' or 'educated–illiterate', and whether we can settle for the designation 'popular' when describing early works.[15] Admittedly, every culture has a

[14] Mikhail Bakhtin, *Rabelais and his World*, trans. Helene Iswolsky (Bloomington: Indiana University Press, 1984), 197 ff.

[15] Gunter Lottes, 'Popular Culture and the Early Modern State in Sixteenth-Century Germany', and Erik Midelfort, 'Sin, Melancholy, Obsession: History and Culture in the Sixteenth Century', both in Steven L. Kaplan (ed.), *Understanding Popular Culture* (Amsterdam: Mouton, 1984) (see p. 114).

social foundation, but, when it comes to the *purimshpil*, the relationship
between culture and society is more complex than the term 'popular culture'
may imply. The Yiddish poet and playwright Itsik Manger (1901–69) may
well have been correct in saying that the real heroes of the *purimshpil* were
the tailors (referring to the fact that the plays were amateur productions).
Nevertheless, the anonymous writers and performers (actors for the occasion), the *balmelokhes* (craftsmen), *batkhonim* (jesters), *klezmorim* (musicians),
and *yeshive-bokherim* (seminary students) who produced the shows and went
from house to house performing them were not illiterate, and the cultural
life of the educated classes was also part of their own lives. In Jewish society,
particularly among its male members, illiteracy had been virtually unknown
since antiquity, and literacy prevailed even during the Middle Ages. The vast
majority of Jews could read and write, and their culture was almost certainly a
written one.[16] The revellers thus had at their disposal a wealth of tradition—
both literary and popular—to draw on. The existence of that tradition,
together with the literacy that made it accessible to the general Jewish public,
to some extent distinguished their folk revels from other expressions of popular culture.

As Jacques le Goff points out, although folk culture is interspersed with
fragments of higher forms of culture, it uses these fragments with a great deal
of creativity.[17] However, the *purimshpil* is not simply an example of *gesunkenes
Kulturgut* (sunken cultural assets)—a term coined by Hans Naumann,[18] who
maintains that popular culture makes use of artistic material that, in previous
centuries, belonged to the upper class but which has fallen into disuse over
the years. However, perhaps more than any other folk tradition, Jewish
popular culture relies to a great extent on the existing 'higher culture'. The
elements of its folk plays betray their closeness to a literary origin, and are
manifested in a rather unusual relationship between high culture and folk
culture. Even the least pretentious versions of the *purimshpil* clearly reveal this
reliance on elements from the learned Jewish sources: the Scriptures, Midrash, Targum Sheni, Agadah, liturgy, and other 'high' genres, including
misogynist poetry. Although the interaction between literary and folk genres
in Jewish society was quite different from that in illiterate societies, the
purimshpil does reveal signs of oral transmission. The handful of *purimshpil*

[16] Beatrice Weinreich and Uriel Weinreich, *Yiddish Language and Folklore* (Amsterdam: Mouton, 1959), 12 ff.

[17] Jacques le Goff, 'The Learned and Popular Dimensions of Journeys in the Otherworld in the Middle Ages', in Steven L. Kaplan (ed.), *Understanding Popular Culture* (Amsterdam: Mouton, 1984), 19–39.

[18] Hans Naumann, *Primitive Gemeinschaftskultur* [Primitive Shared Culture] (Jena: E. Diederichs, 1921).

texts that have remained in print are the survivors of a deep-rooted, time-honoured oral tradition of Purim plays which flourished in the Jewish community in Europe until the early twentieth century. Throughout the generations the plays were transmitted either in writing or, more often, by word of mouth, together with their special melodies and traditional costumes. In many places a *purimshpil* remained in the domain of one family, who produced it by concessional right. Many testimonies make reference to the oral transmission of texts, tunes, and production conventions.

Sigfried Kapper (1821–79) recalls a *purimshpil* held in the Prague ghetto in 1825 and 1826. An old musician known as Itsik the Fiddler would come to Kapper's family home and recount how he had devised an *Akhashveyresh-shpil* that was acclaimed by Jews and non-Jews alike. Late into the night he would recite whole scenes from memory, singing arias, accompanying himself on the violin, and performing the roles of the king, Homen, Mordkhe, and even Queen Esther.[19] Another testimony mentions a baker who was employed only during Passover; the rest of the year he was idle, receiving bread in exchange for *purimshpil* songs, which he knew by heart.[20] Aaron Levdiev tells of a *purimshpil* in Homel in which he participated. Khayim Meyer, a butcher, mastered all the texts, and at Purim time he organized a company of players that went from house to house performing the *shpil*.[21] Mordkhe Chemerinsky recalls the *purimshpil* in the town of Motili, in which the company leader Wolf could recite the entire repertoire and every detail of all the parts.[22]

In the surviving texts we can detect evidence of the original oral form: the way the rhymes are used, the openings and endings, contrasts, repetitions, and refrains. It is evident, for example, that the sound of the rhyme helps the actor to remember the text, as in the song Akhashveyresh sings when he is crowned and mounts the throne: 'Nit tsu hetsn nit tsu shpetsn, nor tsu zetsn afn shtuletsn' ('Not to incite, not to jest, but to sit on the chair').[23] In many instances we can also see how the players used an alternative text when only the sound of the rhyme had been remembered and the original words were long forgotten. In the *Akhashveyresh-shpil* published in Schudt, Mordkhe greets the king:

[19] Sigfried Kapper, *Ahasverus—Ein jüdisches Fastnachtspiel* [Ahasuerus: A Jewish Fastnachtspiel], in *Zeitschrift für Literatur, Kunst und öffentliches Leben*, vol. iv (Leipzig: Deutsches Museum, 1854), 490–7, 529–43.

[20] M. Spektor, 'Velvel der shiber' [Velvel the Baker's Assistant], *Der tog*, 63 (1904).

[21] See Zalmen Zylbercweig (ed.), *Leksikon fun yidishn teater* [Lexicon of Yiddish Theatre] (New York: Elisheva, 1931–70), iii. 1708.

[22] Chaim Chemerinsky, 'Ayarati motili' [My Town Motayali], *Rashumot*, 2 (1927), 74–6.

[23] Ibid.

Du bist der meylekh? Ikh het
   dikh eyer ongezen far eyn vamfm vasher.
Far eyn shtrik treger.
Far eyn moyshev feger.
Far eyn hunt shloger.
Far eyn katsn yeger.
Meakher dos du yo der meylekh bist,
Halt mir der shtekn.
In arsh zolst mikh lekn.

(II. 190–7)

You are the king? You look
   to me like a guts-washer.
Like a rope-bearer.
Like a messy corpse.
Like a dog-beater.
Like a cat-hunter.
If you are the king,
Hold my stick.
And lick my arse.

Two more impulses marked the creative process of the oral transmission of the *purimshpil*, one to circumscribe it, and the other to open it out: while it focused on the essence of the biblical story itself, with a single thread running through the plot, at the same time comic characters and random elements from beyond the world of the biblical myth were used to expand the tale.

As frequently happens in folk plays that appropriate elements wherever they can find them, outright anachronisms appear. In the *purimshpil* on the Megillah theme, Akhashveyresh is described as the king of four continents: Asia, Africa, Europe, and America (*Akta ester mit akhashveyresh*, ll. 357–8). Christianity is the religion of the surrounding non-Jewish world, and all the citizens of Persia are referred to as Christians, including Homen, who wears a cross on his back (*Eyn sheyn purimshpil*, ll. 292–3). In this play, talmudic law is antedated to biblical times and Mordkhe is given the privilege by King Akhashveyresh of pronouncing judgement on what is forbidden and what is permitted (ll. 250–1). Characters from different places and periods are thrown together on the stage. In the *purimshpil* on biblical themes we find dramatis personae who are not connected to the original Bible stories. In *Mekhires yoysef* (The Sale of Joseph, *c*.1707) by Berman Limburg the German jester Pickelherring crops up,[24] while the spy Lizhinsky features among Goliath's men in the play *Dovid un goliyes haplishti* (David and Goliath the Philistine,

---

[24] Bodleian Library, Opp. 8° 1090. *Mekhires yoysef* was performed in Frankfurt in 1707.

1717).[25] In *Mordkhe und ester* (published in the early 1770s)[26] we discover contemporary types such as Shvelie de Metz Gvidrl and Freilein Makhlei, friends of Esther who have distanced themselves from Jewish tradition, while the Devil himself appears in *Akeydes yitskhok* (The Sacrifice of Isaac).[27]

With the narrative continuity supplied by the myth, the play could distance itself from the original narrative and elaborate on the central storyline through the use of extras, comic fragments, local allusions, jokes, liturgical parody, songs, and a medley of gibberish, as well as sketches on local rabbis, doctors, and cantors. The point of departure and the denouement were anchored in the festival myth, enabling the players to elaborate on the storyline dramatically, and then work the many components into a unified whole.

Refrains were added to many of the songs and some of the dialogue. Such creativity is found not only in the use of Scripture stories, but also in the introduction of the Midrashim and Agadah. Different literary materials were also borrowed, such as the misogynistic genre found in *Dos purimshpil*, reconstructed by Samuel Weissenberg. After Vashti's execution the executioner recites a long poem, listing the faults of the biblical mothers of the nation: Eve, Sarah, Rebecca, Rachel, and Miriam. After each one he concludes in refrain:

Darum zog ikh aykh . . .	So I say to you . . .
Un zog es aykh,	And say to you
Yabirin nokh mit eynem,	Never forget,
Hert nit froyen, vaybsgeburt.	Never listen to women, born of women.

(ll. 255–8)

The moral is obvious: a wife should obey her husband.

In the world of the feast, in the break 'betwixt and between' the ordinary flow of time—'neither here nor there, neither one nor the other', as Van Gennep describes the liminal stage—the revellers could afford to parody anything that was sacred, turning it on its head: buffoonery replaced seriousness, the profane subverted the holy. The sanctity of the sabbath and other Jewish holidays, as well as Jewish customs such as dietary laws, were similarly targets for parody. In *Eyn sheyn purimshpil* Mordkhe's description of the high holi-

---

[25] The play *Aktsyon fun kenig dovid un goliyes haplishti* [The Story of King David and Goliath the Philistine], National Library, Jerusalem, was printed in Hanau in 1717. See Shmeruk, *Maḥazot*, 623–706.

[26] See Jacob Shatzky, 'Geshikhte fun yidishn teater' [The History of Yiddish Theatre], in *Algemeyne entsiklopedye* [General Encyclopaedia], 11 vols. (Paris: Dubnov-Fond, 1934–66), vol. ii, cols. 389–414; H. Bar-Dayan, *Lereshito shel maḥazeh hahaskala—al operah komit beyidish* [The Beginnings of the Haskalah Play: On a Comic Opera in Yiddish] (Jerusalem: Second World Congress of Jewish Studies, 1957).   [27] *Akeydes yitskhok*, in Prilutski, *Zamlbikher*, no. 6.

days includes a fantastic dream in which his cow fulfils all the rituals specified in the liturgy: with her hooves shaking the palm branch and beating her breast in a ritual gesture of atonement, she blows the *shofar* (ram's horn) with her buttocks (ll. 573–5).

The mythical heroes of the liturgy, Mordkhe and Esther, become laughing-stocks, and their authority is subverted and ridiculed. In a *purimshpil* from Mogilev, in Russia, which was performed until the beginning of the twentieth century, Mordkhe is introduced thus:

> Fus-yid monderkhe,
> A shleper, a betler, vu a khasene, vu a bris,
> Dortn hot gornit gefelt
> Un a teler geshtelt:
> A portret—af im tsu kukn
> A harb afn rukn,
> Un dr'erd tut er kukn.
> Nokh a simen vel ikh aykh zogn:
> M'hot nit lang im bankes geshtelt tsum rukn.[28]

> Wandering Jew Monderkhe,
> A pauper, a beggar, at every wedding, every circumcision,
> Where nothing is missing
> And everything is laid on the plate.
> What a portrait to look at:
> Hunchbacked,
> Staring at the ground.
> And I will tell you another sign:
> Recently his back was treated with cupping.

In the *purimshpil* 'the world has been miraculously turned upside down', as Mordkhe concludes in *Dos shpil fun mordkhe un ester* (The Play about Mordkhe and Esther).[29] The miraculous match between Esther and the great king, who has dismissed Queen Vashti, provides the perfect pretext for sexual references, for parody on marriages and matches, ill-assorted couples, verbal violence, offensive mockery of the grotesque body, lewd gestures, and attempted rape. The Megillah tells us that King Akhashveyresh commanded his seven chamberlains 'to bring Vashti the queen before the king with the crown royal, to show the people and the princes her beauty, for she was fair to look on' (Esther 1: 11). *Dos purimshpil* makes much of the midrash according to which Akhashveyresh orders Vashti to appear before him totally naked. The displaced awareness of physicality and reference to the naked body violated

[28] B. Gorin, *Di geshikhte fun yidishn teater* [The History of the Yiddish Theatre], 2 vols. (1918; New York: Max N. Mayzel, 1923), i. 60.

[29] Melman Collection, National Library, Jerusalem. See Shmeruk, *Maḥazot*, line 1476, p. 328.

prevailing taboos. In the play the sense of unease that should be elicited by defiance of this taboo is replaced by excitement, with the courtiers crying out in unison: 'Naket un naket mit ir bloyzn layb' ('Naked, naked, in her bare skin', l. 62). In the aria, after her fate is sealed, Vashti sings:

> Farvos zoltsu fargesn ale dayne tsaytn,
> Az du host geton baputsn mayne klore shneyvayse zaytn?
>
> (ll. 145–6)
>
> Why have you forgotten all the times
> When you used to fondle my snow-white breasts?

Such a description might well have transported the audience to the realm of the classical mode, which perceives the human body as harmonious and beautiful. But when a man plays the part—'mit a simen fun a berdl in a kurts shmutsik kleydl, fun velkhn es kukn aroys groyse, grobe shtivl' ('with a trace of a beard, and in a short dirty dress, beneath which one can see great clod-hoppers'), the description given of Vashti in *Der priziv* (The Conscript) by S. Y. Abramovitsh (Mendele Moykher Sforim)[30]—Vashti's reference to her 'snow-white breasts' becomes an absurd parody, and renders the body even more grotesque.

In their memoirs contemporary spectators of *purimshpil* performances record abrupt changes in atmosphere, from laughter to tears and from pathos to low farce.[31] It was this range of responses that gave the performances their popular appeal. The clown's jests intermingled with the nobles' decorum was typical of the *Staatsaktionen* on which the play's form was based, much as a similar blend of the comic and tragic in melodrama ensured its popularity in the late nineteenth century.

Having wept through the dirges of Vashti and Homen before their executions, the audience was immediately compensated by a display of amusing buffoonery. Esther, the fair queen from the Megillah, is introduced by Mord-khe, who compares her to an ugly frog, and calls her the daughter of a whore. She is played by a man sloppily dressed as a woman; together with the king who, in the best midrashic tradition, is always drunk, they create a comic double act, similar to that of the conventional ill-matched married couple in the carnival plays. Mordkhe the matchmaker pushes Esther into Akhash-veyresh's arms, taking advantage of the king's predicament, and mocking him, his bride, and the two of them as a couple. Esther's introduction pro-

---

[30] In *Ale verk fun mendele moykher sforim* [Complete Works of Mendele Moykher Sforim] (Warsaw: Farlag Mendele, 1913), 76–80.

[31] Countless memoirs and stories from the *shtetls* (small towns) in eastern Europe contain accounts of *purimshpil* performances. A bibliography can be found in Zylbercweig, *Leksikon*, iii. 1754–6.

vides a focus for the grotesque description of the body and its functions. In Weissenberg's *Dos purimshpil* (The Purim Play) Mordkhe introduces the bride:

> Her zhe, kindrig, ikh hob fun daynetvegn a meyd,
> Iz zi azoy groys, vi a berisher veyde!
> A tsung mit a por lipn
> Khotsh in der erd araynshtipn;
> Haklal zi iz sheyn
> Mit oysgefortste tseyn;
> Hor mit a shtern,
> Me kon dem gantsn mark oyskern;
> Mit a bleykhn harts,
> Mit a kupernem boykh,
> Un a pipek vi a makrete . . .
>
> (ll. 356–66)

> Look here, little king, I've found you a girl
> Tiny as a bear's tail.
> She has a tongue and a pair of lips,
> And all you have to do is push her to the ground.
> In short, she is pretty,
> With holes in her teeth,
> A brow and thick hair,
> Good to sweep the market with.
> Her heart is made of tin,
> A copper belly,
> And a navel like a rinsing bowl.

And if this was not enough to shock the spectators, he adds:

> Nokh a mayle hot zi, darfstu visn,
> Az ale nekht tut zi zikh bapishn.
>
> (ll. 370–1)

> And another quality you should know:
> Every night she wets her bed.

More taboos are broken and the sexual allusion is even more pronounced when Mordkhe presents Esther to the king and refers openly to genitalia and intercourse. In the 1708 *Akhashveyresh-shpil* he introduces her by asking, 'My king, isn't it a pleasure, to touch the breast of a beautiful girl? They say it's nothing, until you have made it to her bed. And some say that even that is nothing, until you touch her as she is passing water' (ll. 650–6). The images used to characterize Esther's features are a parody of the Song of Songs; however, in the inverted world of the festival, abundant images of animals and their organs, hyperbole, and fantasies rob Esther of her status as a heroine, and degrade her legendary beauty. In *Eyn sheyn purimshpil* animal images are used to describe her physiognomy: her mouth is like that of an old horse, her nose as big as a rabbit's, her ears like a donkey's, and her brow like a bear's bottom (ll. 192–203). In *Akhashveyresh-shpil* her nose is exaggerated and compared to that of a dead donkey (ll. 212–13). At the time such grotesque depictions of the face and body were typical of carnival, which favours characteristics such as protruding eyes, gaping mouths, and excessively large noses symbolic of the phallus.

The introduction of obscenity, pornography, and scatology into the parody of a text of Jewish spiritual values is not surprising. The carnival has always represented the spiritual nature of the world through the body, emphasizing those parts through which the body is open to the world: the nose, the open mouth, the belly, and the reproductive organs. Bakhtin, who studied the popular culture of the Renaissance, noted that underlying all grotesque images was a particular perception of the human body and a representation of physical life quite different from the classical mode or the naturalistic picture of the human form.[32] Unlike classical aesthetics and its artistic canons, in which the body is harmonized, intact, and perfect, the grotesque tradition accentuates bodily functions such as metabolism, reproduction, and death; breasts, phallus, and testicles are often physically exaggerated in dialogue, costume, or performance styles. This convention can be found not only in the carnival tradition, but also in the grotesque tradition of pictorial art, which dates back thousands of years. References to passing water, defecation, and other such bodily functions are common to all festive genres, including ancient Greek comedy. In Aristophanes' *Frogs*, for example, the god Dionysus is portrayed as a fool who defecates in public.

Thus the curses, obscenities, and grotesqueries, all of which mostly pertain to the lower parts of the body, are not merely the scatological obsessions of certain *purimshpil* creators; they are, and always have been, a fundamental and vital feature of popular festive theatre, consistent with the age-old carnival mode, and are integral to folk culture. Moreover, even though they were distortions of 'high culture', these parodies of the orthodox mythology expressed the hopes, aspirations, and problems of the Jews, and the history of the community and its contemporary collective and lower-class experiences, possibly more effectively than the enlightened dramatic literature created for the Orthodox feast. However, like any original art, Jewish folk theatre was not only a complete form in its own right, offering entertainment; it also

[32] Bakhtin, *Rabelais and his World*, 72–97.

performed a serious and subversive social function. The players, who usually belonged to the lower stratum of Jewish society, used the masks of 'national otherness' to express revolt against 'social otherness', and, in doing so, debunked the upper classes by focusing their jibes on the nether regions of the powerful.

II. REPERTOIRE

TWO

Romanticism and the Yiddish Theatre

❧

NAHMA SANDROW

YIDDISH theatre was the last Western theatre—perhaps even the last art form—in the grand nineteenth-century Romantic tradition. Not every Yiddish play was Romantic, nor every production. However, just as many influential theorists of Romanticism loved the very idea of theatre and even wrote plays of their own (among them Schiller, Goethe, Hugo, Coleridge, and Byron), so too the Yiddishists who created the modern secular Yiddish theatre considered it to be, at least potentially, their culture's highest form. Moreover, Yiddish theatre exemplified the Romantic movement in both its development and its philosophy.

The historical development of the Yiddish theatre paralleled that of the Romantic movement. Romanticism appeared in Germany in the 1770s and radiated outwards into other regions and languages. The phrase *Sturm und Drang*, often used to describe Romantic emotionalism, was in fact the title of a play by Friedrich Maximilian, and many other German plays were associated with the appearance of Romantic art, most notably Goethe's *Goetz von Berlichingen* (1773) and *Faust* (begun in the 1780s), and Schiller's *The Robbers* (1781). In the same period Germany was also the wellspring of the Haskalah, the Jewish Enlightenment movement, which then expanded to influence Yiddish-speaking Jews of eastern Europe and Russia. By opening the way for modern secular Yiddish culture, it made professional Yiddish theatre possible.

Certain principles were integral to the soul of the Romantic movement. To the coolness of classicism, Romanticism opposed heat. To order, clarity, and austerity it opposed nature's bursting abundance and infinite variety. To the mind, it opposed the heart and the passions, intuition, and emotion, which it defined as the only authentic routes to truth. Romantic heroes and heroines were people of towering passion, and the ultimate goal of every individual was to attain the full expression of his own individual genius. By extension, Romantics were fascinated with national cultures—individual genius writ large—especially exotic cultures and national pasts. Romanticism carried in it a splendid defiance of the rules, the establishment, the way things had always been done; instead, it valued liberating explosions of natural will.

So too with Yiddish theatre. Its dramaturgy was Romantic in its lavish variety: plots, genres, tone, language. It was Romantic in the primacy it gave to emotion. The two highly emotional and highly Romantic forms, melodrama and expressionism, are also the two genres most typical of serious Yiddish drama. Passions reigned in performance and in the very nature of its heroes. The protagonists of Yiddish plays were often Romantic in that they were nationalistic; they were understood to represent Yiddish or Jewish culture. And Yiddish theatre was a rebel in the Romantic mould. This chapter will trace these four aspects of Yiddish theatre's Romanticism: variety, emotionalism, nationalism, and rebellion.

VARIETY

Romanticism scorns any fixed set of rules and conventions, including, in drama, the Aristotelian unities. Romantic plays typically have momentum, lavish sprawl, even chaos. *Faust*, for example, overflows: folk festivals, Walpurgis night, witches' kitchens, crowds, visions, voices. The plays do indeed tell a story, but plot often progresses through accretion and sensation rather than the conventions of linear development. This is in accordance with the principle articulated by Victor Hugo in the preface to his own play *Cromwell*: 'Genius, which divines rather than learns, devises for each work the general rules . . . The poet should take counsel only of nature, truth, and inspiration . . . Let the poet beware of copying anything whatsoever.'[1]

Yiddish drama never did hold to any one set of rules about form. In any case, Yiddish playwrights had no classical tradition to quote from, to revive periodically—or to stand on its head. Instead, Yiddish plots, especially in the early period, often seem to stride through time and space. Avrom Goldfaden's operetta *Shulamis* (1883) swoops over years. After the lovers meet and vow to be faithful for ever, Shulamis waits and waits while her prince creates and loses a whole second family; then he returns to her, and the second family disappears in the ensuing mass of events. Similarly, the settings range from mountainous waste, to priestly Jerusalem, to a luxurious chamber, to a shepherds' camp fire. 'The Romantic sensibility shifts and spins: Poetry . . . like the upheaval of an earthquake, will . . . set about doing as nature does,

[1] Victor Hugo, 'Préface à *Cromwell*', in Barrett H. Clark (ed.), *European Theories of the Drama* (New York: Crown, 1947), 379; trans. George Burnham Ives, repr. from *Dramatic Works of Victor Hugo* (Boston, 1909), vol. iii.

mingling in its creations—but without confounding them—darkness and light, the grotesque [the Romantics loved the grotesque] and the sublime . . . the body and the soul, the beast and the intellect',[2] explained Hugo, adding that harmony is artificial. Insisting on harmony will inevitably end up forcing the artist to 'mutilate' nature. Thus in *Shulamis* the emotional pitch rockets up and down. There is darkness: the spooky vow and its retribution, the dead child, the grief, and the double abandonment. And there is light: the capers of the servant Tsingitang, the duets of young love, the domestic billing and cooing. These extremes are never harmoniously reconciled; they are 'mingled' but not 'confounded'.

A Yiddish drama may even mingle genres within a single play. Levels of reality and fantasy, implausibility and improbability, slide past each other and collide. Jacob Gordin's *Got, mentsh, un tayvl* (God, Man, and Devil, 1900) starts with a prologue in which angels philosophize in choral blank verse rendered in high Germanic speech, but the action of the play is a melodrama, ranging over time and place, juxtaposing pathos with comic relief. The first scene of Dovid Pinski's *Der oytser* (The Treasure, 1906) promises a domestic family comedy with grotesque touches, but the play becomes increasingly expressionistic and dark as townspeople pour across the stage in choreographed groups. At the end of Act IV, a cheerful domestic moment breaks the mood and signals conventional plot resolution, but this abruptly gives way to the real conclusion, in which ghosts who wander the pre-dawn graveyard muse elliptically about the evils of society. The first and third acts of Peretz Hirschbein's *Di puste kretshme* (The Abandoned Inn, 1911) are domestic and erotic: will the boy get the girl? But the middle act escalates without warning into hallucination as mysterious merchants appear, rich gifts are displayed, and klezmer music rises to a frenzy. H. Leivick's *Shop* (1926) is a drama about a strike, a slice of life with somewhat poetic speech. But in the last act the characters suddenly erupt in a 'Dance of Pressing Irons and Shears', which in the stage directions is explicitly specified as symbolist.

Adapting to different audiences at different times and places—the result of a century of industrialization, immigration, and other violently uprooting experiences—kept Yiddish drama in constant flux. An appropriate image is the evolution of layers of commentary that ring the original text on a page of Talmud. Goldfaden's *Di kishefmakherin* (The Sorceress, 1877), Yitskhok Leyb Peretz's *Baynakht afn altn mark* (A Night in the Old Marketplace, 1907), and S. Ansky's *Der dibek* (The Dybbuk, 1920) are three of the most famous examples of plays created and re-created by directors, each time emerging as something new.

[2] Ibid. 369.

Mixing poetry and prose in the same play is not unique to Yiddish drama. Shakespeare employs the same Western convention, according to which characters who are 'high', whether in social class or honour or nobility of soul, might speak verse, while 'low' characters speak in prose. Early Yiddish theatre created its own version of this polarization: higher characters spoke *daytshmerish*, a heavily Germanic form considered to be fancy, while low characters spoke plain Yiddish, with a larger proportion of words of Slavonic derivation. This is further complicated by the use of *daytshmerish* for realistic character delineation: characters who speak *daytshmerish* (and even German at times) are sometimes held up to ridicule for their pretentiousness.

Yiddish drama typically mixed words and music as well. Operettas and what on Broadway came to be called musical comedies unapologetically punctuated dialogue with songs, which might or might not flow naturally from the scene and further the action. In *Shulamis* the 'Vow' duet is an expression of love, and in fact the lovers' singing of it is the moment that moves the plot. At other points, however, characters simply burst into song for no reason: 'Raisins and Almonds', the most famous song in the score, is a lullaby totally unrelated to the plot.

Music tended to infiltrate Yiddish non-musical plays as well. More intellectually ambitious dramatists tried to make sure that, rather than threaten verisimilitude, music arose naturally and logically from dramatic action. In *Got, mentsh, un tayvl*, for example, Gordin wove a musical setting of Psalm 23 into the action. Freyde sings it to Hershele, and for her it represents their love; Hershele plays it on the violin, and for him it represents his uncorrupted soul. For the audience it symbolizes both: a musical motif functioning in the style of Gordin's Romantic contemporary Richard Wagner. Leon Kobrin's *Yankl boyle* (1913) uses music in a more cinematic fashion; as Yankl's father lies dying in his shadowy room, drunken peasants can be heard singing next door in the tavern, emotionally heightening the scene.

Onstage prayers and cantillation are another overlap of words and music, poetry and prose. *Got, mentsh, un tayvl* includes not only Psalm 23 but also many elements of the liturgy for Yom Kippur, the solemn Day of Atonement: extended quotations from actual prayers, allusions to traditional images of death and final judgement, and even, offstage, the sounding of the ram's horn. Sholem Aleykhem's *Shver tsu zayn a yid* (Hard to be a Jew, 1914) provides a Passover Seder. Osip Dimov's *Der eybiker vanderer* (The Eternal Wanderer, 1907) culminates in the dramatic graveside recitation of the solemn prayer 'El mole rahamim' (God, Full of Mercy).

Of course, 'El mole rahamim', like most Jewish liturgy, is not in Yiddish but in Hebrew. Indeed, a mix of languages is in itself a characteristic sound in

Yiddish drama: Hebrew but also Russian, Polish, German, English, *daytsh-merish*, and the corrupt hybrid 'Yinglish'. Playwrights mixed languages for verisimilitude. Characters, like their audiences, were likely to speak several languages, shifting according to circumstances. In Leon Kobrin's *Riversayd drayv* (Riverside Drive, 1931) immigrant grandparents speak only Yiddish while Americanized grandchildren answer them in English. *Got, mentsh, un tayvl* is only one of many plays in which religious characters (or those who want to appear religious) are distinguished by liberal sprinklings of Hebrew in their speech. On a subtler level such mixing is also organic within the Yiddish language, which normally functions, in true Romantic fashion, in an abundance of distinct language streams 'mingled but not confounded'.

All these contradictory sensations, this sense of flow, the heaped-up riches—and the energy that they generate—the Romantics found in Shakespeare. Johann Gottfried Herder, Lessing's mentor, translated Shakespeare and conveyed his great enthusiasm to other young German dramatists of the *Sturm und Drang* sensibility. Herder himself and many of the younger dramatists, as well as the Schlegel brothers, whose journal *Das Athenäum* is considered the cradle of German Romanticism, all translated Shakespeare's works into German. As Romanticism expanded to France it was a touring English company's performances of Shakespeare in Paris in 1827 that inspired Victor Hugo to write plays. Hugo called Shakespeare 'the god of the stage', describing how he would 'bring Romeo face to face with the apothecary . . . Hamlet with the gravedigger . . . in the scene between King Lear and his jester, mingle its shrill voice with the most sublime, the most dismal, the dreamiest music of the soul'.[3] Hugo compared Shakespeare's works to 'a great animated fair',[4] evoking associations of liveliness, colour, and chaos. Shakespeare was probably performed on the Yiddish stage more than any other non-Yiddish playwright. True, it was generally the same few plays over and over again, most successfully *Lear* and *Hamlet*, and more often adapted than directly translated, but the Yiddish theatre welcomed Shakespeare with genuine relish.

Not only the dramaturgical forms of Yiddish drama but the very nature of Yiddish theatre as an institution was Romantic, repudiating distinctions and purity in favour of variety and abundance. Just as history forced Yiddish theatre to set up stage not only in theatres but in garden cafés and on railway platforms, in libraries and in barns, so too, in addition to the usual genres, Yiddish theatre included cabarets and revues, readings ('word concerts') and art songs. The repertoire included many plays that were originally written not

---

[3] Clark (ed.), *European Theories of the Drama*, 375.   [4] Ibid.

as plays but as dramatizations. Among the best known were Sholem Yankev
Abramovitsh's (Mendele Moykher Sforim) *Masoes binyomin hashlishi* (The
Travels of Benjamin III, 1927) and I. J. Singer's *Yoshe kalb* (Yoshe the Calf,
1932), both from novels by the same name.

Periods were jumbled as well. In the compact history of Yiddish theatre,
eras virtually coexisted. In the early twentieth century a theatregoer could see
a Purim play, an operetta, a melodrama, a problem play, an expressionist
play, a domestic comedy, a variety revue—all in one year, and, all except the
traditional Purim play, professionally produced. Goldfaden wrote the folky
operetta *Di kishefmakherin* in 1877; Gordin 'sat down like a scribe' to elevate
Yiddish theatre with his melodrama *Sibirye* (Siberia) in 1891; and in 1907,
when Asch wrote the naturalistic problem play *Got fun nekome* (God of
Vengeance), Goldfaden and Gordin were still active dramatists.

This chronological overlapping had interesting results. The genres seem to
have actively influenced each other, and authors felt free to try widely varying
styles and genres. So Peretz wrote not only the grim one-act *Shvester* (Sisters,
1906), but also the poetic *Di goldene keyt* (The Golden Chain, 1907). Hirschbein wrote not only the naturalistic *Miryam* (Miriam, 1904) and the symbolist *Tsvishn tog un nakht* (Between Day and Night, 1906), but also the pastoral
Grine felder (Green Fields, 1916). Leivick wrote both *Shmates* (Rags, 1921),
about sweatshop reality and immigrant identity, and *Der goylem* (The Golem,
1920), a symbolist poem about humanity's longing for a spiritually finer
universe. Following Hugo's dictum against 'copying anything whatsoever',
these authors so strove for originality that they did not even copy themselves.

EMOTIONALISM

Yiddish theatre was Romantic not only in its generous, colourful variety but
also in its emotionalism. Emotion was the engine of Romanticism. Schiller
was praising theatre highly when he explained that the theatregoer 'shares in
the general ecstasy, and his breast has now only space for an emotion'.[5] In his
essay 'Shakespeare ad Infinitum' Goethe declared that 'the highest achievement possible to a man is the full consciousness of his own feelings and
thoughts', and added that in Shakespeare 'what the soul anxiously conceals
and represses is here brought freely and abundantly to life'.[6]

[5] Friedrich Schiller, 'Die Schaubuhne als eine moralische Anstalt betrachtet' [The Stage as a
Moral Institution], in John Gassner and Ralph G. Allen (eds.), *Theatre and Drama in the Making*
(Boston: Houghton Mifflin, 1964), 522.

[6] Johann Wolfgang von Goethe, 'Shakespeare ad Infinitum', trans. Randolph S. Bourne, in
Gassner and Allen (eds.), *Theatre and Drama in the Making*, 486.

'Brought abundantly to life' can serve as a metaphor for performance. Romantic actors were known for the immediacy of their emotionalism and the intensity of their temperament. Coleridge described, for example, the famous English actor Edmund Kean (who while on tour in Paris had galvanized Victor Hugo). Kean was a small, homely man with a rasping voice, but Coleridge likened watching him to 'reading Shakespeare by flashes of lightning'.[7] Eyewitnesses claimed just such thrilling power for the Yiddish stars. The ability to tear raw emotion out of oneself makes acting of this type a quintessentially Romantic profession, and Yiddish actors were noted for their emotionalism and temperament.

The journalist Hutchins Hapgood, a close observer of New York's Jewish quarter in the early 1900s, quoted a poetic circular which, in praising the popular actor Boris Thomashefsky, demanded rhetorically of his rivals,

> Are you gifted with feeling
> So much as to imitate him like a shadow?

Trying to describe for his uptown readers the distinctive quality of Yiddish actors, Hapgood concluded that they 'act with remarkable sincerity. Entirely lacking in self-consciousness, they attain almost from the outset a direct and forcible expressiveness. To be true to nature is their strongest passion.'[8] Thus when a modern student of text dismisses Yiddish actors as old-fashioned and hammy, and appreciation of great performance as 'starism', he is denying a profound element of their art.

A corollary is that spontaneous ad libbing can be seen as an assertion of the primacy of what the actor (or the character) feels at that moment. The actor's mission then is to follow recklessly, to plunge after, wherever the actor's own temperament or the role may lead, rejecting the control of a rigid, prepared text. On the other hand, such ad libbing could be the despair of serious Yiddish dramatists. A famous example occurred early in the career of Jacob Gordin. Gordin himself played a Russian policeman sitting in the kitchen of a humble Jewish home. The housewife put fish and schnapps in front of him, and, as he began to eat, the actress turned towards the audience and exclaimed, 'He should only choke on it!' The policeman–playwright slammed the table with the butt of his whip and jumped up, overturning his chair, spilling the schnapps in his fury, and yelled, 'No, no, no! That is not in the script!' But the crowd loved her comment, which surely expressed what was in the housewife's heart.

---

[7] Quoted in Gassner and Allen (eds.), *Theatre and Drama in the Making*, 593.
[8] Hutchins Hapgood, *The Spirit of the Ghetto* (1902; repr. Cambridge, Mass.: Harvard University Press, 1967), 122.

According to the Romantic aesthetic, a great actor abandons himself whole-heartedly in order to serve and embody his own individual nature, his natural genius. Focusing and channelling this natural force into his role generates a powerful charge of theatrical energy, electrifying the audience. His own personal qualities infuse the roles he plays, while at the same time the roles amplify his own persona. No wonder nineteenth-century theatre history—and in Yiddish theatre this continued well into the twentieth century—offered accounts of enthusiastic fans carrying actors on their shoulders in triumph through the streets.

Characters' individual intensity made them vivid beyond the confines of plot. Romantic protagonists were larger than ordinary people. They might be heroes in the most common sense: Bar Kokhba, who defied the Roman army, or Sofia (as Gordin named his modern Sappho), who dared all for love. Some, on the other hand, had greatness conferred upon them only by the sheer magnitude of their passions. Victor Hugo described the actions of such characters as 'the outburst of a soul on fire [which] illumines art and history at once; that cry of anguish is the résumé of drama and of life'.[9] Like Büchner's pathetic barber Woyzeck, maddened by jealousy, Yiddish theatre protagonists include Pinski's frustrated inventor Isaac Sheftl; Yekl in *Got fun nekome*, the brothel-keeper who sets his heart on a mad ideal of purity; and Leivick's inarticulate clay man, the golem himself. Diametrically opposed to Aristotle's conception of the tragic hero, these were 'men of genius' in Hugo's formulation: 'however great they be, [they] have always within them a touch of the beast which mocks at their intelligence. Therein are they akin to mankind in general, for therein are they dramatic.'[10]

Ansky's *Der dibek*, perhaps the best known of all Yiddish plays, employs several typical Romantic techniques to raise the emotional pitch. It is a love story but also something more intense. A young couple fall in love, unaware that their souls are already betrothed because, even before their births, their fathers had pledged them in marriage. When she is forced to marry another, he uses dangerous kabbalistic spells to die and enter her body as a dybbuk. Ansky presents the love between the young couple as not so much a psychological as a spiritual or even mystical union. Such fusion of passion and love with something larger than the personal relationship was particularly congenial to Yiddish culture.

The Romantics also loved the supernatural and the exotic, storms, ghosts, and spooky ruins—all of which heighten the emotional charge of the theatrical experience. *Der dibek* abounds in examples: the wild dance of menacing beggars; the mysterious messenger; the brooding presence of the ancient

---

[9] Clark (ed.), *European Theories of the Drama*, 375.　　　　　　　　　　[10] Ibid.

graves of murdered lovers; the solemn exorcism; and the dybbuk itself speaking from inside the writhing body of his beloved.

When Jewish norms are imposed on Romantic emotionalism, what results is melodrama, the genre most characteristic of Yiddish drama. Melodrama as we know it appeared around the period when Schiller, Hugo, and Ostrovsky were writing their best-known plays. And although, as a distinct genre, melodrama was more widely popular—and popular for a longer period—than those formally Romantic creations such as Schiller's *The Robbers*, Hugo's *Hernani*, and Ostrovsky's *The Storm*, it nevertheless shares many of their qualities.

The essence of melodrama is virtue's ultimate victory over evil. This underlying battle, which is extremely compatible with the traditional Jewish preference for didactic purpose in art, raises the emotional stakes above the specific to the universal.[11] Melodrama taps such strong emotions because audiences sense that what is being enacted touches a larger truth. Schiller said that theatre at its purest is 'where all artifice ends, and truth alone is the judge'.[12] Hutchins Hapgood quoted the typical Lower East Side theatregoer, for whom the highest praise was 'It's true'.[13] (Compare Byron's praise for Edmund Kean: 'Life, nature, truth without exaggeration'.[14]) The tears that we nowadays dismiss as sentimental reaction were valued by nineteenth-century Romantics as nature's free response to truth—an attitude that Yiddish theatregoers preserved well into the twentieth century.

Virtue's struggle to overcome evil drives the action, shaping a plot that scorns unities of action, time, or place as it moves through events to moral as well as artistic closure. Human beings crave affirmation that there is ultimate justice in the world. The human desire for story and for closure, especially with a happy ending, ensures that melodramas remain more universally popular than *Woyzeck*, which ends with murder and inglorious suicide, or *Baynakht afn altn mark*, which ends with a failed attempt to hasten the messianic era. To the extent that actors represent virtue or evil, they are abstractions: larger than ordinary mortals, larger than life. This in turn heightens the effect of their performance and elevates their status as artistic souls.

There are other Romantic elements in melodrama as well. First, like Yiddish theatre in general, it usually includes music. In fact, that is probably

[11] Robert B. Heilman, *Tragedy and Melodrama* (Seattle: University of Washington Press, 1968), 97. For related perceptions see also Peter Brooks, *The Melodramatic Imagination* (New Haven: Yale University Press, 1984).
[12] Gassner and Allen (eds.), *Theatre and Drama in the Making*, 517.
[13] Hapgood, *The Spirit of the Ghetto*, 138.
[14] Gassner and Allen (eds.), *Theatre and Drama in the Making*, 593.

the source of the term itself (from the Greek *melos*, music), thought to have been coined by the voice of Romanticism, Jean-Jacques Rousseau. Also melodrama's juxtapositions in structure and tone, its violent combinations of tragic and merry, high and low, are typically Romantic. Yet another Romantic element is melodrama's characteristic use of touches of the supernatural.

Expressionism was another dramatic form particularly beloved of serious Yiddish audiences. Like melodrama, expressionism is a way to shape a chaos of feelings and behaviour. It is a mix of speech with movement and sound, a mix of purposeful high seriousness with grotesquerie. In most early twentieth-century expressionist theatre the political ideal shaped the aesthetic experience in a way analogous to the structure which the victory of personal virtue provided for melodrama. In both cases the commitment was to art not for its own sake, but rather for the sake of a severer truth. It was in this spirit that Soviet Yiddish director Alexander Granovsky reworked *Baynakht afn altn mark*, the poem which Peretz himself had subtitled *Troym fun a fibernakht*. (Dream of a Fever Night), as a condemnation of pre-revolutionary capitalism.

NATIONALISM

Yiddish theatre was Romantic in its nationalism. Herder, who introduced the young German dramatists to Shakespeare, is best remembered today for his concept of a national soul. Schiller's quintessentially Romantic play *Wilhelm Tell* (1804) celebrates the Swiss hero who fought for national liberation. Peretz was perfectly in tune with Romantic attitudes when he pronounced:

art is the soul of a people, the personality of a nation. . . . To find the heart, the essence of Jewishness in all places and times, in all parts of this scattered, dispersed yet universal people . . . this is the task of the Jewish artist. Creation is an exaltation of the spirit. For the Jewish artist only a Jewish soul, his specifically Jewish soul, can be his Shkhina [an emanation of the Divine Presence], his glory, enthusiasm, creative force.[15]

And indeed with remarkable frequency Yiddish plays turned on, centred on, explored, or celebrated Jewish history or Zionism, communal loyalty or Jewish identity, Yiddish culture or religious Judaism—though this last was rarer, and generally served as metaphor for the others.

A sampling of Yiddish plays reveals many perspectives on nationalism. Goldfaden's hero Bar Kokhba defies Roman rule in ancient Palestine. Goldfaden's hero Ben Ami rejects the Russian diaspora to rebuild Palestine. Aaron

---

[15] Y. L. Peretz, 'What our Literature Needs', in Irving Howe and Eliezer Greenberg (eds.), *Voices from the Yiddish* (Ann Arbor: University of Michigan Press, 1972), 31.

Tseytlin's hero Brenner martyrs himself in the Arab pogrom of 1921. The plot of *Shver tsu zayn a yid* compares the fortunes of a young Jew and a young non-Jew who switch identities in an antisemitic society. In Alter Kacyzne's *Der dukus* (The Duke, 1925) a Christian nobleman converts to Judaism and suffers for his new religious beliefs. Old Reb Moyshe in Pinski's *Di familye tsvi* (The Tsvi Family, also known as *Der letster yid* (The Last Jew), 1905) defends the actual Torah scroll from a peasant mob. In Osip Dimov's *Bronks ekspres* (Bronx Express, 1919) stubborn observance of Yom Kippur is a matter less of piety than of loyalty to fellow Jews. Reb Shloyme in Peretz's *Di goldene keyt* agonizes over ritual practice and commitment to it through generations to come. In Pinski's *Yeder mit zayn got* (To Each his Own God, 1912) refusing to work on the sabbath becomes a metaphor for a humiliated man's last claim to human dignity.

In a number of Yiddish plays the 'nation' itself served as collective hero. Pinski's *Der eybiker yid* (The Eternal Jew, 1906) and Dimov's *Der eybiker vanderer* are allegories of Jewish communities driven by oppression. Pinski's *Di familye tsvi* and Sholem Aleykhem's *Tsezeyt un tseshpreyt* (Scattered and Dispersed, 1903) use families to similar purpose: by making one family member a communist, another a Zionist, a third traditionally pious, and so on, the playwright has created a microcosm of the Jewish world.

Another nationalistic theme is the coming of the messiah. Tseytlin's *Yankev frank* (Jacob Frank, 1929) portrays Shabtay Tsvi, the false messiah of the sixteenth century. Pinski's *Der shtumer meshiekh* (The Mute Messiah, 1918), Asch's *Meshiekhs tsaytn* (The Messianic Era, 1906), and Leivick's *Der goylem* build symbolic plots on messianic longings. The messiah as a recurrent image weaves through many plays, as it does through traditional Yiddish speech.

Mention of the messiah in this sense is an example of yet another affinity with Romanticism: deliberate use of folkloric elements for the sake of colour. In Yiddish theatre, folklore achieved a particularly pungent effect because the theatre existed in a period of violent shifts for the Yiddish-speaking community. Through songs and dances, religious rituals, and above all the language itself, from proverbs to prayers—in all these forms and more, audiences experienced folklore sometimes as distant cultural allusion and sometimes as direct reflection of their daily lives. *Der dibek*, which Ansky based on the gleanings of an anthropological expedition among Ukrainian Jews, is rich in traditional customs that already seemed exotic to urban Jewish audiences. Folklore creates connection to the past, another Romantic predilection and one particularly congenial to Jewish culture. Finally, it enhances a sense of national history.

According to Romanticism, the theatre is in itself a nationalist institution. Schiller made the specific connection to political nationhood when he reflected that 'if the poets were allied in aim, there would be a national stage, and we should become a nation. It was this that knit the Greeks so strongly together.'[16] In this identification of national stage with nationhood itself he was echoed particularly by the nineteenth-century Yiddish intelligentsia who created modern Yiddish literature. For them theatre was the voice and validation of a fine national culture. No wonder Peretz is supposed to have exclaimed after first seeing the Vilna Troupe, 'Congratulations, Jews, we have a theatre!' What he meant was, 'Congratulations! Now that we have a fine theatre, we have finally become a nation as the modern world understands the term!'

REBELLION

Romanticism repudiated more than formal dramaturgical rules. It defied the very notion of submission to rules. The Romantic movement occurred in the period of the French and American revolutions, after all, and Schiller talked about theatregoing as 'emancipation from the chains of conventionality'.[17]

Onstage such emancipation might also mean dramas unfettered by practical demands of stagecraft. The early Romantic dramatists were often poets— Goethe, Schiller, Hugo, Coleridge, Byron—and often their plays were poetic dramas or, more precisely, poems in dramatic form rather than plays at all. *Faust* is an example, as is Byron's *Manfred*. Two of the most famous Yiddish dramas are dramatic poems of this type: Leivick's *Der goylem* and Peretz's *Baynakht afn altn mark*. The former was rarely performed, though Leivick wrote several versions based on the same idea. The latter was performed in very different versions created for the stage by the directors (most notably David Herman in 1928 and Alexander Granovsky in 1925) out of Peretz's free-wheeling original *Dream of a Fever Night*.

Among the best-known protagonists of Romantic plays were the eponymous Goetz von Berlichingen and Faust (Goethe), Hernani (Hugo), and the Prince of Hamburg (Kleist)—all rebels on a splendid scale. Goldfaden's Bar Kokhba, who leads the Jews of ancient Palestine against imperial Rome, is a national hero of the same type. Leivick's *Hirsh lekert* (1931) tells the true story of a shoemaker who in 1902 tried to assassinate the governor of Vilna.

Rebellion against *society* was a recurrent theme. Agitation for political change worked as subtext beneath much of modern Yiddish dramatic literature.

---

[16] Gassner and Allen (eds.), *Theatre and Drama in the Making*, 521.   [17] Ibid. 522.

However, rebellions in Yiddish plays were not necessarily political. For example, Gordin's Sappho rebels against convention by bearing a love child and refusing on principle to marry its father. His Elisha ben Abuyah is a heretic who rebels against rabbinic Judaism. The stand of Mordkhe Maze in Leivick's *Shmates* is both subtler and more abstract; he rejects family ties, American prosperity, and even loyalty to the ideals of his striking co-workers, all in order to remain true to an unattainable ideal of dignity.

Religion was a vivid and powerful element in Jewish cultural life, even among the many intellectuals who had rejected it; religious practice and the very idea of God surfaced in many plays, and rebellion explicitly against God and God's order is a theme in a number of dramas. In *Di goldene keyt* the rabbi tries to prolong the sabbath; he wants to overthrow God's order for the sake of what he conceives to be a holier universe. In *Der dibek* Khonen, like Faust, defies God by striving for unnatural powers, which he uses to unite himself with the woman he loves. The rabbi in *Der goylem* also goes against God and nature when he creates a golem to fight for besieged Jews, for the power to breathe life into clay is God's alone.[18]

One might call the very institution of Yiddish theatre a rebel from birth. Play-acting transgressed traditional prohibitions against men hearing women's voices, men dressing as women, the making of images, and the general frivolity summed up in the words of the psalm as 'sitting in the seat of scoffers'. Unlike Christian folk plays, which despite clowning were essentially pious occasions, associated with the solemnities of the Mass and with the Resurrection, Purim plays were purposely irreverent. They took place outside the synagogue and initially only on a day of foolery. Finally, the Yiddish language itself was a rebel. Hebrew was the aristocrat, the language of prayer and beauty. In the secular sphere German and French, Polish and Russian, were the languages of high culture. In the nineteenth century, when modern secular literary Yiddish was new, a creative institution in the Yiddish language was revolutionary by definition.

Indeed one could think of Yiddish theatre itself as a splendid Romantic rebel, making art in the teeth of starvation, persecution, migration, assimilation, and—as time passed—the ageing of its own artists and audiences. During the last half-century, as Yiddish has fought for its life, its supporters have watched the drama of the embattled institution: a popular image both passionate and grotesque.

---

[18] For many of these examples of rebellion, as well as for other useful suggestions, I am indebted to Joel Berkowitz.

THREE

Jewish Plays on the Russian Stage: St Petersburg 1905–1917

ɞ

BARBARA HENRY

IT has long been assumed that when the tsarist government imposed a twenty-five-year ban on Yiddish theatre in 1883, it prevented all but the most determined of impresarios from staging Yiddish plays in Russia. As a result of the ban, many Yiddish companies left Russia altogether. Those who remained were forced to conceal their identity by billing themselves as German Jewish troupes, or by attempting to charm or bribe local officials, or to avoid them entirely. Official intolerance was thought to be too pervasive for any Yiddish companies of consequence to exist in Russia until the ban expired in 1908. For many years it was believed that only after 1920—when the Yiddish Chamber Theatre of Alexander Granovsky (1890–1937) was included in the Soviet state's network of academic theatres—could Yiddish theatre be regarded as a truly viable art form in Russia.

Recent scholarship based on Soviet and Russian sources and archives, has, however, cast considerable doubt on these assumptions about the history of Yiddish theatre in Russia.[1] That the ban made life difficult for Yiddish companies is certain; but both the long- and short-term efficacy of the ban has been questioned, as has the tsarist regime's motivation in enacting it (see Chapter 9). Convincing evidence that the ban did not—and could not—

I wish to thank Mirosława Bułat, John Klier, Joel Berkowitz, and Jeffrey Veidlinger for their generous help and comments on this chapter. I am also grateful for the support of St Antony's College, Oxford, for their funding of this research through the Max Hayward Fellowship in Russian Literature.

[1] For recent research on the Yiddish theatre in Russia and the Soviet Union, see Evgeny Binevich's numerous articles on the subject, available online from the Jewish Heritage Society at <http://www.jewish-heritage.org>; Jeffrey Veidlinger, 'Let's Perform a Miracle: The Soviet Yiddish State Theater in the 1920s', *Slavic Review*, 57 (Summer 1998), 372–97; Vladislav Ivanov, 'Petrogradskie sezony evreiskogo kamernogo teatra' [The Petrograd Seasons of the Jewish Chamber Theatre], *Moskva*, 2 (1998), 571–97. Ivanov's article is also available online at the Research Library and Archives of Jewish Theater site, <http://www.members.tripod.com>.

suppress Yiddish theatrical performances strongly implies that the tradition may have survived the years of the ban in a better state than was once supposed.

One clear indication of the tsarist regime's failure to extinguish Yiddish theatrical culture, both during the period of the ban's enforcement and in the years following its supposed expiry, is the fact that between 1905 and 1917 more than 160 productions of plays in Yiddish were staged in the heart of the tsarist bureaucracy itself, the capital city of St Petersburg. These productions were the work of both touring companies and, more surprisingly, local Yiddish theatre groups that were established in the last decade of tsarist rule.[2] That the Yiddish theatre not only survived the years of the ban, but produced a new generation of performers, impresarios, and directors during the very period of its suppression, contradicts the conventional view of it as a moribund art form, revived only under the ministrations of the Bolshevik state.

Evidence of a continuing Yiddish theatrical tradition both before and after the ban of 1883 can be gleaned from several sources. One source that has been entirely overlooked by both Western and Russian scholars is that of the plays themselves. Imperial Russian law required anyone wishing to stage a play—anywhere in the empire, in any language—to submit two copies of that play to the central office of censorship in St Petersburg.[3] There the play would be read and either permitted or forbidden to be performed; one copy would be returned to the company wishing to stage the work, and one would remain with the censor in St Petersburg. After the October Revolution the complete collections of tsarist censors' texts were transferred to the St Petersburg Theatrical Library, where they remain today. The Jewish collection (which includes both Yiddish and Hebrew plays) provides ample testimony to the survival of a Yiddish theatrical tradition during the years of the ban. Contrary to expectations, during this very period many hundreds of Yiddish plays were declared suitable for performance by the St Petersburg censors. This does not guarantee, of course, that the plays were actually performed, as local officials

---

[2] Compare this with Mikhail Beizer's statement in his otherwise meticulously researched study *The Jews of St Petersburg: Excursions through a Noble Past* (Philadelphia: Jewish Publication Society, 1989), 146: 'Up to 1919, we can find no significant traces of any Jewish theatrical life in St. Petersburg–Petrograd, even though amateur and occasionally professional groups did come to the city on tour.'

[3] See *Svod Zakonov Rossiiskoi Imperii*, 'Ustav o Tsenzure i Pechati', Sect. 7, Arts. 83–92. These censorship laws were first instituted formally in 1865, and were then periodically amended and updated. Particularly stringent censorship was applied to any theatre that aimed its plays at a working-class or peasant audience. In addition, in certain 'sensitive' areas of the empire, such as the Pale of Settlement and the Caucasus, local officials were also required to give their consent to any plays performed in a language other than Russian, even if the play had been declared suitable by the St Petersburg censor, or had been performed previously.

could still ban a production even if St Petersburg had cleared a play for performance. But the very fact that Yiddish plays *were* cleared in great numbers by St Petersburg throws into doubt the assumption that the tsarist regime was implacably hostile to Jewish theatre. It is also worth noting that the plays rejected by the censor were usually those that featured biblical themes and characters—subject matter that was strictly forbidden on the Russian-language stage as well.

Another important source of information on the Yiddish theatre in this period is the Russian-language press, as advertisements and reviews of Yiddish productions appeared regularly in St Petersburg's daily newspapers and theatre journals.[4] According to reports in the press, the earliest Yiddish theatrical performances in St Petersburg in the period under discussion were those of Yakov Spivakovsky's German Jewish operetta company, which, after apparently having made several unsuccessful attempts to perform in the capital, arrived there in March 1905. According to one scholar, the company had gone so far as to book a theatre in the city in 1898, during the Lenten season, when foreign-language companies traditionally played in Russian cities. Plans fell through, however, as the all-important temporary residence permit, the *pravo zhitel'stva*, which was required for all Jewish performers—indeed for all Jews wishing to visit St Petersburg—was not granted.[5] Other companies had been refused on the same grounds, but Spivakovsky was not so easily defeated. His eventual success in 1905 was achieved with the aid of a charity called the Blue Cross; according to the press, the company had agreed to donate a portion of their profits to the charity in return for its securing them the necessary residence permits. The general liberalization of censorship rules, which Nicholas II had reluctantly introduced late in 1904, may also have had as much to do with the Yiddish company's being allowed to perform in St Petersburg as the charity's intervention itself.

Spivakovsky's company duly advertised their opening at the Nemetti Theatre on 7 March 1905.[6] On the opening night they performed Avrom Goldfaden's *Shulamis*, an appropriate choice since the last Yiddish company St Petersburg had seen was Goldfaden's own, which had performed in the city from July 1881 until April 1882. Spivakovsky's production of *Shulamis* was

---

[4] The newspapers and journals consulted for this research include the St Petersburg journals *Rech'* [Speech]; *Birzhevye Vedomosti* [Stock Exchange News]; *Teatr i Iskusstvo* [Theatre and Art], and *Obozrenie Teatrov* [Theatre Review] for the years 1900–17. The St Petersburg journal *Voskhod* [Rising, or The East] (1881–1906) was, unfortunately, not available for this research.

[5] Evgeny Binevich, 'Gastrolery v peterburge' [Touring Performers in St Petersburg], Preprint 9 of the Jewish Heritage Society, citing 'Khronika' [Chronicle], *Teatr*, 7 Nov. 1898, 3.

[6] The Nemetti Theatre (also known as the Novyi Theatre) seated 1,000, and was located on the 'Petersburg side' (Peterburgskaya storona), a predominantly working-class district of the city.

advertised as being performed in German, but it was a ruse that fooled no one—certainly not the audience who crowded the theatre, nor the critics sent to review it.

Critical opinion of the productions was sorely divided. One reviewer, from the *Peterburgskaya Gazeta*, found the Spivakovsky company engaging, highly musical, and very professional. Another, however, from *Syn Otechestva* (Son of the Fatherland), compared the company unfavourably with Goldfaden's own, which the critic knew well from his time in Warsaw in the mid-1880s. The critic for *Birzhevye Vedomosti* (Stock Exchange News), N. Markov, reviewing a production given early on in the company's run, noted only the theatre's empty seats and yawning patrons glancing at their watches and waiting impatiently for the curtain. 'What's good enough for the depths of the Pale', he sniffed, 'is hardly suitable for the capital. You're not going to astonish St Petersburg with an outfit like this, and I can only think that after "successes" like these, this troupe won't be coming back here any time soon.'[7] Markov was wrong; the balance of evidence points to the company's enjoying a profitable run. Not only did they move to a better theatre, closer to the centre of town, midway through their stay, but they returned to St Petersburg in 1907.

This second tour attracted less notice from the press, and the attention it did gain was largely negative. In a brief review of the Spivakovsky company's production of Goldfaden's *Bar kokhba*, Alexander Kugel (1864–1928), the editor and founder of the journal *Teatr i Iskusstvo* (Theatre and Art), and probably Russia's best-known theatre critic, called the operetta 'naive', and remarked that the music seemed to have been drawn mainly from old Italian operas. He had some praise for the singing, but was very critical of the acting, complaining of its corruption of German Romantic convention and its overly emotive tone.[8]

However, the most memorable events in the life of Yiddish theatre in St Petersburg—events that served as the benchmark for all later Yiddish-language productions—occurred when Avrom Kaminsky's Warsaw-based company toured the capital in 1908 and 1909. Unlike Spivakovsky's company, Kaminsky's was pointedly a 'literary' theatre, and it offered St Petersburg not a single work by Goldfaden or Joseph Lateiner. This should have stood the company in good stead with those critics who had derided the musical repertoire of the Yiddish theatre, but it seems that, initially, the idea of a literary Yiddish theatre was met with suspicion by St Petersburg's critics. They

<hr/>

[7] N. Markov, 'Teatr', *Birzhevye Vedomosti*, 2 Mar. 1905, 6, cited in Binevich, 'Gastrolery v peterburge', 5.
[8] N.N. [N. Negorev (Alexander Kugel)], 'Khronika' [Chronicle], *Teatr i Iskusstvo*, 19 (1907), 309.

greeted the company's initial production, *Di shkhite* (The Slaughter), by Jacob Gordin (1853–1909), with some scepticism.

The company's opening night, 15 April 1908, at the Theatre on Ofitserskaya Street, not far from the city's grand Choral Synagogue, also provided a piece of backstage drama. With the theatre full, the bells for the start of the play having rung, and the house lights dimmed, the curtain failed to rise. There was some confusion, and voices shouting in Yiddish could be heard behind the curtain. The fear, of course, was that at the last minute the police had banned the production. But suddenly the curtain rose. One reviewer described the scene:

They wore wigs, caftans, and yarmulkes; and when it was time to weep they wept long and as one, in simultaneous torment; and when it was time to make merry, they did this too with unvarying, communal gaiety . . . And they sobbed loudly, shrilly, to the point of hysterics, not only on stage but in the house, because it stood to reason that this was how one represented everyday Jewish life, and this was how one created a Jewish theatre.[9]

Another critic, Nikolai Shebuev, reviewed a later performance of the same play. He too noticed the deep emotional response that the performance evoked from the audience. Taking a thoughtful look around him, he remarked:

A Jewish theatre audience is a special kind of audience. They listen with extraordinary attentiveness and sensitivity to every heartbeat . . . In Act IV, during the mad scene, they were weeping in the boxes and the orchestra. Bearded men with greying hair blinked back a secret tear from their red-rimmed eyes, and then went home their separate ways. But these very same grey-haired men had just moments before responded with unrestrained laughter to the jokes of the talented (if somewhat monotonous) Mr Vaysman.[10]

[9] Kin (pseud.), 'Teatr i muzyka—Evreiskii literaturnyi teatr—*Zaklanie*, drama v 4 d., soch. Ya. Gordina' [Theatre and Music—Jewish Literary Theatre—*The Slaughter*, a Drama in Four Acts by Jacob Gordin], *Rech'*, 17 Apr. 1908, 5.

[10] Nikolai Shebuev, 'Di shkhite' [The Slaughter], *Obozrenie Teatrov*, 3 May 1908, 3–4. It is difficult to speculate on the exact composition of the audiences for these plays. The Jewish population of St Petersburg (which one can assume corresponded with the number of Yiddish speakers) never exceeded 2% of the total population of St Petersburg itself, even in 1917, when there were an estimated 50,000 Jews living in the city. It should not necessarily be assumed that only Jews attended Yiddish theatre in St Petersburg. The city was home to several foreign-language companies, and even had a permanent German-language theatre dating to the 18th century. Moreover, foreign companies from as far away as Japan regularly toured St Petersburg, and were a staple feature of the repertoire until 1914. St Petersburg audiences had long been accustomed to theatrical performances in languages other than Russian, and there is every reason to believe that they would have attended Yiddish theatre as well, particularly given the popularity of Jewish themes in the Russian repertoire itself.

But if the reaction of St Petersburg audiences to the Kaminsky company was passionate, the literary quality of the repertoire, which consisted primarily of Gordin's plays, was again the subject of endless complaints from the critics.[11] Reviewers loathed Gordin's plays for their melodrama and their 'ethnographic' elements, and reserved special scorn for what Nahma Sandrow has called the playwright's tendency towards 'moralistic, unnaturally centripetal endings'.[12] The pleasant 'shock of recognition' that one might have expected to greet the depiction of Jews and Jewish subjects on the Russian stage did not apply here. Instead Gordin's dramaturgy came in for heavy criticism because St Petersburg audiences were already quite familiar with Jewish plays.

From 1900 until the revolution the Russian stage saw a continual turnover of very popular plays dealing with Jewish subjects. Some of these plays were translations of Yiddish originals, such as Sholem Asch's (1880–1957) *Got fun nekome* (God of Vengeance, 1907), which opened in St Petersburg in Russian translation in 1907. Others were by Russian Jewish writers such as Semyon Yushkevich (1868–1927) and Osip Dimov (1878–1959), or even by non-Jewish Russian writers, such as Evgeny Chirikov (1864–1932), Leonid Andreev (1871–1919), and Arkady Averchenko (1881–1925). Still others were translations from French, German, and Polish. While the initial production of plays such as Chirikov's *Evrei* (The Jews, 1903) or Dimov's *Slushai, izrail!* (Hear, O Israel!, 1907; later translated into Yiddish) were clearly a response to the pogroms of 1903 and 1905, very few of the works that made up the Jewish repertoire at the beginning of the twentieth century could be considered 'pogrom' plays. As well as issue-based dramas, the repertoire included satires, one-act comedies, and domestic tragedies.

These plays also differed substantially from earlier Jewish plays, such as Gotthold Ephraim Lessing's *Nathan der Weise* (Nathan the Wise, 1779) and Karl Gutzkow's *Uriel Acosta* (1847). These works, all staples of the nineteenth-century Russian repertoire, are set in the past in European locations. The turn-of-the-century Russian Jewish repertoire, in contrast, consisted overwhelmingly of original Russian plays and translations from Yiddish. These plays were local and contemporary, and set within the Pale of Settlement itself,

[11] For their 1908 tour the Kaminsky company performed *Di shkhite*, *Mirele efros*, *Gebrokhene hertser* (Broken Hearts), *Der fremder* (The Stranger), *Talmid khokhem* (Learned Scholar), *Kroytser sonate* (Kreutzer Sonata), *Yankl der shmid* (Yankl the Blacksmith), *Dos vare glik* (True Luck), *Der yidisher kenig lir* (The Jewish King Lear, 1892), *Khasye di yesoyme* (Khasye the Orphan), *Hamlet; oder, Der yeshive bokher* (Hamlet; or the Yeshiva Student, 1899), *Di muter* (The Mother), *Yankev meshulem* (Jacob the True), *Di emese kraft* (The True Power), and Gordin's adaptation of Franz Grillparzer's (1791–1872) *Medea*.

[12] Nahma Sandrow, *Vagabond Stars: A World History of Yiddish Theatre* (Syracuse, NY: Syracuse University Press, 1996), 150.

which, in play after play, takes on a metaphorical significance as a kind of Russian frontier. Like the Caucasus for the nineteenth-century Russian literary imagination, or the American West, the Pale of Settlement becomes more a mythic than an actual landscape, a place where Russia could act out anxieties and fantasies about modernity, money, sex, and her Slavonic 'manifest destiny'. Such was the popularity and familiarity of these plays that part of the harsh critical reaction to Gordin's 'real' Yiddish plays may simply have been a result of their not coinciding with critics' own ideas of what constituted an 'authentic' Jewish play.

When the Kaminsky company returned triumphantly to St Petersburg in 1909, complaints about the repertoire were somewhat assuaged by the inclusion of a greater number of non-Gordin plays.[13] Not even this was entirely safe, though, as a review of Nokhem Rakov's *Talmid khokhem* (The Learned Scholar) indicates. The play, apparently the basis for the 1923 film *East and West*, depicts the mock wedding ceremony of a beautiful, wealthy young woman to an impoverished, long-suffering yeshiva boy, who then insists that the ceremony be honoured as binding.[14] One reviewer declared testily, 'Rakov has created a play that is unnatural in psychological terms, the lowest of farce in comic terms, and lacking in any literary merits.'[15] He then added reluctantly, 'Kaminsky's company played this absurd drama so well that at times one did not even notice its anti-aesthetic character.'[16]

What emerges most strikingly from the Russian-language reviews of Yiddish theatre was the critics' insistence that Yiddish theatre be judged as strictly as Russian theatre. No points were awarded for well-intentioned but

[13] New, non-Gordin plays produced on this tour include Arnshteyn's *Dos eybike lid* (The Eternal Song) and *Der vilner balebesl* (The Petty Householder of Vilna), Sholem Aleykhem's *Tsezeyt un tseshpreyt* (Scattered and Dispersed), Moyshe Rikhter's *Sholem bayis* (Domestic Harmony), Przybyszewski's *Dos glik* (Luck; Polish: *Dla szczescia*), Kaminsky's own *Yidishe aktyorn af der rayze* (Yiddish Actors on the Road), and a quasi-Symbolist work called *Trayhayt* (Loyalty) by a young female playwright called Prilutskaya.

[14] In addition to the connection that *Talmid khokhem* shares with *East and West*, the ultimate source of Rakov's play may be Shakespeare's *All's Well That Ends Well*, with the roles of Helena and Bertram reversed. For an extended discussion of the film, see Jeffrey Shandler, 'Ost und West, Old World and New: Nostalgia and Antinostalgia on the Silver Screen', in Sylvia Paskin (ed.), *When Joseph Met Molly: A Reader on Yiddish Film* (Nottingham: Five Leaves Publications, 1999), 69–101. The St Petersburg Theatrical Library has several copies of Rakov's play (filed under an unorthodox system of transliteration). See 'Der Talmud-Chuchem. Lebensbild in 5 Acten von Rakow' [The Scholar: Portrait of Life in Five Acts by Rakov] (Yiddish, in German transliteration), St Petersburg Theatrical Library, Tsarist Censor's Collection, *fond* 1031, passed for performance in 1909. See also the same play, attributed to a different author and adapted by Jacob Slotnitzky, 'Der Talmud Chuchem. Lebensbild in 5 Akten von Jakobi. Bearbeitet Jacob Slotnitzky, ibid., *fond* 1474, passed for performance in 1908.

[15] 'Teatr i muzyka: *Talmid khokhem*' [Theatre and Music: *Talmid khokhem*], *Rech'*, 4 Apr. 1909, 5.

[16] Ibid.

poorly executed theatre. No indulgence was granted to a theatre that had yet to reach its half-century. From the very outset Yiddish theatre was taken seriously as an art form, and was seen as essential to the Jewish community in St Petersburg. The need for improvement of the Yiddish repertoire, to bring it up to the high literary standard of the Russian repertoire, was taken as given.

This reforming zeal on the part of Russian critics reflects two distinct tendencies within the Russian theatre itself. Historically, theatre in Russia has been seen not just as an art form but as an important public forum, one which could not be ceded to the 'low' tastes of popular culture. Given the place of Jews in Russian culture and society, Yiddish theatre may well have been regarded as of even greater significance in this respect than was the Russian theatre, hence the disapproval when Yiddish theatre did not appear to uphold its artistic and civic duties. Additionally, criticism of the Yiddish theatre and the dismissal of its repertoire reflected a general contemporary tendency within the Russian theatre at the turn of the century. From 1902, when disenchantment with the methods championed by the Moscow Art Theatre set in, until the revolution of 1917, the Russian theatre was widely regarded as being in a state of crisis. For years its practitioners sought (often with little success) to extend the language of the Russian theatre beyond the dominant realist and naturalist mode of the day. While more astute viewers might have seen in the Yiddish theatre's conventions an elaboration of the Romantic theatrical tradition, or even an embryonic expressionism, less imaginative critics may simply have seen naturalism, and not even a terribly accomplished one at that. Whether berated for clinging to the clichés of naturalism, or castigated for inadequate observance of its conventions, Yiddish theatre was bound to come into conflict with any number of existing Russian theatrical prejudices. The severity of the criticism launched against the Yiddish theatre is entirely commensurate with the high expectations that critics and theatrical practitioners had of it.

Suspicion of Yiddish dramaturgy continued to permeate critical appraisal by the Russian press, even as it heaped adulation on the actors who performed this controversial repertoire. This disjunction became particularly obvious at a celebration held in St Petersburg to honour Esther-Rokhl Kaminska's fifteen years on the Yiddish stage. During the ceremonies a Mr Zeldovich spoke on behalf of Kugel's journal *Teatr i Iskusstvo*. His remarks were typical of the theatrical establishment's attitude towards the Yiddish theatre in that they managed to be at once sincere and deeply patronizing. Approaching the great Kaminska, Zeldovich declared, no doubt with good intentions, 'Your language is imperfect, your repertoire meagre and wretched, and you are a queen without royal robes or crown. But a true queen has no need for luxurious trappings, for she is a queen always.'[17]

St Petersburg audiences were not wholly reliant on touring companies or Russian translations for their Yiddish plays. As early as 1907 attempts had apparently been made to establish Yiddish theatre in the capital itself.[18] It was not until two years later, however, in October 1909, that a Yiddish play was produced in St Petersburg: S. A. Melnikov directed two plays, Moshe Rikhter's *Hertsele meyukhes* (Hertsele the Aristocrat) and Goldfaden's *Di kaprizne tokhter; oder, Kaptsnzon et hungerman* (The Capricious Daughter; or, Pauperson and Hungerman, 1887), at the Palm Theatre for a delighted capacity crowd. Reviewers, predictably, were less than impressed. The newspaper *Rech'*'s perennial reviewer of Yiddish theatricals, L. Vasilevsky, praised Melnikov's work as a performer, but found his work as a director 'provincial' and 'slipshod'.[19] Melnikov joined forces the following year with another would-be entrepreneur, Berman-Dvinsky, and the two offered productions of Goldfaden's *Di kishefmakherin* (The Sorceress) and *Shulamis* in early 1910.[20] Unfortunately, no lasting alliance seems to have been forged as a result of this union.

A determination to improve the quality of the Yiddish repertoire was one of the principal aims of St Petersburg's first Jewish Drama Circle, formed in November 1909 as an offshoot of the Jewish Literary Society. The Drama Circle's aim was to establish a repertoire based on both translations of foreign drama and the work of younger Yiddish playwrights such as Peretz Hirschbein (1880–1948) and Dovid Pinski (1872–1959).[21] The semi-professional company was headed by Mark Semyonovich Rivesman (1868–1924), a member of the Jewish Literary Society and a teacher in one of St Petersburg's Jewish primary schools.[22] The Drama Circle's first production, a three-act comedy by Rivesman entitled *Schastlivchik* (The Lucky Man), and a one-act piece called *Blagotvoritel'naya kruzhka* (The Collection Box) took place at a summer theatre

[17] L.K., 'Teatr i muzyka: Chestvovanie R. Kaminskoi' [Theatre and Music], *Rech'*, 20 Apr. 1909, 5.

[18] See Evgeny Binevich, '"Svoi" teatr v peterburge ['Our Own' St Petersburg Theatre], Preprint 39 of the Jewish Heritage Society (Moscow, 1997), 2, citing 'Malen'kaya khronika', *Teatr i Iskusstvo*, 20 (1907), 326. [19] L. Vasilevsky, 'Zal *Pal'ma*', *Rech'*, 10 Oct. 1909, 3.

[20] 'Za nedelyu', *Novyi Voskhod*, 9 (1910), 22; 'Varia', *Rassvet*, 13 (1910), 37; 'Khronika' [Chronicle], *Obozrenie Teatrov*, 29 Mar. 1910, 2. Cited in Binevich, '"Svoi" teatr'.

[21] 'Teatr i muzyka' [Theatre and Music], *Rech'*, 23 Nov. 1909, 3.

[22] For a brief profile of Rivesman, see the entry under his name in the *Evreiskaya entsiklopediya: Svod znanii o evreistve i ego kul'ture v proshlom i nastoyashchem* [The Jewish Encyclopaedia: Collected Learning on the Jews and their Culture in the Past and Present], ed. L. Katsenelson, 16 vols. (St Petersburg: Izdanie Obshchestva dlya Nauchnykh Evreiskikh Izdanii i Izdatel'stva Brokgauz-Efron, 1906–13), xiii. 478. See also the obituary of Rivesman by Alexander Kugel, *Zhizn' Iskusstva*, 26 (1924), 4.

outside the city in August 1910.[23] Thereafter, amateur and semi-professional
companies of Yiddish actors resident in St Petersburg began to perform in the
city and its environs on a fairly regular basis. Occasionally they joined forces
with touring Yiddish actors such as the peripatetic Sam Adler. Rivesman's
company called itself the Jewish Literary-Dramatic Troupe, and had its first performance in the centre of St Petersburg on 15 October 1910, with a programme
of *Schastlivchik* and M. M. Yakhdov's *Nokhn tsholnt* (After the Sabbath Meal) in
Pavlova Hall, 13 Troitskaya Street.[24] Despite the much-vaunted improvements
that local companies would be bringing to the usual repertoire of Yiddish
theatre, little attempt was made to stage the work of modern Yiddish writers.
Although the Drama Circle did stage original plays, primarily the work of
Rivesman (such as his *Di ershte patsyentn*, The First Patients, staged four times
in three years), the company tended to rely on one-act plays adapted from
Sholem Aleykhem (1859–1916), such as *Mazl-tov* (Congratulations) and *Mentshn*
(The Employees) and the much-maligned, but apparently still popular, Gordin. Advertisements for Yiddish theatre did not always carry the name of the
performing company, so it can be difficult to know who performed what. The
lack of any 'names' seems not to have troubled the St Petersburg public, who
seem happy to have had any local Yiddish theatre at all.

 Yiddish theatre in Russia's capital was very much a natural development
in a city that enjoyed a vibrant Jewish cultural life. Newspapers of the time
provide ample testimony to this, regularly carrying advertisements and
reviews of concerts, lectures, and literary evenings in Yiddish, Russian, and
even Hebrew. These events were organized by the two dozen or more Jewish
artistic, philanthropic, scholarly, and political societies active in St Petersburg.[25] In addition to the concerts and lectures of the Society for Jewish Folk
Music, one could attend functions organized by the Society for the Expansion of Education among the Jews of Russia, the Society for the Attainment
of Elementary Education for Jewish Children, the Society for Devotees of the

[23] Although these early performances were in Yiddish, no Yiddish play-titles were supplied in the Russian advertisements. Later productions of Yiddish plays, however, even after the 1915 ban on the use of Hebrew letters in advertising, were often printed in both Russian and Yiddish ('Teatr i muzyka', *Rech'*, 23 June 1910, 3). There is a brief account of the production in Sestroretsk in the 12 Aug. 1910 issue of *Rech'*.

[24] The advertisement, in the 10 Oct. 1910 issue of *Rech'*, attributed *Schastlivchik* to Yakhdov, and *Nokhn tsholnt* to Rivesman, although all previous and subsequent performances of *Schastlivchik* were attributed only to Rivesman.

[25] One example of the variety of events organized was a 'Palestinian evening' which took place on 2 Mar. 1908, in the Pavlova Hall, in aid of settlers and farmers in Palestine. The highlight of the evening was Chaim Nachman Bialik's reading of his own poetry in Hebrew. The event attracted a 'mass of people . . . the overflow was such that at 10 p.m. the police had to close the hall's outer doors and several hundred people were left without any access to the auditorium' ('Palestinskii vecher', *Rech'*, 5 Mar. 1908, 3).

Hebrew Language, the Jewish Artistic Society Betzalel, the Jewish Literary Association, and many others.[26]

But in the autumn of 1913, as the Kiev blood-libel trial of Mendel Beilis (1874–1934) got under way, Petersburg's lively Jewish community went almost completely silent. The lectures, charity evenings, plays, and concerts that so publicly defined Jewish culture in the capital vanished. Given the tremendous unrest that the trial sparked within the Pale of Settlement, and the stringent censorship that surrounded the case, it is perhaps not surprising that nothing so 'provocative' as a Yiddish play should have been staged at this time.[27] It was not until late November, after Beilis had been acquitted, that Jewish cultural life began to re-emerge in St Petersburg, and it was not until January 1914 that a Yiddish play was again staged in the city.[28]

In the months that preceded the outbreak of the First World War a permanent company of Yiddish actors under the direction of S. A. Melnikov was organized in St Petersburg. They tended to perform at charity functions and to stage evenings of Yiddish theatre in a variety of venues. Their first official production was of Sholem Asch's *Got fun nekome*, staged in February 1914. In true Yiddish theatrical tradition a rival company also seems to have formed at this time, this one under the direction of S. M. Gusinov. Gusinov's troupe performed their own Yiddish translation of a popular satire that had been played numerous times in Russian, *Der ayngegebener frak* (The Well-Tailored Frock-Coat).[29] Apparently, the enthusiasm for locally produced Yiddish theatre was infectious, and an amateur production of Sholem Aleykhem's *Mentshn*, with the writer himself playing one of the roles, was also staged as a benefit in May 1914.[30]

[26] For a further listing of Jewish organizations in St Petersburg, see Beizer, *The Jews of St Petersburg*, and 'The Petrograd Jewish Obshchina (Kehilla) in 1917', *Jews and Jewish Topics in the Soviet Union and Eastern Europe*, 3 (Winter 1989), 5–29.

[27] This was not the case, curiously enough, for Russian-language Jewish plays, which remained a prominent feature of the St Petersburg stage. In the weeks preceding and succeeding the Beilis trial, the hit of the Saburov Theatre's season was a Russian translation of a German play called *Gospoda meieri* (Messrs Meyer), which satirized antisemitism, and the Liteinyi Theatre had enormous success with its production of Arkady Averchenko's *Odessity* (The Odessans) an extended Jewish anecdote that had more than a hundred performances.

[28] *Dora; oder, 17 yor in ostrog* (Dora; or, Seventeen Years in Prison), a drama in four acts with songs, by Shlifershteyn, with S. A. Melnikov in the role of the Convict, Zvaikofskaya as Dora, and Sarkanov as Dornbaum, performed on 18 Jan. 1914 at the Serpukhovsky Concert Hall.

[29] There is a Russian translation of this Hungarian play in the St Petersburg Theatrical Library. See G. Dregel, *Khorosho sshityi frak: Komediya v 4-kh deistviyakh. Perevod S. S. Parfenova*, Biblioteka K. P. Larina, no. 12745, n.d. The play was performed first in Russian at St Petersburg's Saburov Theatre in 1912, and was revived several times subsequently. The Yiddish translation, by S. M. Gusinov, *Der ayngegebener frak; oder, Meltser der shnayder*, was performed at the Ekaterinsky Theatre on 8 Apr. 1914 by the Jewish Drama Troupe under Gusinov's direction.

[30] See the review of this production, 'Teatr i muzyka', *Rech'*, 13 May 1914, 6.

With the start of the war patriotic plays came to dominate the repertoire of all Russian theatres for many months and Yiddish theatre productions came to a halt.[31] They did not re-emerge until May 1915, when some 15,000 Jewish refugees, driven from the disintegrating Pale of Settlement by the advancing German army, fled to Petrograd. Their effect on the city's Jewish community was galvanizing; by the spring of 1916 the city once again abounded in charity balls, benefit performances, concerts, and lectures of special interest to the Jewish community.[32] In addition, the refugees brought with them a number of Yiddish actors, including the American operetta singer Clara Young, and quickly set about establishing theatre groups.[33]

The city's hunger for Yiddish plays was such that even the high-minded newspaper *Rech'*, which prior to the war reviewed only the best Yiddish theatrical offerings, now sent one of its sternest critics, I. Rabinovich, to review Young's decidedly lowbrow productions. The plays on offer, such as Boris Thomashefsky's *Di amerikanerin* (The American Girl), Nokhem Rakov's musical farce *Khantshe in amerike* (Khantshe in America, an operetta designed to show off the talents of Bessie Thomashefsky), and a mysterious musical called *Mademoiselle goplya*, were, according to Rabinovich, utterly excruciating. The tedium of sitting through them was made possible only by Clara Young's beauty and vivacity.[34] Apparently completely besotted with Young, Rabinovich selflessly returned to the theatre night after night, so that he

<hr/>

[31] See Hubertus F. Jahn, *Patriotic Culture in Russia During World War I* (Ithaca, NY: Cornell University Press, 1995), which deals with this repertoire and addresses the question of the image of Jews within nationalistic Russian culture of the time.

[32] In one week in March alone one could see the Melnikov company's production of Gordin's *Di brider lurye* (The Luria Brothers) on the 1st, attend a lecture on the 4th on the subject of Jewish sculpture, and take in either a children's matinée *purimshpil* at the Intimnyi Theatre on the 6th, or a matinée on the same day of Melnikov's production of *Sore sheyndl*.

[33] A short piece in *Rech'* noted, 'The idea of opening a travelling Yiddish art theatre is moving towards realization. On 29 February a meeting devoted to this issue was convened by the Jewish Folk Music Society. The meeting recognized the immediate necessity of organizing a Jewish art theatre. A committee was selected comprising O. O. Gruzenberg (chairman), M. S. Rivesman (vice-chairman) and L. L. Levidov (secretary)' ('Teatr i muzyka', 2 Mar. 1916, 6).

[34] Young's earliest performance was 19 Apr. 1916 at a benefit at the Theatre of Comedy, performing in *Di amerikanerin*, a 'sensational play from the lives of American Jews' (advertisement, *Rech'*, 17 Apr. 1916). She performed several times that season, and returned for a lengthy engagement in the autumn of 1916 at the Intimnyi Theatre, where she starred in *Lgunishka*, *Bar kokhba*, *Mademoiselle goplya*, *Shulamis*, *Di amerikanerin*, *Tsezeyt un tseshpreyt* (a memorial tribute to Sholem Aleykhem), *Khantshe in amerike*, *Dos pintele yid*, and others. The 'sensational' lives of American Jews were of interest to Petrograd's wider population, it seems, as one of the most popular plays in the Russian repertoire of this time was a stage adaptation of Montague Glass's *Potash and Perlmutter*. The play had its première at the Saburov Theatre in March 1915. It had more than eighty performances, and was revised for the 1915–16 season and the 1917–18 season. It was also the inspiration for a dire (and probably unauthorized) 'sequel', *Schastlivye dni Potasha i Perlmutra* (Potash and Perlmuter's Happiest Days), which ran for a short time at the Saburov Theatre in March 1916. It was the recipient of hilariously bad reviews and was hastily withdrawn from the repertoire.

might offer lengthy disquisitions on her squandered genius in the newspaper on the following day.[35]

As complaints about the low literary quality of the Yiddish plays performed in Petrograd resounded, plans to remedy the situation revolved around the establishment of the first Jewish Theatrical Society.[36] The idea was first mooted at a national conference on folk theatre held in Moscow from 27 December 1915 to 5 January 1916, at which S. Ansky lectured on the subject of the Jewish theatre.[37] The press reported that the Jewish Theatrical Society was to promote the all-round development of Jewish theatrical enterprise in Russia.[38] Their plans included the opening of affiliated branches in the provinces and the promotion of theatrical productions in Hebrew. According to an article in *Birzhevye Vedomosti*, the society managed, in a six-month period, to decide on a repertoire, hire a company of actors, and come up with enough money to secure a theatre. All that remained was to petition the local authorities for permission to establish a permanent Yiddish theatre in Petrograd. Ten days before the season was set to begin, though, the company's petition was rejected. The reason given was that the plays would be performed in Yiddish. Pointing out that Yiddish plays had been continually staged in Petrograd, Moscow, and other Russian cities outside the Pale did not prove persuasive.[39]

Apparently undaunted, the society reconvened in November 1916. One of the board's members, Lev Levidov, recalled the opening session—attended by the then unknown Alexander Granovsky—as a joyous occasion. 'The hall was filled to overflowing; there were excited faces, triumphant speeches, and an extraordinarily buoyant mood. A new society was born, issuing a call for the creation of a Jewish national, vibrant, artistic theatre!'[40] But the society's next meetings were not convened until December 1916,[41] when a review of the state of Yiddish playwriting was undertaken, and plans were made to establish a Jewish theatrical school and studio.[42] In January 1917 it was reported

[35] Alexander Kugel also wrote an extremely favourable review of the company, and especially Clara Young. See his 'Zametki' [Notes], *Teatr i Iskusstvo*, 43 (1916), 866–9.

[36] For a detailed account of the establishment and workings of the Jewish Theatrical Society, see Ivanov, 'Petrogradskie sezony', 3–8. See also Ivanov's *Russkie sezony teatra Gabima* [Habimah's Russian Seasons] (Moscow: Artist. Rezhisser. Teatr, 1999), which deals in part with the Yiddish theatre in Petrograd. [37] Ivanov, 'Petrogradskie sezony', 21.

[38] 'Teatr i muzyka', *Rech'*, 16 Mar. 1916, 5. See also these periodic updates on the society's progress: 'Teatr i muzyka', *Rech'*, 10 July 1916, 5; 5 Oct. 1916, 4.

[39] 'Zapreshchenie spektaklei na evreiskom yazyke', *Birzhevye Vedomosti*, 25 Aug. 1916, 6; cited in Binevich, '"Svoi" teatr', 4.

[40] L. Levidov, 'Ereiskoe Teatral'noe obshchestvo i Evreiskii Kamernyi teatr; Evreiskii Kamernyi teatr', RO Tsentral'nogo Teatral'nogo muzeya im. A. Bakhrushina, TSPM, *fond* 584, *opis'* 1, *ed. khr.* 90, *l.* 1; cited in Binevich, '"Svoi" teatr', 4.

[41] 'Teatr i muzyka', *Rech'*, 4 Dec. 1916, 6. The society met on 1 and 9 Dec. 1916.

[42] This proved a controversial issue. For a detailed account, see Ivanov, 'Petrogradskie sezony', 3–5.

that the society had opened branches in Irkutsk and Ekaterinoslav, and was preparing once again to stage its own productions of Yiddish plays.[43]

When the February Revolution took place a month later, theatrical life came to a halt in Petrograd for several weeks, recommencing only in mid-March. When the dust had settled, restructuring of many theatrical organizations was undertaken, including the Jewish Theatrical Society. Granovsky, who had quickly emerged as an important member of the society, passionately concerned with establishing a Jewish theatre-training school, abruptly departed for Europe, where he remained until 1918. As Vladislav Ivanov relates, Granovsky's absence occurred at a time of increasing public interest in the Yiddish theatre. In May 1917 a special mass meeting was held in Petrograd, at which the impresario Avrom Fishzon made an impassioned speech calling on the meeting not to abandon the cause of a Jewish theatre. In August that year the society showed further signs of expansion when it proposed to sell shares in its Free Jewish Theatre.[44] The Jewish Theatrical Society was also no longer isolated in its endeavours: in the same month a national convention of the Russian Theatrical Society convened a general meeting in Kiev, in which a representative of the Union of Jewish Performers and Singers also took part.[45] By the time the conference came to a close, in October 1917, whatever plans the participants had made for the future of the Yiddish theatre were very shortly to be superseded.

The October Revolution may have ensured, for a time, the survival of the Yiddish theatre, but it also necessitated a degree of mythologization in order to safeguard its class purity. The popularity of Yiddish theatre in pre-war St Petersburg, and the formation of local Yiddish companies there, could hardly be considered a working-class phenomenon. Until the war the Jews of St Petersburg were, by and large, privileged, educated, Russian-speaking, and assimilated. While the Yiddish theatre of poor *shtetl* Jews was acceptable to the new regime as an expression of both national and working-class culture, the Yiddish theatre of St Petersburg Jews was a 'bourgeois' phenomenon and best forgotten.

Clearly, the legend that there was no sustained Yiddish theatrical culture in Russia prior to the establishment of the State Yiddish Theatres under the

[43] 'Teatr i muzyka', *Rech'*, 5 Jan. 1917, 5; 22 Jan. 1917, 6.

[44] *Rech'* reported that the chairman of the Jewish Theatrical Society, O. O. Gruzenberg, the secretary, L. Levidov, and others were proposing to sell 2,500 shares at 100 roubles each in a joint-stock company called the Free Jewish Theatre (Svobodnyi Evreiskii Teatr) ('Teatr i muzyka', 4 Aug. 1917, 4).

[45] 'Teatr i muzyka', *Rech'*, 22 Aug. 1917, 5. The Russian Theatrical Society was established in 1894 to provide aid for theatre professionals and their dependants. In 1894 it was reorganized as a professional society to promote Russian theatre and to aid its practitioners. In the Soviet period the society was reorganized again as a professional union.

Soviet regime is patently untrue. The Jewish Theatrical Society that was established in Petrograd in 1916 evolved into Alexander Granovsky's Yiddish Chamber Theatre in 1919, and was moved in 1920 to Moscow to become the State Jewish Chamber Theatre, later the celebrated State Jewish Theatre (GOSET). This chain of developments came about as a direct result of Yiddish theatrical activities in imperial Russia's capital in the last decades of tsarist rule. That an energetic, educated Jewish culture thrived in the heart of tsarist Russia, and that Yiddish theatre was performed there for more than a decade before the revolution, did not coincide with the myth of the Yiddish theatre's spontaneous generation under the Soviet regime, and was conveniently ignored.

Now, with Russian archives opened, and with treasure troves of Yiddish theatrical history awaiting investigation in the former Soviet Union, it is time to begin writing the true history of the Jewish theatre in Russia. It promises to be a far richer and more complex story than could once have been imagined.

FOUR

The Text of Goldfaden's Di kishefmakherin *and the* Operetta Tradition

ৡৼ

PAOLA BERTOLONE

DI KISHEFMAKHERIN (The Sorceress, 1877) is one of the first plays of the modern period of Yiddish theatre to be written down. The celebrated poet, journalist, director, and playwright Avrom Goldfaden (1840–1908) chose to give his work the unusual description 'Opperette mit gesänge und tänze' (operetta with songs and dances); in other words, he laid the foundation of the modern course of Yiddish theatre mainly by pursuing the operetta tradition.

A text is more than a mere literary work; it may also be considered a historical and sociological document of a culture. In this chapter I will focus on the theatrical patterns Goldfaden elaborated in writing *Di kishefmakherin*, together with two of the most historically significant productions of the operetta and an analysis of the author's attempts to relate to an 'alien' aesthetic world. finally, I will discuss the performance of *La maga* (the Italian version of *Di kishefmakherin*) given in Trieste in September 1998.

From a sociocultural point of view, theatrical scholarship defines the boundary between modern and pre-modern eras in theatre on the basis of two main factors: the festive or non-festive framework and the amateur or professional organization of the company. I use the word 'festive' to denote not only the special time devoted to sacred celebrations, but also extra-religious ceremonies such as carnival or secular events connected to court life, when various performances took place. The distinction between festivals and what we nowadays consider theatre is an important theoretical question which allows us to follow the rise of professional theatre within the larger festive context.

For centuries festive occasions had been the only circumstance in which theatre was allowed; until the start of the sixteenth century religious and

I should like to offer my sincere thanks to Robert Silverberg, who helped me to translate this chapter.

moral censorship strictly forbade performances outside such occasions. With the modern era came the formation of independent professional theatre companies, a development that first appeared in northern Italy in the mid-1500s; this entrepreneurial phenomenon is usually known as *commedia dell'arte*.[1] From the Middle Ages until the seventeenth century mystery plays, miracle plays, and *autós sacramentales* were staged in European countries where the Church had considerable power. Notable solo performers appeared as well, but, generally speaking, there were no independent companies. In the modern era theatre became a product to be sold to a paying public: from its 'sacred' roots it turned into 'democratic' merchandise.

What had occurred in Western theatre took place within Yiddish culture three centuries later. This gives us the opportunity to study the process by which religious theatre gave birth to 'profane' (or secular) theatre.

Much of the scholarship on Goldfaden describes the transition he initiated as sudden, with almost no antecedents except the Broder singers (with two of whom he created his first troupe). Historians such as Bernard Gorin, Zalmen Zylbercweig, Sholem Perlmuter, Jacob Mestel, and Zaynvl Diamant see Goldfaden as the father of the modern Yiddish theatre.[2] It is easy to infer that the leading role ascribed to Goldfaden in the transition from the old to the new Yiddish theatre derives from the fact that he was a playwright first, and an actor and composer second. It is still common to confuse dramaturgy with the wider history of theatre, and that is one of the reasons for the Goldfaden myth in traditional historiography. It is worth noting that Goldfaden himself helped to create this myth. In his short autobiography he actually claims to be the founder of the modern Yiddish theatre—perhaps, as Zylbercweig maintains, in order to preserve his memory for future generations.[3]

Goldfaden declares in his autobiography, which is written in the third person, signed Voliner, and was published in his newspaper *Di nyu-yorker yidishe ilustrirte tsaytung* (The Yiddish Illustrated Newspaper of New York) on 22 October 1887, that 'he alone built the scene, he painted the stage sceneries, he wrote the play, he collected the music, he taught the mimicry'. It should be

[1] Among the many sources on *commedia dell'arte*, see K. M. Lea, *Italian Popular Comedy: A Study in the Commedia dell'arte, 1560–1620* (with special reference to the English stage) (Oxford: Clarendon Press, 1934; repr. New York: Russel & Russel, 1962), and T. F. Heck, *Commedia dell'arte: A Guide to the Primary and Secondary Literature* (New York: Garland, 1988).

[2] B. Gorin, *Di geshikhte fun idishn teater* [The History of the Yiddish Theatre], 2 vols. (New York: Literarisher Farlag, 1918); Zalmen Zylbercweig, *Leksikon fun yidishn teater* [Lexicon of Yiddish Theatre], 6 vols. (New York: Elisheva, 1931–70), i. 275–367; Sholem Perlmuter, *Yidishe dramaturgn un teater-kompozitors* [Yiddish Playwrights and Theatre Composers] (New York: YKUF, 1952), 51–60; Zaynvl Diamant, *Leksikon fun der nayer yidisher literatur* [Lexicon of the New Yiddish Literature] (New York: Congress for Jewish Culture, 1958), vol. ii.

[3] Zalmen Zylbercweig, *Teater mozayik* [Theatre Mosaics] (New York: Itshe Biderman, 1941), 140.

stressed that the phenomenon of the Broder singers cannot be compared with Goldfaden's theatrical works, not just because their style was more like cabaret as their shows consisted of variety acts, but especially because those who worked with them were not organized into a company. Goldfaden, on the other hand, organized an actors' company that travelled and gave performances in defiance of the religious rules that allowed theatrical shows only within ritual contexts, such as wedding entertainments or Purim celebrations.

Even Goldfaden's biography tells the story of a transition: from Hebrew to Yiddish, from rabbinical schools to the commercial stage, from Haskalah to Zionism. He was able to capture the deep and hidden source of his culture, and quickly evolved into an authority figure. His ultimate destiny, though, was tragic: his old actors left him to join rival companies, so, whereas Moyshe Hurwitz and Joseph Lateiner enjoyed lasting success in New York, Goldfaden spent much of the last twenty-five years of his life shuttling between a number of cultural centres.

Nevertheless, the popularity of many of Goldfaden's plays continued unabated. *Di kishefmakherin*, arranged in five acts and eight scenes, starts with Mirele's seventeenth birthday party, which is interrupted by the arrival of a policeman who has come to arrest her beloved father, Avromtse. The audience learns that Bashe, Mirele's stepmother and Avromtse's second wife, has plotted with her aunt, the sorceress Bobe Yakhne, against Avromtse and Mirele to acquire all their assets. Bashe and the sorceress set a trap that leaves the girl, in Act III, the prisoner of Bobe Yakhne's assistants, who sell her into slavery. Act IV opens in a Turkish café in Constantinople, where Mirele is forced to entertain the customers. After many reversals of fortune, the pedlar Hotsmakh and Marcus, Mirele's fiancé, end up in Constantinople, Marcus having come in search of Mirele, Hotsmakh in search of a new clientele for his merchandise. Act V brings the final family reunion of Mirele, Bashe, Marcus, and Avromtse, who has proved his innocence. Hotsmakh organizes a party at an inn, but Bobe Yakhne puts a sleeping draught in everyone's wine. As they all fall asleep, she sets fire to the inn. But the heroes again turn the tables on the villains, who perish in the fire they started.

Di kishefmakherin is one of the first successful efforts in the Yiddish theatre to channel different tendencies and conflicting impulses into a confluent stream. The fascination of this operetta comes from its proximity to the origins of Yiddish theatre: everything seems possible when a language—an entire culture's theatrical vocabulary, in this case—has yet to be created. It is no accident that *Di kishefmakherin* had a formative influence on the development of Yiddish theatre on at least two continents: most notably, in an 1881 production in New York City, one of the first Yiddish plays performed in

America; and in the Soviet Union with the landmark avant-garde version by the Moscow State Yiddish Theatre (GOSET).[4]

We can see two main strands in the traditions that influenced Goldfaden in writing *Di kishefmakherin*: the 'alien' one of operetta, and Goldfaden's connections, whether conscious or unconscious, with his own roots in Yiddish culture. Leaving aside the operetta for the moment, an examination of the central character of the play reveals the Jewish influence. The theatre historian Béatrice Picon-Vallin has described the sorceress Bobe Yakhne as 'embody[ing] a Jewish reality, the shrew of the *mestechko* (place), the old beggar woman, a bit of a magician, whom people find repugnant but feed nevertheless'.[5] However, I locate the character's origins in a different tradition. Bobe Yakhne is clearly modelled on the well-known character in Slavonic folklore Baba Yaga, to whom many tales and songs are dedicated, including the unforgettable *Pictures at an Exhibition* by Mussorgsky. Baba Yaga is evil personified: her awful tricks seem to arise from a boundless energy that is one of her most characteristic features. The same kind of unceasing activity, always in cooperation with the evil side of mankind, is also Bobe Yakhne's most prominent trait, though in the Yiddish context Goldfaden made fundamental additions as he reworked this figure.

A good example can be found in Act II scene iv, when Bobe Yakhne asks Bashe:

Are you still persuaded that I can make magic spells? Do you still believe that I stir a burning cauldron, make circles in chimneys, burn hairs, thrust stakes into the earth? . . . Does this accomplish anything? I use these tricks just to steal money from those fools who believe in it, but in reality, all this is useless. What do you think all my magic is made of? My great experience of the world, my energy, my knowledge, my skill in cheating people. That's all there is to magic.

In response to Bashe's request for magic (*kishef*) she uses the reasoning of a maskil and agrees to show him the machinery hidden behind the curtain, a metaphor for witchcraft. In this scene we see reflected Goldfaden's own purpose: following the pedagogic and paternalistic principles of the Haskalah, he wanted his audience to be instructed, to 'grow up'. For Goldfaden, theatre was the pre-eminent instrument of reform. Bobe Yakhne, queen of the irrational and lady of Slavonic folklore, had to be adopted and used to destroy the instinctive, primitive, superstitious mentality.

[4] I discuss the GOSET production in greater detail below.

[5] 'Baba Yaga, la sorcière, incarne une réalité juive, la mégère de la mestetchko, vieille femme mendiante, un peu magicienne, qui répugne mais que l'on nourrit pourtant': Béatrice Picon-Vallin, *Le Théâtre juif soviétique pendant les années vingt* [Soviet Jewish Theatre during the 1920s] (Lausanne: La Cité-L'Âge d'Homme, 1973), 73.

In the widely accepted view of Goldfaden's biographers Oyslender and Finkel, his plays can be divided into two periods: the first is characterized by a lighter spirit, while the second is ideologically orientated. These scholars place the turning point in the year 1881, when violent pogroms broke out, demonstrating to Goldfaden the need for nationalistic dramas instead of mere entertainment.[6] However, it seems to me that Goldfaden's style and content do not change dramatically after 1881. Even though historical operettas or operas such as *Bar kokhba; oder, Di letste teg fun tsion* (Bar Kokhba; or, The Last Days of Zion, 1883) and *Dovid bemilkhome* (David at War, premièred in 1906) do come later in his output, there is a clear sense of continuity between the earlier and the later, more 'political', period, both in a strictly formal sense and from the point of view of content. It is true that comic characters are replaced by national heroes, but this is more the effect of a metamorphosis in stylistic conception: it seems evident that Goldfaden tries to purify his later work of 'low' comedy in order to raise it to a 'higher' level of seriousness, as if he was trying to behave properly from both a moral and an intellectual perspective.

The playwright's rationalist attitude is less evident in *Di kishefmakherin*. It can still be found, however, disguised by the lighter genre of the operetta, which is derived from the *opera buffa*, while in his later librettos and scores his devotion to Zionism is expressed in *opera seria*. The Hebrew drama *Dovid bemilkhome*, meanwhile, contains no music at all. This progression reveals the development of his aesthetic values: from the commercial level, associated with music and comedy, to the 'artistic' composition of *Dovid bemilkhome*, where he is unconcerned with public taste or critical success. Deep down these two periods of Goldfaden's works are not so divergent.

From a playwriting point of view Bobe Yakhne's speech can be seen as a direct expression of the author's ideas, particularly his view of magic as superstition, a 'childish' cultural condition that people must go beyond in order to reach a more refined state. It is worth noting that a similar parodic vein appears in Goldfaden's work in relation to hasidism, as in the case of *Di tsvey kuni leml* (The Two Kuni Lemls, 1880).

Bobe Yakhne's false and falsified *kishef* is a vehicle allowing Goldfaden to fill *Di kishefmakherin* with 'theatrical moments'. This technique has similarities to Brecht's theory of alienation, in which, in order to prevent the audience from reacting emotionally rather than rationally, actors are required to adopt a critical attitude towards the characters they play and towards the play as a whole. Although this device was meant to reveal the artifice of drama,

---

[6] Nokhem Oyslender and Uri Finkel, *A. goldfadn: materialn far a biografye* [A. Goldfaden: Materials towards a Biography] (Minsk: Institut far Vayruslendisher Kultur, 1926).

the paradoxical result was an increase in theatrical illusion. Somehow Bobe
Yakhne's rationalistic attitude—to which we can easily add Goldfaden's
maskilic attitude expressed through his character's words and gestures—
strengthens the realm of folklore and popular superstition that he set out to
combat. As Nahma Sandrow has observed, 'He was actually entering and
enriching popular tradition while he thought he was guiding his audience
away from it.'[7] This ambivalence—simultaneously attacking and preserving
folk customs—is typical of many writers of the period, and is in fact typical of
the maskilic approach.[8]

The other main character of the operetta is Hotsmakh the pedlar. Through
him we enter more directly into the Yiddish aspect of the play, simply
because, on a social level, the pedlar figure originates in the reality of misery,
enforced wandering, and petty trading that was the Jewish way of life in the
Pale of Settlement. At the level of textual analysis, Hotsmakh's function is to
be the hero's helper: he is the one who helps Marcus search for Mirele, his
fiancée, at the end of Act IV, and the one who arranges the family reunion in
the last act.

He is a peculiar sort of helper, however. His actions seem to originate
neither from a conscious decision nor, as usually happens in the Western
drama's pattern of the servant–master relationship, from the will of another
such as his master, but rather by accident. He is in the right place at the right
time, for instance at the Turkish café, where he is finally able to 'encounter'
some money, while Marcus finally encounters Mirele; or in Act I, when he is
by chance playing blind man's buff with the other guests when the policeman
arrives. He actually drops into Mirele's birthday party and everyone asks him
to stay and sing. He is a witness rather than an active figure or an 'actor'; since
he moves the narrative forward through his actions, his function is to be a
storyteller, a fundamental function not only of Yiddish tradition but, as far as
is known, one which reaches back to the origins of theatre itself. In other
words, the stage life of Hotsmakh is placed partly outside the action, in the
tradition of the jester, whose role as singer, entertainer, and parodist is typical
of the structure of *purimshpil*.

Di kishefmakherin helps us to understand Goldfaden's aims as he worked to
build a renewed Yiddish theatre. In 1887 Baumritter & Gonsher of Warsaw
published a number of his works: the melodramas *Di kaprizne tokhter; oder,*

[7] Nahma Sandrow, *Vagabond Stars: A World History of Yiddish Theatre* (New York: Harper & Row, 1977; repr. New York: Limelight Editions, 1986, and Syracuse, NY: Syracuse University Press, 1999), 50.

[8] See Dan Miron, 'Folklore and Antifolklore in the Yiddish Fiction of the Haskala', in Frank Talmage (ed.), *Studies in Jewish Folklore* (Cambridge, Mass.: Association for Jewish Studies, 1980).

Kaptsnzon et Hungerman (The Capricious Daughter; or, Pauperson and Hungerman); *Di bobe mitn eynikl* (The Grandmother and her Granddaughter); *Bar kokhba*; *Doktor almosado; oder, Di yidn in palermo* (Doctor Almosado; or, The Jews in Palermo); and the operettas *Di tsvey kuni leml* and *Di kishef-makherin*. In the previous year Goldfaden had published the melodrama *Shulamis*.

Strangely, all these works were published without scores. They were treated as librettos even though Goldfaden, in collaboration with the comic actor Sigmund Mogulesco (and perhaps others), was the chief composer. Even though it seems contradictory, we can infer that Goldfaden did not send the scores to press because he was afraid that if the complete text were published it would be even more difficult to protect his copyrights. On the other hand, he also wanted to make it clear that he was the author, so he published the text without the music: in other words, he compromised.

The 1887 edition of this text thus seems to originate from two opposing forces: Goldfaden's desire to establish his authority and his desire not to be plagiarized by other, newly formed, travelling companies. As a result, as far as I know, the complete score of *Di kishefmakherin* was never published and was probably lost: we possess some music rearranged by his contemporaries just a few years later, such as the violin and piano version arranged by I. R. Berman; and H. A. Russotto, published (undated) by the London Hebrew Publishing Company; in this *Di kishefmakherin* is described as an opera.

In the 1887 Warsaw edition of the libretto the publisher, probably at Goldfaden's suggestion, wrote on the Yiddish side 'Di Kischufmacherin' and on the back cover the German equivalent *Die Zauberin*. The work was labelled an 'opperette mit gesänge und tänze'. I have always considered this description overblown, since an operetta is actually a texture of words, dance, music, and song. Why then did Goldfaden wish to stress the composition? The only answer I can suggest is that he himself was not clear about the style he wanted to adopt; nor was the public, whose experience and knowledge he wanted to enrich with the 'alien' operetta tradition. This semantic uncertainty reveals the true theme of Goldfaden's production: to lay the foundations of the modern Yiddish theatre by building bridges.

The pictures on the covers of the librettos represent, I think, the key scenes or the most crucial moments of the plots. One cover of *Di kishefmakherin* shows a marketplace with a number of benches, and features Mirele, Bobe Yakhne, and Hotsmakh in the foreground. Such an arrangement creates a mass choral effect rather than a scene structured round a small number of actors and singers; to be able to put an entire choir on stage proved Goldfaden's ability to imitate opera's main element—the chorus—but also established his intention to root his work deeply in a popular context, in order to give a mirror to his Yiddish audience.

The image has a focal point and is in perfect perspective. In Goldfaden's mind *Di kishefmakherin* takes place within the ideological context of perspective painting and scenography, that is, it lies within the common pattern of nineteenth-century Western use of theatrical space. With this in mind, it is possible to compare the use of space in *purimshpil* and in the dramaturgy of the Haskalah, since the maskilim staged only salon theatre.

The image of the marketplace attracts our attention by its use of perspective, but the 1887 edition has a different illustration, showing a couple, perhaps a king and queen, seated on thrones, facing a group of dancers. Although this image also uses perspective, the use of theatrical space is of a different kind: the dancers, shown in front of the public, are dancing for the couple's entertainment; perhaps they are a ballet company performing on a festive day. Is the love story of Mirele and Marcus inspired by a biblical royal love story? This is just a hypothesis, but if correct it would show how Goldfaden linked different styles and dissimilar topics, following not a regular canon but a 'cluster structure' or symbolic constellation; his position as an artistic outsider allowed him to select and synthesize his material without cultural prejudice or imitation. The result was an interpretation of the operetta's pattern based on ethics, parody, and elements of epic.

In 1922 Alexander Granovsky, the artistic director of the Moscow Yiddish State Chamber Theatre (GOSET), decided to produce *Di kishefmakherin*. Until then the newly formed Yiddish Theatre Society, which had recently moved from Petrograd to Moscow, had been in search of a stylistic identity, even though Marc Chagall's sets and costumes had already opened the way. In the programme published when the company opened in Petrograd in 1919 a statement written by Rivesman, the literary director, revealed how much Goldfaden's original productions differed from Granovsky's later stylistic choices:

With no literary taste, and no sign of intellectual development, they played, sang, and danced, and were happy when the rich contractors in Romania burst into laughter over their *purimshpil* barbs. Today a lover, the next day a Kuni Leml [*shlemiel*], tomorrow a witch, the Yiddish actors, as it were, felt no shame . . . Then only a year ago a mournful cry was heard: 'How long? Until when will the immortal Kuni Leml and the screaming witch Yakhne dominate?' The cry was issued by the new-born Yiddish Theatre Society . . . [9]

[9] M. Rivesman, 'The Past and the Future of Yiddish Theatre', trans. Benjamin and Barbara Harshav, in *Marc Chagall and the Jewish Theatre* (New York: Solomon Guggenheim Foundation, 1992), 146–7.

Rivesman emphasizes unfavourable critical reactions to *Di kishefmakherin*: Bobe Yakhne, one of the two main characters, is considered a typical figure in the old, shameful, style, in contrast to Goldfaden's Haskalah approach to folklore, superstition, and the popular stage.

Granovsky's production opened on 2 December 1922. The encounter with Goldfaden's dramaturgy had a conclusive impact on the definition of Granovsky's aesthetic style, and it is significant that he chose to perform this particular operetta. The fantastic parody of the traditional world, as it appears in Goldfaden, was replicated by Granovsky in the same spirit of ambivalence that breathes in Goldfaden's text. The GOSET director's purpose was to change the traditional way of performing Goldfaden's operettas and thus reinforce the latter's attempt to rise to a higher artistic level than the *purimshpil* style.

Almost forty years elapsed between Goldfaden's first production and the 1922 performance. How can we account for their aesthetic differences in this period? How can we account for why the same text gave different results, transformed from a commercial and popular production to one hailed internationally as artistic? I believe the answer is to be found in the nature of the Soviet theatre and in the Bolshevik revolution. The actors and singers Goldfaden assembled came from an amateur background or had only a superficial knowledge of theatre life; some of them had cantorial training. The way they worked on *Di kishefmakherin* was based on natural instinct, enhanced by the actors' cultural roots and knowledge of *purimshpil*. In other words, their personal background smothered what was new in Goldfaden's text. GOSET's troupe, on the other hand, was shaped, consciously or unconsciously, by the methods of Stanislavsky, Meyerhold, and Tairov, and by the lessons learned in Reinhardt's theatre by Granovsky; their methods of acting and their use of the stage were theatrical communication far removed from the approach of their non-professional predecessors.

I should like to add a few notes on the Italian version of *Di kishefmakherin*, *La maga*, performed in September 1998 at Trieste's Teatro Miela.[10] The director Giulio Ciabatti adapted the text (with a few suggestions from me), while the composer Alfredo Lacosegliaz arranged the music on the basis of Berman's treatment of the presumed original score. The operetta had to be shortened to make it acceptable to a contemporary audience, and the plot was simplified, becoming the story of Mirele. The frame of the action was changed and

[10] *La maga* was included in the Shalom Trieste festival and was made possible by the municipality of Trieste, the International Association for Operetta, and the Jewish Association, Yashar.

Hotsmakh placed at its centre with the function of storyteller: *La maga* was changed into the living 'pantomine' of Hotsmakh's tale, more or less a parallel with Itsik Manger's 1936 adaptation of the play, *Hotsmakh-shpil* (Hotsmakh Play). Stefano Galante, who played Hotsmakh, also played Bobe Yakhne, with no illusionistic or realistic aim. The anti-realism of the production was underlined at the start by Hotsmakh's addressing his first monologue directly to the public, to whom he tried to sell his odd merchandise, 'Glass garters, rubber eyeglasses, steel suspenders, leather needles, kosher soap, *treyf* purses, *pareve* knives, red envelopes, white sealing-wax, combs, brushes, buttons' (Act I, scene viii). Only afterwards did he evoke Marcus (Elia Dal Maso), Bashe (Elke Burul), Avromtse, and the guests, who entered celebrating Mirele's birthday. The chorus remained on one side of the stage, while a group of actors created the effect of a crowd through choreographic pantomime. We decided the performance had to be in Italian except for the songs, which were in Yiddish (transliterated by me for the soprano Manuela Kriscak, who played Mirele, and the chorus), and the last wedding melody (a liturgical melody not included in the original score) sung by the Trieste cantor Shai Misan, who played Avromtse.[11] The performance made a favourable impression on the public, thanks in great measure to the fairytale atmosphere and the light musical interludes. These elements have been at the heart of this operetta's success in its many incarnations.

Goldfaden's main goal was to amuse and comfort the spectator, an ambition he accomplished with *Di kishefmakherin* and many other works through his elaboration on the operetta model. As he himself remarked, 'In the few hours [the spectator] spends in a theatre, he needs to forget his troubles, he needs to laugh, he needs to listen to the music, he needs to see dancing, so, with a few coins, he buys his great delight. Therefore my project became fixed: only to write comedies with music and dance. These are called operettas.'[12] According to the French director Jacques Copeau, the history of theatre is mainly a '*naissance* tradition'; that is, a chronicle of the new rather than of the usual. This is also the case with Avrom Goldfaden, whose conscious aim was to create a tradition. His work offers us an interesting paradigm that merits further investigation.

[11] I worked on the Italian translation of *La maga* with Marion Aptroot, to whom I am deeply grateful. The translation was published in 1994 as part of an essay dedicated partly to Goldfaden and partly to the connections of Joseph Roth, Marc Chagall, and Franz Kafka with the Yiddish theatre. See Paola Bertolone, *L'esilio del teatro: Goldfaden e il moderno teatro yiddish* [The Exile of Theatre: Goldfaden and the Modern Yiddish Theatre] (Rome: Bulzoni, 1994).
[12] Zylbercweig, *Teater mozayik*, 142.

FIVE

Shulamis *and* Bar kokhba: *Renewed Jewish Role Models in Goldfaden and Halkin*

⁊

SETH L. WOLITZ

WHEN the poet Avrom Goldfaden, the self-appointed and undisputed father of Yiddish theatre, turned from popular satirical musical plays such as *Shmendrik* (1877) and *Di kishefmakherin* (The Sorceress, 1877), with their contemporary Jewish folk types, to plays on biblical and post-biblical themes, he sought not only to reach a wider audience for aesthetic and pecuniary reasons but also to participate further in the incipient cultural nationalist renaissance in eastern Europe by using theatre as a gateway to Jewish history and consciousness. His post-biblical plays *Shulamis* (1880) and *Bar kokhba* (1882), considered by non-Soviet critics to be his masterpieces, reintroduce into theatre these two ancient figures, celebrated in Jewish culture for at least 2,000 years, as classic role models of Jewish identity. For Goldfaden, Shulamis and Bar Kokhba represented centred figures, whole and wholesome as opposed to a marginalized and dilapidated Jewish national identity in need of cultural renovation. For the Soviet Jewish dramatist Shmuel Halkin (1897–1960), working in the late 1930s in the Soviet home-land, these ancient figures in his plays *Shulamis* (1937) and *Bar kokhba* (1938) provide the framework for the modern socialist hero, representing the ideal Jewish man and Jewish woman of the past and of the future restoration. But, as I shall show, Goldfaden's vision and Halkin's interpretation represent different and competing poles of modern Jewish identity sharing the same cultural inheritance.[1]

Yiddish theatre, by its very existence, became an instrument of modern cultural politics. The new institution presented material that broke major

---

[1] Avrom Goldfaden, *Oysgeklibene shriftn: Shulamis un Bar kokhba* [Selected Writings: *Shulamis and Bar kokhba*], ed. Shmuel Rozhansky (Buenos Aires: YIVO, 1963); Shmuel Halkin, *Shulamis* (Moscow: Melukhe-farlag 'Der Emes', 1940), and id., *Bar kokhba* (Moscow: Melukhe-farlag 'Der Emes', 1939) are the editions used in this chapter.

taboos in Jewish orthodoxy and became a new focus for secular Jewish practice. It satirized what it considered to be the agents of backwardness, yet also
acted as a site of resistance to assimilation by putting Jewish history centrestage and rallying its audiences. The theatre provided a repressed people with
a new instrument to express their oppression, to distinguish themselves as a
people, and to project a vision of national recuperation.

A hundred years before Augusto Boal created his Theatre of the Oppressed,
Goldfaden understood the potential of the stage as the setting in which to
question the condition of the Jewish people by representing its history and
thereby mediating the present with alternative visions.[2] By choosing Jewish
historical plays, Goldfaden created a theatre of the Jewish people which
encouraged his audience to recognize and empathize with its subtext. These
historical plays not only recalled the past, looking back to better days, but provided explanations for Jewish defeats. Generally speaking, biblical plays could
pass muster before the Russian authorities as a part of the Western cultural
tradition. Goldfaden's audiences, used to allegory, relived the past of their
ancestors as they watched the drama unfold, and were thereby enabled to conceive a new vision of themselves for the future. The Yiddish theatre, following
the novel, initiated Jews into Western modes of aesthetic expression.

Secular theatre served as an agent of change in Jewish society, opening it
up to new influences. The introduction of Western ways of seeing to a traditional culture with its own religious inheritance had the effect of removing
the aura of sacredness from some long-established modes of expression, but
of renewing the sacred character of others.[3] Using the stage to represent
religious material may have struck a discordant note, especially if a particular
ceremony—such as a priestly blessing—was represented. But theatrical performance can and does create a privileged space in which the sacred can be
enacted in a secular context without offence and, indeed, can lead to a new
understanding of traditional beliefs. In this process, a new site of the sacred is
born: the stage itself becomes the place where a rite is performed, and where a
traditional culture can find fresh expression of its core beliefs. In the context
of Judaism, Yiddish theatre resacralized Jewish history, its traditions, and its
people: the Jewish stage dared to become the lost sovereign land of Israel,
restoring through performance the national homeland of the past and the
future.

The stage is a liminal space in which a rite of passage occurs, in this type
of drama providing the exiled Jews with ownership of home and land. The

---

[2] Augusto Boal, *The Theatre of the Oppressed* (New York: Theatre Communications Group, 1985).
[3] Kees Bolle, 'Secularization as a Problem for the History of Religions', *Comparative Studies in Society and History*, 12 (1970), 242–59.

performance can suspend the outside secular insufficiencies by the holistic transformation of the people into their original sacral role in time and space. The Jewish theatre emerging with Goldfaden's creativity mediated, in the suggestive terms of Hedva Ben-Israel, a 'performance of nationalism' appealing not only to the historical past but to biological continuity, past unity, and the power of nostalgia for an essentialist vision of itself.[4]

From 1877 to 1883 Goldfaden and his troupe toured Ukraine, visiting major cities (such as Odessa, Kiev, and Kharkov) and heavily populated Jewish towns (such as Zhitomir and Homel), and even reached Moscow and St Petersburg. Both the increasingly demanding public and the growing sociopolitical tensions led the dramatist to broaden and deepen his art, and to create his two post-biblical works. Unlike Boal, Goldfaden always had to function within a censorial antisemitic autocracy, and his major post-biblical play, *Bar kokhba*, was denounced as subversive to the tsarist authorities before its performance in 1883, leading to an edict against further theatre in Yiddish. The continual subterfuges used by Goldfaden and other Jewish troupes attempting to survive and perform are no less glorious pages of resistance to intolerance than are street demonstrations or strikes, and belong to any history of a repressed people's theatrical practices. Yiddish theatre was born at the time of the Russian–Turkish war of 1877–8, and its easiest years barely lasted until 1881, when the assassination of Alexander II led to the May laws of 1882, increasing Russification, and pogroms against the Jews. *Shulamis* and *Bar kokhba*, Goldfaden's most elaborate works, reflect the precarious condition of Jewry in tsarist Russia. *Shulamis* functions in a comparative idyll, *Bar kokhba* in a world of catastrophe. Goldfaden's plots display a command of Western literary theatrical form; he created fable-like structures, using mainly one-dimensional figures drawn from earlier times, and through his set-pieces evokes a post-biblical era of an intact Israel, an image intended to raise national consciousness in his audience without flouting tsarist censorship.

Where did Goldfaden find the models for his historical plays? The main characters, Shulamis and Bar Kokhba, were traditional, Shulamis representing in Jewish culture an image of beauty and nobility, and, by extension, Israel itself. Bar Kokhba traditionally projects the image of the national hero and the false messiah. The subject matter has been elaborated from biblical allusions through talmudic legends, midrashim, and numerous commentaries and histories. Goldfaden states that he took the material and plot for *Shulamis* from a narrative poem entitled *Edim ne'emonim* (Trustworthy Witnesses), written by his father-in-law, Eliyohu Verbl, in the mid-nineteenth century, and added elements from Mapu's *Ahavat tsiyon* (Love of Zion). *Bar*

---

[4] Hedva Ben-Israel, 'From Ethnicity to Nationalism', *Contention*, 5/3 (Spring 1996), 52.

kokhba derives from various histories and commentaries. Our interest is the transformation of the subject and characters into a theatrical performance, and here the models become more elusive.[5]

Historians of Yiddish theatre in Soviet Russia, such as Litvakov, Oyslender, Dobrushin, Bilov, and Velednitsky, emphasize the folk origins of Goldfaden's theatre, and use the Purim plays as well as the Yiddish Haskalah dramas as key historical models. Critics, from Gorin and Zylbercweig through Sandrow and Rozhansky to the present, argue that Goldfaden drew on both Jewish and non-Jewish sources, Western classics and European operettas and operas, in a pot-pourri that even included Turkish folk songs.[6] A. Mukdoyni (Alexander Kapel) is the only Western critic to doubt that Goldfaden had catholic tastes.[7]

Surprisingly, no scholar has commented on the generic description that appears below the two titles of each of the two works: *muzikalishe melodrame in raymen in fir aktn un 15 bilder* (a musical melodrama in verse in four acts and fifteen tableaux). Goldfaden knew precisely what he was doing, and his tableaux are perfectly designed to present the main action of each play. Melodrama is a genre that establishes an expectation of larger-than-life characters in settings that test their mettle, guaranteeing the dramatic and exotic while establishing heroic virtue. The continuing appeal of Goldfaden's work is based on his use of *muzikalishe* (musical numbers), within the melodramatic structure. Each of the scenes set inside each tableau is punctuated with choruses,

[5] The complex history of the plot material of *Shulamis* is worthy of a study in itself. The plot line derives from the Babylonian Talmud, *Ta'anit 8a*, but its psychological and social elaborations, which become increasingly sophisticated, pass through Rashi, Tosafot, and *Sefer arukh* (Kholed) to the *Mayse bukh*, story 100. These developments reflect the various forces at play in Jewish society across the centuries until they reach Goldfaden and Halkin. The figure of Bar Kokhba has been addressed in Richard G. Marks, *The Image of Bar Kokhba in Traditional Jewish Literature: False Messiah and National Hero* (University Park: Pennsylvania State University Press, 1994), but this study stops before reaching the secular period and the further reworking of the matter. Bar Kokhba needs a fuller elaboration up to the present as well.

[6] Moyshe Litvakov, *Finf yor melukhisher idisher kamer-teater* [Five Years of the State Yiddish Chamber Theatre] (Moscow: Farlag Shul un Bukh, 1924), 56–72; Yekhezkel Dobrushin, *Binyomin zuskin* (Moscow: Melukhe-farlag, 1939); B. Gorin, *Di geshikhte fun idishn teater* [The History of the Yiddish Theatre], 2 vols. (New York: Literarisher Farlag, 1918), vol. i; 'Goldfaden, Avrom', in Zalmen Zylbercweig (ed.), *Leksikon fun yidishn teater* [Lexicon of Yiddish Theatre], 6 vols. (New York: Elisheva, 1931–70), i. 275–366; S. Bilov and A. Velednitsky, Introduction to Avrom Goldfaden, *Geklibene dramatishe verk* [Selected Dramatic Works] (Kiev: Melukhe-farlag, 1940), 3–64; A. Mukdoyni [Alexander Kapel], 'Avrom goldfaden', in Jacob Shatzky (ed.), *Goldfaden-bukh* (New York: Yiddish Theatre Museum, 1926), 6–8; Nokhem Oyslender and Uri Finkel, *A. Goldfaden: materyaln far a biografye* [A. Goldfaden: Materials towards a Biography] (Minsk: Institut far vaysruslendisher kultur, 1926); Nokhem Oyslender, *Yidisher teater, 1887–1917* (Moscow: Melukhe-farlag, 1940); Shmuel Rozhansky, Introduction to Avrom Goldfaden, *Oysgeklibene shriftn* [Selected Writings] (Buenos Aires: YIVO, 1963), 23–31; Nahma Sandrow, *Vagabond Stars: A World History of Yiddish Theater* (Syracuse, NY: Syracuse University Press, 1999), 40–69.

[7] Mukdoyni, 'Avrom Goldfaden'.

individual songs, duets, and voice against chorus. The musical component is essential to each of his works. The singing acts as an important channel for emotional expression, thereby justifying the hybrid nature of 'musical melodrama'.

The dramatic verse both supplies the characterization and moves the plot forward, while the music arrests the progress of the plot to focus sharply on the intense emotion and meaning of the moment. The purely orchestral numbers enhance the dramatic action; they accompany the dance sequences and herald important scenes, and provide music's emotional charge to accomplish the full theatrical experience. Goldfaden followed the theatrical conventions of the surrounding cultures, which he absorbed and brought over to a Jewish world just becoming secular and breaking away from the taboo of dramatic representation.

Goldfaden's melodrama corresponds to the Italian opera not only in structure, plot, and character elaboration, but also in its various if simplified uses of music, alternating *grandes scènes* with intimate personal and love scenes in which spoken dialogue replaces the traditional recitative. (The use of spoken dialogue derives from French melodrama, which evolved into vaudeville, a play alternating dialogue and song, as does Beethoven's *Fidelio*.) Internal evidence in his work shows that Goldfaden was aware of and influenced by Italian and French opera and operetta elements, theme, plot, and characterization. But he had closer at hand, in Ukraine, the distinct Russian and Ukrainian musical melodramas that were being performed in all the major towns. These works engaged particularly in the imaginative restoration of their national histories and consciousnesses. Sokalsky's *Mazeppa* (1858), Artomovsky's *Zaporozhets za Dunayem* (Cossack on the Danube, 1863) and Vakhnyanin's *Kupalo* (Pentecost, 1870) celebrated Ukrainian historical moments and religious holidays. The subject matter and general theme expressed national aspirations, but structurally the works followed European models of plot and characterization. The unique contribution of these works erupts in the colourful native melodies used in the various songs and dances. These Ukrainian works, themselves influenced by Austrian, Czech, Polish, and Russian models, could easily have served Goldfaden as living examples. We may infer this from the fact that *Shmendrik*, a comedy with dance and music and studded with Jewish folk types, was performed in Moscow, where, Goldfaden noted, half of the audience was non-Jewish. Evidently, he was working in known east European cultural structures but proffering the 'exotic' quality of Jews on stage through their melodies.

What the Italian and European Romantic opera tradition offered Goldfaden, besides the formal structures, were the specifically Israelite setting and biblical stories considered so attractive in the new orientalist vogue, which, in Italy particularly, took on a unique cultural and political role, for Bellini's *Norma* (1831), Verdi's *Nabucco* (1842), and even Goldmark's *Die Königin von Saba* (1866–75) (which includes a Shulamis!) express national humiliation and national renewal, and these Italian operas served to rally the Risorgimento. Most of the plots of these works centred on the conflict of love and duty among the heroes, a conflict in which the national good prevailed as the first duty—the long heritage of the Cornelian neoclassical tragedy. Goldfaden saw such works, which were part of the standard repertoire in tsarist Russian opera houses, performed in Russia and in the opera house of Odessa. Goldfaden's Yiddish theatre therefore drew on a musical and melodramatic world that had already evolved a highly developed formulaic ordering. What makes his historical plays *Shulamis* and *Bar kokhba* so remarkable are his skills in verse, plotting, characterization, spectacle, and, not least, musical composition.

The musical melodrama *Shulamis* reveals a mastery of the *pièce bien faite* ('well-made play'): Act I portrays Shulamis as a devoted daughter following her father on his pilgrimage, but he sends her back home. Lost in the desert, she falls into a well. She is rescued by Avisholem, a noble youth of Maccabean descent returning to Jerusalem, and they swear an oath of fidelity to each other, with the well and a wildcat as witnesses. Act II develops Avisholem's return and his unexpected choice of wife, Avigayil, in the vineyard. Scene ii, the classical ballet act, concludes with dance, music, and the great Priest blessing them on their knees *à la chrétienne*. Act III, two years later, reveals a loyal, unhappy Shulamis being pressed by suitors. To escape rather than become mad, like Bellini's Elvira or Donizetti's Lucia, Shulamis feigns madness, to everyone's horror. The scene shifts back to Jerusalem, where Avisholem and Avigayil are contentedly celebrating their second year of marriage when the nurse enters to reveal in a *coup de théâtre* that their second child has drowned in the well (the first having been strangled by a wildcat). Revealing his broken oath, Avisholem must leave, and his wife withdraws in bitter understanding. He enters a shepherd's camp, learns the sad tale of Shulamis, and declares that, as a doctor, he will cure her. Act IV concludes with the happy reunion and a final grand scene in which Avisholem and Shulamis receive the priestly blessing, again on their knees, at the great Temple.

The text is laden with fluent verse, mainly rhyming pentameters, creating a glow of orientalism drawn from Western literary and musical sources. The play has a religious frame, for the father has set off on a pilgrimage from Bethlehem to Jerusalem for Sukkot. The Temple becomes the heart of the play, for that is where the nation's life is reinstituted and renewed as the couple receives the priest's blessing. Microcosm and macrocosm are fused: Israel with the Creator, and Avisholem (who is of Davidic descent and thus prefigures the messiah) with Shulamis (allegorically Israel). The repeated image of the Temple in Jerusalem underscores its cultic power as the omphalos of Jewry.

The play's alternative title, *Bas yerushalayim*, suggests that Shulamis is the daughter of Jerusalem. This image ties her to her namesake in the Song of Songs, the Shulamis of Jerusalem, and to Abishag the Shunamite, the young handmaid of King David. As noted above, the Davidic presence is evident in the name of her lover, Avisholem, the rebellious son of King David and Avigayil, his first wife, further linking the action to David's reign. By joining Bethlehem, David's home town, to Jerusalem, with the subtextual allusion to the Davidic kingdom, the play projects an elegiac, if not nostalgic, pastorale of Jewish wholeness, sovereign and secure in a quasi-sacral biblical or post-biblical world. The daughter of Jerusalem, Shulamis becomes the image of the Jewish Everywoman, the woman of valour (*eyshes khayl*) praised in Proverbs and the symbol of Jewish feminine virtues. But Goldfaden's characters are in fact in the mould of the Western Romantic operatic model of noble, upright, and passionate figures, where the hero, after passing through a crisis of egotism, attains a new moral stature. Goldfaden's Shulamis is such a Romantic figure, playing the mad recluse and patiently awaiting her beloved.

If today Goldfaden's Shulamis projects a vision of a Romantic Jewess in the mould of the Western woman of *nobilitas*, we also recognize that her character reflects the Western model of love as an individuated experience that valorizes the woman and threatens the traditional hierarchy. The use of the Israelite setting and the historical Jewish milieu allows the dramatist to project both the conscious and the unconscious stresses of contemporary society beside the purely nationalist element. Shulamis's kindly, old-fashioned father wants to respect his daughter's preference in men; but he cannot refuse all her suitors so has to choose a demeaning process, the use of lots, by means of which one of them will become her bridegroom. Her feigned madness, which drives her father to despair, represents the emerging tensions in the Jewish world as it secularized. Unlike Lucia di Lammermoor, the heroine of Donizetti's opera, who marries and then goes mad, the Jewish heroine is made of stronger stuff. Both characters can be seen to represent feminist protest, highlighting the strains on a society facing the erosion of patriarchal absolutism. Shulamis refuses marriage, using her native intelligence and ability to resist. Her loyalty to the love sworn between her and Avisholem at the well gives her strength, both emotionally and because it represents a legal contract. Indeed, Avisholem insisted that their meeting was *bashert* (fated), even though Shulamis emphasized that she was not from his class but, in contrast to his Maccabean nobility and links with the city, was from the middle class, and tended the flock (as indeed King David originally did in Bethlehem).

These class tensions reflect the conditions of Goldfaden's day, as Jews moved from the countryside and *shtetls* to the larger cities, testing and reject-ing older hierarchies. While Shulamis recognizes the dangers inherent in their social differences, they elude Avisholem, who fails to understand this key factor which precipitates the dramatic development. Throughout the play Avi-sholem, whose name ironically means 'father of peace', remains a rather good historical namesake of the rebellious son of King David, for, though he even-tually repents, he is unfaithful. The oath of love between him and Shulamis is an iconic expression of operatic Romanticism, which the Yiddish culture of Goldfaden's time was appropriating and giving secular overtones: love was now seen as an individuating force, a destroyer of patriarchy, a challenger of class divisions, and a creator of new references of identity. The play's Roman-tic theme of love conquering all is not without its demonic streak, for it causes the deaths of two children and the collapse of a successful marriage. The sworn oath takes precedence over these later developments, and, as the pin-nacle of values, parallels duty to the state in Western plays. This distinctively Jewish feature runs through early Yiddish theatre, and even serves as the basis of Ansky's *Der dibek* (The Dybbuk). Shulamis is within her rights on two levels: legal and emotional. The oath expresses an act of intention, and has legal status.

Shulamis appears as the first full-blooded woman on the Yiddish stage whose actions are based on her own will. She is in control of her choices and decisions, and the songs she sings, like arias, reflect the emotional states she passes through. Her role is to a large extent determined by the genre in which Goldfaden was working. He made use of the Romantic musical melodrama with its Western expectations, especially in its treatment of plot, theme, and characterization. He elaborated a Jewish heroine based on Western models of female behaviour. He Judaized as much as possible any hint of Christian elements, but the rhetorical and elegant verse cannot avoid reflecting its origins in the high-caste (Christian) women of Western opera. (Nor in 1880 would Goldfaden have known, from archaeological evidence, what the Temple would have looked like.) He relied on his European models with their Chris-tian inheritance, appropriating them and keeping whatever he considered not blatantly offensive to Jewish sensibilities. Indeed, the novelty of his Shulamis lay in projecting on stage the classic Jewish heroine in the European mould, whose traditional beauty, brains, and ethical behaviour represented a true daughter of Jerusalem: speaking and singing Yiddish, in love, and ultimately able to get her way. Her mythic past becomes an immediate presence, and a possible role model.

The historical plays emerged in counterpoint to the earlier ones, which depicted contemporary one-dimensional folk types. Soviet Jewish critics consider *Shulamis* and *Bar kokhba* inferior works, lacking historical colour and characterization,[8] while the so-called 'nationalist' critics appreciate the unique characterizations. Both critical schools ignore the fact that these ancient characters are based on Western modes of depiction, for Yiddish culture had no distinctive visual or theatrical tradition. The novelty of seeing Jewish heroes speaking *mame-loshn* and acting nobly brought Goldfaden remarkable success. He was offering another road to modernity—that of the maskilim, who wanted to reclaim Jewish history from a purely religious interpretation. He was also offering another human dimension—the aesthetic—as represented by Shulamis (for the female) and Bar Khokhba (for the male).

In the Soviet Union forty years later Goldfaden's popularity was still not exhausted, and in 1922 Alexander Granovsky, the director of the Moscow State Yiddish Theatre (GOSET) rewrote Goldfaden's *Di Kishefmakherin* with the help of Yekhezkel Dobrushin, 'in order that its staging should resonate in the present, with contemporary political questions'; as Picon-Vallin notes, 'The Sorceress (*kishefmakherin*) throttles the synagogue, beginning the assault on the temple by means of prayers or religious ceremonies that she voids of their divine context.'[9] GOSET whittled Goldfaden's plays into a director's enterprise with a new political orientation: the Bolshevik demystification of religion and the expulsion of bourgeois nationalist chauvinism. During the 1920s and well into the 1930s this defined the orientation of this famous Yiddish theatre. As Sandrow among others has noted, Lazar Kaganovich, the sole Jewish member of the Politburo at the time, appeared at GOSET in the 1935–6 season and requested plays depicting Soviet Jews building new lives. Where were the Maccabees and where was Bar Kokhba?[10] At a time of ideological tensions, purges, anti-nationalist expression, and disappearing writers, such thoughts appeared to the assembled Jewish actors to be a 'provoca-

---

[8] Bilov and Velednitsky, Introduction, 62.

[9] Yosef Shayn, *Arum moskver yidishn teater* [Around the Moscow Yiddish Theatre] (Paris: Éditions Polyglottes, 1964), 43; Béatrice Picon-Vallin, *Le Théâtre juif soviétique pendant les années vingt* [Soviet Jewish Theatre during the 1920s] (Lausanne: La Cité-L'Âge d'Homme, 1973), 83.

[10] Sandrow, *Vagabond Stars*, 242; Yekhezkel Dobrushin, 'Moskovskii Evreiskii Teatr', in *Teatral'naya Entsiklopediya*, ed. S. S. Morkul'sky, 6 vols. (Moscow: Gos. nauch. izd-vo 'Sov. entsiklopediya', 1961–7), iii. 936.

tion'.[11] But the troupe set about the task, and Shmuel Halkin reworked Gold-faden's *Shulamis* as a play of Soviet socialist expression with a positive hero-ine; it reached the boards in 1937, to great success.

The reasons why the new Communist Party line encouraged works pre-senting national heroes who conform to socialist ideals have not yet been thoroughly explored, but, as the historian Sheila Fitzpatrick has noted, the party constantly harassed the cultural intelligentsia, and in the late 1930s con-ditions deteriorated.[12] The party's proletarian focus used folk culture as a weapon against the intelligentsia with their bourgeois origins and their cul-tural interests. As Shayn quotes from the newspaper *Sovetskoe Iskusstva*, '*Shu-lamis* must serve as a penance to overshadow Granovsky's *Kishefmakherin* with its aesthetic excesses. Theatre will henceforth make full use of folklore and the popular traditions of folk art.'[13] The article notes that *Shulamis* is based on a folk epic, like '*Kiz-Zhibak* among the Cossacks and *Abisalam and Eter* among the Georgians'.[14] From an official newspaper, such remarks safely grounded Halkin's new work in pure folkloric legend, which assured its conformity to the party's aesthetic dictates. That Halkin chose the Shulamis theme may not be entirely accidental. The late 1930s was also a period of much concern about the role of women and women's liberation in the Soviet Union: the importance of recognizing women as individuals was par-ticularly stressed at the peasant level and among the national minorities.[15]

The work, dedicated to Goldfaden on his centennial year (1940), further aligned Halkin with a 'folk national tradition'. Cultural milestones such as Pushkin's centenary in 1937 were celebrated as part of the drive to *kul'turnost'* in the world of socialist realism.[16] As Zachary Baker has also noted, the celebration of Sholem Aleykhem's eightieth birthday on 19 April 1939 in the Kremlin's Hall of Columns added to the new freedom to appeal to Jewish national sentiments.[17] The folklorization of Goldfaden belongs to a study of Yiddish cultural history, for this interpretation does an injustice to both the dramatist and his works. But it also allowed Halkin to publish *Shulamis* in 1940 under his own name rather than as an adaptation.

[11] Yosef Shayn, 'Yidisher teater in sovetn-farband' [Yiddish Theatre in the Soviet Union], in Itsik Manger, Jonas Turkow, and Moyshe Perenson (eds.), *Yidisher teater in eyrope tsvishn beyde velt-milkhomes: sovetn-farband, mayrev-eyrope, baltishe lender* [Yiddish Theatre in Europe between the World Wars: The Soviet Union, Western Europe, and the Baltic Countries], 2 vols. (New York: Congress for Jewish Culture, 1971), 138.
[12] Sheila Fitzpatrick, *The Cultural Front: Power and Culture in Revolutionary Russia* (Ithaca, NY: Cornell University Press, 1992).   [13] Shayn, 'Yidisher teater in sovetn-farband', 137.
[14] Ibid.   [15] Fitzpatrick, *The Cultural Front*, 234.   [16] Ibid. 225.
[17] Zachary Baker, 'Yiddish in Form and Socialist in Content: The Observance of Sholem Aleichem's Eightieth Birthday in the Soviet Union', *YIVO Annual*, 23 (1996), 210.

Halkin essentially retained the basic plot line but created a *dramatishe poeme* distinctly his own and a product of his Soviet reality. Lev Pulver provided the music, elaborating Goldfaden's melodies and his own, but Halkin's text only alludes to which passages should be sung. Goldfaden's work was an integrated ensemble of one creator, whereas Halkin's *Shulamis* is a separate 'dramatic poem' and its performance a result of the collaboration of poet, composer, actor, and theatre people. The dichotomy between text and performance is made clear by the generic definition.

Halkin's play is in three acts, unlike Goldfaden's four-act structure so reminiscent of late nineteenth-century operatic tradition and Russian theatre. Halkin's first act corresponds to Goldfaden's, with the exposition of Shulamis lost in the desert, Avisholem as her rescuer, and the well as a witness to their oath of love. Halkin then fuses Goldfaden's second and third acts by removing the elaborate dance scene and the Temple scenes. Thus, while Avisholem's choosing Avigayil absorbs Goldfaden's Act II, in Halkin it also includes the longer second scene in the tent of Manoyekh, her father, and the mad scene with the suitors. Halkin's Act III takes place in Avisholem's house, where his servant Tsingitang, a character modelled on Shakespeare's Caliban, reveals to Avigayil that the source of the familial unhappiness resides in the oath to Shulamis. After Avisholem has declared that he will honour the oath, Avigayil lets him depart. From the shepherds he learns of Shulamis's madness; around Manoyekh's tent a Molièresque group of doctors, charlatans, and townsfolk discuss her fate. The final scene reveals Avisholem and a cured Shulamis together at last. Although Halkin's basic plot line parallels Goldfaden's version, his world-view, the internal structuring of the scenes, the characters, and the social, cultural, and historical representations emerge quite differently.

In Halkin's text the secure and irenic religio-aesthetic world-view Goldfaden conjures in his *Shulamis*, with its Sukkot tonality of ripeness, joy, and order, transmogrifies into a state of alarm: the nation is invaded by an enemy advancing on the capital. The pastoral idyll becomes a mere decorative backdrop. The shepherds of Bethlehem are off—not on religious pilgrimage, but to defend the fatherland—and Avisholem, transformed from a Maccabean aristocrat into a shepherd, emerges as the natural leader. The entire work projects a bizarre peasant or proletarian vision of the single-class state, with the remnants of other classes in retreat. Goldfaden's effort to resurrect a lost Jewish realm through the Romantic operatic tradition translates in Halkin's work into a setting of folkloric fantasy closer to Rimsky-Korsakoff's *Sadko* (1898) or *The Legand of the Invisible City of Kitezh and the Maiden Fevroniya* (1907). Halkin sharpens this perception with the use of the Russian-style folksinger (*skazitel'*), who sings *byliny* (ballads), giving the story a strong flavour of Slavonic folklore. The folksinger thereby establishes the context in which the audience should interpret the play, and reinforces the fantastic quality of the story line. His ballad about the well, *Brumem fun farlibte tsvey* (The Well of the Loving Pair), serves to define the character of the work in microcosm. The singular event at the well in Goldfaden's play is transformed by Halkin into a folktale, a recurrent leitmotiv in his work, of which the elaboration in this drama is but one more retelling.

In each version, the way in which the love story of Shulamis and Avisholem develops around the well points up the vast ideological difference between the authors, even if for both the well is the archetypal symbol of femininity, its pure water the traditional symbol of life and renewal. For Goldfaden it becomes, at the microcosmic level, the manifest symbol of the love of Shulamis and Avisholem—purity, unity, and renewal. The desert setting and betrothal recall the beginning of the love between God and Israel as told in Jeremiah: 'I remember the devotion of your youth, how as a bride you loved me and followed me through the desert.' The contemporary Jewish audience watching Goldfaden's *Shulamis* would be intensely aware of the resonance of the love stories in Genesis which begin around a well. The story of Isaac and Rebecca (Gen. 15: 11–26), who gives Abraham's servant water from the well, and the encounter of Jacob with Rachel (Gen. 29: 1–12), both focus on the well, giving it potent symbolic value in Jewish historical and religious consciousness; its presence silently confirms Israel's providential continuity and God's love of Israel. For Goldfaden, the Shulamis love story symbolized by the well and its water is linked to and embedded in the sacral— the Sukkot celebrations in Jerusalem to which her father goes in pilgrimage and, particularly, the ceremony of *simkhas beys hasho'eva* (Rejoicing at the Place of Drawing Water) at the Pool of Siloam—for this 'well of salvation' was used to anoint the Davidic dynasty, bringing salvation both to the dynasty itself and to all Israel. Thus the two wells are joined, and the oath between Avisholem and Shulamis (with their Davidic ties) is a further link in the liaison of Bethlehem and Jerusalem with the Davidic inheritance, placing the oath (which, if unfulfilled, will bring not salvation but retribution) doubly within divine protection.

Halkin, on the other hand, removes all scenes at the Temple and any religious allusion implied in the images, making the story line a mere folk legend showing the power of love. It is de-Judaized but for the names. Goldfaden's powerful religio-national and historical texture is replaced by a Slavonic atmosphere of jolly peasants and folksingers, and legends of lovers, magic wells, and beasts, with threatening enemies relegated to the periphery.

Halkin has reduced Goldfaden's historical and aestheticized ritual to mere folklore based on vapid universalization.

In both Goldfaden and Halkin, Shulamis is drawn as the Romantic woman; however, she is not drawn true to type: unlike the heroines of nineteenth-century opera, she does not become mad but only feigns madness as a ploy.[18] She is a strong-willed lady. In both cases she displays her loyalty to the family and community, and above all to her love, but at the same time she has a sense of her own uniqueness. Goldfaden's Shulamis is a woman in love whose lyrical feelings are strongly tied to the loyalty of the oath. As Avisholem departs, she repeats:

> Af viderzeyn, mayn liber, mayn reter, mayn lebn!
> Avisholem, farges nit di shvue, vos du host gegebn!
>
> Au revoir, my beloved, my knight, my life!
> Avisholem, do not forget the oath you have sworn![19]

Love and insecurity, sensitivity and intelligence. Halkin's Shulamis, a true Soviet heroine in the Cornelian mould, states to Avisholem departing for war:

> Mayn libster, mayn giber, mayn har,
> Bist tsen mol mir liber derfar . . .
> Nu gey hob a gliklikhn veg.
>
> My dearest, my hero, my lord, you are ten
> times dearer to me [for your patriotic act].
> Go, then; may your path be bright.[20]

When he does not come back to her, her lamenting is no less intense, but the time factor has been mercifully shortened—as has her mad scene, which has a touch of parody. The restoration in the final act has less the nuance of evolving emotional recuperation than a sense of the necessary reunion after the quacks have had their day attempting to restore Shulamis to sanity for Avisholem's return.

Both versions of Shulamis are idealized visions of the modern Jewish woman placed in the context of ancient times, with Goldfaden drawing on the Western operatic tradition and Halkin on the Soviet made-to-measure template. Neither seeks to project a Jewish woman in the contemporary mould, but rather one based on non-Jewish literary and ideological sources. Yet both are grounded in ancient Jewish subject matter—whether strongly or weakly depends on each dramatist's political orientation. By choosing to create this idealized image, Goldfaden had no choice but to use the contemporary stage

---

[18] This motif of feigning madness first appears in the *Sefer arukh*, Kholed. This text contains essentially the entire plot of Goldfaden's *Shulamis* but not the name!

[19] Goldfaden, *Oysgeklibene shriftn: Shulamis*, 53.   [20] Halkin, *Shulamis*, 16–17.

successes of the West. For Halkin, the use of Shulamis was a device permitting the hint of a Jewish past that was acceptable to the party in that period; when the party line changed he paid for it with a long period of imprisonment. The character of Shulamis as the vision of an authentic, positive Jewish woman, worthy of imitation by those of either a nationalist or a communist persuasion, today suggests a more clearly feminist interpretation.

Halkin's success—or rather the acceptance of the *Shulamis* production in 1937—allowed the company daringly to comply with Kaganovich's request in 1938 for a play on Bar Kokhba.[21] This play moved almost blatantly from folk epic to a tale of historical and national consciousness, and, even though he was protected by Goldfaden's earlier play and by his legitimization as a folk dramatist, Halkin went to great lengths to keep the plot line of the battle of an oppressed people fighting a ruthless, exploitative oppressor. And he did not forget class conflict: the legitimate uprising occurs thanks to the working class with its sense of justice, as opposed to the traitorous, collaborating bourgeois class, whose members care for peace only in order to protect their wealth. Their lack of a sense of civic duty and of respect for civil rights and dignity condemns them. With cautious craft even the rabbis are brought into the conflict, for the Bar Kokhba story without Rabbi Akiba would have been unthinkable. (Nevertheless, to avoid the false messiah theme becoming dominant over that of the military hero Goldfaden did not use the character.) Rabbi Akiba becomes a spiritual and intellectual leader for the uprising, a sagacious figure who anoints Bar Kokhba as the true leader and judge. Eliezer, the leader of the peace party in Goldfaden's play and ultimately the victim of Bar Kokhba's hubris, becomes in Halkin's version the image of the counter-revolutionary who must be condemned to death:

> Farlorn geyn muz der dem veg tsum folk farlorn.
>
> Astray must he go who has strayed from the people.[22]

In wartime the people come before Torah and law, says Elisha, the *vox populi*.[23] The last desperate battle against Rome fully brings out the socialist hero in Bar Kokhba. As the leader of the oppressed, he calls them to arms:

> A knekht, vi er nemt di shverd in hant,
> Er vert oys knekht.
>
> A slave, just by holding a sword in his hand,
> Is no longer a slave.[24]

---

[21] Lazar Moisevich Kaganovich, the one Jew in the Politburo and close to Stalin, appeared at the Moscow Yiddish State Theatre and asked to see Jewish historical and Soviet heroes like Bar Kokhba on the stage. See Sandrow, *Vagabond Stars*, 242–3.

[22] Halkin, *Bar kokhba*, 122.   [23] Ibid. 121.   [24] Ibid. 126.

When a child fighter dies and the father asks for sympathy, Bar Kokhba answers:

> Nit veyn! Dayn kind unz alemen gehert!
>
> Do not weep! Your son belongs to all of us.[25]

And with the freedom of theatre and the demands of socialist realism, Bar Kokhba's death and the defeat of Israel for 2,000 years is postponed to the specious but thrilling:

> Vayl vemen shtarbt s'iz bashert
> Far frayhayt fun zayn folk—blaybt lebn shtendik.
> [*Es derhert zikh a trompeyt.*]
> In shlakht! In shlakht! Di shlakht iz nit farendikt!
>
> For whoever is fated to die
> For freedom for his people, lives on for ever.
> [*Trumpet calls.*]
> To battle! To battle! The battle is not over![26]

Halkin has created a positive hero in both action and example, the friend of the people and a true leader. One cannot but recognize in this the hero of Sergei Eisenstein's film *Alexander Nevsky*. Eisenstein was constructing the same type of heroic figure in the context of Russian history, in preparation for the feared war with the Germans. Indeed, the Roman salutes in *Bar kokhba* are used, no doubt, to allude to the fascists. In Halkin's play history is suspended to allow a Marxist interpretation. This battle is not a conclusion, but an episode in the fight for human freedom. Its meaning is projected into the future, when historians will record and applaud the nobility of the action whether won or lost.

Ironically, Goldfaden's ending is not very different, in spite of adhering to the European Romantic convention of the hero's death, drawn from neo-classical models. Goldfaden's Bar Kokhba faces his *anagnorisis*, and admits wronging Eliezer, who pursues him like the ghosts at Bosworth Field in Shakespeare's *Richard III*, prophesying that he will lose the battle.

> Ze, der groyser giber beygt far dir di kni . . .
> Ikh vel shtarbn, yo, nor loz mikh shtarbn vi a held . . .
> Loz mikh khotsh zayn der letster af dem blutikn shlakhtfeld . . .
>
> Behold, the great hero bends his knee before you . . .
> I shall die, yes, only let me die like a hero . . .
> Let me at least be the last on the bloody battleground.[27]

---

[25] Ibid. 127.   [26] Ibid.   [27] Goldfaden, *Oysgeklibene shriften . . . Bar kokhba*, 204.

Then, giving what is perhaps the classic rabbinic interpretation of these events, Bar Kokhba states:

> Yo, brider, farges shoyn fun haynt on in dem zig
> Unzer land vet ir shoyn nit opnemen mit krig . . .
> Nor af eybik untergevorfene—denkt shoyn nit afile oykh,
> Az got vil nit, iz umzist dem gibers koyekh!
> [*In dem moment hert men a trompeytn-shal un a geshrey fun a sakh roymishe militer.*]
> Neyn, soyne. Frey dikh nit! Az ikh ken shoyn gor nit nemen bay dir—
> Eyns vel ikh bay dir: dayn shtolts iber mir!
> Nit dayn fayl zol durkhboyern di brust fun dem giber—
> Fun mayn hant aleyn iz mir tsu shtarbn liber!

> Yes, brethren, forget victory henceforth
> You will not retake our land by war
> For ever cast down—never think otherwise;
> If God does not will it, the hero's strength is in vain!
> [*A trumpet blast; cries of many Roman soldiers.*]
> No, foe! Rejoice not that I can no longer overcome you—
> I wish to take back but one thing, your overweening pride over me!
> Not your arrow will pierce the breast of this hero—
> But by my own hand is it better to die![28]

The tragic flaw is pride, the one failing of the perfect Aristotelian hero. Goldfaden captures both the hero's fall in the catastrophe and the *nobilitas* essential to the tragic character.

The figure of Bar Kokhba restores a vision of a Jewish hero fighting nobly for his country against impossible odds, and his death does not conclude the melodrama. In the tumultuous clash of Roman soldiers and Jewish fighters an important Jewish turncoat dies—a psychological retribution. The final scene builds dramatically as defence walls collapse to reveal the burning of the Betar fortress, and then freezes into a tableau of Roman soldiers killing a Jewish child defended by its mother, an old man about to lose his head, and a Roman soldier standing above a Jew and spearing him in the final fray. Strikingly, Goldfaden's play ends with the people a victim. In 1882 this scene must have been extremely powerful, and contained a message of caution, for it represented the repeated pogroms of 1881 and 1882. Goldfaden's choice of this national tragedy as a subject of theatrical representation was not without irony, and the resulting play is ambivalent as a restorative drama. The use of the tragedy serves as both a cautionary tale and a historical goad to action. Yiddish theatre provided a place of secular lamentation through the ritual of

---

[28] Goldfaden, *Oysgeklibene shriften . . . Bar kokhba*, 204–5.

theatre and also a site of memory and renewal. The representation of Israel on the stage, proffering as it did the possibility of national restoration, prepared a public for political Zionism twenty years later. Restoration was very much in the air after the pogroms of 1881, and the theatre became the focal point for the ritual re-enactment of the Jewish community's suffering and its hope for the future. Goldfaden's hero, based on contemporary Western operatic models, provided through theatre a leadership that paved the way for the modern Jewish leader—perhaps Herzl himself, whose noble bearing was so much admired in eastern Europe. Goldfaden's Bar Kokhba was the first secular Jewish hero in Yiddish theatre, and remarkable as a model of Jewish pride.

Halkin provided the same character with the heroic values of the Soviet regime but with a sufficient element of national historical past, if necessarily deformed to induce a consciousness of a worthy folk inheritance within the mould of the positive Soviet socialist folk hero. Halkin's Bar Kokhba chides Yoysi, the national chauvinist worker who wishes to cast out Kosi (from *kuti*: Samaritan) and other non-blood members of the nation (perhaps an allusion to the Arab–Jewish clashes in Palestine in the late 1930s and the anti-Zionist attitudes in the party line). Bar Kokhba's line 'ver s'geyt bafrayen, yenems iz dos land' ('whoever goes to free the land, the land belongs to them')[29] fits the inclusive national folk hero as the correct vision of proletarian nationalism. Significantly, the word Israel is never mentioned in the text. Halkin's hero, then, is a hero without a named country, loving all people who serve the nation and are all equal fighting oppression—quite different from Goldfaden's national hero with his sin of pride.

In the two distinct Yiddish theatres and plays of Goldfaden and Halkin, two ideologies hidden beneath the shared plot lines and characters project the shared intention of offering a new image of the Jewish hero, male and female, drawn from the past and serving the future; the Shulamis plays provide the strong, new, independence-loving Jewish female ideal, and the Bar Kokhba plays the strong male Jewish leader. Both types are created from ultimately non-Jewish theatrical sources, for the Yiddish theatre, like any Third World theatre today without an established secular traditional theatre, can only begin by adopting and adapting from Western models and allying them to indigenous subject matter and native codes of cultural expression. The act of going to a Yiddish play in Goldfaden's time was revolutionary, and the site of a stage performance a new rite of passage to the past and to the future. For Halkin's GOSET theatre in the Moscow of 1938–47, simply to attend was also a fairly daring act, for, even if the plays were acceptable to the party, the entire Yiddish enterprise was under suspicion; and indeed it was suddenly

[29] Halkin, *Bar kokhba*, 108.

closed down. Nevertheless, GOSET performed such works by Halkin, and permitted a people to find a remnant of secular modern expression for their threatened national cultural identity. Yiddish theatre found in its two character creations, Shulamis and Bar Kokhba, metaphors and allegories of Jewish continuity.

III. REGIONAL CENTRES

SIX

Yiddish Theatre in Vienna
1880–1938

&

BRIGITTE DALINGER

VIENNA is famous for the many notable Jewish authors and scientists who lived and worked there at the beginning of the twentieth century: for example, Arthur Schnitzler, Sigmund Freud, and the physician Julius Tandler. Their lives and works must be seen in the context of a special circumstance—the meeting of German and Jewish cultures. But from the beginning of the century until 1938 a less celebrated facet of Jewish culture had a home in Vienna: Yiddish culture, which was represented by Yiddish journalists and writers, the newspapers and books they produced, and the Yiddish theatre. Only the end of the twentieth century, however, has seen the beginnings of scholarly research on these topics.[1]

Yiddish theatre was brought to Vienna by immigrants, who came mostly from Galicia, Bukovina, Russia, and Romania.[2] They had left the *shtetl* in search of a better life in the great capital of the Austro-Hungarian monarchy. Staging Yiddish productions in German-speaking Vienna meant restricting the possible audience to a small section of the population. Between 1890 and 1910 an estimated 175,318 Jews lived in Vienna (8.63 per cent of the city's

---

[1] See A. Eidherr, '"Auf stillem Pfad . . .". Jiddische Schriftsteller in Wien' ['On a Silent Path . . .': Yiddish Authors in Vienna], *Literatur und Kritik*, 273–4 (1993), 47–55; Gabriele Kohlbauer-Fritz, 'Jiddische Subkultur in Wien' [Yiddish Subculture in Vienna], in Peter Bettelheim and Michael Ley (eds.), *Ist jetzt hier die 'wahre Heimat'? Ostjüdische Einwanderung nach Wien* [Is this the 'True Homeland'? East European Immigration to Vienna] (Vienna: Picus Verlag, 1993), 89–115; Gabriele Kohlbauer-Fritz (ed.), *In a Schtodt woss schtarbt—In einer Stadt, die stirbt. Jiddische Lyrik aus Wien* [In a Dying City: Yiddish Poems from Vienna] (Vienna: Picus Verlag, 1995); Thomas Soxberger, 'Jiddische Literatur und Publizistik in Wien' [Yiddish Literature and Publishers in Vienna], MA thesis, University of Vienna, 1994; id., 'Strukturen des jiddischen Kulturlebens in Wien. Verlage und Druckereien, Vereinswesen' [Structures of Yiddish Cultural Life in Vienna: Publishing Houses and Presses, Associations], unpublished manuscript; Brigitte Dalinger, *'Verloschene Sterne'. Geschichte des jüdischen Theaters in Wien* ['Extinguished Stars': The History of the Jewish Theatre in Vienna] (Vienna: Picus Verlag, 1998).

[2] See Brigitte Dalinger, 'Poczatki Teatru żydowskiego w Wiedniu' [The Beginnings of the Yiddish Theatre in Vienna], in Anna Kuligowska-Korzeniewska and Malgorzata Leyko (eds.), *Teatr żydowski w Polsce* [The Jewish Theatre in Poland] (Łódź: Wydawnictwo Uniwersytetu Łódzkiego, 1998), 331–41.

inhabitants); about 40,000 of them came from Galicia,[3] and one can assume that a majority of them spoke or understood Yiddish. During the First World War an estimated 50,000[4] to 125,000[5] Jewish and non-Jewish refugees from Galicia, Bukowina, and Russia arrived in Vienna. About 25,000 of them settled down,[6] and their efforts led to a flowering of Yiddish literature and theatre at the beginning of the 1920s. Some years later most of the Yiddish writers and publishers had left Vienna for Vilna, Warsaw, or New York, where they saw better opportunities for Yiddish culture. The percentage of the Jewish population decreased; in the 1930s about 176,000 Jews lived in Vienna (9.4 per cent), and it is not clear how many of them spoke Yiddish.

The reception of Yiddish theatre in Vienna was determined by two factors: first, Yiddish speakers were a small proportion of the city's inhabitants, and second, they were not very popular with the Viennese Jewish community. The so-called Ostjuden (Jews from eastern Europe) and their Yiddish culture were alien to the acculturated, German-speaking Jews, whose families had settled in the city some decades before the immigrants from eastern Europe. These Viennese Jews felt at home in German language and culture. When they were confronted with Yiddish literature and culture they reacted in a variety of ways: some avoided it; some, such as Schnitzler, expressed a friendly interest; others saw Yiddish as a basic ingredient of a Jewish cultural renaissance and Jewish identity, as illustrated by the careers of the cultural activist Nathan Birnbaum and the Zionist Otto Abeles, who wrote reviews of Yiddish plays in the 1920s.[7]

Until the 1920s Yiddish language and theatre were expressions of a small minority of Viennese Jews—and were little valued outside their circle. With the rise of Zionism and a longing for Jewish national identity this attitude changed. It was the interaction between the Yiddish language and its speakers on the one hand, and the German-speaking Jews on the other, that determined the history and development of the local Yiddish theatre.

---

[3] See Ivar Oxaal, 'Die Juden im Wien des jungen Hitler. Historische und soziologische Aspekte' [Jews in Vienna when Hitler was Young: Historical and Sociological Aspects], in Gerhard Botz, Ivar Oxaal, and M. Pollak (eds.), *Eine zerstörte Kultur. Jüdisches Leben und Antisemitismus in Wien seit dem 19. Jahrhundert* [A Devastated Culture: Jewish Life and Antisemitism in Vienna since the Nineteenth Century] (Buchloe: Obermayer Verlag, 1990), 49.

[4] See Ruth Beckermann, 'Die Mazzesinsel' [The Island of Matzah], in ead. (ed.), *Die Mazzesinsel: Juden in der Wiener Leopoldstadt 1918–1938* [The Island of Matzah: Jews in Vienna's Leopoldstadt, 1918–1938] (Vienna: Löcker Verlag, 1984), 16.

[5] See Michael John and Albert Lichtblau, *Schmelztiegel Wien—Einst und Jetzt. Zur Geschichte und Gegenwart von Zuwanderung und Minderheiten* [Melting-Pot Vienna—In Former Times and Now: Immigration and Minorities in History and Today] (Vienna: Böhlau Verlag, 1993), 114.

[6] In 1923 there were 201,513 Jews in Vienna. See John and Lichtblau, *Schmelztiegel Wien*, 157.

[7] Some of the ways in which Jewish nationalists, Zionists, and acculturated Viennese Jews responded to Yiddish theatre are described in Dalinger, 'Verloschene Sterne', 157–95.

In 1880 Moyshe Hurwitz (1844–1910; his name is in the German files as Moses Horowitz) went with his ensemble to Vienna, to perform at the Ringtheater. In 1877, after his first play was rejected by Avrom Goldfaden, he set up his own ensemble, performing in Romania, Poland, Russia, and Vienna; in 1886 he left Europe for New York.[8] In 1880 Hurwitz staged in Vienna his version of a dybbuk play, *Der Dibick; oder, Der Wundermann, Posse in 5 Akten*[9] (The Dybbuk; or, The Miracle Worker, a Farce in Five Acts), but negative reviews soon left the company playing to an empty house. The troupe left Vienna in a sad condition and penniless. The reception of this first staging of a Yiddish play in a large Viennese theatre explains why Yiddish theatre was never really acknowledged in the city: the reviews displayed not only an anti-semitic attitude towards that part of the audience which understood the Yiddish used on stage, but also a strong bias against the Yiddish language itself, which it often dismissed as a *zhargon* rather than a fully developed language. As one critic put it, 'The language of the negroes living in the Congo sounds no less alien to us than the gibberish we had to listen to today.'[10]

There is no evidence of any Yiddish theatrical activity in Vienna between 1880 and 1890. In 1890 a company from Lemberg (present-day Lviv, Ukraine) led by Khayim-Binyomin (Charles) Treytler[11] (1853–1916) wanted to perform on another important stage, the Carltheater. Like all other theatres and ensembles, the Treytler troupe had to submit the text of the play—Avrom Goldfaden's *Shulamis; oder, Bas yerushelayim* (Shulamis; or, The Daughter of Jerusalem)—to the Theatrical Censorship Board prior to production, in order to ensure that the play did not include material critical of the Austro-Hungarian authorities. Since the language of the play was Yiddish, the censors passed the text on to the representative communal body of Viennese Jewry, the Israeli-tische Kultusgemeinde. Representatives of the latter body advised against the staging of *Shulamis* because they feared that speaking *zhargon* on the stage of a German-speaking theatre might provoke antisemitic attacks.[12] Consequently,

[8] See Nahma Sandrow, *Vagabond Stars: A World History of Yiddish Theater* (New York: Harper & Row, 1977), 104–5.

[9] This spelling follows the German spelling in the documents of the Theaterzensurbehörde. The documents are located in the Niederösterreichisches Landesarchiv, St Pölten, Austria, Theater-zensursammlung, *Ringtheater* 1880, file 7687/P. The play itself is lost, but the file contains a report on the opening night.

[10] *Neue Freie Presse*, 12 Dec. 1880. See also *Neue Freie Presse* and *Neues Wiener Tagblatt*, both 16 Dec. 1880.

[11] For further information on Treytler, see Zalmen Zylbercweig (ed.), *Leksikon fun yidishn teater* [Lexicon of Yiddish Theatre], 6 vols. (New York: Elisheva, 1931–70), ii. 892–3, and B. Gorin, *Di geshikhte fun idishn teater* [The History of the Yiddish Theatre], 2 vols. (New York: Max N. Mayzel, 1923), ii. 142, 149, 153.

[12] See 'An die löbliche k.k. Polizei-Direction Wien! Vom Vorstand der israelitischen Kultus-gemeinde' [To the Laudable Police Department of Vienna! From the Board of the Jewish Com-

the Treytler troupe never performed in Vienna, and Yiddish ensembles learned to avoid the city's most important theatres.

As a result, Broder singers and Yiddish actors started to perform in small taverns and inns. A group of singers, the so-called Polnischen (Jews from Poland), gave performances in Vienna from 1900 to 1905, mostly in an inn by the name of Leopoldstädter Volksorpheum, where they performed folk songs and excerpts from plays. The Polnischen, who also played in Bosnia and Herzegovina, Bulgaria, and Turkey, adapted their Yiddish to the language of the country in which they performed, so one can assume that in Vienna they spoke a kind of Yiddish that could be understood by a German-speaking audience. The star of the Polnischen was Pepi Litman (1874–1930), described here (along with the atmosphere in the Volksorpheum) by the German Jewish author Felix Salten (the author of *Bambi*):

In the Roten Sterngasse there was a small inn called Edelhofers Volksorpheum. . . . You could see east European Jewish folksingers there every day. There was an absolute genius of a woman among them. She never wore women's clothing, but dressed like a boy. . . . She sang a couplet with the refrain: 'God in his goodness will make it happen. We will live to see it!' She sang one verse anticipating the acquittal of Alfred Dreyfus. And she sang another about the antisemitic mayor of Vienna, predicting blindness and terminal illness. She sang the refrain: 'God in his goodness will make it happen. We will live to see it!' She clapped her hands and the audience applauded wildly night after night.[13]

The description shows a number of striking features of the popular Yiddish theatre in Vienna: the noisy, uninhibited atmosphere; the popularity of actresses in men's dress; and, although the full text of Litman's couplet has been lost, one can conclude that the Polnischen referred to current affairs in their songs. This is one of the most important and exciting features of the Yiddish, and German Jewish, theatres in Vienna: the creation of songs and dramas with topical themes.

munity], Archiv der Bundes-Polizeidirektion Wien, Karton Carltheater 1890/91, file Z 55452/3206 P.B., Z 2098/1890. The text of the Israelitische Kultusgemeinde's decision to reject Treytler's production of *Shulamis* is partly reprinted in Brigitte Dalinger, 'Jüdisches Theater in Wien' [Jewish Theatre in Vienna], MA thesis, University of Vienna, 1991, 41.

[13] Felix Salten, 'Gedenkrede für Theodor Herzl. Zum fünfundzwanzigsten Jahrestag seines Todes' [Memorial Speech for Theodor Herzl on the Twenty-Fifth Anniversary of his Death], *Neue Freie Presse*, 23 June 1929. 'In der Roten Sterngasse gab es ein kleines Wirtshaus, das sich Edelhofers Volksorpheum nannte . . . Dort also produzierten sich täglich ostjüdische Volkssänger. Darunter eine Frau von absoluter Genialität. Sie trug nie Frauenkleider, sondern das Kostüm eines Bochers. . . . Sie sang ein Couplet, das den Refrain hatte: "Der gute Gott wird geben, wir wer'n das auch erleben!" Sie sang eine Strophe, die den Freispruch des Alfred Dreyfus prophezeite. Und sie hatte eine Strophe, die dem antisemitischen Bürgermeister tödliche Krankheit und Erblinden weissagte. Sie sang den Refrain: "Der gute Gott wird geben, wir wer'n das auch erleben!" Sie klatschte dazu in die Hände, und der Saal erdröhnte vor Beifall Abend für Abend.'

Additional evidence to support this view can be found in a Yiddish play of which only a German version has been preserved, *Jüdaly mit dem Wandersack* (Jüdaly and his Travelling Bag; Jüdaly (in Yiddish, Yudele) is a diminutive of Jude: Jew). Billed as a 'realistic picture with songs and dances in three scenes by S. Laresku',[14] the play was staged in the Volksorpheum in 1904 in honour of the recently deceased Theodor Herzl. The action revolves around a rich assimilated Jewish banker named Bauchfett (literally, Belly-fat), who wants to marry off his daughter Rebecca to a non-Jewish baron. Rebecca is in love with Albert Kohn, a young Zionist, and asks her father's permission to marry him. Bauchfett, whose goal is total assimilation into non-Jewish aristocratic society for himself and his daughter, refuses. Rebecca and Albert struggle to stay together, and to achieve their goal of going to Palestine. With the help of Albert's uncle Jüdaly, a Jew searching everywhere for a home but rejected because he is poor, and the real-life character of the prominent Zionist Samuel Pineles,[15] the young couple discuss Zionism and the future of Palestine with Bauchfett. Impressed by the opportunities Palestine has to offer, the banker talks to Pineles and agrees to his daughter's marriage to Albert. The story shows a problem typical of many acculturated Viennese Jews: the conflict between complete assimilation into non-Jewish society on the one hand and a strong Jewish identity on the other. The play mixes Viennese and Yiddish theatrical traditions. It uses a love story as a vehicle for addressing assimilation and Zionism, while the dramatis personae resemble those of the Altwiener Volkstheater, Viennese comedies written and staged in the nineteenth century with stock characters such as a tailor and a butcher, whose names illustrate their personalities or occupations.[16]

The Jüdische Bühne, the first permanent Yiddish theatre in Vienna, was established in 1908 in a hall at the Hotel Stefanie. This hotel still stands on the Taborstrasse, near the Praterstrasse, the district in which the Jewish immigrants from eastern Europe arrived and settled. The first leader of the Jüdische Bühne was Maurice Siegler, an actor who went to Bucharest in 1915, where he founded the Siegler–Pastor troupe, which performed in Vienna in the 1920s and 1930s. After Siegler the former Broder singer Schulim Podzamcze

[14] 'Jüdaly mit dem Wandersack. Realistisches Bild mit Tanz und Gesang in 3 Szenen von S. Laresku' [Jüdaly and his Travelling Bag: A Realistic Picture with Songs and Dances in Three Scenes by S. Laresku], Niederösterreichisches Landesarchiv, Theaterzensursammlung, Volkssänger box 14, Edelhofer 1904, file Z 22/13 P.B. 24.11.1904. Apart from this text there is no further information about the author or the production.

[15] Samuel Pineles (1843–1928) was an early member of the Zionist movement in Romania and one of the founders of the Jewish Colonial Trust.

[16] See Brigitte Dalinger, '"Jüdaly mit dem Wandersack" bricht "auf nach Tel Aviv". Zionismus und populäres jiddisches Theater' ['Jüdaly and his Travelling Bag' Goes 'to Tel Aviv': Zionism and Popular Yiddish Theatre], *Das Jüdische Echo. Zeitschrift für Kultur und Politik*, 47 (Oct. 1998), 250–6.

became head of the Jüdische Bühne until 1938. The Jüdische Bühne staged operettas, melodramas, and comedies by Hurwitz, Joseph Lateiner, and Jacob Gordin, which were much loved by the audience. The repertoire also reflected contemporary events in Austria, especially during the First World War. In those years about 100,000 refugees from eastern Europe arrived in Vienna, among them the young Galician watchmaker and author Abish Meisels (1893–1959). There he started to write plays for the Yiddish troupes. Two of them have survived (in German versions) at the Theaterzensurbehörde (Board of Censors): *Die jüdische Heldin; oder, Herz und Hand fürs Vaterland. Komödie in vier Aufzügen* (The Jewish Heroine; or, Heart and Hand for the Fatherland, a Comedy in Four Acts), staged in 1916, and *Der Traum des Reservisten. Märchen in vier Aufzügen* (The Dream of a Reserve Officer, a Fairy Tale in Four Acts).[17] In *Die jüdische Heldin* Meisels deals with a very topical problem: the response of the Jews in the east European war zone to the Russian, Austrian, and German occupations. The play emphasizes the harmonious relations between Jews, Germans, and Austrians, with its hero-ine, Lila, intercepting a secret order from the Russians and passing it on to German officers. Meisels also responded to the increasingly antisemitic reac-tion to the refugees from eastern Europe by stressing the Jews' love for the Austrian emperor Franz Joseph. *Die jüdische Heldin* was staged successfully in March 1916 and remained in the repertoire for a whole year.

From time to time the Jüdische Bühne also attempted to stage modern Yiddish dramas such as Ansky's *Der dibek* (The Dybbuk) and successful operettas from the German stage in Yiddish translation, such as Emerich Kalman's operetta *Csárdásfürstin* (literally Princess of Csárdás; the *csárdás* is a Hungarian dance), both in 1921. Most popular were the comedies with a girl dressed as a boy, such as *Yankele* with Molly Picon, who performed with the Viennese ensemble in 1921. In addition to staging popular operettas and comedies, the Jüdische Bühne performed two important social functions: as a first port of call for Yiddish actors from eastern Europe looking for an engage-ment, and as a meeting place for immigrants, and, in wartime, for refugees, from the east. The atmosphere at the Jüdische Bühne was always noisy; the audience came not only to see a play, but also to meet *landslayt* (people from the old country) and speak in their mother tongue.

The German actor Egon Brecher (1880–1946), the actor and writer Jacob Mestel, and the actor Isaac Deutsch (1884–1934) founded the Freie Jüdische Volksbühne (Free Jewish People's Stage) in 1919 in order to show modern Yiddish dramas in cultivated Yiddish. The company stayed together until 1923. Some of its actors, such as Deutsch, Jonah Reissmann (1862–1932), and

---

[17] Both plays are in Niederösterreichisches Landesarchiv, Theaterzensursammlung, box 729.

Lea Weintraub-Graf (1888–*c*.1938), came from the Jüdische Bühne; some were new to theatre, such as Yude Bleich (1901–61), Michael Preiss (1904–78), and Ben-Zion Witler (*c*.1900–61); yet others came from abroad, such as Paul Baratoff from Russia and Noemi and Simkhe Natan from Łódź. The Volksbühne's most successful productions were *Isaac sheftl* by Dovid Pinski, *Got fun nekome* (God of Vengeance) by Sholem Asch, and *Der fremder* (The Stranger) by Jacob Gordin.

The first performances of the Volksbühne took place in the halls of hotels and on German stages such as the Rolandbühne. In 1920 the ensemble opened its own theatre, the Jüdische Kammerspiele, in Vienna's second district. The Volksbühne did not confine itself to the Jewish district; it was invited to perform at the Theater in der Josefstadt, a well-known, sophisticated theatre that was later managed by Max Reinhardt. In June 1921 on that stage the Volksbühne performed *Got fun nekome* and *Der fremder*, in addition to *Shma yisroel* (Hear, O Israel) by Osip Dimov and *Tkies-kaf* (The Vow) by Peretz Hirschbein. These plays brought Yiddish theatre to a wider audience in Vienna, including non-Jewish theatregoers. The Volksbühne received excellent reviews, and Jewish and non-Jewish critics started to write about the Yiddish language, literature, and theatre. Zionist critics such as Otto Abeles, who published in the only daily Zionist newspaper in the German language, the *Wiener Morgenzeitung*, began to regard Yiddish theatre as one of the most important manifestations of Jewish national life. He saw it as an important medium to bring the Jewish audience 'back to its roots'. Writing about a performance of A. Vayter's *Der shtumer* (The Mute), Abeles observed, 'The figures of the fathers and mothers show us, their Western successors, a very lusty Jewish people, and, deeply touched, we learn to see them as our people.'[18] The non-Jewish newspapers responded positively to the actors and directing, but received the dramas themselves less favourably. A critic asked of Hirschbein's *Tkies-kaf*, for example, 'This is a drama? — Not in our sense. Lamentation, reflection, expressing one's feelings, variation. Father, mother, daughter. And two minor characters. Five concise acts. The real hero is the grim old god of the Ostjuden.'[19] Antisemitic newspapers such as *Deutsches Volksblatt* and *Reichspost* were quite fond of the Yiddish theatre and expressed their desire for an explicitly 'Christian' theatre.[20]

---

[18] Otto Abeles, 'A. Weiters. *Der Verstummte*' [A. Vayter: *The Mute*], *Wiener Morgenzeitung*, 4 Feb. 1920.

[19] *Illustriertes Wiener Extrablatt*, 17 June 1921; repr. in *Freie Jüdische Volksbühne. Pressestimmen* [Free Jewish People's Theatre Organization: Press Commentaries] (Vienna: Gründungskomitee der Jüdischen Künstlerbühnen, 1921), 19.

[20] See *Deutsches Volksblatt*, 12 and 15 June 1921; *Reichspost*, 15 June 1921. Parts of these reviews are published in Dalinger, '*Verloschene Sterne*', 78 ff.

Yiddish culture flowered in Vienna for a short period in the late 1910s and
early 1920s owing to the presence of Yiddish-speaking refugees from eastern
Europe. The Volksbühne staged ambitious dramas, while Yiddish writers
and journalists published their works in limited-circulation but highbrow
journals such as *Di kritik* (Criticism) and through the publishing house Der
Kval (The Source). Soon, however, the prospects of Yiddish culture declined,
and most of the authors left Vienna for Warsaw, Vilna, and New York. Two
of the founders of the Volksbühne emigrated to New York, where they continued their stage careers: Jacob Mestel[21] in the Yiddish theatre, and Egon
Brecher, who performed on both the Yiddish- and English-language American stages.

The Volksbühne ensemble broke up in Romania, where it was touring
during the 1922–3 season. The mid-1920s were a different time for Yiddish
theatre in Vienna; the Volksbühne had fallen apart and the Jüdische Bühne
had trouble finding an appropriate stage on which to perform. But as always
throughout the decades of its existence, it found a home and started to perform again, with actors such as Jonah Reissmann and Isaac Deutsch returning from the disbanded Volksbühne.

In 1925 the Jüdisches Künstlerkabarett, founded by the actor Max Streng
and the actress Paula Dreiblatt, opened on 60 Praterstrasse. The Künstlerkabarett presented such plays as *Di rumenishe khasene* (The Romanian Wedding) and so-called *lebnsbilder* (literally, pictures of life), melodramas with
songs which were constructed like musicals. One of these, by an unknown
playwright, was *Bankrot* (Bankrupt). The first Yiddish revue (in the sense of
musical show), Meisels's *Fun sekhistov biz amerike* (From Sechistow to America), presented at the Künstlerkabarett in February 1927, comes very close to
this aesthetic form.[22]

At the beginning of the 1920s operettas and revues were very popular on
German stages in Vienna. Some of the songs from the productions became
popular in their own right; they were recorded and published individually
and were performed in people's parlours. In 1926 Meisels attempted to bring
these popular genres to the Yiddish stage by writing *Fun sekhistov biz amerike*.
His musical production presented the journey of a traditional Jewish family
from Galicia to America, where Reb Hersh, an innkeeper and the head of the
family, is to claim an inheritance. The first scenes show the family—Reb

---

[21] In New York Mestel wrote and published studies of the Yiddish theatre. His major works are
Undzer teater [Our Theatre] (New York: YKUF, 1943), and *70 yor teater-repertuar* [Seventy Years of
Theatre Repertoire] (New York: YKUF, 1954).

[22] Abish Meisels, *Von Sechistow bis Amerika / Fun sechisstow bis amerika. Eine Revue in 15 Bildern / A
rewi in 15 bilder* [From Sechistow to America: A Revue in Fifteen Tableaux], ed. and trans. Brigitte
Dalinger and Thomas Soxberger (Vienna: Picus Verlag, 2000).

Hersh, his wife, Sheyndl, their daughter Rokhele, and her fiancé, Shmulik—at their Galician home, learning of the inheritance, saying farewell to their friends, and taking the train to Vienna. Meisels, himself an immigrant from the east, used the opportunity to describe the situation of an immigrant arriving in Vienna. His life was affected by the antisemitic Viennese on the one hand and the internal strife of the Jewish community on the other. *Fun sekhistov biz amerike* has a bleak ending: the inheritance turns out to be very small, and the family finds itself disappointed and homeless.

Some months later Meisels wrote another ending that gave his musical a new direction. Aware of the small size of the inheritance, the family decides to go to Tel Aviv, where all of them lead a fulfilled life working on a farm free from antisemitic attacks. The revised play was given a new title, *Auf nach Tel Aviv*[23] (Let's Go to Tel Aviv), and was the first in a series of new Yiddish musicals in Vienna to convey Zionist ideas, though similar sentiments had been expressed in Yiddish plays dating back to the early 1880s.

The Jüdische Künstlerkabarett did not last very long. Following the death of its founder, Max Streng, in 1928, several actors tried to run the establishment, but without success. In 1931 the Jüdische Bühne moved in.

The Jüdische Künstlerspiele, established in 1927 at 34 Praterstrasse, was more successful, playing until 1938. With the help of guests from East and West, the Künstlerspiele was able to put on not only comedies, melodramas, and Zionist musicals, but also modern dramas from world literature translated into Yiddish, including *The Father* by August Strindberg, *Die Sendung Semaels* (Semaels's Mission) by Arnold Zweig, and *Hinkemann* by Ernst Toller. Most of the actors who played in this ensemble had also been on other Yiddish stages, such as Mina Deutsch (b. 1887), Paula Dreiblatt, Clara Meisels (1896–1960), Lea Weintraub-Graf (b. 1888), Ben-Zion Sigall (1900–41), and Ben-Zion Witler. Isaac Deutsch made a guest appearance in 1928. Vera Kaniewska, Paul Breytman, and Simkhe Natan from Poland appeared in 1928. Members of the Vilna Troupe played at the Künstlerspiele in 1930. In 1931–2 Gisa Haiden and Salo (Shloyme) Prizament were seen there, as were Paul Baratoff and Meyer Tselniker. The Siegler–Pastor troupe from Bucharest made the Künstlerspiele the most successful Yiddish theatre in the 1930s.

The Künstlerspiele presented popular operettas and melodramas in ambitious stagings, but one of its biggest hits was Meisels's *Auf nach Tel Aviv*. In subsequent years Meisels would write more Zionist comedies in Yiddish, which are known only by their German titles: *Die Wiener Rebbyzin* (The Viennese Rabbi's Wife, January 1929), *Ohne Zertifikat nach Palästina* (To Palestine without a Certificate, May 1935), *Hallo! Hallo! Hier Radio Jerusalem*

[23] In the Viennese sources the title was not printed in Yiddish.

(Hello! Hello! This is Radio Jerusalem, May 1936), *Chassene im Städtel* (A Wedding in the *Shtetl*, December 1936), and *Kol Nidre im Galuth* (Kol Nidre in the Diaspora, January 1937). All of these works were very popular, especially when staged by members of the Siegler–Pastor troupe, led by its star, Sevilla Pastor. And Meisels's musical comedies brought an advantage to the Künstlerspiele: for the first time in the history of Yiddish theatre in Vienna, official representatives of the Jewish community attended performances, such as when the leader of the Israelitische Kultusgemeinde, Desider Friedmann, went to see *Auf nach Tel Aviv*. From the mid-1930s onwards the Künstlerspiele was supported by several Jewish associations and clubs which bought out whole shows, thus enabling the company to continue operating until 1938.

In addition to these light offerings and translations of European dramas, the Künstlerspiele offered ambitious Yiddish plays such as *Baynakht afn altn mark* (A Night in the Old Marketplace) by Yitskhok Leyb Peretz; *Der zinger fun zayn troyer* (The Singer of his Sorrow; also known as *Yoshke muzikant* or Yoshke the Musician) by Osip Dimov, and *Grine felder* (Green Fields) by Peretz Hirschbein. In the 1930s, with Nazi Germany as a neighbour, some of these dramas—such as Toller's *Hinkemann* and Sholem Aleykhem's *Shver tsu zayn a yid* (Hard to be a Jew)—became unexpectedly contemporary, and the reviewers took the performances as a point of reference to write about the growth of antisemitism, the danger of National Socialism, and their fear of an approaching war. Most of the performances of translated or modern dramas were directed by guests from abroad, such as Baratoff, Simkhe Natan, Shmuel Iris, and Alex Stein. Such plays gave Viennese Yiddish actors the opportunity to perform in sophisticated dramas as well as in the operetta and melodramatic repertoire still preferred by the audience.

Vienna's Yiddish stages attracted the attention of non-Jews and non-Yiddish-speaking Jews only on a few occasions—for example, when the Freie Jüdische Volksbühne played at the Theater in der Josefstadt and when famous ensembles and artists from abroad made guest appearances. In the 1920s and 1930s many famous Yiddish stars played in Vienna: Molly Picon and Jacob Kalich in 1920 and 1921, the Vilna Troupe in 1922–3, Maurice Schwartz and his Yiddish Art Theatre in 1924 and 1936, the Moscow State Yiddish Theatre with director Alexander Granovsky in 1928, and the Hebrew Habimah from Russia in 1926, 1928, and 1938. They all attracted much attention and serious reviews.

By the 1930s the attitude of acculturated German-speaking Jews in Vienna towards the Yiddish language, literature, and theatre had changed considerably. That Yiddish was now seen as a language worthy of being staged as well as read and translated into German was illustrated by the existence of the Jüdisches Kulturtheater, a German-speaking company that performed Yiddish dramas in German translation, such as Peretz's *Di goldene keyt* (The Golden Chain) and Dimov's *Shma yisroel*. The aim of the company's founders was to create a common Jewish identity by bridging the gap between the Jews from eastern Europe (the Ostjuden) and their more acculturated brethren. Since the Kulturtheater did not open until December 1935, it could not achieve its aim, although it was able to provide refugees from Germany with short engagements and performed dramas that dealt seriously with the rise of Nazism in Germany. This soon became a reality for Jewish cultural life in Vienna as well; after the *Anschluss* in March 1938 the Jüdische Kulturtheater was destroyed by members of the Hitler Youth.

The Jüdische Bühne and the Jüdische Künstlerspiele were still performing as late as March 1938. In the summer of 1938 the heads of both ensembles asked for permission to play in the coming season. Their petitions, handed to the Reichstheaterbehörde (Reich Theatre Department), were never answered.

Vienna never became a primary centre for the development of the Yiddish theatre. No internationally famous troupes originated there, and the conditions to support a literary Yiddish stage in Vienna never lasted long. Nevertheless, the city boasted a durable Yiddish theatre scene, with about a hundred actors, directors, and playwrights, mostly from eastern Europe. Their art should be remembered as a part of Viennese as well as Yiddish culture, and is a reminder that for every Moscow, New York, or Warsaw, there were many Kharkovs, Philadelphias, and Viennas.

Flagellatio Judaica. 353.

1. Seventeenth-century sketch of a *purimshpil*.
From *Philologus Hebraeo-Mixtus*, 3rd edn. (Leyden, 1699), by Dutch Hebraist
Johannes Leusden. From the Dorot Jewish Division, the New York Public
Library, Astor, Lenox, and Tilden Foundations

2. Frontispiece of one of several published texts of Goldfaden's *Di kishefmakherin* (Warsaw, 1887). From the Dorot Jewish Division, the New York Public Library, Astor, Lenox, and Tilden Foundations

3. Actress Clara Young, darling of theatre critics in St Petersburg in the early 1900s, in a photo taken in the 1920s. Courtesy of the YIVO Institute for Jewish Research, photo archives

סקאצעל קומט, מיסטער שונד איז ווידער דאָ!

טהעאַטער-קריטיקער: — טפֿררר! — טפֿררר! — הע, מר. שונד, דענקסט שוין טאַקע אַזוי אַבריִטען אויף "משה'ן" דעם גאַ
צען סיזאָן? — ער איז אַ שרעקליכער פֿערד! — ער קען דיר די ביינער צוטראַנען!

שונד: — נעוואַר מיינד, וועט ער בלייבען רוהיג, וואָרף איך אַריבער דעם אַנדער פֿוס, און ס'געהט אַ גאַנצ. נאָ
טאָמער שטעלט ער זיד אָווק אויף צוויי פֿיס... איז מיט איין שפֿרונג בין איך אוים די צייט.

4. The theatre critic seating *shund* (popular plays; literally 'trash') on the back of 'Moyshe', the Yiddish audience. Critics and satirists frequently characterized the Yiddish audience not only as children, but as animals as well. From *Der groyser kundes*, 29 September 1909. From the Dorot Jewish Division, the New York Public Library, Astor, Lenox, and Tilden Foundations

5. Actor/manager Jacob P. Adler breast-feeding 'Moyshe' (the Yiddish audience) as his competitors look on in dismay. From *Der groyser kundes*, 19 September 1913. From the Dorot Jewish Division, the New York Public Library, Astor, Lenox, and Tilden Foundations

ליי פיינמאן און לודװיג זאץ, אין יאזעף מארקאװיטש'ס „פארשידענע
גליקען", געשפילט אין לאנדאן, אין 1913.
LUDWIG SATZ and LILLY FEINMAN, as they appeared in a scene
from *Farshidene Glicken*, by Joseph Markovitch.

6. Ludwig Satz and Lilly Feinman in Joseph Markovitsh's
Farshidene glikn (London, 1913). Courtesy of the YIVO Institute
for Jewish Research, photo archives

7. Maurice Schwartz as Uriel Mazik in Jacob Gordin's *Got, mentsh un tayvl*
(Yiddish Art Theatre, New York, 1919). Courtesy of the YIVO
Institute for Jewish Research, photo archives

8. Alexander Stein and Miriam Orleska as Khonen and Leah in the Vilna Troupe's production of Anski's *Der dibek* (Warsaw, 1920). Courtesy of the YIVO Institute for Jewish Research, photo archives

9. *left to right*: Egon Brecher, Paul (Benzvi) Baratoff, and Isaac Deutsch, the leading figures behind Vienna's Freie Jüdische Volksbühne (1919–23). Courtesy of the YIVO Institute for Jewish Research, photo archives

10. Maurice Schwartz as the Bobe Yakhne in Goldfaden's *Di kishefmakherin* (Yiddish Art Theatre, New York, 1925). Courtesy of the YIVO Institute for Jewish Research, photo archives

11. A scene from H. Leivick's *Der goylem* (Lublin, *c.*1925). Courtesy of the YIVO Institute for Jewish Research, photo archives

12. Marketplace scene in a stylized revival of Goldfaden's *Di kishefmakherin* (Yiddish Art Theatre, New York, 1925). Courtesy of the YIVO Institute for Jewish Research, photo archives

13. Corpses rising from the dead in the Vilna Troupe's production of I. L. Peretz's *Baynakht afn altn mark* (Warsaw, 1928). Courtesy of the YIVO Institute for Jewish Research, photo archives

14. Unidentified production at the Jüdische Künstlerspiele or Jüdische Bühne, Vienna, early 1930s. Courtesy of the YIVO Institute for Jewish Research, photo archives

15. Sleeping shepherds in the desert in Goldfaden's *Shulamis* (Varshever Yidisher Kunst Teater, Warsaw, 1938). Courtesy of the YIVO Institute for Jewish Research, photo archives

16. Postcard advertising Joseph Kessler's production of Lateiner's *Di seyder nakht* (Pavilion Theatre, London, 1928). Courtesy of the YIVO Institute for Jewish Research, photo archives

17. Zygmunt Turkow in the title role of Sholem Aleykhem's *Tevye der milkhiker*. Courtesy of the YIVO Institute for Jewish Research, photo archives

18. Abish Meisels in his London office, *c.*1945.
Courtesy of the YIVO Institute for Jewish Research, photo archives

19. Michal Szwejlich as Hotsmakh in Yankev Rotboym's *A goldfaden kholem*
(Warsaw, 1970s). Courtesy of the YIVO Institute for Jewish Research, photo archives

Stories in Song:
The Melo-deklamatsyes *of*
Joseph Markovitsh

๕

DAVID MAZOWER

I N the early decades of the twentieth century the American Yiddish stage star Tsili (Celia) Adler made regular guest appearances at the Pavilion Theatre in London's East End. In her autobiography she recalls those years and her many British colleagues, among them Whitechapel's Yiddish playwright Joseph Markovitsh, 'who so easily manufactured new plays, practically to order'. Adler relates how Markovitsh was approached by a disgruntled theatregoer in the Pavilion's lobby late one evening about 1912, after a performance of one of his plays:

'You're Mr Markovitsh, aren't you? You know, I always like your plays, but somehow today's I didn't enjoy. Something was missing, it just didn't sparkle.'

Markovitsh wasn't annoyed; he just asked the man: 'What line of work are you in?'

'I'm a tailor.'

'All right. Let's say my wife or I order an expensive new garment from you. We'll pay whatever you ask, but we must have it finished in two hours. How do you think it would turn out?'

'I wouldn't take it on—it wouldn't be any good.'

So Markovitsh said: 'You're a lucky man. You can afford to lose the few pounds, but I don't have a choice. About twenty families depend on my decision—I must fulfil the order. So you must forgive me if, once in a while, one of my shows doesn't please you.'[1]

I am grateful to all those who helped to unearth Markovitsh's long-lost compositions: Rosalind Gold (daughter of the Yiddish actor Yidel Goldberg) and the Yiddish actors Dora Krelman, Shifra Lerer, and Anna Tzelniker. I benefited greatly from Joel Berkowitz's invaluable editorial advice and improvements. Above all, however, I should like to thank the Yiddish actor Bernard Mendelovitch, a true friend, my Yiddish-language oracle, and an indefatigable collaborator in the quest to trace Markovitsh's work. To him, as a small token of my gratitude and deep affection, I dedicate this chapter.

[1] Tsili Adler with Yakov Tikman, *Tsili Adler dertseylt* [Celia Adler Relates], 2 vols. (New York: Tsili Adler Foundation un Bukh-Komitet, 1959), 202–3.

The lack of vanity and the homespun comparison are typical of Markovitsh. But Tsili Adler's anecdote demonstrates a more fundamental issue for historians of the Yiddish theatre: the predicament of the Yiddish playwright. The jobbing Yiddish writer, dismissively dubbed a 'baker' by his theatrical colleagues, had the herculean task of satisfying the often conflicting demands of the audience, his fellow actors, the highbrow critics, and his own artistic conscience.

Clearly, Markovitsh was only too well aware of the compromises forced on him by the system in which he worked. However, a few years after the encounter in the Pavilion Theatre he appears to have found a way of minimizing these conflicting demands, while giving free rein to his many talents as a writer, composer, lyricist, and singer. The format he hit upon was that of a dramatic concert piece for voice and instrumental accompaniment, a fusion of theatre song, opera aria, and *khazones* (cantorial music). Markovitsh called these distinctive pieces *melo-deklamatsyes* (dramatic poems set to music) and he wrote at least eight of them. They were performed throughout the Yiddish-speaking world by Markovitsh himself and other leading actors until the 1950s, but very few were recorded or published.[2]

A few years ago, curious to see what remained of Markovitsh's creative legacy, I began to track down these long-forgotten compositions. Thanks to the combined efforts of several veteran Yiddish actors (many of whom had worked with Markovitsh), these remarkable pieces gradually emerged, mostly written in neat Yiddish script in old notebooks unearthed from cupboards in New York, London, and Tel Aviv. The *melo-deklamatsyes* are noteworthy for several reasons: formally, for their attempt to extend the traditional boundaries of the theatre song; thematically, for their focus on the class divisions and corrosive poverty of *shtetl* life; and musically, for revealing Markovitsh to be a gifted composer and songwriter whose work deserves to endure.

MARKOVITSH'S LIFE

Joseph Markovitsh was born in about 1880 into a poor Jewish family in Fastov, near the Ukrainian city of Kiev.[3] His formal schooling was minimal, and his

---

[2] The *melo-deklamatsye* 'Berke goylem' (Berke the Fool) was published in A. N. Shtentsl (ed.), *Yoyvl almanakh, loshn un lebn 1956* [Jubilee Almanac of the Loshen un Lebn (Language and Life) Society 1956] (London, 1956) 140–2.

[3] Biographical information about Markovitsh has come from three main sources: first, the entry about him in Zalmen Zylbercweig (ed.), *Leksikon fun idishn teater* [Lexicon of Yiddish Theatre], 6 vols. (New York: Elisheva, 1931–70), ii. 1265–6; secondly, Markovitsh's own autobiography, covering the years until 1914, which appeared towards the end of his life in twenty-one instalments in a London Yiddish weekly: Joseph Markovitsh, 'Fun mayne fuftsik yor in England' [About My Fifty

childhood unconventional: he was a gifted child singer with a fine alto voice, and his parents apparently agreed to let him leave home at the age of 9 to accompany an itinerant *khazn* (cantor). Markovitsh and the cantor spent the next three years travelling throughout southern Russia, stopping every sabbath in a different *shtetl*. Their business partnership finally came to an end in the town of Radomishl, where the child soloist was heard by the great *khazn* Yankev Shmuel Morogowski (1856–1942), popularly known as Zaydl Rovner, who took him into his synagogue choir.

Years later Markovitsh would describe himself, with uncharacteristic lack of modesty, as 'the most famous alto in the whole Russian empire, almost a child prodigy'.[4] He would recall with pride the formidable list of cantors with whom he had worked, among them some of the most celebrated composers and performers of Jewish liturgical music of the late nineteenth century. In addition to Zaydl Rovner, they include Pinchas Minchovski (1859–1924) and Nusn Spivak, better known as Nisn Belzer (1824–1906).

At the age of 15 Markovitsh left home for good, and settled in Kiev. There he continued to work as a *meshoyrer* (chorister) and began to study music. Eventually his voice settled into a lyric baritone, and he joined the chorus of Schwartz's Russian Opera and Operetta Company. This sort of curriculum vitae was by no means unusual for its day; indeed, Markovitsh's biography suggests a fruitful area for further research: the close triangular relationship between the synagogue choir, the world of Russian classical opera, and the Yiddish theatre.[5]

By the age of 20 Markovitsh had begun to sing solo roles in Schwartz's company and seemed set for a career in opera. Then he was called up for military service. After six weeks in the Russian army he deserted, made his way

Years in England], *Di idishe shtime* [The Jewish Voice], 13 Nov. 1953–9 Apr. 1954; thirdly, the detailed recollections of Irenee Peterman, the granddaughter of Markovitsh's lifelong partner, Becky Goldshteyn (personal correspondence between Irenee Peterman and the author, 1995–2000). Markovitsh's date of birth is unclear: Zylbercweig, and Morris Myer, in his book *Idish teater in london, 1902–1942* [Yiddish Theatre in London, 1902–1942] (London: M. Mayer [1943]), both give 1884, *Di idishe shtime* (26 Feb. 1954) suggests 1883, and Markovitsh's tombstone indicates 1879/80.

⁴ *Di idishe shtime*, 13 Nov. 1953.

⁵ The route from religious chorister to Yiddish theatre chorister or soloist was a well-travelled path; for example, the 9-year-old Boris Thomashefsky, future star of the New York Yiddish stage, also joined Nisn Belzer's choir as a boy. But there are also many examples of links with Russian opera. The conductor of Schwartz's Russian Opera Company was the former *batkhn* (Jewish wedding entertainer) Moyshe Tzhizhik, who had Russified his name to Tzhizhikov. Another example is that of Nisn Belzer's eldest son, Alter, who became the conductor of the St Petersburg Opera. Among the memoirs and scholarly studies that document the connection between the *meshoyrerim* and the professional Yiddish theatre are: Mark Slobin, *Tenement Songs: The Popular Music of the Jewish Immigrants* (Urbana: University of Illinois Press, 1982); Joseph Rumshinsky, *Klangen fun mayn lebn* [Echoes of My Life] (New York: Itshe Biderman, 1944); Victoria Secunda, *Bei mir bist du schon: The Life of Sholom Secunda* (New York: Magic Circle Press, 1982); and Boris Thomashefsky, *Mayn lebns-geshikhte* [My Life Story] (New York: Trio Press, 1937).

to Hamburg, and boarded a ship for London. He stepped off the boat at London Bridge on a damp, foggy day in about 1900. With no friends or relatives to assist him, Markovitsh's first stop was the Poor Jews' Temporary Shelter in London's East End. Registering on arrival, he described himself as 'a Russian actor'. Officials at the shelter immediately lined up a job for him— in a tailoring factory. But Markovitsh was determined to find work in the theatre; as he later recalled, he may have been a *griner* (newcomer), but he was 'keyn griner af der bine' (no newcomer to the stage).[6] Quick-witted, resourceful, and sure of his own abilities, he was an experienced singer and a skilled musician, who had no trouble working out an instrumental arrangement and writing out the different parts.

Wandering the streets of the East End, Markovitsh was soon directed to a Whitechapel pub called the York Minster, where Yiddish variety entertainment briefly flourished around the beginning of the century in a first-floor room crammed with wooden benches.[7] There, to his great embarrassment, he made his debut singing Yiddish and Russian songs in a bizarre costume of Russian military boots, trousers, and an overcoat open to the waist with wide lapels and large buttons of varying colours. Desperately poor, he also began to earn a little money writing songs for himself and the other actors. Two early efforts were 'Aleyn in a fremd land' (Alone in a Strange Land) and 'A kholem' (A Dream), songs about poverty and the alienation of the new immigrant: 'I dreamed that I was a rich man. . . . and when I came to London, Rothschild received me as a son-in-law. . . . I bathe in milk and eat fish with *khreyn* [horseradish] . . . ah, a dream, a dear and lovely dream.'[8]

Despite his unpromising situation Markovitsh was lucky in one respect. His arrival in London coincided with the first efforts for many years to establish a permanent Yiddish theatre in the East End. Fifteen years before, a kosher butcher named David Smith had converted a Spitalfields workhouse into a Yiddish theatre for the popular dramatic actor Jacob Adler. The Princes Street Club did good business, confirming the commercial potential of this new form of entertainment. But the tragedy at the club in 1887, when panic following a false fire alarm led to seventeen deaths, blighted this early promise and prompted many actors to leave for America. More than a decade would elapse before Yiddish theatre in London gained a comparable venue. In the 1890s one of the Princes Street Club chorus girls, Jenny Kaiser, formed her own company, performing in halls in London and the provinces. At the same

[6] *Di idishe shtime*, 27 Nov. 1953.

[7] Among the actors who performed there were Paul Muni's parents, Fayvl and Saltshe Vayznfroynd, who stopped in London en route to America. See David Mazower, *Yiddish Theatre in London*, 2nd edn. (London: Jewish Museum, 1996), 17–18.   [8] *Di idishe shtime*, 4 Dec. 1953.

time Yiddish theatre and opera gained a brief foothold in a hall in Vine Court, off Whitechapel Road. Finally, in the late 1890s, matinée performances of Yiddish drama began to feature in the cavernous Victorian playhouses of the East End, the Standard Theatre in Shoreditch, and the Pavilion Theatre in Mile End. From 1906 onwards the Pavilion, known as 'the Drury Lane of the East', became the new home of Yiddish drama in London.[9]

Markovitsh soon graduated from Yiddish music hall to the mainstream stage, making his debut as a *shoykhet* (ritual slaughterer) in a production of Joseph Lateiner's play *Blimele* at the Pavilion Theatre. A few years later his career as a dramatist began with a commission from the celebrated actor–manager Sigmund Feinman. This was a huge honour for the little-known Markovitsh. Feinman, born near Kishinev in 1862, was a veteran of Avrom Goldfaden's company, a distinguished figure on the Yiddish stage, and a noted playwright. In 1906 he took up residence at the Pavilion Theatre and became an immediate favourite of the London Yiddish public. Markovitsh describes him as 'a true man of the theatre, a great artist who could make stones weep with his davening [praying] in his play *Shabes koydesh* [The Holy Sabbath]'.[10] Initially commissioned by Feinman to write a song, Markovitsh resolved to try his hand at a drama, a task he recalled as being 'harder than marrying off a daughter without a dowry'. Having written his play, about a Russian Jewish radical named Zaretsky, he nervously took it to read to Feinman:

Then I came to the moment where Zaretsky has to sing. At this point Feinman sprang up like a fiend, banged his fist on the table and yelled:

'Who's singing? How come a person with such feelings, who's just come back from Siberia, starts singing? You *khutspediker* [impudent person], you! Your mother's milk is still wet on your lips and you're already slipping into trashy ways, tickling the audience with a tune. Shame on you!'

I felt like a dead man and began to tremble all over. Nevertheless, I started to explain to Feinman that my hero Zaretsky wasn't singing to the audience, but when his beloved Liza sits at the piano, he sings to her of his sorrows.

'All right, let me hear the song.'

I sang the song, ending with the chorus:

> 'Ven vet shoyn kimen di gliklikhe tsayt
> Mir zoln shoyn hern fun noent un fun veyt
> Az in rusland iz likhtig, in rusland iz fray
> *Zdravstvuyet svoboda!* Arunter nikolai!'

> [When better times come
> We will hear from far and wide
> A new day has dawned in Russia: Russia is free.
> Long live freedom! Down with Tsar Nicholas!]

[9] See Mazower, *Yiddish Theatre in London*.   [10] *Di idishe shtime*, 15 Jan. 1954.

The song won Feinman over and the rest of the reading went more smoothly. At the end Feinman said: '*Mamzer!*' [Bastard]—that's what he used to call me—'I'll take the play.'[11]

Markovitsh's play *Der revolutsyoner* (The Revolutionary) was staged at the Pavilion Theatre in November 1906. It launched his career as London's leading Yiddish dramatist, the undisputed successor to Nokhem Rakov, who produced a stream of topical Yiddish plays in Whitechapel in the 1890s.[12] Over the next fifty years Markovitsh became known in the world of the Yiddish theatre as a prolific author of dramas, operettas, and musical comedies. He wrote at least forty, and probably many more. The dramas include: *Der apikoyres* (The Heretic), *East end vest* (East End West [End]), *Der goldener shlisl* (The Golden Key), *Despot* (The Despot), *Farshidene glikn* (Assorted Luck), *In di keytn fun libe* (In the Chains of Love), *Der zapasner zoldat* (The Reserve Soldier), *In vald* (In the Forest), *Der brodyaga* (The Vagabond), *Der gembler* (The Gambler), *(Tsvey) Khaveyrim* ([Two] Comrades), *Der midber* (The Desert), and *Grazhdanin* (Citizen); among the musical comedies and operettas are: *Di vaybershe melukhe* (Women's Realm), *Pariz baynakht* (Paris at Night), *Serkele di grefin* (Countess Sarah), *Di sheyne miryam* (Beautiful Miriam— a musical reworking of Jacob Gordin's drama), *A milyon far a yidn* (A Million for a Jew), *Selima, Grefin pototski* (Countess Pototski), and *Di importirte dinst; oder, Domestik servis* (The Imported Maid; or, Domestic Service). In addition, Markovitsh wrote several *tsaytbilder* (topical plays), including *Mendel beylis protses* (The Mendel Beilis Trial), *Konvenshon* (The [Anglo-Russian Military Service] Convention), and *Yisroel lebt un lakht* (Israel Lives and Laughs). Markovitsh's plays were performed in all the main centres of Yiddish theatre by many of its leading actors, including Jacob Adler in New York; Sigmund Feinman and Maurice Moskovitsh in London; Zalmen Zylbercweig and Dina Halpern in Poland; Ludwig Satz in London, Paris, and elsewhere; and Julius Adler in Poland.[13]

Throughout his years in London Markovitsh combined the roles of playwright and character actor. His partner on- and off-stage was the Yiddish

[11] *Di idishe shtime*, 15 Jan. 1954.

[12] According to most accounts, the Russian-born Rakov arrived in England about 1887 and left for America about 1902. Described by his contemporaries as morose, semi-reclusive, and an alcoholic, Rakov's work deserves fuller critical attention. See Sholem Perlmuter, *Yidishe dramaturgn un teater-kompozitors* [Yiddish Playwrights and Theatre Composers] (New York: YKUF, 1952), 184–8; Zalmen Reyzen, *Leksikon fun der yidisher literatur, prese un filologye* [Lexicon of Yiddish Literature, Press, and Philology], 4 vols. (Vilna: B. Kletskin, 1926–9), iv. 243–7; Zylbercweig (ed.), *Leksikon fun yidishn teater*, iv. 2497–2506.

[13] Selective lists of Markovitsh's plays can be found in Zylbercweig (ed.), *Leksikon fun yidishn teater*, and Myer, *Idish teater in london*. See also Leonard Prager, *Yiddish Culture in Britain: A Guide* (Frankfurt am Main: Peter Lang, 1990), 439.

actress Rebecca Goldshteyn. Madame Goldshteyn, as she was known in the profession, had come to London as a child in the 1880s and joined the Yiddish theatre after working briefly in a shirt factory. In her twenties, married with four children, she defied her husband's demand that she should leave the stage and walked out on him. Her relationship with Markovitsh, well before the divorce came through, scandalized the East End. Headstrong, resourceful, vivacious, and gregarious, Goldshteyn was the perfect foil to the laconic, sceptical, and self-effacing Markovitsh.

For almost fifty years Markovitsh and Goldshteyn were regulars in the London Yiddish theatre, first at the Pavilion, and later at the Grand Palais in Commercial Road. While Markovitsh played mainly character parts, Goldshteyn was a leading lady and *muter-rolist* (specialist in mother roles). They frequently toured together, visiting France, Belgium, and Germany repeatedly in the years before the First World War. In 1914 they were staying in Berlin when war broke out, and Markovitsh was arrested on suspicion of being a Russian spy. He spent almost two years in a German prison camp, emerging severely emaciated and suffering from gastric ulcers that persisted for many years. In the 1920s and 1930s Markovitsh and Goldshteyn also toured South America and South Africa as part of a company of London Yiddish actors, staying away for months at a time.

Like virtually everybody in the Yiddish theatrical profession (except the theatre owners), Markovitsh and Goldshteyn lived extremely frugally. Until the late 1920s they rented rooms in the East End (occasionally above Abrahams Restaurant in Whitechapel, which was owned by Goldshteyn's sister and her husband) or lived in boarding houses while touring. But in about 1930 their joint earnings enabled them to buy a comfortable three-storey Edwardian house in Spurstowe Road, Hackney. Goldshteyn's eldest son had just lost his job, and she invited his family of four to move in with them. Her granddaughter Irenee Peterman vividly recalls their life in the 1930s:

Becky loved her role as a benevolent hostess. On warm summer evenings Marchy [Markovitsh] strung up fairy lights in the garden and she gave parties outside and invited any of the actors who were able to come. Marchy was well-known and treated almost as a celebrity in those days when the theatre was doing well despite the lack of employment elsewhere . . . the long narrow garden was Marchy's domain and delight during his leisure periods. He grew all the flowers which are rarely seen today, 'tobacco plant' with its heady smell, tea roses, foxglove, delphiniums, Michaelmas daisies and beautiful bronze spiky chrysanthemums . . . grandmother and grandfather had brought back many gifts and wonderful things from their South American trip: crocodile handbags, silk shawls and silver and turquoise jewellery. These were all kept in a marvelous large trunk with a deep rounded lid,

Mazower

bound with bamboo and lined with striped linen. . . . Joseph listened to Chaliapin and Caruso on the gramophone . . . he played the piano and also gave singing lessons for a time . . . he read a great deal: Jack London, Dickens and Voltaire, Victor Hugo and volumes such as 'Great Tales of the World'. He also read the Yiddish newspapers and the *Daily Worker*, and he could read and write in Russian as well as Yiddish in a beautiful flowing hand.[14]

Mention of the *Daily Worker* highlights an important influence on Markovitsh's personality and writings—his deeply held left-wing politics. He seems to have been a strong sympathizer with, if not perhaps a card-carrying member of, the Communist Party, certainly until the Second World War. His experiences as a youth in Russia had left him with a burning sense of injustice, and his radical political views were matched by an equally strong contempt for what he saw as the hypocrisy of organized religion. In short, he was a humanist, a passionate champion of the working man and woman. His politics inform almost everything he wrote, from early verses about the alienation and poverty of immigrant life, to the classically Marxist song 'Kapital':

> Dos gelt tsit arop di hoyt fun di beyner
> Dos gelt shaft unz tsures a kval,
> Es arbetn toyzenter, raykh vert nor eyner
> Eyner vert raykh mit a groys kapital.[15]

> Money tears the skin right off the bone
> Money creates a whole lot of trouble,
> Thousands work, but only one gets rich
> One gets rich with huge capital.

By the late 1940s Markovitsh and Goldshteyn had both retired from the stage and moved into a small flat in Fieldgate Street, near Commercial Road. However, in 1951, after a break of two years, Markovitsh was invited to rejoin the company at the Grand Palais, and he remained there until well into his seventies. By now white-haired and frail, he took care not to exert himself, but played small character roles and also revived some of his own plays for the company. His keen sense of the theatre was matched by a wicked sense of humour, well remembered by his colleagues: 'One evening when the midweek attendance at the Grand Palais was particularly thin, in one play a young actor asked Markovitsh: "Tate, vus veynsti?" [Father, why are you crying?]. Markovitsh didn't answer but merely extended his arm with a sweeping gesture towards the auditorium!'[16]

[14] Irenee Peterman, correspondence with the author.
[15] From a copy of the MS in the author's possession.
[16] Bernard Mendelovitch, interview with the author.

Markovitsh died in London following a heart attack on 25 October 1965. His tombstone records his age as 85 and describes him as 'the celebrated composer and playwright of Yiddish plays and music'.[17] Becky Goldshteyn died seven years later at the Jewish Blind Home in Dorking.

THE *MELO-DEKLAMATSYES*

In his lifetime Markovitsh was known mainly as a playwright, but, as his tombstone suggests, he perhaps deserves posthumous recognition primarily as a composer and songwriter in the tradition of Avrom Goldfaden and Shloyme Prizament. For almost sixty years he produced a voluminous output of musical items for his own use, as numbers within his operettas, or as concert pieces for colleagues. Many of these compositions were extremely popular, but very few were preserved for posterity. However, with the rediscovery of the *melo-deklamatsyes*, and the recovery of other songs from Markovitsh's memoirs, old programmes, and the memory of former colleagues, enough material has now emerged for us to form a picture of his legacy as a composer.

Markovitsh's songs range from the briefest of *kuplets* (witty or satirical rhyming couplets) to long multiple-verse compositions; they include comic songs, polemics against tsarism and capitalism, quarrel duets, *lebns-lider* (character portraits), and lyrical depictions of *der heym* (the Jewish homeland), which for Markovitsh always meant Russia, never Palestine. Many of the lyrics from his first decade in London reflect his strongly held socialist beliefs: 'Ven vet kumen di gliklekhe tsayt' (When Better Times Come) is typical, with its Siberian setting and a chorus looking forward to the downfall of the tsar and a new era of freedom. 'Der shatkhn' (The Matchmaker) was in the repertoire of character comedians all over the world; it is a catchy double-entendre number sung by the hapless matchmaker who complains that his clients always ask for the impossible. Asked to describe the bridegroom, the chorus provides the answer: 'Er hot, er hot, er hot, er hot . . . dos vos ale yidn' ('He has, he has, he has, he has . . . what every Jew has'). There follows a similar assessment of the bride's qualities. 'Aheym tsurik' (Returning Home) tells the story of an elderly Orthodox Jew who comes to live with his children in the West after his wife dies. However, he soon becomes disillusioned with the modern way of life and decides to go 'aheym tsurik in der alter velt' ('back home to the old country'). 'Ukrayine' is for Markovitsh a rare, nostalgic look at his native country in lyrical rhyming verse:

---

[17] Markovitsh is buried in the United Synagogue cemetery at Waltham Abbey, Essex.

Oy mayn sheyne ukrayine, mit dayne stepes lang un breyt
Mit velder tife, felder grine, vi kavyorn oysgeshpreyt.[18]

Oh my beautiful Ukraine, with your broad long steppes,
With deep forests, green fields, spread out like carpets.

For all their undoubted charm, inventiveness, rhyming facility, and typical Yiddish melodies, these songs all proceed along fairly standard lines. Not so the *melo-deklamatsyes*. Undoubtedly the jewel in the crown of Markovitsh's musical legacy, these remarkable virtuoso pieces are distinctive, dramatic poems for voice and orchestral accompaniment with frequent changes of mood, tempo, and musical idiom. It is not clear exactly how many there are, or exactly when Markovitsh wrote them, although most appear to have been written by the late 1920s. The second volume of Zylbercweig's *Leksikon* (published in 1934) lists eight by name: 'Berke goylem; oder, Di oreme khasene' (Berke the Fool; or, The Paupers' Wedding), 'Kol nidre; oder, Kidesh hashem' (All Vows; or, Sanctification of the Holy Name), 'Shma yisroel' (Hear, O Israel), 'Der shtot meshugener' (The Village Idiot), 'Seydi' (Sadie), 'Tsu der khupe; oder, A khasene in a kleyn shtetl' (Under the Wedding Canopy; or, A Small-Town Wedding), 'Opgegebn broyt' (Come-uppance), and 'Ven leybke iz keyn amerike geforn' (When Leybke Went to America), often simply called 'Leybke' or 'Reyzl'.[19] Of these eight compositions, we now have lyrics for seven, music for three of those seven, and, in the case of 'Kol nidre', a complete private recording.[20]

'Kol nidre' was a well-known and popular concert item in the 1920s and 1930s. Set during the First World War, the action takes place in a crowded synagogue on the eve of Yom Kippur in a Jewish town caught between German and Russian forces.[21] The piece opens in a measured, minor key with a description of the deserted *shtetl* at sundown, the old synagogue crowded with worshippers as the *khazn* begins to sing the Kol Nidre prayer. Then,

---

[18] From a copy of the MS in the author's possession.

[19] Zylbercweig (ed.), *Leksikon fun yidish teater*.

[20] In the 1930s or 1940s the London Yiddish actor and singer Yidl Goldberg made a private recording of 'Kol nidre', accompanied on the piano by the synagogue choirmaster Aaron Sorokin. Goldberg knew Markovitsh well, and regularly performed his pieces with the composer's full support. Despite its poor sound quality, his recording is therefore especially valuable as a close expression of the composer's intentions. (The family still has the original glass LP; a cassette copy is in the author's possession.)

[21] We do not know when 'Kol nidre' was written, nor whether it is based on a particular incident. However, there are similarities between the text and a sketch entitled 'Der shpyon: A milkhome bild fun di letste teg fun a idish shtetl' [The Spy: A War Sketch of the Last Days of a Jewish Town], which appeared in the London Yiddish daily *Di tsayt* [The Jewish Times] on 11 June 1915. Written by Dovid Lifshits, the sketch describes the Russians and Germans fighting a pitched battle for control of a *shtetl*, but ends with the death of Khaym Zlotshever as he returns to the ruins of his home to retrieve some holy books.

changing to a march tempo, Markovitsh shows the rival armies closing in on the besieged town:

> Dos shtetl iz umringelt fun ale zaytn
> Fun shvere kanonen zenen di vent
> Di rusn un daytshn haltn in shtraytn
> Un dos shtetl vert langzam farbrent.

> The *shtetl* is surrounded on all sides
> The walls assailed by cannon fire
> The Russians and Germans do battle
> And the *shtetl* slowly burns.

Terrified and exhausted, the Jews take refuge in the synagogue. From the fields outside, the German and Russian armies can be heard approaching, their marching songs carried on the evening air:

> In di velder, in di felder,
> Makht der daytsher mit zayn shtarker hant,
> *Mein heimat, mein heimat, das lieber Faterland* . . .
> Fun der tsveyter zayt zingt der rus un shrayt:
> *Soldatushki der bravere Yatushki*
> *Da gdye zhe vashi matki* . . .

> In the forests, in the fields,
> The German gestures with his strong hand,
> 'My homeland, my homeland, the beloved Fatherland . . .'
> While from the other side the Russian sings and shouts:
> 'Little soldiers of the brave Yatushki
> Where are your mothers?'

With the earth shaking under the impact of the heavy guns, the *khazn* continues with the Kol Nidre service. Suddenly German troops enter the synagogue, bayonets at the ready, and a bellowing voice interrupts the service:

> 'Ich bin ein deutscher Offizier, ich verbiete jedes Wort,
> Ruhe! Ruhe! Und bleiben auf dem Ort.
> Ach, wie schmutzig! Gerade wie in einem Pferdestall
> Wo ist der "Aufseher" von diesem Lokal?
> Dann hören sie doch, Kreuz Donnerwetter noch einmal.'
> Der alter rav geyt shver, vishndik a trer
> Un mit shrek fregt er, 'Vos farlangt der her?'

> 'I am the German commander and I forbid you to say a word,
> Silence! Silence! Stay where you are!
> Ugh! It's filthy in here, just like a stable
> Who's in charge here?
> For God's sake, just you listen to me.'
> The old rabbi walks with difficulty, wiping away a tear,
> And fearfully asks, 'What is the gentleman's command?'

The German officer accuses the Jews of concealing a spy inside the synagogue, and threatens to kill everyone inside unless the spy is handed over. With the music building to a climax, the rabbi asks the congregation whether there is a spy in their midst. Suddenly, an old, blind man shouts: 'Dos bin ikh, rebe' ('It's me, Rabbi'), and the music comes to an abrupt stop as the incredulous crowd exclaims:

> Moyshe der blinder balegole a shpyon?
> Moyshe der blinder balegole a shpyon?
>
> Moyshe the blind coachman a spy?

Moyshe the coachman steps forward, explaining that he is giving up his life on this holy day to save the rest of the community from a similar fate. He is taken out and shot, and the piece ends with the congregation resuming the Kol Nidre service:

> Un der oylem in shul vi shtark er klogt
> Ful mit trern ven der khazn zogt:
> 'Oy!! Kol nidre.'
>
> And how strongly the assembled crowd weeps
> Full of tears when the cantor says:
> 'Oy!! Kol nidre.'

With 'Kol nidre' Markovitsh's ability to integrate various voices, languages, and musical idioms produces a powerful, expressive, and intensely dramatic composition. In a piece lasting no more than five minutes, there are seven different voices (the narrator, the *khazn*, the German and Russian troops, the German officer, the rabbi, and Moyshe the blind coachman); four languages (Yiddish, Hebrew, German, and Russian); and frequent changes of tempo and musical style (including *khazones*, recitative, march, military songs, and unaccompanied declamation).

The Jews in 'Kol nidre' are victims of external forces beyond their control. But in several other *melo-deklamatsyes*, just as in many of Markovitsh's plays, the main theme is class conflict and injustice within the *shtetl* itself. 'Tsu der khupe' (Under the Wedding Canopy) opens with preparations for a wedding in a small town. Amid the excitement as the bridegroom's party is seen arriving on the road, a dark tale of thwarted love, snobbery, and communal intrigue is revealed. The bride's father, Reb Groynem, is an Orthodox Jew, whose chief concern is not his daughter's happiness but his own status as a leading member of the town's powerful religious elite:

> Mit yikhes iz zayn gantse mishpokhe
> Nishto afile keyn eyn bal-melokhe

Nor shoftim, rabonim, dayonim, khazonim
Ay! . . . a bande ganovim mit berd.

His whole family is prestigious,
Not one ordinary worker among them
They're all ritual slaughterers, rabbis, religious judges, cantors
Ay! . . . a bunch of thieves with beards.

When his daughter Freyda falls in love with the son of Zorekh the tailor, Reb Groynem conspires with the local Russian authorities to have the boy banished to Siberia, and arranges for Freyda to be married to a yeshiva student. The day of the wedding arrives, but Freyda stays in her room, grief-stricken and inconsolable. As the music abruptly switches from funereal lament to a hectic dance, Markovitsh brilliantly contrasts her despair with the forced jollity of the party-goers.

Un di kale zitst nebekh in ir kheyder
Ongeton oy vey in di khupe kleyder
Un zi klogt un zi veynt keseyder:
'Ver ken den visn vi dos harts vert tsurisn
Fun trern ver ikh bald dershtikt
Mayn lebn tsebrokhn, mayn gelibtn fartribn
In kaltn sibirn farshikt.'
Ay! Ay! Ay, ay, ay, ay!
Yakhne, sose, khane, dvose, sore, rifke, tsipe,
Loyfn ale tsu der kale firn tsu der khupe.

And the poor bride sits in her room
Wearing her wedding dress
And she weeps and wails without pause:
'Who can know how my heart is in shreds
I am choking with tears
My life in ruins, my beloved driven away from me,
Banished to cold Siberia.'
Ay! Ay! Ay, ay, ay, ay!
Yakhna, Sosa, Khana, Dvosa, Sora, Rivka, Tsipa,
All run to the bride to lead her to the wedding canopy.

With the party in full swing, Zorekh suddenly arrives, confronts Reb Groynem, and demands to know what has happened to his son. He is thrown out, and the bride is led to the wedding canopy. Suddenly she produces a small bottle of poison, swallows it, and, with her dying breath, implores her father to write to her beloved in Siberia, and tell him of her love. The last word goes to Zorekh, who is watching through a window and wishes Reb Groynem a bitter 'mazl tov' ('congratulations') on his daughter's wedding day.

Power and influence in the *shtetl* are also the underlying theme of 'Berke goylem' (Berke the Fool). Pesl, an orphaned girl, is old enough to be married, but her lack of a dowry presents the community with a problem. The elders of the town think they have found the perfect solution and nominate Berke, the local dimwit. Markovitsh's description of the bridegroom illustrates another of his strengths as a lyricist—his mastery of idiomatic Yiddish and rhyming verse:

> Berke iz dem khosns nomen
> Bay vayse khevre heyst er homen
> Vayl ven men shlogt im bay der megile
> Farkrimt zikh berke nisht afile.
> A shtile nar, kimat a goylem, er badint dem gantsn oylem
> Un derfar krigt berke take, ale yontev a groyse make.
> Purim trogt er shalekhmones, an oysher vert er gor sakones.
> Fun di heshaynes heshayne rabe, krigt er a barg mit oylem habe.
> Tilim zogt er, bay toyte klogt er, vaser trogt er
> Un vos farmogt er?

> Berke is the bridegroom's name
> But the pranksters call him Haman
> Because when they hit him with their rattles during the reading of the Megillah
> He doesn't even wince.
> A quiet fool, almost an idiot, he's at the community's beck and call,
> And that's why, as a reward, on festivals all he gets is a plague.
> He carries the gifts on Purim, and he becomes rich with troubles.
> From the willow twigs on Hoshanah Rabbah, he gets nothing in this world.
> He recites psalms, he wails over the dead, he's a water-carrier,
> But what does he possess?

The wedding is fixed and the big day arrives, but an unexpected hitch occurs at the last moment. To everyone's amazement Berke reveals himself to be a shrewd tactician; he refuses to go ahead with the ceremony until a dowry is hurriedly collected from the assembled guests.

Happy endings, however, are a rarity in the *melo-deklamatsyes*, as in Markovitsh's work as a whole. 'Shma yisroel' (Hear, O Israel), one of his bleakest compositions, is a stark portrayal of *shtetl* poverty, and a bitter attack on religion. In a dark basement on a cold winter's evening, a mother sits watching over her sick child and weeping. As the child's life ebbs away, she begs her deeply religious husband to go out and earn some money to buy food and ease their desperate poverty:

> Gazlen, roytsekh, ikh red dokh tsu dir
> Yankl! Meshumed! Vos entferstu nisht mir?

> Robber, murderer, I'm talking to you
> Yankl! Convert! Why don't you answer me?

The more she harangues him, the more fervently he prays, appealing to God to show mercy and save the child. The piece ends with the child's death and the father still praying, his faith unshaken: 'Shma yisroel, adoyshem eloy-keynu, adoyshem ekhad' ('Hear, O Israel, the Lord our God, the Lord is One).

'Shma yisroel' highlights another noteworthy feature of Markovitsh's work: his sympathy for the plight of women in the traditional world of the *shtetl*. In 'Leybke' he focuses on a tragic but common phenomenon during the years of mass Jewish emigration. Leybke sets off for America, reassuring his wife and child that he will soon be sending them tickets to join him in the New World. While they wait for a letter, he prospers in business, meets another woman, and gets engaged. One day, to his wife's delight, a letter finally arrives; when she opens it, her joy turns to horror as she discovers a bill of divorce rather than the tickets she was expecting.

Whereas 'Shma yisroel' and 'Leybke' feature intimate, domestic settings, 'Der shtot meshugener' (The Village Idiot) and 'Opgegebn broyt' (Come-uppance) are much closer to conventional melodrama. Dramatic tales of revenge and mistaken identity, they read rather like play synopses, their action tele-scoped from three or four acts to a few minutes. In 'Der shtot meshugener' a young man, Khayim Zeydl, tells his story to a group of yeshiva students. Abandoned by his father as a child, he and his mother live in wretched cir-cumstances. As his mother lies dying, he discovers that his father lives nearby, leading a wealthy and dissolute life. He confronts his father, pleads with him to send a doctor to help save his mother's life, but is rebuffed. Finally, over-come by emotion, he shoots him and is declared insane. He ends by asking his listeners:

> Un mentshn mit kep, advokatn, doktoyrim kluge
> Hobn derklert az ikh bin meshuge!
> Nu, bin ikh meshuge? Nu, bin ikh meshuge?

> And people with brains, lawyers, clever doctors,
> Pronounced me crazy!
> Well, am I crazy? Well, am I crazy?

'Opgegebn broyt' also starts with a mother and son, although its focus is more overtly political. Avram Zilbershteyn is a revolutionary, on the run from the tsarist authorities. When officers come to arrest him, his mother pleads with the chief of police, Count Trubetskoy, to spare her son. However, he kicks her so hard that she dies on the spot, and her son vows to avenge her death. Ten years later the tables are turned when Zilbershteyn, now a Bol-shevik soldier, finds himself billeted in Trubetskoy's palace. When the count's aged mother begs him not to arrest her son, Zilbershteyn answers her in the same words that Trubetskoy used ten years earlier:

> Ir zent far dem rusishn folk a mageyfe.
> Loz up mayne fis, du alte makhsheyfe!

> You are a plague on the Russian people.
> Let go of my feet, you old witch!

The piece ends with Zilbershteyn killing the old countess with a kick, telling Trubetskoy: 'Dos iz opgegebn broyt!' ('This is a taste of your own medicine!'). A striking feature of this *melo-deklamatsye* is the way Markovitsh interweaves Yiddish and Russian words, especially in the conversation of the young Soviet troops who turn up at Trubetskoy's palace (Russian words in italics):

> *Tovarishchi*, ir kent banutsn ot di ale zaln
> Ober keyn skandaln. *Do svidaniya!*
> *Rebiata, davay piesna.*

> Comrades, you can use all these rooms
> But no bad behaviour. Farewell!
> Lads, let's have a song.

The blend of languages is surely being used to make a political point: Markovitsh seems to be suggesting that in the new Soviet Russia Jews and non-Jews will coexist happily, just as Yiddish and Russian will intermingle in everyday speech.

These brief summaries indicate Markovitsh's bleak vision of life in his native Russia, his radical political views, and his sympathy for the poor and oppressed. But while their story lines are quintessential melodrama, the *melo-deklamatsyes* stand out by virtue of the sheer artistry of their construction and Markovitsh's skilful juggling of different languages and musical styles. As a composer, Markovitsh is closer in spirit to the songs of Avrom Goldfaden and Shloyme Prizament than the Yiddish theatre show tunes of New York's Second Avenue; his melodies have the simplicity and intimacy of Yiddish folk music, combined with his evident fondness for *khazones* and his frequent use of snatches of prayers. In 'Shma yisroel' the hapless husband offers his prayers to God; in 'Kol nidre' the old *khazn* prays fervently for God to save the community from the violence engulfing it; and 'Leybke' ends with the *khazn* blessing the marriage vows of Leybke and his new bride.

At their best, Markovitsh's *melo-deklamatsyes* are masterpieces of compression, musical parables that bring a large cast of characters vividly alive in a matter of minutes. Their complexity and richness of texture were surely important factors in their appeal to public and performers alike. With their multiplicity of voices and musical styles, they were the perfect virtuoso vehicle, and it is no surprise that they featured in the repertoire of many leading actors. Their best-known interpreter was undoubtedly the Yiddish stage star Samuel Goldenburg (b. 1886). The Russian-born Goldenburg arrived in London as a young man in 1907, and soon joined an amateur Yiddish company. By the time he left England several years later as a highly regarded professional, he would undoubtedly have known Markovitsh well. A talented pianist, fine singer, and dramatic actor, Goldenburg was ideally suited to perform the *melo-deklamatsyes*. By the 1920s he was singing them all over the world, frequently accompanying himself at the piano, and he recorded at least one ('A khasene in a kleyn shtetl') and possibly more. Besides Goldenburg and Markovitsh himself, many other actors regularly featured the *melo-deklamatsyes* in their concert repertoire, among them Herman Fenigshtayn (1893–1972), Henry Gerro (*c*.1918–80), Renye Glickman (d. 1961), Isaac Krelman (1892–1966), Mark Markov (1905–83), Isaac Samberg (1889–1940s), Meyer Tzelniker (1898–1980), Ben-Zion Witler (*c*.1900–61), and Dovid Zayderman (b. 1895).[22] Interestingly, anecdotal evidence and the surviving recordings indicate that the *melo-deklamatsyes* were performed both as 'straight' dramatic pieces and as parodies. In Goldenburg's American recording, for example, there is much use of circus-style trombone and brass clowning with exaggerated glissandos, effects which sit uneasily with Markovitsh's pared-down folk style.

Markovitsh's *melo-deklamatsyes* constitute what may be a unique body of work within the repertoire of the Yiddish theatre, which is not generally known for innovations in form. The relentless demands of the popular Yiddish stage affected all who worked in it, but none more than its resident writers. Lack of subsidy, low budgets, and tight deadlines ensured that companies worked at a breakneck pace; dwindling audiences and the domination of the star system helped to reinforce a fear of failure. Taken together, these factors produced a theatre that put a premium on virtuosity and all-round

---

[22] In an obituary the Polish-born Yiddish actor and playwright Harry Ariel recalled the first time he heard Markovitsh's work: 'I was ten years old when I first heard the great American star Samuel Goldenburg reciting Markovitsh's "Kidesh hashem" in Łódź. He accompanied himself on the piano and I remember as a child how a shudder went through my body at the words and music which painted such a tragic picture of the anti-Jewish pogroms' ('Yozef markovitsh o.h.', *Loshn un lebn* (Oct.–Dec. 1965)). Isaac Krelman's MS copy of 'Der shtot meshugener' records that Markovitsh made him a present of the piece for a special evening to mark Krelman's thirty-fifth stage anniversary at Stoke Newington Town Hall, London, on 11 Sept. 1952. According to Bernard Mendelovitch, however, although many actors used Markovitsh's material, only Samuel Goldenburg and Henry Gerro ever paid him a fee for performing his work.

performance, but left little room for innovation or experimentation. As concert pieces, the *melo-deklamatsyes* offered Markovitsh an opportunity to develop a different type of musical theatre composition, combining elements from both Jewish music and the classical tradition allied to his own distinctive voice as a lyricist.

For all their formal novelty, however, the *melo-deklamatsyes* rely on conventional, old-fashioned story lines. In part, this is undoubtedly due to Markovitsh's own personality, which combined radical political views with a generally traditional outlook on life. But it also reflects the state of Yiddish culture in Britain. In contrast to the situation in the United States, where there was considerable interaction between the Yiddish playhouses on Second Avenue and theatre on Broadway, Yiddish theatre in the East End remained, by and large, a world apart, less susceptible to modern trends in the theatre or society at large. Wider demographic trends also played an important role: the relatively small size of the Yiddish-speaking community and the dearth of new immigrants after about 1910 determined the fate of Yiddish theatre in Britain as almost entirely a one-generational phenomenon, certainly as far as its audience was concerned. With few exceptions, Whitechapel's Yiddish theatre patrons were born between about 1865 and 1895, a generation whose formative years, like those of Markovitsh, were mostly spent in the Pale of Settlement.

Unfortunately, comparisons between the history of Yiddish theatre in Britain and its counterparts elsewhere are difficult given the paucity of detailed research on the subject. Despite the pioneering studies of Leonard Prager, the cultural life of Britain's Jewish immigrant communities remains an almost entirely neglected area of scholarly enquiry. Sadly, an enormous amount of valuable source material — not least concerning the Yiddish theatre — has now been lost to historians owing to a combination of British institutional negligence, Jewish communal indifference, and the effects of the Blitz and wartime dislocation. By the time the YIVO Institute in New York began to solicit donations of British Yiddish material in the 1960s, it was almost too late.

Markovitsh's missing legacy offers a depressing case-study. In his lifetime he published virtually nothing of his rich output. (This was partly because of the fragile economy of the Yiddish theatre community, where copyright protection was almost non-existent, prompters were notorious for selling unauthorized copies, and original scripts were jealously guarded.) After his death a sizeable collection of manuscripts remained within the family, including many complete play scripts. These were eventually made available to other Yiddish actors in Britain, who later threw them out. Virtually all the photographs, posters, and other memorabilia collected by Markovitsh and

Goldshteyn over their long careers were also lost. Not until the 1980s, when the newly created Museum of the Jewish East End mounted a comprehensive exhibition of London's Yiddish theatre history, was any concerted attempt made to collect surviving archival material.

And yet, as the process of recovering the *melo-deklamatsyes* indicates, even at this late stage it is still possible to find unique documents and important primary materials for the study of Yiddish theatre in private hands. Much valuable biographical information can still be obtained by consulting and interviewing relatives of actors, playwrights, and theatre composers. The importance of such fieldwork for the study of Yiddish theatre's great actors and dramatists is self-evident. However, there are many other figures who are less well known but whose posthumous obscurity is undeserved. One such is Joseph Markovitsh — an inventive composer and an original and witty lyricist whose distinctive voice deserves greater recognition.

EIGHT

From Goldfaden to Goldfaden in Cracow's Jewish Theatres

🎭

MIROSŁAWA M. BUŁAT

O N 27 APRIL 1939 a soirée entitled 'From Goldfaden to Goldfaden' was held in Cracow.[1] The event was organized by the Cracow Jewish Theatre Society, one of the first Jewish social organizations of its kind in Poland, which, from 1926 onwards, acted as a patron to the endeavours of the Jewish theatre in the city. That evening Simkhe Natan sang popular arias by the 'father of professional Yiddish theatre' which were already part of the cultural tradition of Jewish theatre. Also at the event was the outstanding director Zygmunt Turkow who outlined the premisses of his original interpretation of one of Goldfaden's most popular plays, *Shulamis*, which was to be performed in Cracow the following day by a troupe from Lviv. The evening was introduced by the influential theatre critic Mojżesz Kanfer, a co-founder and active member of the Theatre Society. Kanfer was a representative of that generation which, in its youth, had seen the plays put on by friends and colleagues of Goldfaden himself (often in barns or stables), and, as adults, had seen modern interpretations of those same plays which equalled the best non-Jewish performances.

As a centre of Jewish theatre Cracow was not as influential as Vilna or Warsaw. With a Jewish population of 20,939 in 1890, 45,229 in 1921, and 64,348 in 1938, and the reputation for being a 'bavuste festung fun asimilatsye' (a well-known stronghold of assimilation),[2] it could not foster such a variety of forms of theatrical creativity as those towns. Fortunately, a group of devotees of Yiddish theatre strengthened Cracow's ties with Yiddish culture by organizing guest performances of the best troupes and artists. I have chosen to explore not only performances by local professional ensembles, but also

---

[1] 'Z teatru, literatury i sztuki' [From Theatre, Literature and Art], *Nowy Dziennik*, 23 Apr. 1939; 'Od Goldfadena do Goldfadena; [From Goldfaden to Goldfaden], *Nowy Dziennik*, 25, 26, 27 Apr. 1939.

[2] Gezelshaft Krokever Yidish Teater, 'A briv in redaktsye' [A Letter to the Editor], *Literarishe bleter*, 14 (1927), 281.

those by visiting troupes, and in what follows I will trace the changing approaches to Goldfaden's works as they were presented to the Jewish audience in Cracow over a period of sixty years.

'FROM GOLDFADEN': 'AS WRITTEN' — 'IN THE SPIRIT OF THE TIME'

The first documented performance in Cracow of a play in Yiddish took place on 13 July 1887.[3] The Polish Jewish Theatre Company, directed by Khayim-Binyomin Treytler, staged Goldfaden's *Di kaprizne tokhter; oder, Kaptsnzon et hungerman* (The Capricious Daughter; or, Pauperson and Hungerman) under the title *Der kortnshpiler* (The Gambler). The same ensemble performed Goldfaden's biblical operetta *Shulamis* in 1888. We have no details of either of these performances. They may have been influenced by the original staging supervised by the author himself, since Treytler and his daughter Malvina had played under his direction in the Zhignitse Theatre in Bucharest,[4] but this is only conjecture. In about 1889 Goldfaden's biblical operettas were performed in Cracow by Kalmen Yuvelir's troupe.[5] Unfortunately, no critical reviews of these performances have been preserved.

Plays by Goldfaden were a permanent part of the repertoire of the Jewish theatre which operated at 7 Bocheńska Street from 1917 or 1918 to 1922, when it was managed by Moses Yakob.[6] We know for certain that the much-admired operettas *Akeydes yitskhok* (The Sacrifice of Isaac), *Meshiekhs tsaytn* (The Messianic Age), *Dos tsente gebot; oder, Loy sakhmoyd* (The Tenth Commandment; or, Thou Shalt Not Covet), *Ben ami*, and *Bar kokhba* were staged in 1918, and the last of these again in 1919. The theatre revived *Akeydes yitskhok* and *Bar kokhba* in 1920 and 1921, and also staged *Kenig akhashveyresh* (King Ahasuerus) in each of those years. No details of any performances of Goldfaden's plays in 1922 have been preserved, but the sources relating to those years are incomplete. The theatre manager Yakob, a professional censor and a teacher of the 'Mosaic religion' in state schools, had neither the interest nor

---

[3] See the poster for this performance, preserved in the Biblioteka Jagiellońska, Cracow.

[4] Zalmen Zylbercweig (ed.), *Leksikon fun yidishn teater* [Lexicon of Yiddish Theatre], 6 vols. (New York: Elisheva, 1931–70), ii. 892–3.

[5] See Rachela Holcer, 'Teatr żydowski w Krakowie' [Jewish Theatre in Cracow], in Jan Michalik and Eugenia Prokop-Janiec (eds.), *Teatr żydowski w Krakowie: Studia i materiały* [Yiddish Theatre in Cracow: Studies and Materials], trans. Anna Ciałowicz (Cracow: Księgarnia Akademicka, 1995), 199.

[6] On the Cracow Jewish Theatre managed by Moses Yakob, see Mirosława Bułat, 'Kraków—żydowska mozaika teatralna' [Cracow—Jewish Theatre Mosaic], in Michalik and Prokop-Janiec (eds.), *Teatr żydowski w Krakowie*, 30–8.

the qualifications to manage his institution, which he treated merely as a source of income. He skimped not only on scenery, but also on essential furniture and repairs. Perhaps it was for this reason, and because of his incompetence as a director, audience preferences, and the actors' strengths—which were more vocal than dramatic—that Yakob emphasized the musical and vocal interpretations of Goldfaden's performances.

Several members of Yakob's troupe, such as Zalmen Libgold, Sammy Urich, and Adolf Meltser, may have met the author of *Shulamis* himself or worked alongside his collaborators, first of all in Lviv.[7] On Meltser's ability to act in Goldfaden's plays, Leon Herbst (or Staw), an actor in the Cracow Jewish Theatre and a historian of Jewish theatre, wrote in 1929:

The thirty-five-year history of the Jewish theatre in the former Galicia is associated with the name of Adolf Meltser. I have in mind the old, authentic theatre of Goldfaden, Lateiner, Richter, Gordin . . .

Meltser was the single true interpreter of Goldfaden's 'history' (historical operettas are called 'history' in Jewish theatre). He bore on his shoulders the whole of Goldfaden, the father of our theatre. And he really was a strong man . . .

Adolf Meltser was the master of Jewish song in our theatre.

And it was the folk song which gave birth to Jewish theatre.

Song in our theatre amounts to Goldfaden, and Meltser is the best singer. This is precisely what he is known for.[8]

In 1924 *Shulamis* and *Bar kokhba* were still being played in Cracow, but we have no details of these performances. The same applies to the performance of *Akeydes yitskhok* on 11 January 1925, at the theatre on Bocheńska Street now managed by Meltser. These performances must have followed the rather traditional style typified by *Di tsvey kuni leml* (The Two Kuni Lemls) as performed by Avrom Kompaneyets's troupe from Łódź on 14 February 1926:

The actors performed *The Two Kuni Lemls* without over-acting or use of the grotesque, but rather in the spirit of the time. We have to agree that they achieved much, although here too the performance should have been cut considerably. The performers, in particular old Kompaneyets, reminded us how such parts used to be acted, which was good because we could see that old Jewish actors are also able to play their parts correctly. . . . The audience enjoyed the play very much, though there were few songs.[9]

[7] On Libgold, Urich, and Meltser, see Zylbercweig (ed.), *Leksikon fun yidishn teater*, ii. 1025, i. 44–5, and ii. 1352–4 respectively. On Meltser, see also Leon Herbst, 'Adolf Melzer, 35 lat teatru żydowskiego w b. Galicji' [Adolf Melzer, Thirty-Five Years of Jewish Theatre in the Former Galicia], *Nowy Dziennik*, 14 Aug. 1929.   [8] Herbst, 'Adolf Melzer'.

[9] M.K. [Mojżesz Kanfer], 'Z teatru żydowskiego: *Obaj Kuni Lemel*' [From the Jewish Theatre: *The Two Kuni Lemls*], *Nowy Dziennik*, 19 Feb. 1926.

In his youth Avrom Kompaneyets had performed with the Broder singers. Influenced by Goldfaden, he dedicated himself to the Jewish theatre. In the early period he was an outstanding interpreter of Goldfaden's comic characters, especially in the breeches role of the title character in *Di kishefmakherin* (The Sorceress). In Cracow he played Kuni Leml, which he regarded as his most successful role; he had witnessed the famous comedian Sigmund Mogulesco interpreting it under the direction of the author himself.[10]

In June and July 1926 *Di tsvey kuni leml*, *Akeydes yitskhok*, *Shulamis*, and *Bar kokhba* were staged in the summer theatre in Wasserlauf's restaurant garden. The troupe was directed by Meltser and Shloyme Prizament, the son of Moyshe Prizament, at that time one of the most popular *batkhonim* (wedding entertainers) and folksingers in Hungary and a personal friend of Goldfaden,[11] a fact that suggests that the performers may have kept to the original traditions of performing Goldfaden's plays. This is confirmed by a review of *Akeydes yitskhok*:

The Jewish theatre presently in the garden of the Londyński Hotel presented *The Sacrifice of Isaac* by A. Goldfaden.

I went to the performance because I feel some warmth for the father of the Jewish theatre. Obviously, the nicest memories of youth are essential; I mean the times when I was not sitting in a reviewer's chair and was not a stern critic, but rather 'experienced' plays directly. . . . I now find that Goldfaden is still alive and well. He needs only to be 'modernized', stripped of German barbarisms and correctly staged. The secret of his vitality lies in a profound feeling for melody, and an eternal feeling for performance. Goldfaden's music . . . is smooth, fluid and melodious. . . . Obviously *The Sacrifice of Isaac* lost much of its charm when presented on a small and extremely primitive stage reminiscent of the old Shakespearean theatre. However, we stayed until the end.[12]

In the summer of 1927 *Shulamis* was staged again in the summer theatre in Wasserlauf's restaurant garden. Goldfaden's operettas were still being performed on the summer stage of the Londyński Hotel garden, at least in 1931 (*Akeydes yitskhok* and *Shulamis*), in 1933 (*Bar kokhba* and *Shulamis*, staged by a troupe including Dovid Zeyderman and Khane Lerner), and in 1934 (when the theatre was managed by Beno Jakubowicz; the troupe, including Miriam Koralova and Leon Libgold, the son of Zalmen Libgold, staged *Shulamis*).

The Vilna Folks-teater (People's Theatre) inaugurated the third season of the Krokever Yidish Teater (Cracow Jewish Theatre) in 1928 with a performance of *Akeydes yitskhok*. In a speech given before the performance the troupe's

[10] Zylbercweig quotes a funny anecdote connected with this role, told by Avrom Kompaneyets himself: Zylbercweig (ed.), *Leksikon fun yidishn teater*, vi. 5416–17.   [11] See ibid. iii. 1873.
[12] M.K., 'Teatr żydowski: Żywotność Goldfadena' [Jewish Theatre: The Vitality of Goldfaden], *Nowy Dziennik*, 13 June 1926.

representative, Leyb Shriftzetser, explained the reasons for that choice, emphasizing that 'the theatre plays Goldfaden not to show off its capabilities but to repay the moral debt the Jewish theatre owes to Goldfaden'.[13] Kanfer observed the reception of the play by the Cracow audience:

The old theatregoers who used to visit the Jewish theatre at a time when it was just taking its first steps, when it still aimed to reach the widest audience and not only the intelligentsia, must have been moved to witness that primitive plot, clad in a regal coat of melody which, later, became a folk song. And those young ones who know Goldfaden only from the stylized productions of modern directors could see the plentitude of motifs and the warm beauty of Goldfaden's works. . . . Our current theatre has given us Goldfaden in his original state, and, at last, achieved considerable success. It was Goldfaden who triumphed, although he was neither given a Cubist setting, nor distorted into the form of a grotesque.[14]

This last comment relates to the innovative productions by Alexander Granovsky in Moscow (*Di kishefmakherin*, 1922; *Dos tsente gebot*, 1926), Maurice Schwartz in New York (*Di tsvey kuni leml*, 1924; *Di kishefmakherin*, 1925—see Plates 10 and 12; *Dos tsente gebot*, 1926), and Zygmunt Turkow in Warsaw (*Di tsvey kuni leml*, 1924; *Dos tsente gebot*, 1926).

'TO GOLDFADEN': ADAPTATIONS, MODERNIZATIONS . . .

This phase was initiated by the guest performance by the Warsaw Yiddish Art Theatre (VYKT) of Goldfaden's play *Di tsvey kuni leml*, directed by Zygmunt Turkow in 1924.[15] The first performance in Cracow was on 6 July 1924.[16]

Reb Pinkhesl, a wealthy hasid, seeks a suitable match for his stepdaughter Carolina. A young man named Kuni Leml comes from a fine family but has his shortcomings: he stutters, is blind in one eye, and lame. He is also, by Carolina's modern standards, a religious fanatic. Her soulmate, Max, devises a plan to save her from an unwanted marriage by disguising himself as Kuni Leml—a feat he pulls off with such skill that he makes the foolish Kuni Leml doubt his own identity. Meanwhile, when the stepfather seems about to abandon his plan, Carolina declares to his amazement that she has nothing

---

[13] M.K., 'Pierwsza premiera teatru żydowskiego w Krakowie' [The First Performance of Jewish Theatre in Cracow], *Nowy Dziennik*, 14 Oct. 1928.   [14] Ibid.

[15] On modernized versions of Goldfaden's plays performed in the United States, see Joel Berkowitz, 'The Tallis or the Cross? Reviving Goldfaden at the Yiddish Art Theatre, 1924–26', *Journal of Jewish Studies*, 50 (Spring 1999), 120–38.

[16] See 'Ostatnie przedstawienia W.I.K.T.u' [The Last Performances of VYKT], *Nowy Dziennik*, 3 July 1924; 'Ostatnie występy W.I.K.T.u' [The Last Performances of VYKT], *Nowy Dziennik*, 10 July 1924; M.K., 'Ostatnie występy W.I.K.T.u (dokończenie)' [The Last Performances of VYKT (Conclusion)], *Nowy Dziennik*, 12 July 1924.

against it. Pinkhesl now suspects that the insignificant stutterer must be a *lamed-vovnik*—according to Jewish tradition, one of the thirty-six righteous men in every generation on whom the continued existence of the world depends. Max confirms this when, still in disguise, he convinces Pinkhesl of his ability to commune with the spirits by putting on, with the help of fellow students, a dance of the dead. Finally, Max becomes engaged to Carolina, while Kuni Leml is left with the matchmaker's daughter Libe, who is unimpressive but eager to marry.

The critics emphasized that the producer had preserved the nature of the primitive folk scenery, while giving it a modern setting.[17] They also identified in the production inspiration from the *commedia dell'arte*,[18] and an intense theatricality visible not so much in the sets as in the action.[19]

Another adaptation of *Di tsvey kuni leml* was staged in Cracow by the manager of the Cracow Jewish Theatre, Menakhem Rubin. Rubin's production, which featured local actors, had previously appeared in Riga, Warsaw, and New York, and made its Cracow debut on 11 November 1933.[20] Rubin enabled the ridiculous Reb Pinkhesl to develop as a character: although he remains religious, he becomes less narrow-minded.[21] Instead of Goldfaden's music, Rubin introduced melodies by a Moscow composer, Shaynin. He staged the opening of the play against the backdrop of the title-page of an old edition of the work, decorated with original Jewish ornaments.[22] In the company's productions elsewhere a narrator stood outside the proscenium commenting on the action in comic verse. But Polish theatres in Cracow hosted Yiddish troupes rarely and unwillingly, and the only Jewish theatre in town was small, primitive, and lacking in both space and machinery. Thus it was impossible to construct a proscenium in the building on Bocheńska Street and there was no narrator.[23] Comparing Rubin's modernization with the achievements of Granovsky and Schwartz, Kanfer saw that the Cracow approach was a middle way between Moscow's grotesque and satire, which served propagandistic purposes, and New York's spectacular fable.[24]

---

[17] See 'Ostatnie przedstawienia W.I.K.T.u.   [18] See 'Ostatnie występy W.I.K.T.u.'
[19] See M.K., 'Ostatnie występy W.I.K.T.u (dokończenie)'.
[20] On Menakhem Rubin's staging of *Di tsvey kuni leml* (The Two Kuni Lemls) in Cracow, see M.K., 'Niespodzianka, jaką nam przygotowuje Menachem Rubin' [The Surprise that Menakhem Rubin is Preparing for Us], *Nowy Dziennik*, 12 Nov. 1933; M.K., 'Teatr żydowski w Krakowie: Gościnne występy Menachema Rubina, *Kuni Lemel*, komedia muzyczna wg Goldfadena w inscenizacji Menachema Rubina' [Jewish Theatre in Cracow: The Guest Performances of Menakhem Rubin. *Kuni Leml*, a Musical Comedy Based on Goldfaden, Produced by Menakhem Rubin], *Nowy Dziennik*, 15 Nov. 1933; R.W., 'Głos aktora o przedstawieniu *Kuni Lemel*' [An Actor's Opinion of the Performance of *The Two Kuni Lemls*], *Nowy Dziennik*, 29 Nov. 1933.
[21] See M.K., 'Niespodzianka'.   [22] See M.K., 'Teatr żydowski w Krakowie'.
[23] See M.K., 'Niespodzianka'.   [24] See M.K., 'Teatr żydowski w Krakowie'.

Di tsvey kuni leml was a starting point for Mikhl Weichert's staging of *Trupe tanentsap* (The Tanentsap Troupe)[25] by the Yung Teater (Youth Theatre) in Warsaw in 1933 and in Cracow in 1936.[26] The staging was a response to the second prohibition issued by the censor of Yung Teater's play *Boston*, a dramatization of the Sacco and Vanzetti affair. *Trupe tanentsap* was to be an expression of the problems the artists and the Jewish theatre had to face from the very beginning. They included conflicts with Russian, Austrian, and Polish officials, as well as within the Jewish community itself.

Weichert's satirical play within a play, subtitled *A goldfaden-shpil in a galitsish shtetl* (A Goldfaden Play in a Galician *Shtetl*), showed how Goldfaden's comedy *Di tsvey kuni leml* might have been staged by a Galician travelling company in the 1890s. Although such a troupe had existed, with a manager named Tanentsap, Weichert's aim was not theatrical biography. He built a temporary stage in the hall, as in the pioneering days of Yiddish theatre. The stage was located in a stable, vacated for the duration of the performance and built from boards set on beer barrels. It was lit with kerosene lamps of the type used by carters. A brightly coloured, floral-print cloth on a string served as the curtain. Weichert situated the play's prologue among the audience. First the embarrassed manager of the Tanentsap troupe himself appears, followed by his wife and daughter. Another character tries to get in without paying. The comedians' performance attracts the typical *shtetl* personalities: a simple tailor's apprentice and his fiancée, a servant, a local rich man, a *magid* (preacher) from Lithuania, a Hungarian officer, a Czech gendarme, and a Russian policeman.

[25] For the preface to, and text of, *Trupe tanentsap*, see Mikhl Weichert, *Trupe tanentsap: a goldfaden-shpil in a galitsish shtetl* [*The Tanentsap Troupe*: A Goldfaden Play in a Galician *Shtetl*] (Tel Aviv: Hamenorah, 1966). I would like to thank Jan Adamczyk from the Slavic and East European Library of the University of Illinois at Urbana-Champaign for making this book available to me. See also Yosef Glikson, 'Yung-Teater', in Itsik Manger, Moyshe Perenson, and Jonas Turkow (eds.), *Yidisher teater in eyrope tsvishn beyde velt-milkhomes* [Yiddish Theatre in Europe between the Two World Wars], 2 vols. (New York: Congress for Jewish Culture, 1968), i: *Poyln* [Poland], 127–47. For reviews of the Warsaw productions, see 'B', 'Zza kulis teatralnych: Wizyta w żydowskim "Studio" Teatru Młodych' [From behind the Scenes: A Visit to the Jewish Experimental Youth Theatre], *Ilustrowany Kuryer Codzienny*, 30 Sept. 1933; Jakub Appenszlak, 'Żydowskie Studio Teatralne "Teatr Młodych": *Trupa Tanencapa*' [The Jewish Experimental Theatre "Youth Theatre": *The Tanentsap Troupe*], *Nasz Przegląd*, 12 Oct. 1933; Stefan Rumelt, 'U progu nowego sezonu w teatrach żydowskich' [On the Threshold of a New Season at the Jewish Theatres], *Opinia*, 22 Oct. 1933. For a review of the Vilna productions, see Wilhelm Mermelstein, ' "Jung-Teater": List z Wilna' ['Yung Teater': A Letter from Vilna], *Nasza Opinia*, 31 May 1936. For reviews of the Cracow productions, see M.K., '*Trupa Tanencapa*' [*The Tanentsap Troupe*], *Nowy Dziennik*, 27 Dec. 1936; H.W., 'Wartości plastyczne w "Teatrze Młodych"' [Stagecraft in 'Youth Theatre'], *Nowy Dziennik*, 16 Jan. 1937. See also Mirosława Bułat, ' "Jung Teater" i "Naj Teater" w Krakowie' ['Young Theatre' and 'New Theatre' in Cracow], *Pamiętnik Teatralny*, 3–4 (1996), 515, 517–18, 520–1.

[26] The first performance in Cracow was on 25 Dec. 1936.

After the prologue *Di tsvey kuni leml* begins. Tanentsap's audience reacts vocally to the action on the stage, telling the characters what to do and requesting their favourite songs. The actors repeat the comments of these spectators, with which they agree, and carry out their requests, regardless of its effect on the logic of the action and the integrity of the play within the play. The first conflict takes place in the Odessa scene. Student characters, following the mood of Goldfaden's text (in which Max and his fellow students sing a tribute in Yiddish to the tsar), sing 'Bozhe, tsarya khrani' (God Save the Tsar) in front of the Russian emperor's portrait. Representatives of the authorities object, stating that the performance is taking place in the territory of the Austro-Hungarian empire. Tanentsap quickly replaces the beard on the tsar's portrait with whiskers. Having 'disguised' Nicholas to look like Franz Joseph, he orders the orchestra to play the Austrian anthem, 'Gott erhalte, Gott beschütze'. The officer, the gendarme, and the policeman salute. The disorder in the audience reaches its peak when Max and his friends play ghosts in order to advance his plan to marry Carolina. When a hasid from Warsaw objects to the ungodly ridiculing of the dead, the gendarme forbids the troupe to continue its performance. Tanentsap makes a speech expressing his love of the Jewish theatre and his regret over the oppression to which his company has been subjected, and points to his closed mouth. The unmoved representative of the authorities disperses Tanentsap's audience, and so ends Weichert's play.

Reviews of the Cracow productions did not concentrate on the political aspect of the staging—the problem of censorship and the authorities' hostility to Yiddish theatre. Instead, the production was looked at in terms of its historical authenticity. As a boy Mojżesz Kanfer, the Cracow reviewer, had witnessed a similar play performed by the real Tanentsap's troupe in his home town of Buczacz. He may not have been the only member of the audience to have had this experience, as many Cracow Jews had previously lived in other Galician towns. In Kanfer's view, the staging was generally faithful to the historical reality. He pointed out only a single error, which was not significant in a production that was aiming to do more than merely reconstruct the past:

Being an eyewitness . . . I can confirm that Weichert's staging is authentic. One detail, however, does not correspond to reality: the manager Tanentsap was not an actor himself and did not take part in the performances. Still, he used to make speeches to the audience. Buczacz was a progressive town, famous for its maskilim. . . . That is why the hasidim did not demonstrate here; I can imagine that in other towns where the hasidim were in the majority, such demonstrations against blasphemers, which these comedians were thought to be, were quite likely.[27]

---

[27] M.K., '*Trupa Tanencapa*'.

The production was staged 220 times in Warsaw, but only ten in Cracow.

A few years after Weichert's production, the writer Itsik Manger and the director Yankev Rotboym collaborated on another of Goldfaden's most popular musical comedies, *Di kishefmakherin*. The adaptation was first performed in Warsaw in 1937, and made its debut in Cracow on 12 February 1938.[28] The performance was to be the inaugural production and a flagship for the newly established Folksteater un Teater far Yugnt (Folk and Youth Theatre), managed by Clara Segalovitch. The group was formed to discourage the Polonization of Jewish youth, especially students in Polish high schools and private high schools where Polish was the language of instruction. Goldfaden's play was well suited to be the first performance by the new theatre since, being a work of the 'father of the Jewish theatre', it was among the Jewish classics, and also, because of its fairytale character, it could be staged so as to make it attractive to an audience with a poor command of Yiddish.

Jews in Cracow, especially educated ones, were more Polonized than Jews elsewhere in Poland. In the 1930s Polonization proceeded apace, especially among the younger generation. The performance of *Di kishefmakherin*, which incorporated vivid action, visuals, music, and sound and light effects, was intended by the producers and the local Jewish Theatre Society that had invited the troupe to attract Jewish children and young people with little or no

[28] For the text of Itsik Manger's adaptation, see Avrom Goldfaden, *Czarownica* [The Sorceress] (typescript in Yiddish), Archiwum Ringelbluma, Archiwum, Żydowski Instytut Historyczny, Warsaw, call no. I/613. On Itsik Manger and Yankev Rotboym's version of *Di kishefmakherin*, see Yankev Rotboym, 'Itsik mangers debyut als dramaturg (zikhroynes fun a rezhiser)' [Itsik Manger's Debut as a Dramatist (Director's Memoirs)], *Folks-sztyme*, 18 Oct. and 1 Nov. 1991; Dina Halpern, 'Mayne bagegenishn mit itsik manger'n' [My Encounters with Itsik Manger], *Folks-sztyme*, 23–30 Dec. 1988. For reviews of the Warsaw productions, see Zastępca, 'Żydowski teatr dla młodzieży: *Czarodziejka*' [Jewish Youth Theatre: *The Sorceress*], *Nasz Przegląd*, 16 Mar. 1937; N.M., 'Ershte oyf-firung in'm "Teater far yugnt"' [The First Performance of the 'Youth Theatre'], *Literarishe bleter*, 11 (1937), 180. For reviews of the Cracow productions, see Moyshe Blekher, 'Der vunderlekher kishef-nign' [The Wonderful Magic Tune], *Di post*, 20 Feb. 1938; Mojżesz Kanfer, 'Krakowski Teatr Żydowski: *Czarodziejka* (*Baba Jachne*)' [Cracow Jewish Theatre: *The Sorceress* (*Bobe Yakhne*)], *Nowy Dziennik*, 15 Feb. 1938; m., 'Prawdziwy wywiad: Żydowski Teatr Ludowy dla Dzieci i Młodzieży' [A Real Interview: Jewish Folk Theatre for Children and Youth], *Nowy Dziennik*, 25 Feb. 1938. See also: Shloyme Mendelson, 'Der tuml arum *Bobe yakhne*' [The Stir around *Bobe Yakhne*], *Folkstsaytung*, 9 Apr. 1937; A. Grafman, 'Di bobe-yakhne un ir kishef-lid' [Bobe Yakhne and her Magic Song], *Moment*, 16 Mar. 1937; A. L. Taf, 'Der spektakl inem "Teater far yugnt": di oyffirung fun der *Kishefmakherin* (*Bobe yakhne*)' [A Performance in 'Youth Theatre': The Production of *The Sorceress* (*Bobe Yakhne*)], *Der yunger dor*, 4 (1937), 7; 'A nay idish teater in varshe far kinder' [A New Jewish Theatre for Children in Warsaw], *Haynt*, 18 Feb. 1937; A. Foygl, 'A vikhtiger kultur-gesheyenish in varshe' [An Important Cultural Event in Warsaw], *Haynt*, 9 Mar. 1937; Elkhonen Tseytlin, 'A vort in der diskusye (Arum der polemik vegen der *Kishefmakherin*)' [A Word in the Discussion (About the Dispute over *The Sorceress*)], *Unzer ekspres*, 16 Apr. 1937; Moyshe Perenson, 'Goldfaden un manger: tsu der oyffirung fun di *Kishefmakherin*' [Goldfaden and Manger: On the Production of *The Sorceress*], *Naye folkstsaytung*, 29 Mar. 1937. I would like to thank Anna Hannowa of Wrocław for sharing with me the latter newspaper clippings from Yankev Rotboym's personal archives.

Yiddish. A newspaper article addressed to this potential audience and written in Polish told them about the origins of the professional Yiddish theatre and its founder.[29]

In its original version the play tells the story of 16-year-old Mirele. Her mother has died giving birth to her, and her father, Avrom, has been imprisoned following a false accusation. The girl is left at the mercy of her evil stepmother, Bashe, whose aunt, the sorceress Bobe Yakhne (customarily played by a man), imprisons her with a group of other girls and finally sells her into white slavery. Luckily, Mirele's beloved, Marcus, frees Avrom from prison and finds Mirele in a café in Istanbul. He manages to free her with the help of a wandering pedlar, Hotsmakh. Having learned of their return, Bashe and Bobe Yakhne plan to stop them on their way, induce them to sleep in an inn, and burn them while they are asleep. But the tables are turned, the virtuous are rescued, and the villains die in the fire.

Manger preserved only two scenes from Goldfaden's plot: those in Mirele's house and at the market square. He changed the thrust of the plot, which was no longer driven by Bashe's desire to seize Mirele's and Avrom's property. In Manger's version Bobe Yakhne takes revenge on Avrom for sharing the miraculous song of liberation and happiness she has written rather than keeping it to himself. In place of one Hotsmakh—a poor travelling salesman—the adapter introduced three Hotsmakhs, rendering him more explicitly a symbol of an entire social group: the oppressed Jewish masses. However, this change shifts the focus from the tragic fate of an innocent girl to the troubles of the pedlar. In this version Hotsmakh wanders all over the world in search of the song of liberation, and, having found it, learns from Bobe Yakhne that it was not meant for him and that the Hotsmakhs (the Jewish masses) need a different kind of song.

Rotboym's direction drew out the nuances of the adaptation and emphasized the spectacle of the play. The stage was transformed into an enchanted mirror on which images from the borderline between reality and dream appeared. Audiences were very impressed by the first scene, in which three beautiful girls wearing tulle dance and sing while preparing magic incense for Bobe Yakhne; they also praised the scenes with the three Hotsmakhs. At one stage two children appeared in front of the curtain to point out specific members of the audience to whom the performance was addressed. The charm of the primitive and fairytale atmosphere this created was enhanced by elements of the tragic nature of contemporary Jewish life. In Kanfer's opinion[30] the Polish set designer, Jan Kosiński, although not a Jew himself, had successfully entered into the spirit of Jewish folklore, creating colourful and original sets,

---

[29] See m., 'Prawdziwy wywiad'.   [30] See Kanfer, 'Krakowski: Teatr Żydowski'.

costumes, and lighting effects. The beautiful music, composed by Henekh Kohn, based on folk motifs both naive and romantic, and in the spirit of the fantastic whole, contributed to the fairytale atmosphere of the performance; especially memorable was the enchanted melody which brings luck. The influence of the *commedia dell'arte* was evident in the actors' performances. Besides tripling the number of Hotsmakhs, perhaps the most novel feature of Manger and Rotboym's adaptation was that, rather than following the tradition of casting a man as Bobe Yakhne, they cast the exceptionally beautiful actress Dina Halpern.

The production raised much controversy over the limits of a producer's creative freedom. Yekhezkel-Moyshe Neyman, the reviewer for the Warsaw daily *Haynt*, argued that, as a significant author in the history of Jewish theatre and drama, Goldfaden should not be improved upon, but played with respect.[31] The actor Avrom Morevski accused Manger of a 'cultural and moral offence worse than plagiarism' by allowing Goldfaden's name to be printed on the poster instead of his own.[32] Manger was defended by Rokhl Oyerbakh (his wife), who claimed that he had not committed any literary *khilel-hashem* (blasphemy), but had only fulfilled his aim, which was to modernize the play for contemporary children and young people. She argued further that Manger's activity so far had proved his love of the Jewish cultural tradition and his fidelity to its spiritual heritage.[33] A public discussion was held in Warsaw, labelled 'The Mock Trial of Manger's *The Sorceress*'.[34] The roles of the prosecutors were taken by Neyman, Nakhman Meisel, and Yehoshua Perle (who acknowledged the value of the adaptation, but viewed it as a new work based on motifs drawn from Goldfaden). The defence claimed that great creators could be recognized by their unceremonious handling of their material. A report of these debates was published in the Cracow Polish-language Jewish daily *Nowy Dziennik*, whose influential reviewer, Kanfer, felt that the fact that Goldfaden himself could be called the 'king of plagiarism' released his adapters from any obligation to stick to the letter of his scripts, provided they remained true to their 'spirit'.[35] This view was evidently shared by the Jewish intelligentsia in Cracow, who were open-minded and well acquainted with modern productions in European theatres.

[31] See M.K., 'Notatki teatralne: Jak *Czarownica* zaczarowała Mangera' [Theatrical Notes: How *The Sorceress* Bewitched Manger], *Nowy Dziennik*, 11 Feb. 1938.

[32] See Avrom Morevski, 'Kulturlozikeyt' [Culturelessness], *Literarishe bleter*, 14 (1937), 221–2. See also 'A. Morewski przeciwko Mangerowi' [Avrom Morevski versus Manger], *Nowy Dziennik*, 3 Apr. 1937.

[33] See Rokhl Oyerbakh, 'A mayse mit a kultur-moral' [A Story with a Cultural Message], *Literarishe bleter*, 16 (1937), 256.

[34] See M.K., 'Notatki teatralne'.   [35] Ibid.

Another outstanding staging of a Goldfaden play was brought to Cracow from Lviv. The VYKT production of the 'historical pastorale in three acts (six scenes)' *Shulamis*, adapted and directed by Zygmunt Turkow, had its première in Lviv in 1938 and in Cracow on 28 April 1939.[36]

Shulamis tells of the fatal consequences of breaking a vow. Shulamis is lost in the desert on her way from Jerusalem to Bethlehem and desperate for water. She climbs down a well, but is unable to get out again. She is saved by Avisholem, a Jewish noble returning to Jerusalem for the Sukkot holiday. They fall in love and vow eternal loyalty to each other, with a wild desert cat and the well as witnesses. When the lovers part, however, Avisholem forgets Shulamis and marries Avigayil, the daughter of a temple priest; they have two children. In the meantime, Shulamis asks the witnesses to the oath, the wildcat and the well, to avenge her. She rejects numerous suitors, including an illustrious warrior, a man of great wealth, and a respected priest. Finally, unable to postpone marriage in any other way, she feigns insanity. When Avisholem and Avigayil's children die tragically—one killed by a wildcat, the other drowned in a well—their father remembers his oath, leaves his wife, and is reunited with Shulamis.

Turkow adapted *Shulamis* to counter the spread of Nazi ideology and antisemitism with positive images of Jewish life based on examples drawn from the past. He wanted to emphasize what he felt were common Jewish characteristics: love of one's neighbour, a predilection for farming, an attachment to nature, and the ability to feel unselfish love.[37] He made a number of changes that allowed him to comment on the contemporary situation of the Jews. For example, Shulamis was shown as having given up a life of ease to stay with a simple shepherd; in Goldfaden's original she lives with her father in their poor home in Bethlehem, while her beloved is a wealthy soldier, almost a prince. Avigayil became the new, Jewish embodiment of Medea. Yet, lacking the vindictiveness and cruelty of her Greek equivalent, she suffers in silent

---

[36] For reviews of the Lviv productions, see Z. Sinkaver, 'Goldfadens *Shulamis* in a nayem levush baym "VIKT" in lemberg' [Goldfaden's *Shulamis* in a New Garb at 'VYKT' in Lemberg], *Di post*, 22 Jan. 1939; Itsik Shiper, 'Avrom goldfadn—azoy vi er iz . . .? (Randbamerkungen tsu z. turkovs oyffirung fun *Shulamis*)' [Avrom Goldfaden—Such as he is . . .? (Marginal Remarks on Zygmunt Turkow's Production of *Shulamis*)], *Di post*, 22 Jan. 1939; Yisroel Ashendorf, '*Di Shulamis*-oyffirung baym "VIKT" in Lemberg' [The Production of *Shulamis* at 'VYKT' in Lemberg], *Literarishe bleter*, 1 (1939), 12–13; A. Teatral, 'Tsu der *Shulamis*-oyffirung in "VIKT" (Etlekhe bamerkungen)' [On the Production of *Shulamis* at 'VYKT' (A Few Remarks)], *Di post*, 14 May 1939. For reviews of the Cracow productions, see M.K. and [Henryk] Apte, 'Wieczory teatralne: Zaczarowany świat sielanki miłosnej' [Nights at the Theatre: The Enchanted World of the Love Pastorale], *Nowy Dziennik*, 30 Apr. 1939.

[37] On why *Shulamis* was chosen by Zygmunt Turkow to be staged, see id., 'Dlaczego wystawiłem *Sulamitę*' [Why I Staged *Shulamis*], *Nowy Dziennik*, 28 Apr. 1939.

heroism.[38] The song 'Rozhinkes mit mandlen' (Raisins and Almonds) was reworked so that it no longer expressed dreams of becoming rich through trade, but linked the future of Jewish children with the development of knowledge and technology.[39]

Thus Turkow injected his own social commentary into Goldfaden's story by modifying several of the characters. Avisholem, a wealthy soldier, becomes a common shepherd. He does not own (or want to own) slaves since he believes it to be the first step towards a country's enslavement. His friend Khananye, formerly a peripheral character, now delivers slogans about justice. Avisholem's black-skinned servant Tsingitang, traditionally a comic figure, becomes an exponent of protest by coloured people against repression by the white race.

The scenery, designed by Fryc Kleinman, combined static with dynamic and multicoloured elements. Sets and costumes were given a period feel. The choreographer, Bella Kats, hindered by the lack of source material on Jewish dances in Palestine in those days, used instead the folk dances of neighbouring nations as models. Shloyme Prizament's music blended so well with Goldfaden's that it was difficult to distinguish the two.[40]

The production was a great success. In Cracow as in Lviv all kinds of people came to see it: older people who had grown up with the traditional Jewish folk theatre, devotees of the non-Jewish stage, regular theatregoers and those who did not normally attend Yiddish performances, young people, the intelligentsia, ordinary people, and even non-Jews. By 11 June forty performances had been given in Cracow, with a total attendance of 12,500 people.[41] This was the biggest audience for any Yiddish play in Cracow at the time.

The success of the new version of *Shulamis* led Turkow to stage a modified version of another popular Goldfaden play, *Bar kokhba*.[42] VYKT's production,

---

[38] Yitskhok Shiper noted that Goldfaden's original play contained some negative features of the stereotypical Jew, e.g. breaking promises, the greed of the communal leaders, gluttony, and the habitual drunkenness of the priests. See Shiper, 'Avrom goldfadn—azoy vi er iz . . .?'

[39] Unfortunately, Turkow's text of 'Rozhinkes mit mandlen' is not available, and the preserved reviews do not indicate more specific changes to the song's lyrics.

[40] See M.K. and Apte, 'Wieczory teatralne'.

[41] See 'Trzeci dzień niebywałego powodzenia *Sulamity*' [The Third Day of the Exceptional Success of *Shulamis*], *Nowy Dziennik*, 14 May 1939; (gr.), 'Z życia teatru: Rzadki jubileusz' [From Theatrical Life: A Rare Anniversary], *Nowy Dziennik*, 15 May 1939; 'Dziś nieodwołalnie po raz ostatni *Sulamita*' [Today *Shulamis* Plays Irrevocably for the Last Time], *Nowy Dziennik*, 25 May 1939; (gr.), 'Wymowa liczb' [The Significance of Figures], *Nowy Dziennik*, 11 June 1939.

[42] On Turkow's staging of *Bar kokhba*, see: A. Teatral, 'Naive "oystaytshung" tsi beyzvilike felshung? (Kritishe bamerkungen tsu der *Bar-kokhba*-oyffirung in "VIKT" loyt der baarbetung fun i. ashndorf)' [Naive 'Interpretation' or Malevolent Forgery? Critical Comments on the Production of *Bar kokhba* at 'VYKT' in Yisroel Ashendorf's Adaptation)], *Di post*, 7 July 1939; M.K., 'Wieczory teatralne: Goldfaden czy Aszendorf?' [Nights at the Theatre: Goldfaden or Ashendorf?], *Nowy*

with a script rewritten by Yisroel Ashendorf,[43] had its première in Lviv in February 1939, and in Cracow on 16 June the same year. In Goldfaden's version, a musical melodrama in four acts with a prologue, the introduction sketches the main forces at work in the drama. God seems to have turned his back on the Jews and left them to the mercy of the Romans. Eliezer speaks for those in the community who desire peace. An opposing faction, headed by Bar Kokhba and supported by his beloved, Eliezer's daughter Dina, insists on an uprising.

When Dina rejects the courtship of the Samaritan Papus, a rich jeweller who is black, half-blind, and lame, he vindictively advises the Romans on how to overcome the insurgents. The Roman governor, Turnus Rufus, invites Dina and her father to his palace, and holds her captive in order to lure Bar Kokhba into a trap. The Jewish hero, however, uses his tremendous physical strength to break his shackles, and escapes on the back of the lion that has been loosed upon him. Dina is held hostage and made to work like a slave; in addition, she has to resist the sexual advances not only of Papus, but also of the Roman governor. Ultimately, when used as a 'living shield' in the tower of the fortress being stormed by the Jewish insurgents, Dina commits suicide so that nothing should hold back Bar Kokhba's troops. Meanwhile, Bar Kokhba, incited by Papus, asks the Sanhedrin to judge Eliezer. Dina's father is mortally wounded by an enemy soldier, and Papus leads the Romans into the fortress. Bar Kokhba is willing to fight to the end, but, having seen the ghost of Eliezer, who tells him that it was Bar Kokhba's own inflated ego and hubris that brought defeat to the insurgents, he throws himself on his sword. Jews and Romans fight on the fortress walls. The Roman soldiers spare neither women, the elderly, nor the children. The fortress burns down.

While Goldfaden concentrated on the tragedy of an individual, shown against the backdrop of the first-century Jewish revolt against the Romans, Ashendorf introduced the historical character of Rabbi Akiva, a spiritual leader of the revolt, and representatives of various social groups (priests, assimilationists, small merchants), thus providing a cross-section of society. In the new version Bar Kokhba breaks down, not because of a personal drama, but because of the tragedy of the whole nation; he is defeated only after being confronted by a chorus of widows and mothers asking for the return of

Dziennik, 18 June 1939; M.K., 'Wieczory teatralne: *Bar Kochba* jako widowisko' [Nights at the Theatre: *Bar Kokhba* as a Spectacle], *Nowy Dziennik*, 20 June 1939; [Henryk] Apte, 'Z teatru żydowskiego: *Bar Kochba* Goldfadena' [From the Jewish Theatre: Goldfaden's *Bar Kokhba*], *Nowy Dziennik*, 27 June 1939; H.W., 'Dekoracja *Bar Kochby*' [The Scenery for *Bar Kokhba*], *Nowy Dziennik*, 1 July 1939.

[43] For the author on his adaptation, see Yisroel Ashendorf, 'Jak opracowałem *Bar Kochbę*' [How I Adapted *Bar Kokhba*], *Nowy Dziennik*, 16 June 1939.

their husbands and sons. Ashendorf also gave the role of Papus a more solid psychological base, making him commit treachery, not out of revenge for his rejection by Dina or jealousy of Bar Kokhba, but, in an echo of the opening soliloquy of Shakespeare's *Richard III*, because he feels unfairly treated by nature, and so avenges himself on his fellow man.

Ashendorf saw in Goldfaden's familiar play a means of empowering his fellow Jews, who had been charged with cowardice by their enemies, and of providing them with the incentive to do battle in the future. However, he needed to alter the play's apocalyptic ending. Although the outcome of the historic last Jewish revolt against the Romans could not be changed, the mood at the end of the play could be. Ashendorf therefore ended his historical folk opera not with the death of the protagonist, but with Akiva's optimistic encouragement to his followers to survive, assuring them of the immortality of the Jewish people. Ashendorf's adaptation caused some controversy, especially among those who did not share his political views.[44] On this occasion, however, nobody denied him the right to an interpretation different from that of the author.

The inventiveness of Zygmunt Turkow, the director, was praised, specifically in relation to the staging of the Hamlet-like struggle between Bar Kokhba and the victims' ghosts, Eliezer's death, the well-organized crowd scenes, and the powerful final scene. The designer, Fryc Kleinman, kept the set uncluttered, relying instead for effect on allusion and suggestive detail. For instance, pillars in the Jewish buildings were decorated with Hebraic motifs; in non-Jewish buildings they were decorated with Roman ones. The emblem of freedom and the Jewish rebels who fought for it was the lion, whereas the symbol of the ruling classes was the eagle. The Romans wore gaudy clothing embellished with shiny gold and magic symbols, while the costumes of the Jews were white. Akiva's costume was decorated with a *talit* motif.

Turkow's staging, though impressive, was blamed for having too weak a foundation in the original play. A similar objection was advanced about *Shulamis*.

Architecture is a very subtle art, although from the outside it impresses us with its force. The first rule of architecture is not to erect mighty colossi on foundations designed for light, airy villas. Zygmunt Turkow does not always observe the rule. He loves theatre so much, he has so much to say, he is so full of ideas that, incautiously, he places too much burden on the foundations. For example, *Shulamis* is supposed to be a historical pastorale, yet in some places it is an oratorio, in other

---

[44] See e.g. M.K., 'Wieczory teatralne: Goldfaden czy Aszendorf?' and Teatral, 'Naive "oystaytshung"'.

places an ancient Greek opera, not to mention the utterly grotesque emphasis on the . . . black equal rights movement.[45]

Yet, despite extensive departures from the original versions in both cases, this time the critics did not accuse the director and adapter of being unfaithful to the author. The new versions achieved the same objectives as those that guided Goldfaden when he wrote the original plays. They cheered the spirit, awakened national pride, and strengthened the bonds with the nation's past. This seems to have fully absolved Ashendorf and Turkow.

This survey of productions of Goldfaden's plays on the Yiddish stages of Cracow raises several points. First, it demonstrates the way in which the plays of the 'father of the Yiddish Theatre' remained in the repertoire while, almost indiscernibly, their meaning was transformed. In the process the generally accepted limits on the freedom to adapt them for modern audiences were redefined. Initially audiences hoped to return to pleasant memories of the past, to bask in nostalgia among Goldfaden's music and songs performed in familiar ways, so they were offended by attempts to smuggle in new contextual and formal elements. Then they began to acknowledge the right of the producer and director to discover new meaning in the plays, especially if such discoveries were accompanied by sensitivity to the needs of the contemporary audience. Adaptations were valued when they were perceived as fulfilling a significant social and national role, lifting the audience's spirits and awakening pride in their history and culture.

This brief examination has also shown how conservative the staging process was on the provincial scene, including in Cracow. While Goldfaden's plays were successfully modernized in the Soviet Union and the United States, and even in other centres of Jewish theatre in Poland such as Warsaw, the audiences in Cracow—and not only the less educated, more conservative ones, but also those acquainted with Polish and European dramatic theatre—continued to support these works in their traditional form until the 1930s. It should also be remembered that when the original adaptations were brought to Cracow (since none of them originated there), they did not supersede traditional stagings, and for some time the two styles coexisted.

This discussion also provides insight into the evolution of Jewish theatrical ambitions, based on the example of a single town. Originally audiences and reviewers were satisfied with competently performed songs and background music, and general adherence to the spirit of the time, with primitive sets and

[45] M.K., 'Wieczory teatralne: Goldfaden czy Aszendorf?'

effects. Later, under the influence of the Polish theatre, which was patronized by the Jewish intelligentsia, the Jewish theatre was expected both to achieve an artistic standard equal to that of reputable non-Jewish theatres, and to contribute to the discussion about modern Jewish identity and the future of the nation. The eminent creators of the Jewish theatre in Poland in this period seem to have been successful in fulfilling these expectations. In the exchange with other Yiddish theatre centres Cracow benefited more than it contributed, but Cracow Jews were responsive to the changing trends in staging.

IV. CENSORSHIP

NINE

'Exit, Pursued by a Bear': The Ban on Yiddish Theatre in Imperial Russia

ॐ

JOHN KLIER

'CULTURE WARS', both symbolic and actual, play such an important part in modern societies that there is an understandable temptation for scholars to seek historical parallels. The Russian empire would seem to offer a very appropriate example. The politics of language played a prominent role in what might anachronistically be termed Russia's 'ethnic politics'. Every Polish rebellion that was quashed was followed by restrictions on the use of the Polish language in education and civic life in the Kingdom of Poland. Polish influence in the western provinces was undermined by a series of policies collectively known as Russification, of which language restrictions formed a central part.[1] Fearful that the Poles were using the nascent Ukrainian national movement to sow discord in the disputed borderlands, the Russian government notoriously placed a ban on Ukrainian in 1876.[2] In 1885 the governor of Bessarabia refused permission to a Romanian-language theatre troupe to perform in Kishinev on the grounds that the use of Russian was spreading too slowly in Bessarabia and separatism had not yet been fully extinguished.[3]

Tsarist language politics could hardly avoid the Jews. Indeed, the empire's first attempt to frame a comprehensive code for the Jews in 1804 included incentives to master non-Jewish languages.[4] In 1862 the Ministries of

---

[1] One of the first after-effects of the rebellion of 1863 was the replacement of the bilingual Polish–Russian *Vilenskii Vestnik* (Vilna Herald) by a purely Russian version. For the impact on other nationalities, see David Saunders, 'Russia and Ukraine under Alexander II: The Valuev Edict of 1863', *International History Review*, 17/1 (1995), 23–50; id., 'Russia's Ukrainian Policy (1847–1905): A Demographic Approach', *European History Quarterly*, 25 (1995), 181–208; and John D. Klier, 'The Polish Revolt of 1863 and the Birth of Russification: Bad for the Jews?', *Polin*, 1 (1986), 91–106.

[2] See Fedir Savchenko, *Zaborona ukrainstva 1876 r.* [The Suppression of Ukrainian Activities in 1876] (Kharkiv: Derzhavie vidavnitstvo Ukraini, 1930; repr. Munich: Wilhelm Funk Verlag, 1970).

[3] Michael F. Hamm, 'Kishinev: The Character and Development of a Tsarist Frontier Town', *Nationalities Papers*, 26/1 (1998), 25.

[4] John D. Klier, *Russia Gathers her Jews* (DeKalb: Northern Illinois University Press, 1986), 136.

Education and Internal Affairs exchanged opinions over whether a ban on Yiddish publishing might expedite the process of Jewish acculturation.[5] Thus, the decision to outlaw the public performance of Yiddish plays—directed at a population group within these same disputed Russo-Polish territories— would seem to be redolent with political significance. The ban undoubtedly had great significance for the cultural history of east European Jewry. 'The father of the Yiddish theatre', Goldfaden, is reported to have cried out 'My child has perished in broad daylight!' when he first received news of the prohibition.[6] Yet the origins of the ban and the intentions of the authorities remain unclear to this day. Confirming the axiom that rumour expands to fill the vacuum left by the absence of facts, a series of myths and legends grew up surrounding the ban.

Many of these stories were prompted by another obscure episode, the presumed lifting of the ban in 1905. Early in that year a number of newspapers reported—erroneously, it seems—that the ban had been withdrawn. This prompted a spate of stories about how it had been imposed in the first place. In March 1905 the *Peterburgskaya Gazeta* carried an article which claimed that the St Petersburg *gradonachal'nik* (town governor), General P. A. Gresser, had been present at a performance of *Doktor almosado* (Dr Almosado) by Goldfaden's troupe in 1883. He had been struck by one scene in which an actor burst into tears, as did many in the audience. What was the reason for the tears, he asked Goldfaden. 'The actor is weeping onstage because the Jew is persecuted everywhere. He does not have a refuge since everywhere he is told: "Go! Go!" As a result he has nowhere to lay his head and hasn't even a crust of bread.' General Gresser frowned, then announced: 'Well, if you are complaining that you are without bread, then you don't need an audience', and the right to perform was withdrawn.[7] While this anecdote may convey the sense of administrative capriciousness that bedevilled the Jewish theatre, it does not satisfactorily explain a nationwide ban.

The Jewish press also debated the ban. In January 1905 the *Nedel'naya Khronika Voskhoda* (Weekly Chronicle of Sunrise) reprinted a story about the

---

[5] The proposal foundered on the opposition of the minister of education, who feared that a ban on Yiddish would merely raise its status in the eyes of the devout (P. S. Usov, 'Iz moikh vospominanii', *Istoricheskii Vestnik*, 11 (Jan.–Mar. 1883), 342–3. The discussion of Yiddish paralleled a similar discussion about tolerating Ukrainian.

[6] L. O. Tretsek, 'O vozrozhdenii evreiskogo teatra' [The Resurrection of the Jewish Theatre], *Nedel'naya Khronika Voskhoda*, 12 (24 Mar. 1905), 45. Goldfaden is said to have received the news during the interval after Act IV of *Bar kokhba*, at the time of its fifth performance. This conjecture may be the source of another legend, put forward by Soviet researchers, that the 'Zionism' of *Bar kokhba* was responsible for the ban.

[7] Evgeny Binevich, *Nachalo evreiskogo teatra v Rossii* [The Origin of the Jewish Theatre in Russia] (Moscow: Jewish Heritage Society, 1994), 6.

lifting of the ban that had first appeared in *Odesskie Novosti* (Odessa News) from the pen of L. O. Tretsek. Tretsek attributed the original ban to the minister of the interior, N. P. Ignatiev, who had issued it as a temporary measure 'at the very height of the Jewish pogroms in 1883'. The reported cause was a denunciation sent to the minister by a representative of the London Missionary Society, Dr Ben-Tsion. The motive of his denunciation was Goldfaden's refusal to produce plays written by Ben-Tsion, which had a Christian message.[8] Even at the time this account was challenged. N. Prizhansky, also writing in *Nedel'naya Khronika Voskhoda*, claimed to have seen Ben-Tsion's plays, denied that they had a Christian message, and attributed Goldfaden's refusal to the simple fact that they were 'very bad'. As for denunciations to the authorities, Prizhansky pointed out that the aggressively antisemitic *Novorossiiskii Telegraf* (Novorossiisk Telegraph), published in Odessa, had conducted a regular campaign against the young Jewish theatre, and might serve as a more realistic culprit.[9]

Dmitry Elyashevich, the leading contemporary researcher on tsarist censorship and the Jewish question, has attempted to find a factual basis for these stories by establishing the identity of Dr Ben-Tsion, and has identified him as the young Jewish religious reformer Ya. M. Priluker, then active in Odessa. In 1882 Priluker published a book devoted to the reform of Judaism under the pseudonym Emmanuel Ben-Sion.[10] He later converted to Christianity and emigrated to England. He had links to the censor of Jewish plays N. D. Rapoport. (As an additional irony, his collaborator in the project of radical Jewish religious reform was Jacob Gordin, who, after emigrating to New York, became one of the leading lights of the American Yiddish theatre.)

Despite the many coincidences, Elyashevich himself admits that there are a number of problems with his theory. Priluker was never a representative of a London missionary society and, despite a wide-ranging literary career, never wrote plays in any language. Nor do the dates fit. In 1883 Priluker was a 23-year-old assistant schoolmaster resisting efforts by the Jewish community to dismiss him from his post because of his eccentric religious views. He was

---

[8] 'Bibliografiya' [Bibliography], *Nedel'naya Khronika Voskhoda*, 4 (27 Jan. 1905). In his memoirs, published in 1913, Avrom Fishzon also attributed the ban to the intervention of Ben-Tsion. See A. Fishzon, 'Zapiski evreiskogo antreprenera' [Notes of a Jewish Entrepreneur], *Biblioteka 'Teatra i Iskusstva'*, 12 (1913), 18.

[9] N. Prizhansky, 'O vozrozhdenii evreiskogo teatra' [On the Revival in Jewish Theatre], *Nedel'naya Khronika Voskhoda*, 8 (24 Feb. 1905). The articles in question appeared in *Novorossiiskii Telegraf*, 2381 (9 Jan. 1883), 2404 (6 Feb. 1883), and 2440 (23 Mar. 1883). It should also be noted that Ignatiev was not then the minister of the interior.

[10] E. Ben-Zion, *Evrei reformatory* [Jewish Reformers] (St Petersburg: no publisher given, 1882).

not a doctor of any sort.[11] The Ben-Tsion whom both Tretsek and Prizhansky claimed to know well was a man of some means who was prominent in the community. This identification simply will not serve for Priluker. The role of the censor Rapoport must remain conjectural without the discovery of documentary proof of his involvement.[12]

A curious file in the archive of the Department of Police of the Ministry of Internal Affairs (MVD) suggests that the origin of the ban was an almost casual decision, and certainly one that lacked real political weight. It also provides evidence that, in consequence, the ban was strikingly ineffective. In doing so, it permits us a glance into the travails and triumphs of the travelling Yiddish theatre in the late Russian empire.[13]

ORIGINS OF THE BAN

The police agencies of the tsarist regime were assiduous readers of the press. In early 1879 an article in the provincial newspaper *Odesskii Vestnik* (Odessa Herald) caught the eye of an official of the Chief Office of Press Affairs, the GUpDP (i.e. the censorship agency). It reported that a play had been presented in Odessa in the Jewish *zhargon*, the standard term for Yiddish. The play had been directed by a Russian subject from Mitau, a certain Obershneder, and the director of the Bucharest Jewish Company, Goldfaden.[14] The company had presented a series of musical-literary evenings at the Craftsmen's Club and the Odessa Mariinsky Theatre. The sharp-eyed censor was curious since he could not recall any play in Yiddish ever having been submitted to the theatrical censor.

A query to the *gradonachal'nik* of Odessa elicited the explanation that the play in question had been reviewed by the local censor of Jewish texts, Yu. M. Bardakh. Since there was no legal ban on such performances, the police had issued the necessary permission. The *gradonachal'nik* himself had no

---

[11] For Priluker's recollections of these days, see Jaakoff Prelooker, *Under the Czar and Queen Victoria* (London: no publisher given, 1895), 22–42.

[12] See the discussion in D. A. Elyashevich, *Pravitel'stvennaya politika i evreiskaya pechat' v Rossii, 1797–1917* [Government Policy and Jewish Printing in Russia, 1797–1917] (St Petersburg: Mosty Kul'tury; Jerusalem: Gesharim, 1999), 475–8. Elyashevich makes the important point that the prohibition was directed *only* against the Yiddish theatre. Yiddish book and newspaper publishing was allowed to continue (p. 478).

[13] The file in question, covering the period 1883–1904, is that of the Second Section of the Department of Police, in the Gosudarstvennyi Arkhiv Rossiiskoi Federatsii (State Archive of the Russian Federation), Moscow (GARF), *fond* 102 (2-oe deloproizvodstvo), *opis'* 40, *delo* 287, *ll.* 99. Citations from this source will be simply to 'GARF', followed by page number.

[14] Names in this chapter are translated from their Russian forms, as found in official documentation, with the exception of a few especially well-known figures.

objections. Quite the contrary: he saw the Jewish theatre as a healthy moral influence on the Jews. He was convinced that the Jewish popular theatre, properly supervised, could help to guide the Jewish masses to a healthier understanding of their civil and state obligations.[15] The GUpDP informed the *gradonachal'nik* in turn that review by the local censor was not enough; all plays had to be submitted to a special theatrical censor. The Odessa authorities responded by sending all the plays in the repertoire of the Jewish theatre for approval. (One source claims that Goldfaden himself made the journey to St Petersburg to shepherd the scripts through the censorship.[16]) On 3 January 1880 permission was granted for the presentation of Jewish plays in St Petersburg itself, and plays began to flood in to the censor. If the GUpDP had sought to make more work for itself, it had succeeded.

The censors were not pleased when they began to delve into the Yiddish repertoire. The theatrical censor found them 'inconvenient' (*neudobno*) for presentation on the stage and was puzzled as to how they had ever passed a censor's review. Worse, the number of plays presented for consideration was growing by the day. On 27 July 1883 the head of the censorship office, E. M. Feokistov, reported to the director of police, V. K. Pleve, that 'the minister' (not further identified) was amazed that public performances in Yiddish, which he assumed had not taken place before 1879, were now being permitted. He announced that the police were henceforth to impose a ban on dramas presented in Yiddish. On 17 August 1883 the deputy minister of internal affairs sent a circular to all governors. It was direct and to the point: 'In recognition of the fact that some plays in Yiddish, which have been authorized at the present time, appear to be quite inappropriate for stage presentation, it has been seen as necessary to prohibit any future theatrical presentations in conversational Jewish.' Since all theatrical performances had to be approved by the police, the circular noted, the withholding of police approval would be the obvious way to enforce the ban.

What made the content of Yiddish plays 'inconvenient'? Some clues may be found in a circular sent to governors under the signature of the minister of internal affairs, D. A. Tolstoy, dated 18 August 1883, which noted that

in the course of 1880, 1881, 1882 and 1883 there emerged a number of Jewish troupes which were permitted to perform plays in Jewish *zhargon*, the plays themselves

---

[15] GARF, *ll.* 1–4ᵛ. Russian officials were not always so sanguine about the uses of popular theatre. In 1888, fearing the potential of theatre to 'corrupt the masses', the Ministry of Internal Affairs created a special censorship board with a mandate to oversee popular theatres. See E. Anthony Swift, 'Fighting the Germs of Disorder: The Censorship of Russian Popular Theatre, 1888–1917', *Russian History*, 18 (Spring 1991), 4. In its casual level of organization, and the random nature of its repertoire, the Russian popular theatre displayed many affinities with the Yiddish theatre in Russia and abroad.   [16] Binevich, 'Nachalo', 21.

having been submitted to the censor in the Jewish alphabet. The inconvenience of such a procedure soon became evident. Governors and the police authorities encountered extreme difficulties in controlling the performance of plays owing to the absence of responsible persons who knew *zhargon*. It also became evident that Jewish entrepreneurs were abusing the ignorance of the language on the part of the local authorities and were putting on the stage not only material which was permitted, but also that which was directly forbidden. This circumstance was the cause, in part, of the dissatisfaction of the clerical authorities, when scenes from the Holy Scriptures insulting to Christian religious feelings began to appear on the stages of Jewish theatre.[17]

This documentation offers little to go on, since the file lacks details that might have confirmed Tolstoy's claim. His pretext resembles the warning, given decades before, by the governor-general of Odessa to the Jewish newspaper editor O. A. Rabinovich: 'If something appears in your paper that does not please me, or if it should bore me when I read it, or if I just feel like it, or if perhaps my stomach aches, I will close your paper down immediately.'[18]

But something is missing from this picture. The authorities most involved in the ban were policemen, not censors. Had there been an ideological or political aspect to the case, we might have expected to find the comments of censors taking issue with the content of the plays which they had read. There were certainly specialist censors for Jewish materials in Hebrew and Yiddish attached to the St Petersburg Censorship Directorate.[19] Moreover, we know that the most popular works in the pre-ban repertoire had been passed by the censor. (In 1909 the German Jewish Troupe in Warsaw was able to produce Yiddish-language plays which carried the seal of the Chief Office for Press Affairs and the legend 'Plays Permitted for Performance'. It is unclear from the documentation when these approvals were given.[20]) There is no trace of critical comment from the censors in the file, nor complaints from the Russian public that might have triggered an investigation, as was a common

[17] Elyashevich, *Pravitel'stvennaya politika*, 477. It is this latter, religious, concern that Elyashevich connects to the religious reformer Priluker (ibid.). The first complaint about the religious content of Yiddish plays to be found in the file under examination dates to 1890. See Table 9.1, 1890 (Jewish Theatrical Troupe) and 1900.

[18] Yu. I. Gessen, 'Smena obshchestvennykh techenii. II. "Pervyi russko-evreiskii organ"' [The Shift of Social Trends, II: The First Russian Jewish Periodical], *Perezhitoe*, 3 (1911), 57 (hereafter 'Pervyi'). Matters were not helped by the negative opinion that the authorities had developed of Goldfaden. One report characterized him as a person who had a 'bad reputation' and was an 'immoral individual' who was known only as a theatrical producer and a 'compiler of harmful plays' (Elyashevich, *Pravitel'stvennaya politika*, 703).

[19] I. P. Foote, 'The St Petersburg Censorship Committee, 1828–1905', *Oxford Slavonic Papers*, NS 24 (1991), 69.   [20] GARF, *l.* 91ᵛ.

phenomenon of the time.[21] While the police authorities may well have been troubled by their inability to monitor Yiddish-language plays properly, it is curious in the extreme that the clerical authorities would have any knowledge at all of the contents of the Yiddish stage. Perhaps the negative criticism of the *Novorossiiskii Telegraf* did have a role to play here, but again the documentation has not come to light.

It should be borne in mind that, while plays had to be approved by the censorship authorities, this did not guarantee their production. According to Article 135 of the Russian Criminal Code, *all* public performances and activities were subject to approval by the police. A good case could be made that the ban grew out of public order considerations. The Ministry of Internal Affairs was Janus-faced: one face was that of the sophisticated censor, the other that of the policeman. It is to the latter that the ban may well be traced.

Certainly the MVD continued to worry about pogroms and the possibility that they might arise from public gatherings, such as theatrical presentations. The riotous fairs that initiated the celebration of the Russian Orthodox Easter were curtailed during this period in order to reduce the chance of clashes between Christians and Jews. During the 1882 Russian Christmas holidays in Berdichev all businesses, as well as the Jewish theatre, were closed as a precaution.[22] At least one pogrom in 1882 arose from a dispute over the performance of a Jewish puppet theatre in the *shtetl* of Irkmeev, in Poltava province.[23] At the very beginning of the ban the Moscow police chief, A. A. Kozlov, sought to have it extended to include Russian-language performances in private theatres which lampooned Jews 'and which could easily lead to the arousal of disdain and ill feeling towards the Jews'.[24] On the other hand, the 1883 ban hardly occurred at the height of the pogroms. The phenomenon of mass pogroms had been halted by 1883. That year saw only one major pogrom, in Ekaterinoslav.

The ultimate answer may be simpler still. It should be remembered that the Jewish theatre was a novelty in Russia, so that a performance in Odessa was unusual enough to catch the eye of a St Petersburg official in 1879. The appearance of troupes in the Russian capital itself necessitated requests for residence permits, the right to hire theatres and halls, and the certification of

[21] See e.g. the Kiev archives for a copy of a Yiddish theatrical poster sent to the office of the governor-general of Kiev in 1876. It advertises 'a selection of scenes from Jewish life' performed by a Jewish troupe under the direction of Avrom Fishzon (Tsentral′nyi Gosudarstvennyi Arkhiv Ukrainy, Kiev, *fond* 442, *opis′* 57, *delo* 1 (25 Apr. 1876), *l.* 28).   [22] *Rassvet*, 2 (12 Jan. 1882).
[23] GARF, *fond* 102, *opis′* 39 (1882–5), *delo* 280, *chast* 12, *ll.* 21–3.
[24] GARF, *l.* 9ᵛ. On this occasion Pleve rejected a specific ban on such productions, suggesting instead that the police use their powers to ban public performances. Binevich also points to the fear of pogroms as a major motivation for the ban ('Nachalo', 22).

the repertoire.[25] As we have seen in Tolstoy's circular, this placed demands on the uniformed police and on the censorship bureaucracy. The Jews were, in effect, asking for favours. This was a time, moreover, when the authorities were hardly in the mood to make the lives of the empire's Jews easier or to grant them what might be seen as new prerogatives. To legalize the Jewish stage meant to take a positive step. It was much more convenient for officials to follow the Russian legal tradition that held that 'everything that is not specifically permitted to the Jews is to be considered forbidden'. The decisive word here is the one that continually reappeared in correspondence concerning the theatrical ban: the presentation of Yiddish plays was 'inconvenient'.

This interpretation gains force when it is recognized that the ban was implemented in the form of a police order. The circular banning Yiddish plays was sent under the name of the deputy minister of internal affairs, P. A. Orzhevsky, whose job was primarily to supervise the police. The ban was clearly made the brief of the police, since the instruction emphasized that it was the police who were charged with authorizing public performances.[26] In short, it appears to have lacked an ideological motivation. It fell into the category of low-level antisemitism, which permeated so much of the official treatment of the Jews after 1881: when given the choice, the authorities found it easier to be unpleasant to Jews rather than nice to them. Still less was it convenient to grant them new 'privileges'.

FAILURE OF THE BAN

Since, in my interpretation, the ban itself was casual and offhand, it is not surprising that little thought had been given to methods of enforcement. Indeed, the ban seems to have belonged to that category of restrictive legislation on Jews that existed primarily to supplement the income of the notoriously underpaid local police. This would explain its widespread failure. The guile of Jewish theatrical entrepreneurs is well known: they renamed their troupes 'German Jewish', and pretended to perform in German, as a means of circumventing the law. Yiddish producers submitted German versions of Yiddish plays to the theatrical censor in Warsaw, where they were approved.[27]

---

[25] Efforts have been made to identify the audience for early Jewish theatrical efforts in Bucharest. It would be useful to have a study of the audience in St Petersburg, which was large enough to keep the companies busy before—and after—the ban.

[26] It is significant that the first enquiries about enforcement of the new ban were handled by the police. Besides the enquiry in 1883, by the police chief in Moscow, it was the Department of Police which helped the governor of Tambov to decide whether the ban extended to plays with stereotypical Jewish characters speaking in a Russian-Yiddish mishmash (GARF, *ll.* 13–14).

[27] GARF, *l.* 91ᵛ.

These texts could then be shown to the local police in order to secure permission for a performance. As Tolstoy had lamented, there were few jurisdictions in which the policemen were fluent in Yiddish and could ensure that the text, as performed, was German and not German Jewish. Even allowing for this ruse, the fact remains that the local police, of high and low rank, were willing to authorize the performances of almost any Jewish theatre group that entered their jurisdiction. In 1888 the GUpDP in St Petersburg complained to the governor-general of the north-west (Vilna, Kovno, and Grodno provinces) that it had received numerous theatrical posters that clearly demonstrated that Jewish theatrical troupes were widely performing unapproved plays in Yiddish.[28] Exhortations to prevent such activities were clearly unsuccessful. In a confidential circular to governors in 1891 the MVD complained that Jewish companies were moving freely from town to town, 'with the permission of police chiefs and *ispravniki* [local police officials]'.[29] They performed classics of the Yiddish theatre, and nobody was fooled that these performances were in anything but *zhargon*. (See Table 9.1 for information on such performances gleaned from Moscow and provincial archives.)

The leaders of the young Yiddish theatre, many of whom claimed to be operating from altruistic rather than mercantile motives, continued to bombard the MVD with requests for an exemption from the ban in the cause of the greater good. Lazar Tsukerman submitted a petition to the tsar in 1884 arguing that his company sought to influence in a positive manner 'a certain class of the Jewish population'. Moreover, he noted, his troupes gave employment to more than 200 artists.[30] In 1898 a former military doctor (and thus a member of the Russian Jewish intellectual elite), A. B. Rosenbaum, asked for permission to stage one Yiddish play, as a controlled experiment, with the objective of encouraging the Jews to undertake honest and productive labour.[31] In 1905 Mark Arnshteyn sent a telegram to the tsar asking for permission to open a Yiddish-language Jewish Popular Theatre with the aim of spreading 'true enlightenment' among Warsaw Jews.[32] In September 1905 Elizaveta Vasilevna Kivshenko, the widow of no less than a professor at the Imperial Academy of Art, sought to sponsor a tour of the Pale by a Yiddish theatre company.[33]

All of the above requests were denied, along with many others. Most of the would-be impresarios accepted their refusal with good grace. Avrom Fishzon was a striking exception. In 1888, according to police records, he founded a Yiddish-language troupe and began to travel about the Pale. When the police

[28] Lietuvos Centrinis Valstybinis Archyvas (Central State Archive of Lithuania), Vilnius, *fond* 378, *opis'* 180, *delo* 82 (24 Oct. 1888), *l.* 2ᵛ.   [29] GARF, *l.* 20ᵛ.   [30] GARF, *ll.* 15–18.   [31] GARF, *ll.* 21–6.   [32] GARF, *ll.* 45ᵛ–46.   [33] GARF, *ll.* 79–80.

Table 9.1 Performances of Yiddish theatre groups in the Russian empire (actual and proposed) under the ban of 1883

Date	Company	Director/artistic director	Location and/or itinerary	Repertoire (where available)	Comments
1883[a]	Moscow Jewish Dramatic and Opera Troupe	L. S. Gartenshteyn	Minsk		One of the first cases of the ban
1884–5[b]	German Jewish troupe	n.a.	Vitebsk province		Sought permission from the authorities
Before 24 Oct. 1888[c]	n.a.	Avrom Fishzon, Tantsman, N. K. Shaykevitsh, and others	Governor-general of the north-west (Vilna, Kovno, Grodno provinces)		Complaint of GUpDP to governor-general of north-west
1888–90	Unnamed	Avrom Fishzon	Rovno (1890); towns near Pale		
1890	Society of Operetta Artists	Avrom Fishzon	Rovno	Goldfaden, *Fanatik* (The Two Kuni Lemls)	With permission of police authorities
	Company of Russian–German Operetta Artists	V. Antsipovich	Belz	*Bal-tshuve* (Penitent); *Fanatik*; *Razbitoe schastie* or *Evreiskii pan* (Broken Happiness; or, The Jewish Gentleman); *Inkvizitsiia* (The Inquisition)	With permission of local police
	Jewish Theatrical Troupe	Avrom Kaminsky	Łódź, Kiev, Odessa, Gomel, Mogilev, Kovebkov (Chernigov province)		Denounced to police by Mikhail Kazansky for presenting plays in Yiddish that were 'insulting to the [Russian] Orthodox faith'
1890–1	Troupe of K. Branitsky	K. Branitsky	Ekaterinoslav (2 Dec.); Pavlograd (22 Dec., 9 Jan. 1891); Aleksandrovsk (12, 22, 28 Jan. 1891)	*Evreiskii pan* (The Jewish Gentleman); Goldfaden, *Fanatik, Doctor Almosado Shmendrik, Kapriznaia doch'* (The Capricious Daughter), *Kaptsnzon et hungerman, Shulamis, Koldunye* (aka *Di kishefmakherin*, The Sorceress)	All with permission of police authorities
1893	German Operetta Artists	V. Antsipovich and K. Branitsky	Vinnitsa (2 Nov. 1893)	*Shulamis*	Russian translation had been prohibited

Date	Company	Director/artistic director	Location and/or itinerary	Repertoire (where available)	Comments
1898	German Troupe of Kompaneyets	Yankl Goltsman	Minsk		
1899	German Dramatic–Operetta Troupe	Yakov Spivakovsky (director); Avrom Fishzon (artistic director)	Odessa (22–8 Sept. 1899)		Run stopped by Odessa police chief
1900	n.a.	Avrom Fishzon (artistic director)	Simferopol	*Zhertvoprinoshenie Isaaka, ili, Sodom i Gomorra* (The Sacrifice of Isaac; or, Sodom and Gomorrah) by Stambulka (9 Mar. 1900)	Complaints from Holy Synod about motifs 'insulting to Christianity', incl. depiction of biblical figures; inspired MVD circular to governors reminding them to enforce Yiddish ban
1901					
	Unnamed German Jewish theatrical troupe	Tolpud	Pinsk, Bobrinsk		Permission refused
12 Mar.	German Jewish troupe	n.a.	St Petersburg	*Velizarii*; *Evropeitsy v Amerike* (Europeans in America)	
2 Oct.	Warsaw German Dramatic–Operetta Troupe	M. O. Vaysfeld	Rostov-na-Donu	*Doktor Yozelman* ([*sic*]: *Rebbe Yozelman*)	
1905 14 Feb.	Unnamed troupe	Nosn Rosenblum (director); Avrom Fishzon (artistic director)	Peschanka		Permission refused
18 Feb.	n.a.	n.a.	Vitebsk		Permission refused
15 Mar.	The Lovers of the Dramatic Arts of the *Shtetl* of Dunaevich, Podolia province	Iakov Vasserman (artistic director); Asher Aberbakh (asst. artistic director)	Dunaevich	*Uriel acosta* by Karl Gutzkow; Goldfaden, *Koldunye*, *Kenig akhashveyresh* (King Ahasuerus), *Di bobe mitn eynikl*, *Di tsvey kuni leml*; *Bar kokhba*; *Shulamis*; *Zhidovka* (La Juive) by Eugène Scribe, *Razvod* (Divorce) by Temoramo	
20 Mar.	n.a.	n.a.	Zhitomir		Permission refused
26 Mar.	n.a.	Kantor	Pereiaslav	Goldfaden, *Kapriznaia doch'*	Permission refused

Table 9.1 (*cont.*)

Date	Company	Director/artistic director	Location and/or itinerary	Repertoire (where available)	Comments
1905 (*cont.*)					
27–31 Mar.	German Jewish troupe	Yakov Spivakovsky (director); Sam Adler (guest director)	St Petersburg (from Odessa)	*Sore-sheyndl* by Adler; *Dovids fidele* (David's violin) by Lateiner; *Bar kokhba* by Goldfaden	Also appeared in Rostov-na-Donu, Vilna, and 'in and out of the Pale of Settlement'
Sept.	German Theatre Troupe	Ilia Feldman	Mogilev		Permission given to perform in German but not Yiddish
1909 Mar.	German Jewish troupe	Zhitomirsky	Kremenchug		Permission refused by local authorities; appealed to Dept. of Police
18 July[d]	n.a.	Avrom Fishzon	Vitebsk province		Reported in *Vitebskie Gubernskie Vedomosti*

Russian titles are translated into English; Yiddish titles, including variants, are given when known. The names of artists and directors are given in Yiddish transliteration where known.

n.a. = not available.

Sources: Gosudarstvennyi Arkhiv Rossiiskoi Federatsii (State Archive of the Russian Federation), Moscow, *fond* 102 (2-oe deloproizvodstvo), *opis'* 40, *delo* 287, *l.* 99, for all items except the following:

- [a] *NIARB* (Minsk), *fond* 295, *opis'* 1, *ed. khr.* 3824, *l.* 175.
- [b] Ibid., *fond* 1430, *opis'* 1, *ed. khr.* 37623.
- [c] Lietuvos Centrinis Valstybinis Archyvas (Vilnius), *fond* 378, *opis'* 180, *delo* 82, *l.* 2ᵛ.
- [d] *NIARB* (Minsk), *fond* 1416, *opis'* 6, *ed. khr.* 872.

interfered with his activities, most notably in Odessa in 1899, he submitted letters of complaint to higher authorities. In February 1900 he petitioned the MVD and the Chief Office of Press Affairs to remove the 'temporary regulations of the circular of 1883'. When his petition was rejected, he submitted formal complaints against the MVD in 1901.[34] It was his petition to the tsar in 1904 which, legend has it, led to the lifting of the ban in 1905. In his telegram to the tsar Fishzon invoked the usual maskilic justifications for the Jewish theatre in Yiddish: 'pursuing along with the Russian theatre the goal of enlightenment, serving as a true mirror of the life of the Jewish masses, mercilessly scourging the dark forces of stagnation and fanaticism, it is a factor in the cause of enlightening the benighted Jewish masses'.[35] The newspaper report claimed that the government had responded positively to Fishzon's plea, but correspondence in the MVD casts doubt on this claim.

[34] GARF, *ll.* 36–38ᵛ.   [35] 'Bibliografiya'.

Despite the uniformly negative attitude at the centre, the Yiddish theatre clearly continued to thrive in the provinces. Many of the refusals were directed to companies already in existence for performances that had already been scheduled. Indeed, requests to the centre for permission were often a 'last gasp' by entrepreneurs when something had gone wrong at the local level and the local police had denied or withdrawn permission. More frequently, the show went ahead. So widespread were Yiddish performances that some provincial authorities assumed that the ban had been lifted. On 2 April 1905 Maksimovich, the governor-general of Warsaw, contacted the Department of Police. He had good grounds for assuming that the 1883 ban had been lifted since, accompanying his letter, was a theatrical poster announcing that the Odessa-based German Jewish troupe of Yakov Spivakovsky had given eight performances of three plays by the 'American' guest director Sam Adler between 27 and 31 March.[36] The performances had been held—in St Petersburg! On receiving a reply that the ban still stood, Maksimovich took up the cudgels for the Yiddish theatre, and sought to make the Department of Police recognize reality. Yiddish plays were being widely and continually presented in Poland and in and out of the Pale of Settlement:

Taking into consideration that most of the plays written in Yiddish have a historical or everyday character, include nothing contrary to morality, and are incapable of arousing interracial hatred, I would assume that the considerations that served as the basis for the publication of the circular of 1883 hardly seem to apply to these plays. Therefore, while it is not within my own competence to recommend the possibility of ending this abolition for all the provinces of the empire, I consider it my duty to ask Your Excellency [the director of the Department of Police] whether it might not be possible, as an exception to the general rule, to permit for the time being the staging of plays in the conversational Jewish tongue, the so-called *zhargon*, in the Privistula region [i.e. the Kingdom of Poland].[37]

Governors-general could not be fobbed off in the brusque fashion reserved for Jewish theatrical directors, and the Department of Police asked the Chief Office of Press Affairs on 7 June 1905 for a full report on the legal status of the Jewish theatre. These were troubled times, as Russia lurched towards the 1905 revolution. Typical of the governmental delays and indecision in dealing with urgent social issues that were to provoke rioting and a general strike in October 1905, the GUpDP chose to rely on a classic Russian bureaucratic ploy. On 1 July 1905 its director informed the Department of Police that the whole question of theatrical performances was under review, so it would be

---

[36] Since Adler had worked in the United States from 1888 to 1890, his publicity referred to him as 'Sam Adler from America', although he was based in Europe at this time. I thank Nina Warnke for this information. [37] GARF, *l.* 72ᵛ.

inopportune to abolish the rule of 1883 (which had most recently been confirmed on 1 September 1898), even if only for the Privistula lands. The apparent anomaly of the German Jewish Troupe's appearance was easily explained: they had performed entirely in German.[38]

The general relaxation of censorship that accompanied the 1905 revolution did not apparently extend to the Yiddish stage, despite the claims of the Jewish press and subsequent scholarship.[39] On 17 June 1906, in response to an enquiry from the office of the governor-general of Kiev as to whether or not the ban was still in place, the Department of Police announced that it was indeed still operative. The enquiry triggered a debate with the Ministry of Internal Affairs and a game of bureaucratic 'pass the parcel'. On 3 July 1906 the director of the GUpDP announced that his agency had no authority to decide whether or not the ban on Yiddish plays could be lifted because its imposition had been a purely police measure. (This further confirms my hypothesis that the ban arose not out of ideological considerations, but as a public order measure.) In response, the MVD's Department of General Affairs announced that it too lacked any authority over the question. On 12 July 1906 Kiev was informed that the ban was apparently still in force.[40]

This raises the interesting question of precisely when the ban on the Yiddish stage was lifted. The authorities themselves were not certain. In January 1909 the new governor-general of Warsaw sought to clarify the situation he had inherited from his predecessor, Maksimovich. He noted that Warsaw had been informed in 1905 that the ban was still in place subject to the revision of regulations governing controls on theatrical productions. While there was no formal announcement, the Warsaw police had received copies of Yiddish plays bearing the stamp of the GUpDP that they were 'permitted to be performed'. This implied that the ban had been lifted. The Department of Police replied on 29 March 1909 in the negative. The ban remained, and even plays passed by the GUpDP could not be performed if they were in Yiddish.

The last piece of evidence comes from an appeal of a German Jewish troupe, led by a certain Zhitomirsky, which found itself stranded in Kremenchug in March 1909, when the local authorities refused it permission to perform. It

[38] GARF, *ll.* 76–77[v].

[39] Khone Shmeruk assumed that the ban had been lifted in 1905, since a work of Sholem Aleykhem was staged in Yiddish in Warsaw by Mark Arnshteyn. See '"Tsezeyt un tseshpreyt" le-sholem aleykhem vehahatsagot shel hamaḥazeh besafah hapolanit bevarshe beshanim 1905–1910' [Sholem Aleykhem's Comedy *Tsezeyt un tseshpreyt* and its Performance in Polish in Warsaw in 1905 and 1910], in Ezra Mendelsohn and Khone Shmeruk (eds.), *Kovets mekharim al yekudei polin: sefer lezikhro shel paul glikson* [Studies on Polish Jewry: Paul Glikson Memorial Volume] (Jerusalem: Hebrew University, 1987), 79–95. This may be an illustration of the general confusion in the Warsaw governor-generalship concerning the status of the ban.   [40] GARF, *ll.* 87–8.

sent a telegram to the Department of Police seeking permission to stage productions so that it might raise enough money to leave the town. The MVD
asked the governor of Poltava province for the reasons why permission had
been withheld. He offered three: the 1883 ban on Yiddish plays; the public
order risks of permitting a performance; and the lack of a sufficient number of
policemen who knew Yiddish and could supervise what was happening on
the stage. The governor informed the MVD that he had asked for clari-
fication on this very matter in October 1908 and had been informed by the
Department of Police that 'although there has been no change in the law
regarding permission for the stage performance of plays in Jewish *zhargon*',
the police and the provincial administration, on the basis of Articles 7 and
135–8 of the Statute on the Prevention of Crime, could prevent Yiddish stage
plays if, under local conditions, they were a threat to law and order. Clearly,
as late as 1909 some authorities were enforcing the ban on Yiddish plays, citing the 1883 decree as well as public order concerns. It had evidently become a
local issue, however, since the central authorities no longer appeared to have
a consistent, empire-wide policy.

In my reading of the episode, the ban on Yiddish theatre lacked any ideological underpinning, with the possible exception of the concern expressed by
some sections of society or the Russian Orthodox Church that certain plays,
specifically those with a biblical theme, were insulting to Christian beliefs.
The ban was imposed largely as a police measure, and emanated from the
Department of Police of the MVD. It may be seen as part of a wider Russian
policy not to permit 'new' rights to the Jews in the conservative atmosphere
that followed the pogroms of 1881–2. Since the ban depended on the participation of the local police authorities in provincial Russia, who were neither
numerous nor professional, but were notoriously bribable, it was easily
circumvented. The ban's continuing existence came to light only by chance,
usually when Jewish entrepreneurs appealed against a local decision to deny
them the right to perform. Such appeals were invariably denied, with a pro
forma invocation of the 17 August 1883 decree. It is clear from police reports
and enquiries, as well as from theatrical posters and handbills, that the Yiddish theatre continued to perform—sometimes, but not always, under the
protective identity of a 'German Jewish' group. There seems little doubt that
these performances were in Yiddish.

  The casual nature of the ban made it difficult to enforce, but equally difficult to repeal, even when this was the recommendation of figures as lofty as
governors-general. Thus, the ban apparently escaped repeal amid the general

relaxation of censorship during the 1905 revolution. As late as 1909 the authorities were unclear who had ultimate responsibility for the ban, the GUpDP or the Department of Police.

The files of the Department of Police provide useful information on the growth of the Yiddish theatre in Russia. They allow us to identify a number of entrepreneurs and their troupes, their geographical range, and the nature of their repertoire. They offer an eloquent demonstration of the failure of Russia's ethnic politics at the end of the nineteenth century. For this information, at least, the cultural historian has reason to be grateful for the efforts of the Russian police.

TEN

The Censorship of Sholem Asch's Got fun nekome, *London*, *1946*

ɞ

LEONARD PRAGER

THE banning of Sholem Asch's *Got fun nekome* (God of Vengeance) by the Lord Chamberlain's Office in London in 1946 is in itself a drama worthy of the proverbial 'two hours' traffic of our stage'. Lacking that much time, let me preview the many acts that make up this extraordinary pageant by putting it in context and summarizing the plot of the play within the play.

1946: NEW HORIZONS AFTER THE DARK HOLOCAUST YEARS

The year 1946 was a relatively rich one for the Yiddish theatre in Britain. The East End of London still had something of a Jewish population, though it was much smaller than before the war. Many who no longer lived in the East End continued to work there. Greater London still contained a sizeable population of Yiddish speakers, a core of whom were veteran theatregoers. Two Yiddish theatres in London had full seasons and circulated in the provinces as well; there was also at least one visiting group from Paris. The New Yiddish Theatre (Nay Idish Teater), starring Meyer Tselniker, celebrated the seventieth anniversary of the Yiddish theatre, nominally founded in 1876. Dovid Pinski, in many respects the personification of quality Yiddish theatre, was honoured with a performance of his *Yankl der shmid* (Yankl the Blacksmith) forty years after its first staging.

The New Yiddish Theatre also revived the most popular of all original British-produced Yiddish plays, Shmuel Yankev Harendorf's *Kenig fun lampedusa* (The King of Lampedusa). The international star Dina Halpern captivated London audiences with her appearance in such classic plays as Gordin's *Mirele efros* (Kafka's friend Dora Diamant reported her visit at length in Avrom-Nokhem Shtentsl's *Loshn un lebn* (Language and Life) in September 1946).

Peretz Hirschbein's popular success *Grine felder*[1] was revived at the Grand
Palais Theatre. The New Yiddish Theatre, committed to producing only 'cultural' plays, commissioned a new production of Shakespeare's *The Merchant
of Venice* and received a grant from the British Arts Council. The atmosphere
in Yiddish cultural circles was upbeat—quality was sought. And thus was
born the plan to revive Asch's admittedly stormy *Got fun nekome*, forty years
old but still seen as a vehicle of dramatic power. It seemed a very good choice
to the director and actors, for here was a play that was both popular and critic-
ally—if not universally—respected.

In the wider Jewish world 1946 was a period of conflict in Palestine between
the British Mandatary power and the Yishuv (Jewish community). In late
1944 Lord Moyne had been executed by the Stern Gang. In 1946 the Kielce
pogrom further fired Zionist resolve to open the gates of Palestine to Jewish
immigration.[2] In January 1946, when London's New Yiddish Theatre, under
the leadership of its licensee, the baker and theatre enthusiast Nathan Beitler,
began rehearsing *Got fun nekome*, an Anglo-American Commission of Inquiry
on European Jewry and Palestine held sittings in London.

Another significant event of the year 1946—significant, that is to say, for
a small group of academics, for this was an event with no apparent political
or public reverberations—was the publication of Gershom Scholem's *Major
Trends in Jewish Mysticism*. This scholarly work was a reminder that normative
rabbinic Judaism never enjoyed exclusive sway over Jewish communities;
there were always mystics with esoteric beliefs and, we may add, the 'folk',
with superstitious ones.

WHAT HAPPENS IN *GOT FUN NEKOME*

The eminent Shakespearean John Dover Wilson sat down one day to describe
the plot of *Hamlet* and ended up writing an entire book called *What Happens
in Hamlet*. A sizeable work could be compiled from various descriptions of
the plot of *Got fun nekome*, for plot summaries of this play tend at one point or
another to become interpretations. The bare bones of the action can be sum-
marized as the efforts of a brothel-keeper, Yankl Tshaptshovitsh, and his wife,
Sore, a former prostitute, to preserve the innocence of their 17-year-old
daughter Rifkele by putting a copy of a Torah scroll in her room as a kind of

[1] Peretz Hirschbein, *Grine felder: komedye in 3 aktn (a mayse fun idish dorfishn leben)* [Green Fields: A Comedy in Three Acts (A Story of Jewish Village Life)], in *Gezamlte dramen* (New York: Literar-ishe-dramatishe fareynin in amerike, 1916), v. 255–318.
[2] The same year saw the rejection by the Jewish side of the Morrison–Grady plan to partition Palestine, a plan that left much of the country in British hands.

talisman. Planning to marry her off to a respectable young man, they forbid her contact with the prostitutes in the brothel that is directly beneath their home. She nevertheless comes to know them, and one of them, Manke, becomes her lover. Another prostitute, Hindl, in the hope of marrying the young pimp Shloyme and establishing her own brothel, helps Manke and Rifkele to flee. The father, devastated by the collapse of his hopes for his daughter, turns against the 'God of vengeance' who punishes children for the sins of the parents. By bribing the pimp, Sore finds her by no means penitent daughter. The distraught father, seeing he has failed to preserve his daughter's purity, gives away the scroll and orders mother and daughter down to the brothel below.

This summary gives a totally inadequate sense of all that happens in a performance of the play. Plot summaries are even less reliable when summarizers improvise, as Liptzin does in his *History of Yiddish Literature* when he tells us that at the end of the play Yankl Tshaptshovitsh 'hurled God's Torah from the upper storey down to the abode of sin and horror'.[3] Some director may have added this flourish in some production, but it is not in the text. The last action before the final curtain is the brothel-keeper restraining Reb Eli, the middleman and *folks-shatkhn* (marriage broker for the lower classes), and exclaiming: 'Dos seyfer-toyre nemt aykh mit, ikh darf es shoyn nisht mer!' (You can take the Scroll of the Law with you now, I don't need it any more!').[4] In the long history of this play's reception, this Scroll of the Law has proved impossible to set aside. Indeed, no more problematic prop is known in Yiddish theatre history.

THE LORD CHAMBERLAIN'S PLAYS

The Licensing Act of 1737 required the Lord Chamberlain to license a new play before it could be publicly performed on the stage. This practice continued until 1968. Few people realize that Yiddish plays and play synopses were similarly presented for decades to the Lord Chamberlain's Office (LCO) for licensing.[5] Since 1880 Yiddish troupes in Britain have staged at least a thousand different works, but they do not seem to have applied for permis-

---

[3] Sol Liptzin, *A History of Yiddish Literature* (Middle Village, NY: Jonathan David, 1972), 147–8.

[4] Sholem Asch, *Dramatishe shriftn* [Dramatic Works], 3 vols. (Vilna: Sholem Ash Komitet, 1922), iii. 96.

[5] John Johnston, in his *The Lord Chamberlain's Blue Pencil* (London: Hodder & Stoughton, 1990), makes no mention at all of Yiddish plays. Copies of all plays licensed between 1824 and 1968 formerly held in the LCO are now in the British Library, together with all correspondence and examiners' reports, where these survive. Plays can be searched through a card catalogue of titles and through bound volumes in which plays were recorded by the LCO as received. Yiddish plays can be

sion to perform as many as a quarter of them. From the late 1890s until the
1940s the practice appears to have been for a Yiddish theatre manager—if he
bothered at all—to submit an English synopsis of the Yiddish play together
with two guineas for the registration fee. Sometimes a printed or manuscript
text accompanied the synopsis, which was generally poorly written and sloppily presented. The examiners had additional cause for irritation when the fee
was late in arriving. If the play was in Yiddish, they felt careful attention to its
contents to be superfluous. This indifference bordered on contempt.[6]

A low-key domestic antisemitism warmed by current political tensions
related to events in Palestine may have nourished this contempt. But its principal source was doubtless a disdainful attitude towards immigrant Yiddish
culture, an attitude shared by sections of Anglo-Jewry. Here is the first letter
in the LCO correspondence concerning *Got fun nekome*. The reader, H. C.
Game, writes:

Another play about brothels and the White Slave Traffic, fortunately in Yiddish. I
must ask the Lord Chamberlain to read the precis submitted, as if I wrote another,
it would only be a condensed version, and he had better have all the facts available.

As far as one can judge it seems a sordid story with a moral purpose. The licensing of these Yiddish plays is in actual fact a mere formality, and as far as censoring
goes, a farce, but I do not see what we can do about it.

Under the circumstances all I can do is to
Recommend the Play for license.

H. C. Game

found only through their translated English titles, a formidable obstacle. Assembling the lists given
in the appendix to this chapter taxed my familiarity with the language of Yiddish play titles: by
searching for certain words and themes, I gradually uncovered the plays of a fair number of playwrights. These lists can doubtless be extended. (This paragraph paraphrases Leonard Prager and
Brad Sabin Hill, 'Yiddish Manuscripts in the British Library', *British Library Journal*, 21/1 (Spring
1995), 93).

[6] Asch's play appeared on the Yiddish stage in London in the mid-1920s and again in 1935. The
1935 examiner made it clear that the play could not have been licensed had it been in English but in
Yiddish it could, reluctantly, be allowed. Here is G. S. Street's report of 1935: 'This play is said to
have been performed in Yiddish at the Pavilion Theatre, Whitechapel, 10 or 12 years ago. I have no
recollection of it, if it was licensed it must have been with some reluctance, the story being excessively ugly. . . . The brothel business is in the background. That being so, I think the play might be
licensed in Yiddish. . . . But it is rather reluctantly | Recommended for License.' The play was per-
formed at His Majesty's Theatre (*God of Vengeance*, British Library, LCP No. 1935/23, 19 Sept. 1935,
Reader's Report no. 14068, by G. S. Street). In the same year another LCO examiner, H. C. Game,
passed Jacob Gordin's *God, Man and the Devil* as adapted by Maurice Schwartz: 'From the synopsis
in the program this play appears to be all right, but as it is in Yiddish, it would not matter very
much if it wasn't. Recommended for Licence' (British Library, LCP no. 1935/21, 24 Aug. 1935,
Reader's Report no. 14017).

Under this we find a pencilled note: 'Ask for script and have it read by some-one.' And in ink below we read: 'You ask for script and have it read by some-one. The Chief Rabbi would be a suitable person, and I think till we get his report and opinions it is best not to sign the Licence.' It is signed 'C.'[7]

In a letter that followed, we overhear one civil servant speaking familiarly to another:

Burghclere 29 January 1946[8]

My Dear Norman[9]

I do not think I should send that brothel play to the Chief Rabbi, as it is so obviously an improving play for Jews, and he may write us off as a bit dense for not realizing it. What you might do is write on the general question to the C[hief] R[abbi] & ask him, if at any time he receives complaints about Jewish theatres, he will pass them on to us. You could also, so as to show that the Censor is awake and watchful, summon the manager of the New Jewish Theatre (or whatever it is called) & ask him a few questions about the play.

Personally I don't think it matters a tuppeny damn what the yids do among themselves as long as their plays are neither subversive or [*sic*] obsene [*sic*]; it is what they do amongst the Christians for the sake of shekels that concerns us!

I don't think there is the least danger of their Yiddish plays offending against their religious susceptibilities.[10]

W. Henry[?][11]

In speaking of 'their Yiddish plays' and 'their religious susceptibilities', the writer of this letter lumps all Jews together. But the Jews who were drawn into the controversy over Asch's *Got fun nekome* were far from being of one mind. Our letter-writer was sure that the play would not offend Jewish reli-gious sensibilities, but the play was nonetheless finally banned because it did disturb the religious susceptibilities of a few highly placed people, none of whom was actually conversant with the Yiddish stage.

Deputy Chief Rabbi Harris M. Lazarus was an English-born Jew, a gradu-ate of Jews' College in north London interested in *masora* (the traditional

[7] This is Item 1 in the correspondence in the British Library, LR 1946. It is a typescript with additions in hand. At the top we read '"God's Punishment" (synopsis from the Yiddish) | 3 acts | Folk House | Shalom Asch'.

[8] Burghclere, in the Wessex Downs, is known for its gentle rolling hills; it is also home to the Stanley Spencer murals in the Sandham Memorial Chapel, which show the horrors of war.

[9] This was presumably addressed to Colonel N. W. Gwatkin, Assistant Comptroller in the LCO. In *Who Was Who*, vii: *1971–1980* (London: Adam & Charles Black, 1989), 326, we read: 'Brig. Sir Norman (Wilmshurst) Gwatkin. GCVO 1963 (CVO 1946; MVO 1937); KCMG 1964; DSO 1944; Comptroller, Lord Chamberlain's Office, 1960–1964. b. 2 Aug 1899–d. 16 Feb 1972. retired pay 1946. Educ. Clifton.'

[10] British Library, LR 1946, Item 20; this is among the first items—the lower the number the earlier the date.   [11] I am not certain that I have deciphered the signature correctly.

pointing and transmission of the text of the Hebrew Bible), which he studied all his life. He was the rabbi of Brondesbury Synagogue in north London, a mainstream Orthodox synagogue. Chief Rabbi Hertz had died in January 1946 and Israel Brodie did not succeed him until May 1948. In the interim period of over two years Rabbi Lazarus served as acting chief rabbi.[12]

On 13 February 1946 Rabbi Lazarus wrote to Colonel Gwatkin: 'I have now read the play in the full Yiddish text. There are heavy pencil deletions whether intended merely for *our* reading or actual expurgation for producing the play, I cannot say.' Notice how the Jewish religious leader ingratiates himself with that convivial 'our' and the implied untrustworthiness of the Yiddish theatre director. The deputy chief rabbi is firm: 'But even with the expurgations, the theme is offensive and not fit for the public stage.'[13] And he further remarks: 'This play could not have been intended for the stage either in Russia[14] or in any other Jewish centre. It is a sordid theme, repulsive in personnel and diction, and offensive to any feeling of decency in the use of the Scroll for such purpose. It is sure to evoke violent expressions of resentment.' On the following day Colonel Gwatkin wrote to Nathan Beitler: 'I am desired by the Lord Chamberlain to inform you that he regrets he is unable to issue a licence for the public performance of the above play.'

Ironically, it was the director of the New Yiddish Theatre himself who recommended Lucas Quixano Henriques, warden of the Bernhard Baron Settlement, as an arbiter.[15] Basil Henriques was the scion of a distinguished Anglo-Jewish family. His paternal grandfather was Jacob Henriques; his mother was a great-niece of Sir Moses Montefiore and a granddaughter of the

[12] I am grateful to Professor Chimen Abramsky and David Mazower for information on Dayan Lazarus.

[13] Most of Lazarus's exposition of the plot is straightforward and knowledgeable; he knows Yiddish and he knows about the customs surrounding the copying of a Torah. Yet he confuses reality with the script when he writes: 'A day is fixed, when a pious scribe brings that Scroll to be completed [i.e. the last sentence which is written in outline is filled in in the presence of the purchaser by way of its dedication by him].' In fact no such ceremony is enacted in the play. Again Lazarus writes: 'When the scribe learns to his horror that the Scroll is to be placed in the girl's bedroom, he declares this to be an act of sacrilege. His fears are allayed by the marriage-broker who assures him that it is soon to be donated to the Synagogue.' The text that Lazarus read may have run along these lines, but differs from the printed text, where the scribe's fears are of a general kind: does his client know how to relate to a Scroll of Law? The marriage-broker assuages the fears of the scribe by stressing the plan of making the scroll part of the bride's dowry to her future husband; there is no mention of giving it to a synagogue, which is, of course, what happens in reality.

[14] The first production of *Got fun nekome* was in Russian in 1908 in St Petersburg, where it was a resounding success. It was eventually played in virtually every Yiddish repertory theatre.

[15] A day after Lazarus's letter was received, a letter informing Nathan Beitler of the banning of *Got fun nekome* was sent out. H. C. Game tells us in one of his letters that 'Henriques . . . was the man to whom the producer suggested sending the play after he had heard what the Office of the Chief Rabbi said.'

mathematician Benjamin Gompertz; he married Rose Loewe, a sister of Herbert Loewe, a Semitics scholar. He was educated at Harrow and Oxford and was a valiant tank corps officer in the First World War. Yet he chose to become a social worker in the East End, and was a proud Jew—though his Jewishness was purely religious rather than ethnic or cultural.[16] The irony of this man being called upon to judge a Yiddish play is great. In one of his books he writes:

Not only was I not very Semitic in appearance, but I was utterly ignorant of Orthodox Judaism with its rites and ceremonies. One of my earliest experiences was a visit to a little shop which sold Yiddish newspapers and Hebrew books, and which had black straps hanging from a shelf. 'I see you are a saddler' I said. 'No' replied the old man; 'those straps are what we Jews call Tephilin (phylacteries).' I had never before in my life seen what every Jewish boy in St. George's was familiar with from before the age of thirteen.

I could not speak Yiddish, and cannot today, partly because I cannot learn it, knowing no German, but chiefly because I won't, for I consider it the duty of every resident alien to learn English. This is a handicap when a Yiddish-speaking man or woman seeks my advice.[17]

It is also something of a handicap to judge a play with an explicit lesbian theme when you have written: 'Nothing is more objectionable than the feminine male or the manlike female. We want our boys to become as manly as possible and our girls as womanly as possible.[18]

Henriques wrote to the censors:

I have read through the *synopsis* of the enclosed play, and my wife has glanced through the text. We are both convinced that it would only be harmful to pass such a play. The attitude of the Rabbi [Lazarus at least knew there was no rabbi in the play] is immoral as well as being offensive to the whole Rabbinate. The superstition connected with the most sacred part of the Jewish religion gives an entirely false place to the Scroll of the Law in the life of the Jew, and is a perversion of what that ought to be.

I am quite convinced that to show such a play would do only harm by causing ever greater misunderstanding between Jews and Christians who saw and understood it

---

[16] Basil Henriques (1890–1961). His grandfather (b. Jamaica 1811) was a Justice of the Peace; he emigrated to England in 1845 and established the firm of D. Q. Henriques & Co., Import and Export Merchants. Basil Henriques was a magistrate and later chairman of East London Juvenile Court. Made a CBE in 1948, he was knighted in 1955 for his contribution to youth welfare. He contributed much to the boys' club movement, was an active leader of the Oxford and St George's Boys' Clubs, and played a role in creating the National Association of Boys' Clubs. He founded the Jewish Fellowship in 1941 'to build up a non-Zionist fellowship of Jews who justified their Jewishness by their religion'. See L. L. Loewe, *Basil Henriques: A Portrait* (London: Routledge & Kegan Paul, 1976), and Basil Henriques, *Club Leadership* (London: Oxford University Press, 1933); *The Indiscretions of a Magistrate: Thoughts on the Work of the Juvenile Court* (London: Harrop, 1951).

[17] Henriques, *The Indiscretions of a Magistrate*, 91.   [18] Ibid. 79.

[were Christians flocking to the Yiddish theatre?] and at the same time would be offensive to all high-minded religious Jews.

The boss 'C' wrote: 'I agree that Henriques's letter fully justifies the banning of this play.'

IS THE PLAY 'IMMORAL'?

Those who claim that the play is 'immoral' invariably stress the placing of a Torah scroll in the brothel-keeper's home. Morris Myer, the editor in the early 1940s of the London Yiddish daily *Di tsayt*, makes the obvious point that the scroll in the play is not a real Torah scroll, but merely a stage prop. Moreover, it is explicitly employed in a superstitious manner that could not possibly be taken as a comment on Jewish law or custom. Myer concludes: 'Es kumt nit for keyn shum farletsung fun an emesn religiyezn gefil' ('There is no violation of any genuine religious feeling').[19] The scroll was a bold theatrical stroke. In a sense, Asch is punning on the words *reynikayt*, a synonym for *seyfer toyre* (the Scroll of the Law), and *reynkayt* (cleanness).[20] The scroll as a talisman is a folkloristic improvisation—the *folks-shatkhn* who arranges for the writing of the scroll is not, as so many readers and reviewers mistook the matter, a rabbi, but merely a *reb*, a 'mister'.

   The alleged immorality of the play derives from the theme of prostitution compounded by supposed sacrilege and also lesbianism. Lazarus and Henriques are not alone in failing to mention the lesbian theme. Whether from embarrassment or lack of interest, it is not often addressed in the reviews. Morris Myer saw *Got fun nekome* as a highly moral play with two major motifs: the thirst for purity in both the brothel-keeper and his prostitutes, and the impossibility of buying one's way out of punishment for sin. But Myer could not acknowledge that Rifkele and Manke are lovers. His Rifkele is drawn downstairs solely out of the need for companionship: 'es iz nit velkhe s'iz libe' ('it is not love of any sort')[21] And the principal danger to her *onshtendikkayt* (respectability) stems from Hindl and her marriage hopes, a view that ignores the role of Manke.

   The lesbian theme was also denied by the critic who, more strongly than any, and earlier than any (in 1908), defended Rifkele and Manke's relationship from charges of wantonness.[22] Shmuel Niger wrote:

[19] Morris Myer, *Idish teater in london, 1902–1942* [Yiddish Theatre in London, 1902–1942] (London: M. Myer [1943]), 109.
[20] See Max Weinreich, *Geshikhte fun der yidisher shprakh* [History of the Yiddish Language] (New York: YIVO, 1973), i. 206.   [21] Myer, *Idish teater in london*, 109.
[22] S. Niger, 'Der novi fun der erd [The Prophet of the Earth]: Sholem ash', *Literarishe monatshriftn*, 4 (1908), cols. 113–42; repr. in id., *Sholem ash, zayn lebn, zayne verk* [Sholem Asch: His Life

Do you recall the most beautiful, most poetic scene in *Got fun nekome*, when Manke, the goddess of 'Sin', bewitches, hypnotizes Rifkele—the slave of innocence—to get her to leave her father's house? The lower dwelling wishes to conquer the upper one. Two souls, two yearnings, meet: Rifkele's pure, celestial soul yearns for a body to burn in like a wick in a candle. And Manke's 'earthly', sinning body seeks a soul to reign over . . .[23]

Such schematic idealizations are not very likely in the altered atmosphere of today.

AN UNCONTESTED VERDICT

Rabbi Lazarus was a *dayan*, a religious court judge; Henriques was a justice of the peace in a magistrate's court. Both men were experienced in weighing moral and ethical issues and both wished to serve the public interest. While the lives of both centred on Judaism, their versions of Jewish thought and practice were alien to a great many Yiddish-speakers. Nor were they any more capable of viewing drama as an autonomous art form than was the LCO, whose role as moral policeman for the nation's stage ensured acceptance of their harsh recommendations. They consulted no one associated with the theatre. Lazarus was aware of the scandal surrounding the play, but does not seem to have known of its artistic success in Max Reinhardt's German production in Berlin in 1910 and its subsequent place in the best Yiddish repertory theatres.[24] Nathan Beitler offered to cut objectionable lines and scenes, but he could not override the voices of the two pillars of the Jewish community, Lazarus and Henriques. What the New Yiddish Theatre saw as a 'cultural' play was an abomination to those empowered to suppress it.

The censorship of Asch's *God of Vengeance* in a New York Broadway theatre in 1923 was an altogether different matter. The New York production was in English rather than in a minority language. It was played in a central theatre district, not in an immigrant neighbourhood. The director and actors were briefly imprisoned: here was an issue of freedom of expression whose salacious features helped to stir popular interest. In recent years not only has

and Work] (New York: S. Niger Book Committee of the Congress for Jewish Culture, 1960), 17–39. Niger does not find the play as a whole successful but is transported by the lyricism of Act II. He writes: 'The second act of *God of Vengeance* . . . is Asch's and only Asch's. Here Asch's strength emerges in its total honesty, the strength to beautify what others disdain, to raise up the fallen, to make clean the unworthy, to purify the sacred sparks embedded in Sin—this is Asch's, this pious, endlessly chaste poem which only tasteless, or just plain depraved, crude persons could find "wanton" . . .' (p. 22).   [23] Ibid. 26.

[24] Nor does he appear to have known of the famous Vilna Troupe's altercations with the LCO in their 1923 production of *Got fun nekome*; however, that was not banned.

the translated play been revived in fresh productions,[25] but the 1923 New York trial has itself become the stuff of drama. In mid-June 1999 the Playwright's Forum in New York made the following announcement:

The 1923 Broadway production of *The God of Vengeance*, Sholom Asch's explosive Yiddish drama, created quite an uproar when its creators were arrested for obscenity. Now, a work in development at the Yale School of Drama, entitled *The People vs. The God of Vengeance 1923*, explores a myriad of controversial issues, including censorship and gender identity, that resonate today much as they did over 70 years ago. Join us for a fascinating evening with director/playwright Rebecca Taichman. Experience scenes of the play, text from the obscenity trial, inflammatory letters from the ACLU [American Civil Liberties Union] and the *New York Times*. Your input, reaction and thoughts will be valuable tools for the further development of this cutting-edge work.[26]

In London, however, the banning of Asch's *Got fun nekome* was without public repercussions. The New Yiddish Theatre management apparently decided to hush up the matter. In any event, to date no report of it is known to have reached any section of the press. There was no response from the ideologically committed secular Yiddishists to whom Yiddish theatre was so important. Neither the still substantial body of Yiddish-speaking *folksmentshn* (the folk) nor the far larger wholly Anglicized Anglo-Jewish community was in the least aware that anything resembling a civil libertarian issue was brewing in the Jewish East End. The only place in which one might have expected to read about the censorship of Asch's play was in Shtentsl's *Heftlekh* (Notebooks), which appeared until the end of 1945, or his *Loshn un lebn*, which was its continuation from 1946 onwards.

In late 1945 and 1946 the principal question raised in discussions on the London Yiddish theatre by Shtentsl and members of his circle was the perennial one of how to ensure quality productions as opposed to light entertainment and *shund* (cheap and vulgar productions). Shtentsl had the temerity to suggest that the two Yiddish troupes operating in the East End, the London Yiddish Theatre (London Yidisher Teater) under the direction of Mark Markov and the New Yiddish Theatre starring Meir Tselniker, should unite to form a single repertory theatre. Attacked on all sides, Shtentsl retreated: 'iz dokh dos yidishe teater do in unzere vaytshepler geslekh der eyntsiker shtolts nokh vos

---

[25] Joachim Neugroschel's new translation was published in *Der pakntreger*, 23 (Winter 1996), 16–39. Caraid O'Brien translated and produced the play at the Henry Street Settlement in New York in 1999. There was also a production at a small theatre in Hackney, London, in 1999. See David Mazower's review of current and past productions in 'Unkosher Sex', *Jewish Chronicle*, 28 May 1999, 29.

[26] Yiddishnet: News Forum Yiddishnet List on Shamash (Reyzl Kalifowicz-Waletzky), <http://shamash.org/listarchives/yiddishnet>.

mir farmogn do un mit vos mir groysn zikh. . . . tsvey teaters oystsuhaltn
. . . maskim!' ('After all, the Yiddish theatre here in Whitechapel's narrow
lanes is all we still have and we are proud of it. . . . Support two theatres? . . . I
agree!')[27]

In 1946 the management of the New Yiddish Theatre was too busy competing with the London Yiddish Theatre to relish negative criticism of any
kind, whether it emanated from the West End or percolated locally. The competing troupe played at the Grand Palais Theatre with its almost 500 seats,
whereas the New Yiddish Theatre had to make do with a hall in the Adler
Street Folk House. Moreover, the New Yiddish Theatre may very well have
felt that any sign of official disfavour could compromise its application to the
British Arts Council for a grant (which it used to produce Shakespeare's *The
Merchant of Venice*). In January 1947 the New Yiddish Theatre sent a delegation to the United States in connection with plans to construct a new Yiddish
theatre. The members of the delegation were the New Yiddish Theatre's
principal patron, Nathan Beitler, and its director, Abish Meisels. Beitler was
almost certainly the Maecenas behind the bilingual (Yiddish and English)
Theatre Mirror (variously titled in Yiddish): it was he who had initiated the
extraordinary practice of paying actors annual salaries, and it was he who had
brought the star Dina Halpern to London for a month of performances.

Kafka's friend Dora Diamant (in the *Loshn un lebn* circle she was Kafka's
almone, or 'widow') could barely contain herself regarding Halpern's visit:
'Az m'lebt derlebt men—take derlebt tsu zen oyf a yidisher bine in vaytshepl
emesdike teater-kunst, fun a groysn farnem' ('If you live long enough, you
live to see things—I have lived to see true theatrical art on a grand scale on a
Whitechapel stage').[28] Beitler was the chief negotiator for the New Yiddish
Theatre in its relations with the LCO. Brimming with plans, he put the banning of the Asch play behind him and forged ahead.

SHARDS OF ONCE BRIGHT VESSELS

When Beitler died two decades after his futile dispute with the LCO, *Loshn
un lebn* wrote an obituary entitled 'Vi "aynzam" men shtarbt in london' (How
'Lonely' One Dies in London). Were it not for Brad Sabin Hill's rediscovery
of the Yiddish materials among the Lord Chamberlain's plays at the British
Library, the entire incident of the censorship of Asch's *Got fun nekome* would
have remained as forgotten as is the baker patron of Yiddish theatre, Nathan
Beitler himself. Sifting through the often tattered and illegible papers that

---

[27] (*Shtentsls*) *Heftlekh*, 71 (Dec. 1945), 46.   [28] *Loshn un lebn* (Sept. 1946).

make up these archival remains of decades of Yiddish theatre in Britain, one experiences a sense of unmediated participation in that quite remarkable institution. There is much to be seen here if one has the patience and perseverance to look carefully—these are fragments waiting to be pieced together.

For most of the Yiddish plays licensed between 1880 and 1961 there are only poor English plot abstracts, but there is also Yiddish-language material, both printed and in manuscript. The plays run the gamut from raucous musicals, sentimental operettas, and tear-jerking melodramas to serious art theatre. It will not be possible to write a full history of Yiddish theatre in Britain without close study of these materials. Selecting a single item of correspondence at random we find the following:

> 17, High Road
> South Tottenham
> 29 June 1899

W. Schaffer
Manager
The London Hebrew Operatic and Dramatic Company

Dear Sir:

Enclosed please find cheque value £2.2.0 as fee for registration for the enclosed Hebrew Piece called A Second Haman or King for a day [*sic*]. Please send receipt, and the Permit to be forward to the Standard Theatre, Shoreditch.

oblige

yours respectively [*sic*],

W. Schaffer

This letter is itself highly informative. Nowhere has the name of a W. Schaffer, the manager of the London Hebrew Operatic and Dramatic Company, been recorded. (It is missing from my *Yiddish Culture in Britain*!)[29] His Yiddish name was probably Shafer, which means both 'creator' and 'raiser [of funds]'. He may indeed have been creative and practical, the right qualities for a theatre manager. His English was not perfect, but he could follow the LCO regulations. He submitted the two-guinea fee—the same fee that was in effect in 1946, but whose value in 1899 was about twenty times greater. The address he gives could be his own—the London Hebrew Operatic and Dramatic Company was using the Standard Theatre in Shoreditch in 1899. Of greater interest than the letter is what accompanied it: a 128-page printed Yiddish copy of *Kenig über ein nacht: historische roman fun schomer* (standard Yiddish: Kenig iber a nakht: historishe roman fun shomer).

---

[29] Leonard Prager, *Yiddish Culture in Britain: A Guide* (Frankfurt am Main: Peter Lang 1990).

The letter speaks of an enclosed 'Piece', i.e. play. As was common on the European stage, it has a double title: 'A Second Haman; or, King for a Night'. The first title names a proverbial enemy of the Jews and the second condenses the notion of fleeting power in a familiar phrase. Both titles are appropriately brief for a stage production. But alas, no 'Piece' was submitted. What the LCO received was the lengthly narrative from which the company carved a stage play rather than the required play script—an early symptom of a farcical relationship which continued for decades. It was pure effrontery for the Yiddish theatre manager to submit a text that could have little relation to the actual stage production. The examiners certainly did not read the 128 pages (in Yiddish!) by the pioneer of Yiddish fiction and author of mammoth potboilers Nokhem Meyer Shaykevitsh (1846–1905). Popularly known by the acronym Shomer, this extraordinarily prolific writer was savaged by Sholem Aleykhem, but is seen in a more positive light by present-day scholars.[30]

Many of Shomer's plays were dramatizations of his novels, often with altered titles, and many were staged in Britain. The famous star Jacob P. Adler played in Shomer's *Kean* in London as early as 1889. The narrative text submitted to the LCO also points to a practice that eventually helped throttle the Yiddish theatre—dependence on adaptations of fictional works rather than encouragement of original writing for the stage. Significant too is the Yiddish troupe's title—London Hebrew Operatic and Dramatic Company—as well as its manager's use of the term 'Hebrew Piece'. The term Hebrew was felt by both Jews and non-Jews to be more dignified and less prejudicial than 'Jewish', and the term 'Yiddish' was not yet in wide use, either as a term for the Yiddish language or as a descriptor of literary and dramatic works in that language. Recognition of the artistic vitality of the Yiddish theatre and acceptance of the term 'Yiddish' go hand in hand.

Shomer's works were generally read avidly, and thus many of his books and plays have bibliophilic as well as literary and historical value. The copy of Shomer's play sent by the London Hebrew Operatic and Dramatic Company to the LCO bears the stamp of the bookseller Feldman of 27 Fashion Street, Spitalfields—another forgotten figure to brighten somewhat our dim perception of the Yiddish cultural scene in late nineteenth-century Britain. The LCO materials will yield many significant details, and they can be scrutinized in a number of ways: for instance, how did an improvising director slice up a narrative text to produce a script for the stage? Many other questions will arise in the minds of researchers who hold these ephemera in their hands, turning their pages, looking for signs of the life behind these fragments.

[30] See esp. Sophie Grace-Pollak, 'Shomer in the Light of "Shomer's Mishpet"', *Ḥuliyot*, 5 (Winter 1999), 109–60.

APPENDIX
APPLICATIONS TO THE LORD CHAMBERLAIN'S OFFICE, LONDON, FOR LICENCES TO PERFORM YIDDISH PLAYS

Table 10.1 Alphabetical listing by author

Author	Play	LCP no.	Licensing date[a]
Not known	Argentine Nights	1932/06	10 Feb. 1932
	Broken Mirror	1911/19	10 July 1911
	Jewish Emigration	1898/11	53693 (no. 108)
	Jewish Zaza	1907/11	24 May 1907
	King Pharaoh	1896 (lost)	no. 662
	Leye lubliner	1946/15	8 May 1946
	Motke from Slobotke	1943/33	13 Dec. 1943
	Palestinian Life	1946/15	8 May 1946
	Professional Socialist	1908/04	3 Mar. 1908
	The Shlemihl	1949	13 Jan. 1949
	Traffic in Souls	1922/19	1922
	Yosele un feygele	1944/04	14 Feb. 1944
Aksenfeld, Israel[c] (1787–1866)	The Jewish Soldier	1880/1–2	53231 (no. 28)
Ansky, S.[c] (1863–1920)	Day and Night	1923/23	14 Sept. 1923
	Dibbick [Dybbuk]	1922/26	13 Oct. 1922
	Dybbuk [Eng.]	1927/12	17 Mar. 1927
	Dybbuk [Eng.]	1930/58	31 Dec. 1930
Arensztejn, Marek, *see* Arnshteyn, Mark			
Arnshteyn, Mark (1878–1940s)	Singer of Vilna	1912/16	19 Apr. 1912
Arnstein, Mark, *see* Arnshteyn, Mark			
Asch, Sholem (1880–1957)	God of Vengeance	1935/23	19 Sept. 1935
	God's Punishment	1946	refused
	His Own People	1923/30	20 Nov. 1923
	Motke the Thief	1944/03	4 Feb. 1944
	Supreme Sacrifice	1934/12	22 Mar. 1934
	Uncle Moses	1943/25	15 Oct. 1943
	Vengeance	1923/26	9 Oct. 1923
Auerbach, I., *see* Oyerbach, Yitskhok			
Bergelson, Dovid (1884–1952)	Breadmill	1934/14	11 Apr. 1934
Bloom, Abraham, *see* Blum, Avrom			
Blum, Avrom[c] (1893–1960)	Motke in America	1949/21	6 Apr. 1949
	Sun Rises Again [Eng.]	1945/40	1945
Dimov, Osip (pseud. 1878–1959)	Jossek the Musician	1946/04	6 Feb. 1946
Dorfson, S.-Y. (pseud.), *see* Harendorf, Shmuel-Yankev			
Dymov, Ossip (pseud.), *see* Dimov, Osip			
Faynman, Zigmund (Asher-Zelig Faynman), *see* Feinman, Sigmund			
Feinman, Sigmund (1862–1909)	Jews in Morocco	1907/05	1 Mar. 1907
	Knave of Hearts	1907/20	17 Sept. 1907
	Mother's Sacrifice	1907/20	17 Sept. 1907

Author	Play	LCP no.	Licensing date[a]
Feinman, Sigmund (*cont.*)	My Wife's Friend	1908/21	20 Oct. 1908
	Nightingale of Jerusalem	1908/04	3 Mar. 1908
	Rabbi Leib Sepharde	1906/30	17 Oct. 1906
	Shattered Lives	1907/20	17 Sept. 1907
Freiman, Louis (pseud.; Layzer Genyuk; 1892–1967)	Tsipke fayer	1949	1949
Freiman(?), Louis	Jewish General	1933/33	16 Oct. 1933
Freyman, Luis, *see* Freiman, Louis			
Gable, Max (Nokhem Menakhem-Mendl; 1877–1952)	Father and Mother's Sorrows	1906/12	24 Apr. 1906
Goldfaden, Avrom (1840–1908)	Bar Cochlar [Bar Kokhba]	1896/10	53611 A–N
	Bar Cochba, the Son of the Star [Bar Kokhba]	1901/42	18 Dec. 1901
	Judas Maccabeus	1904/22	19 Sept. 1904
	Judith and King Alferius	1902/19	2 June 1902
	King Ahasuerus	1902/11	17 Mar. 1902
	Messiah's Times	1945/40	31 Dec. 1945
	Reb yoslman [Rebbe Yozlman]	1896 (lost)	no. 661
	Sulamita [Shulamis]	1896/9–10	53610 M
	Tenth Commandment	1901/36	4 Nov. 1901
	Two Koonylemmels [The Two Kuni Lemls]	1924/12	1 Apr. 1924
	Witch	1946/15	8 May 1946
	—	1947/04	31 Jan. 1947
Gordin, Jacob (1853–1909)	Alisheva [Elisha ben-avuya(?)]	1902/26	24 Aug. 1902
	Beautiful Miriam	1908/02	30 Jan. 1908
	Broken Hearts	1905/07	21 Mar. 1905
	God, Man, and the Devil	1906	12 Nov. 1906
	Jewish King Lear	1901/25	1 Aug. 1901
	Kreutzer Sonata	1904/27	28 Nov. 1904
	Kreutzer Sonata [Feinman]	1907/05	1 Mar. 1907
	Kreutzer Sonata	1944/01	11 Jan. 1944
	Lured from Home	1900/12	22 Aug. 1900
	Meturef (The Abnormal Man)	1906/24	15 Aug. 1906
	Mirele efros	1957/17	26 Mar. 1957
	Miryam efros [*sic*]	1906/09	11 Apr. 1905
	Muriel efros [*sic*; synopsis]	1925/49	17 Dec. 1925
	Myer yosovitch [Mayer yozefovitsh]	1906/26	13 Sept. 1906
	Own Blood	1924/06	16 Feb. 1924
	Real Power	1908/09	11 May 1908
	Solomon kans	1906/24	30 Aug. 1906
	Two Worlds	1908/10	11 May 1908
	Widower	1907/24	15 Oct. 1907
rev. Ida Kaminska	Meyer ezefowitch [Mayer yozefovitsh]	1957/17	26 Mar. 1957
rev. Maurice Schwartz	God, Man, and Devil	1935/21	24 Aug. 1935
Gutzkow, Karl Ferdinand[b] (1811–78)	Uriel acosta	1905/28	25 Nov. 1905
Halpern, Leivick, *see* Leivick, H.			
Harendorf, Shmuel-Yankev (1900–69)	King of Lampedusa	1943/35	30 Dec. 1943
Hirschbein, Peretz (1881–1948)	Blacksmith's Daughter	1924/12	1 Apr. 1924
	Groene weiden [Grine felder; Green Fields]	1922/29	1 Nov. 1922
	Neweile [Carrion]	1922/29	1 Nov. 1922
	Puste kretschme [The Idle Inn]	1922/29	1 Nov. 1922
	Quiet Corner	1923/28	13 Nov. 1923

Table 10.1 (*cont.*)

Author	Play	LCP no.	Licensing date[a]
Hochberg, J.	Resele [Reyzele]	1925/50	24 Dec. 1925
Hofer, A.	Kollegen	1904/5	4 Mar. 1904
Horowitz, M.	Spanish Gypsy Girl	1902/15	28 Apr. 1902
Hurwitz, Yisroel-Zalmen, *see* Libin, Z.			
Jacobs, A.[c]	Blind Man's Buff [Eng.]	1927/12	1927
Jacobs, J.	Bielastock [Białystok] Massacre	1906/22	30 July 1906
Jewry, E. [pseud.]	Unwedded Wife	1906/23	30 July 1906
Kalman(?), Emerich	Gypsy Princess	1899	no. 155
	Gypsy Princess	1944	21 Jan. 1944
Kalmanovitsh, Harry (1885/6–1966)	Forgotten Children	1925/35	26 Sept. 1925
Kobrin, Leon (1872–1946)	Back to his People	1922/31	11 Nov. 1922
	Dorfsjung	1922/29	1 Nov. 1922
	Love against All	1907/28	25 Nov. 1907
Kolar, J.	Jew of Prague [Yiddish?]	1921/14	2 June 1921
Kornblith, Zishe (1872–1929)	Real Happiness	1906/35	3 Dec. 1906
Kowinsky, E.	Adoption	1920/29	2 Dec. 1920
Labiner, F.	King David and King Saul	1898/9–10	53610A
Latayner, Yosef/Yozef/Yoysef, *see* Lateiner, Joseph			
Lateiner, Joseph (pseud.;	Blemele	1901/34	28 Oct. 1901
Yosef Finklshteyn; 1853–1935)	Broken Hearts	1906/11	16 Apr. 1906
	Eva	1901/38	2 Dec. 1901
	Ezra	1901/42	18 Dec. 1901
	Gabriel	1906/11	16 Apr. 1906
	Golden Wedding	1908/25	9 Nov. 1908
	Great Inquisitor	1908/16	6 Aug. 1908
	Jewish Crown	1913/01	23 Dec. 1912
	Jewish Minister	1906/16	29 May 1906
	Jewish World	1902/18	26 May 1902
	Man and Wife	1909/06	8 Mar. 1909
	Power of Music	1900/13	30 Aug. 1900
	Romanian Jew	1903/17	7 July 1903
	Virtuous Woman	1902	10 Mar. 1902
Leivick, H.	The Golem	1931/01	1 Jan. 1931
(pseud.; Leivick Halpern; 1886–1962)	Professor Schelling	1939/35	2 June 1939
	Rags	1924/12	1 Apr. 1924
Libin, Z. (pseud.; 1872–1955)	(?)Emigrants	1945/40	31 Dec. 1945
	Justice	1912/32	12 July 1912
	On Our Own Soil	1945/30	24 Oct. 1945
Markovitsh, Joseph (1882–1967)	Israel Lives and Laughs	1945/26	14 Sept. 1945
	Jewish Student	1906/36	3 Dec. 1906
	Mendl beylis	1913/37	24 Oct. 1913
	[Mendl beylis protses]		
	Paris at Night	1926/16	26 Mar. 1926

Author	Play	LCP no.	Licensing date[a]
Nager, Aaron (1880–1930s)	Benjamin's Brother	1915/28	29 Oct. 1915
Nomberg, Hersh-Dovid (1876–1927)	Mischpoche [Family]	1922/29	1 Nov. 1922
Olshanetski, Alexander (Yehoshue (Shue) Olshanetsky; 1892–1946)	Americana Litwak [Amerikaner litvak]	1943/26	22 Oct. 1943
	My Baby	1927/42	29 Oct. 1927
Olshanski, Alexander, *see* Olshanetski, Alexander			
Oyerbach, Yitskhok	Bostenoi	1902/07	24 Feb. 1902
	Daughter of Jerusalem	1901/39	2 Dec. 1901
Perelman, Joseph/Yosef/Yoysef, *see* Dimov, Osip			
Pinski, Dovid (1872–1959)	Jacob the Smith [Yankl der shmid]	1946/04	6 Feb. 1946
	Jankel der smid	1922/29	1 Nov. 1922
	Yekel the Smith	1910/18	18 July 1910
Rabinovitsh, Shalom, *see* Sholem Aleykhem			
Rackow, N., *see* Rakov, Nokhem			
Rakoff, Nahum, *see* Rakov, Nokhem			
Rakov, Nokhem (1866–1927)	Back to the Faith	1918/19	19 Nov. 1918
	Bigamist	1907/01	8 Jan. 1907
	Factory Girl	1907/32	21 Dec. 1907
	Jewish Heart	1909/16	5 July 1909
	Persecution of the Jews in Portugal	1896/3–4	53596 A–Q
	Persecution of the Jews in Portugal	1902/14	28 Apr. 1902
	Return to Zion	1902/01	13 Jan. 1902
Rapoport, Shloyme-Zaynvil, *see* Ansky, S.			
Richter, Moses, *see* Rikhter, Moyshe			
Rikhter, Moyshe (1871–1939)	Rabi [Rabbi] Gershon's Curse	1902/12	9 Apr. 1902
	Too Late	1925/13	8 Apr. 1925
Rotbaum, Jacob, *see* Rotboym, Yankev			
Rotboym, Yankev (1901–94)	Goldfadn Dream	1947/04	31 Jan. 1947
	Goldfadn Dream	1961	—
Rozenberg, Yisroel (1885–1963)	Maschka	1946/15	16 Apr. 1946
Schiller, Johann Christian Friedrich[b] (1757–1805)	Kabale und Liebe	1902/06	11 Feb. 1902
Schomer, *see* Shaykevitsh, Nokhem Meyer			
Schorr, Anshel, *see* Shor, Anshl			
Schorr, Moses, *see* Shor, Moyshe			
Schwartz(?), Maurice (1888?–1960)	Under One Roof	1932/13	20 Apr. 1932
Seifert, Moshe, *see* Zeifert, Moyshe			
Sharkanski, Avrom-Mikhl (1869–1907)	Father's Sacrifice	1901/09	25 Mar. 1901
	Golden Land of America	1902/15	28 Apr. 1902
	Moses chayit	1906/13	24 Apr. 1906
	Rabbi Amnon	1907/26	15 Nov. 1907

Table 10.1 *(cont.)*

Author	Play	LCP no.	Licensing date[a]
Sharkansky, A. M./Abraham M., *see* Sharkanski, Avrom-Mikhl			
Shaykevitsh, Nokhem Meyer (Shomer; 1846–1905)	Kenig far a nakht	1899	29 June 1899
Sharman, Joseph, *see* Sherman, Yosef			
Sherman, Yosef	Child of Warsaw	1914/38	24 Dec. 1914
	Emigration from Kishinev	1903/17	7 July 1903
Sholem Aleykhem (pseud. Sholem Rabinovitsh; 1859–1916)	Great Prize	1923	4 Oct. 1923
	Hard to be a Jew	1935/23	19 Sept. 1935
	It's Hard to be a Jew	1924/12	1 Apr. 1924
	Tevye the Dairyman	1924/12	1 Apr. 1924
	Tevyeke the Milkman	1957/17	26 Mar. 1957
Shomer, Avrom[c] (1876–1946)	Devil Dick [Eng.]	1922/29	1 Nov. 1922
Shor, Anshl (1871–1942)	Song of Love [Shir hashirim]	1912/27	5 June 1912
	Song of Songs	1943/33	13 Dec. 1943
Shor, Moyshe (1872–1949)	Romanian Wedding	1925/36	10 Oct. 1925
Siegal, William (1893–1966)	American Rebitzen	1943/35	29 Dec. 1943
Singer, I. J. (1893–1944)	Brother Aschkenazi	1938/37	24 June 1938
	Yoshe kalb	1935/29	17 July 1935
Sloves, Chaim (b. 1905)	Baruch of Amsterdam	1961	1961
Voynich, E.	Marriage [Yiddish?]	1925/36	10 Oct. 1925
Zangwill, Israel[b] (1864–1926)	King of the Schnorrers	1930/36	8 Aug. 1930
	Melting Pot	1908/17	17 Aug. 1908
Zeifert, Moyshe (1851–1922)	Thirty Years in Siberia	1896/10	53611
Zolotarevsky, Yitskhok (1875–1945)	Expressman	1909/16	13 July 1909
	Mother	1909/07	22 Mar. 1909
	Mother's Sacrifice	1916/12	27 May 1916
	Rabbinicle shtudent [Rabbinical Student]	1903/17	7 July 1903
	(?)Steiger Trial	1926/18	12 Apr. 1926
	Three Brides	1925/38	22 Oct. 1925

The spelling of play titles is as found in the applications to the Lord Chamberlain's Office.

[a] Prior to 1900 plays were consecutively numbered upon receipt; where it has not proved possible to determine the date of licensing, this number is given as an aid to researchers.

[b] Playwrights translated into Yiddish.

[c] Playwrights translated from Yiddish into English.

Table 10.2 Chronological listing by date of licence

Licensing date[a]	Author	Play	LCP no.
155	Emerich (?)Kalman	Gypsy Princess	1899
661	Avrom Goldfaden	Reb yoslman [Rebbe Yozlman]	1896 (lost)
662	—	King Pharaoh	1896 (lost)
53231 (no. 28)	Israel Aksenfeld	The Jewish Soldier	1880/1–2
53596 A–Q	Nokhem Rakov	Persecution of the Jews in Portugal	1896/3–4
53610 M	Avrom Goldfaden	Sulamita [Shulamis]	1896/9–10
53611	Moyshe Zeifert	Thirty Years in Siberia	1896/10
53611A–N	Avrom Goldfaden	Bar Cochlar [Bar Kokhba]	1896/10
53610A–N	F. Labiner	King David and King Saul	1898/9–10
53693/99(?) (no. 108)	—	Jewish Emigration	1898/11
1899			
29 June	Nokhem Meyer Shaykevitsh	Kenig far a nakht	1899
1900			
22 Aug.	Jacob Gordin	Lured from Home	1900/12
30 Aug.	Joseph Lateiner	Power of Music	1900/13
1901			
25 Mar.	Avrom-Mikhl Sharkanski	Father's Sacrifice	1901/09
1 Aug.	Jacob Gordin	Jewish King Lear	1901/25
28 Oct.	Joseph Lateiner	Blemele	1901/34
4 Nov.	Avrom Goldfaden	Tenth Commandment	1901/36
2 Dec.	Joseph Lateiner	Eva	1901/38
2 Dec.	Yitskhok Oyerbach	Daughter of Jerusalem	1901/39
18 Dec.	Avrom Goldfaden	Bar Cochba, the Son of the Star [Bar Kokhba]	1901/42
18 Dec.	Joseph Lateiner	Ezra	1901/42
1902			
13 Jan.	Nokhem Rakov	Return to Zion	1902/01
11 Feb.	Johann Christian Friedrich Schiller	Kabale und Liebe	1902/06
24 Feb.	Yitskhok Oyerbach	Bostenoi	1902/07
10 Mar.	Joseph Lateiner	Virtuous Woman	1902
17 Mar.	Avrom Goldfaden	King Ahasuerus	1902/11
9 Apr.	Moyshe Rikhter	Rabi [Rabbi] Gershon's Curse	1902/12
28 Apr.	Nokhem Rakov	Persecution of the Jews in Portugal	1902/14
28 Apr.	M. Horowitz	Spanish Gypsy Girl	1902/15
28 Apr.	Avrom-Mikhl Sharkanski	Golden Land of America	1902/15
26 May	Joseph Lateiner	Jewish World	1902/18
2 June	Avrom Goldfaden	Judith and King Alferius	1902/19
24 Aug.	Jacob Gordin	Alisheva [Elisha ben-avuya(?)]	1902/26
1903			
7 July	Yitskhok Zolotarevsky	Rabbinicle shtudent [Rabbinical Student]	1903/17
7 July	Joseph Lateiner	Romanian Jew	1903/17
7 July	Yosef Sherman	Emigration from Kishinev	1903/17
1904			
11 Jan.	Jacob Gordin (Faynman)	Kreutzer sonata	1904/05
4 Mar.	A. Hofer	Kollegen	1904/05
19 Sept.	Avrom Goldfaden	Judas Maccabeus	1904/22
28 Nov.	Jacob Gordin	Kreutzer sonata	1904/27
1905			
21 Mar.	Jacob Gordin	Broken Hearts	1905/07
11 Apr.	Jacob Gordin	Miryam efros	1906/09
25 Nov.	Karl Ferdinand Gutzkow	Uriel acosta	1905/28

Table 10.2 (*cont.*)

Licensing date[a]	Author	Play	LCP no.
1906			
16 Apr.	Joseph Lateiner	Gabriel	1906/11
16 Apr.	Joseph Lateiner	Broken Hearts	1906/11
24 Apr.	Max Gable	Father and Mother's Sorrows	1906/12
24 Apr.	Avrom-Mikhl Sharkanski	Moses chayit	1906/13
29 May	Joseph Lateiner	Jewish Minister	1906/16
30 July	J. Jacobs	Bielastock [Białystok] Massacre	1906/22
30 July	E. Jewry [pseud.]	Unwedded Wife	1906/23
15 Aug.	Jacob Gordin	Meturef (The Abnormal Man)	1906/24
30 Aug.	Jacob Gordin	Solomon kans	1906/24
13 Sept.	Jacob Gordin	Myer yosovitch [Mayer yozefovitsh]	1906/26
17 Sept.	J. Jacobs	Solomon the Siberian	1906/27
17 Oct.	Sigmund Feinman	Rabbi Leib Sepharde	1906/30
12 Nov.	Jacob Gordin	God, Man, and the Devil	1906
3 Dec.	Zishe Kornblith	Real Happiness	1906/35
3 Dec.	Joseph Markovitsh	Jewish Student	1906/36
1907			
8 Jan.	Nokhem Rakov	Bigamist	1907/01
1 Mar.	Sigmund Feinman	Jews in Morocco	1907/05
1 Mar.	Jacob Gordin (Feinman)	Kreutzer sonata	1907/05
24 May	—	Jewish Zaza	1907/11
17 Sept.	Sigmund Feinman	Shattered Lives	1907/20
17 Sept.	Sigmund Feinman	Mother's Sacrifice	1907/20
17 Sept.	Sigmund Feinman	Knave of Hearts	1907/20
15 Oct.	Jacob Gordin	Widower	1907/24
15 Nov.	Avrom-Mikhl Sharkanski	Rabbi Amnon	1907/26
25 Nov.	Leon Kobrin	Love against All	1907/28
21 Dec.	Nokhem Rakov	Factory Girl	1907/32
1908			
30 Jan.	Jacob Gordin	Beautiful Miriam	1908/02
3 Mar.	—	Professional Socialist	1908/04
3 Mar.	Sigmund Feinman	Nightingale of Jerusalem	1908/04
11 May	Jacob Gordin	Two Worlds	1908/10
6 Aug.	Joseph Lateiner	Great Inquisitor	1908/16
17 Aug.	Israel Zangwill	Melting Pot	1908/17
20 Oct.	Sigmund Feinman	My Wife's Friend	1908/21
9 Nov.	Joseph Lateiner	Golden Wedding	1908/25
1909			
8 Mar.	Joseph Lateiner	Man and Wife	1909/06
22 Mar.	Yitskhok Zolotarevsky	Mother	1909/07
22 Mar.	Jacob Gordin	Real Power	1909/07
5 July	Nokhem Rakov	Jewish Heart	1909/16
13 July	Yitskhok Zolotarevsky	Expressman	1909/16
1910			
18 July	Dovid Pinski	Yekel the Smith	1910/18
1911			
10 July	—	Broken Mirror	1911/19
1912			
19 Apr.	Mark Arnshteyn	Singer of Vilna	1912/16
5 June	Shor Anshl	Song of Love [Shir hashirim]	1912/27
12 July	Z. Libin	Justice	1912/32
23 Dec.	Joseph Lateiner	Jewish Crown	1913/01

Licensing date[a]	Author	Play	LCP no.
1913 24 Oct.	Joseph Markovitsh	Mendl beylis [Mendl beylis protses]	1913/37
1914 24 Dec.	Yosef Sherman	Child of Warsaw	1914/38
1915 29 Oct.	Aaron Nager	Benjamin's Brother	1915/28
1916 27 May	Yitskhok Zolotarevsky	Mother's Sacrifice	1916/12
1918 19 Nov.	Nokhem Rakov	Back to the Faith	1918/19
1920 2 Dec.	E. Kowinsky	Adoption	1920/29
1921 2 June	J. Kolar	Jew of Prague [Yiddish?]	1921/14
1922 —	—	Traffic in Souls	1922/19
13 Oct.	S. Ansky	Dibbick [Dybbuk]	1922/26
1 Nov.	Peretz Hirschbein	Groene weiden [Grine felder; Green Fields]	1922/29
1 Nov.	Peretz Hirschbein	Neweile [Carrion]	1922/29
1 Nov.	Peretz Hirschbein	Puste kretschme [The Idle Inn]	1922/29
1 Nov.	Leon Kobrin	Dorfsjung	1922/29
1 Nov.	Hersh-Dovid Nomberg	Mischpoche [Family]	1922/29
1 Nov.	Dovid Pinski	Jankel der smid	1922/29
1 Nov.	Avrom Shomer	Devil Dick [Eng.]	1922/29
11 Nov.	Leon Kobrin	Back to his People	1922/31
1923 14 Sept.	S. Ansky	Day and Night	1923/23
4 Oct.	Sholem Aleykhem	Great Prize	1923
9 Oct.	Sholem Asch	Vengeance	1923/26
13 Nov.	Peretz Hirschbein	Quiet Corner	1923/28
20 Nov.	Sholem Asch	His Own People	1923/30
1924 16 Feb.	Jacob Gordin	Own Blood	1924/06
1 Apr.	Sholem Aleykhem	It's Hard to be a Jew	1924/12
1 Apr.	Sholem Aleykhem	Tevye the Dairyman	1924/12
1 Apr.	Avrom Goldfaden	Two Koonylemmels [The Two Kuni Lemls]	1924/12
1 Apr.	Peretz Hirschbein	Blacksmith's Daughter	1924/12
1 Apr.	H. Leivick	Rags	1924/12
1925 8 Apr.	Moyshe Rikhter	Too Late	1925/13
26 Sept.	Harry Kalmanovitsh	Forgotten Children	1925/35
10 Oct.	Moyshe Shor	Romanian Wedding	1925/36
—	E. Voynich	Marriage [Yiddish?]	1925/36
22 Oct.	Yitskhok Zolotarevsky	Three Brides	1925/38
17 Dec.	Jacob Gordin	Muriel efros [synopsis]	1925/49
24 Dec.	J. Hochberg	Resele [Reyzele]	1925/50
1926 26 Mar.	Joseph Markovitsh	Paris at Night	1926/16
12 Apr.	Yitskhok Zolotarevsky(?)	Steiger Trial	1926/18

Table 10.2 (*cont.*)

Licensing date[a]	Author	Play	LCP no.
1927			
17 Mar.	S. Ansky	Dybbuk	1927/12
—	A. Jacobs	Blind Man's Buff [Eng.]	1927/12
27 Oct.	Alexander Olshanetski	My Baby	1927/42
1930			
8 Aug.	Israel Zangwill	King of the Schnorrers	1930/36
31 Dec.	S. Ansky	Dybbuk	1930/58
1931			
1 Jan.	H. Leivick	The Golem	1931/01
1932			
10 Feb.	—	Argentine Nights	1932/06
20 Apr.	Maurice Schwartz(?)	Under One Roof	1932/13
1933			
16 Oct.	Louis Freiman(?)	Jewish General	1933/33
1934			
22 Mar.	Sholem Asch	Supreme Sacrifice	1934/12
11 Apr.	Dovid Bergelson	Breadmill	1934/14
1935			
17 July	I. J. Singer	Yoshe kalb	1935/29
24 Aug.	Jacob Gordin, rev. Maurice Schwartz	God, Man, and Devil	1935/21
19 Sept.	Sholem Aleykhem	Hard to be a Jew	1935/23
19 Sept.	Sholem Asch	God of Vengeance	1935/23
1938			
24 June	I. J. Singer	Brother Aschkenazi	1938/37
1939			
2 June	H. Leivick	Professor Schelling	1939/35
1943			
15 Oct.	Sholem Asch	Uncle Moses	1943/25
22 Oct.	Alexander Olshanetski	Americana Litwak [Amerikaner litvak]	1943/26
13 Dec.	—	Motke from Slobotke	1943/33
13 Dec.	Anshl Shor	Song of Songs	1943/33
29 Dec.	William Siegal	American Rebitzen	1943/35
30 Dec.	Shmuel-Yankev Harendorf	King of Lampedusa	1943/35
1944			
11 Jan.	Jacob Gordin	Kreutzer sonata	1944/01
21 Jan.	Emerich (?) Kalman	Gypsy Princess	1944
4 Feb.	Sholem Asch	Motke the Thief	1944/03
14 Feb.	—	Yosele un feygele	1944/04
1945			
14 Sept.	Joseph Markovitsh	Israel Lives and Laughs	1945/26
24 Oct.	Z. Libin	On Our Own Soil	1945/30
—	Avrom Blum	Sun Rises Again [Eng.]	1945/40
31 Dec.	Avrom Goldfaden	Messiah's Times	1945/40
31 Dec.	Z. Libin(?)	Emigrants	1945/40

Licensing date[a]	Author	Play	LCP no.
1946			
6 Feb.	Osip Dimov	Jossek the Musician	1946/04
6 Feb.	Dovid Pinski	Jacob the Smith	1946/04
—	Yisroel Rozenberg	Maschka	1946/15
8 May	—	Palestinian Life	1946/15
8 May	—	Leye lubliner	1946/15
1947			
31 Jan.	Yankev Rotboym	Goldfadn Dream	1947/04
1949			
13 Jan.	—	The Shlemihl	1949
6 Apr.	Avrom Blum	Sun Rises Again [Eng.]	1945
—	Louis Freiman	Tsipke fayer	1949
1957			
26 Mar.	Sholem Aleykhem	Tevyeke the Milkman	1957/17
26 Mar.	Jacob Gordin	Mirele efros	1957/17
26 Mar.	Jacob Gordin, rev. I. Kaminska	Meye ezefowitch	1957/17
1961			
—	Yankev Rotboym	Goldfadn Dream	1961
—	Chaim Sloves	Baruch of Amsterdam	1961

The spelling of play titles is as found in the applications to the Lord Chamberlain's Office.

[a] Prior to 1900 plays were consecutively numbered upon receipt; where it has not proved possible to determine the date of licensing, this number is given as an aid to researchers.

V. CRITICISM

ELEVEN

The Child Who Wouldn't Grow Up: Yiddish Theatre and its Critics

 ❧

NINA WARNKE

A ROUND the beginning of the twentieth century a vibrant Yiddish theatre culture flourished on New York's Lower East Side. Several large theatres and their stars vied for audiences, offering historical operas, melodramas, musical comedies, and realist dramas. For the predominantly lower-class and minimally educated immigrants, most of whom had little theatre experience in eastern Europe, the stage quickly developed into the primary institution for entertainment. It was an unruly, boisterous place which entertained its audience primarily with plays that emphasized spectacle over text, visual attractions over logical plot development, slapstick over emotional subtlety, entertainment over education.

The community's intellectual leaders—the journalists, writers, and political activists belonging to the radical camp—monitored the theatre's achievements and failures and attempted to steer it from its lower-class roots and *shund* (literally, trash), as they called it, to a high-art theatre modelled on the dominant artistic trends in Europe. In order to bring realism to the stage, these critics, in conjunction with Jacob Gordin (1853–1909), 'the reformer of the Yiddish theatre', educated both the actors and the public about contemporary perceptions of art. Newspapers, journals, and special pamphlets printed hundreds of reviews, essays on the history of the European theatre or the 'deplorable' state of the Yiddish stage, and articles on the laws and significance of realist drama, creating an intense public discourse which enveloped all segments of the immigrant population. Given the charged political atmosphere in the turn-of-the-century Jewish community, much of this writing was partisan and polemical, guided by personal friendship, animosity, or newspaper

Publication of this chapter was made possible in part through the financial assistance of the Indiana University Russian and East European Institute through their Andrew W. Mellon Foundation Endowment.

politics.[1] Despite the massive quantity and impassioned quality of these articles, they have largely been overlooked by theatre critics and scholars. Zalmen Zylbercweig (1894–1972), for example, whose *Leksikon fun yidishn teater* (Lexicon of Yiddish Theatre) is an essential resource for historians of the Yiddish stage, clearly underestimated the volume and impact of theatre-related articles in the American Yiddish press before the First World War.[2] Subsequently, other Yiddish theatre critics dismissed the value of these texts as serious criticism because of their often personal nature and their lack of certain essential components of theatre reviews (for example, detailed discussions of the staging and the acting).[3] This body of critical writings, however, is significant not only for its scope but also because it displays a clear underlying intellectual framework, which informed the discourse at the time and to this day shapes much of our perception of the nature and development of the Yiddish theatre.

Influenced by the pervasive concept developed by Hegel and Marx of society and culture developing in stages, and of progress as a historical law, these critics perceived Yiddish theatre, and by extension the east European Jewish masses, to be at the beginning of a historical process that had started with the Haskalah and would eventually lead to a mature culture and society. This notion of the linear progress of all cultures from 'primitive' to highly 'developed' served many critics as a model to assess the state of Yiddish theatre.[4] Intent on spurring on this process in order to catch up with the 'developed' level of European culture, they made a concerted effort to teach immigrants to appreciate contemporary, and to a lesser degree classical, drama and literature. Numerous works discussed the European theatrical tradition or modern European dramatists. Gordin, in particular, translated and adapted plays

[1] Most notorious, although not exceptional, were the partisan reviews of Jacob Gordin's plays and the polemics for and against him, in which all Yiddish papers participated. For a discussion of the editor of *Forverts*, Abraham Cahan's, personally motivated attacks on Gordin, see Ronald Sanders, *Downtown Jews: Portraits of an Immigrant Generation* (New York: Harper & Row, 1969). Similarly, during his brief visit to America in 1906–7 Sholem Aleykhem became the victim of politically motivated criticism. See Nina Warnke, 'Of Plays and Politics: Sholem Aleichem's First Visit to America', *YIVO Annual*, 20 (1991), 239–76.

[2] *Leksikon fun yidishn teater*, 6 vols. (New York: Elisheva, 1931–70). In response to the justified criticism that the bibliographies in vol. i of his *Leksikon* were incomplete, Zylbercweig asserted that until the First World War 'very little was written about Yiddish theatre' and that he had cited every review. He was also unaware that theatre journals were published during these years. See Zylbercweig, 'Ven a kritiker aylt zikh' [When a Critic Hurries], in Zalmen Zylbercweig, *Teater mozayik* [Theatre Mosaics] (New York: Itshe Biderman, 1941), 97. Unless otherwise noted, all translations from Yiddish are my own.

[3] See Jacob Mestel, *Undzer teater* [Our Theatre] (New York: YKUF, 1943), 62.

[4] For a discussion on the radicals' concept of 'development', see Steven Cassedy, *To the Other Shore: The Russian Jewish Intellectuals who Came to America* (Princeton: Princeton University Press, 1997), 38–9, 68–9.

from the European repertoire in order to familiarize audiences with Shake-speare as well as German and Russian dramatic literature. Radical intellec-tuals regarded *Bildung* (broad-based education) as a key element in bringing the Jewish masses into the orbit of the modern world and in creating more conscious and, in their parlance, 'developed' workers. This model of cultural and societal progress, however, limited the critics' ability to recognize the stratification of taste and cultural needs according to class as a legitimate factor in the creation and reception of artistic products.

One of the central metaphors writers employed to describe the state of Yiddish theatre was that of a child in its early stages of development. No one expressed these interrelated concepts of theatre as 'child', cultural 'progress', and societal 'development' more succinctly than Khonen Minikes (1867–1932), the editor of the 1897 volume *Di idishe bine* (The Yiddish Stage), published in celebration of the twentieth anniversary of the Yiddish stage. In rhetoric typical of the time he presented some of the central notions about the role of Yiddish theatre within the Jewish community on the one hand and with respect to non-Jewish culture on the other:

Yiddish theatre is turning twenty this month. It has been only thirteen years since the first Yiddish theatre was founded in New York. . . . The young Yiddish theatre child has made such progress here in America that its importance is beginning to make itself felt in Jewish life. . . . finally the time has come to regard Yiddish theatre as an important educational force, as the Christians regard their theatres. . . . The twenty-year existence of Yiddish theatre marks an important period in the intellec-tual development of our brethren, and the anniversary should be celebrated by the entire Jewish intelligentsia.[5]

This image of the child served to express multiple relationships. It denoted Yiddish theatre's relationship to non-Jewish theatre culture: its 'youth' and its 'less developed' state in comparison to the national theatres of Europe. It also signified the relationship of Yiddish cultural leaders to the theatre as an insti-tution. Avrom Goldfaden (1840–1908) perceived himself and was generally acknowledged to be the 'father of Yiddish theatre'; the 'reformer' Jacob Gordin (1853–1909), too, saw himself as a paternal figure. Given the 'youth' of the Yiddish theatre, intellectuals created their own paternalistic relationship to it, regarding it as a child that required constant vigilance and guidance to grow into a respectable, mature institution. They extended this relationship to the

---

[5] Khonen Y. Minikes, 'Hakdomes hameasef' [Introduction to the Collection], in id. (ed.), *Di idishe bine* [The Yiddish Stage] (New York: Katzenelenbogen, 1897), unpaginated. Minikes, whose introduction is dated March 1897, is not exact with his timeline: Goldfaden did not begin his activ-ities in March 1877, as the article suggests, but in the autumn of 1876, and the first Yiddish perform-ance in New York took place not thirteen but fifteen years earlier (in 1882).

audiences, the intellectually 'undeveloped' immigrants whom they depicted as either naive or obstinate. While the critics generally agreed that the theatre had progressed during its few decades of existence and even, at times, were optimistic that through the efforts of individual writers it was about to reach the artistic level of European art theatres, they often deplored the fact that this process was too slow and suffered constant setbacks.

There was general consensus that Yiddish theatre owed its existence to one particular creator, Avrom Goldfaden, who had laid its 'cornerstone' when he began collaborating with the Broder singers Grodner and Goldstein in Jassy, Romania, in autumn 1876. Despite centuries-old traditions of Jewish performance, Goldfaden was acknowledged as the father of Yiddish theatre because under his—a writer's—leadership, the theatre was put into the service of the Haskalah. If one accepts that it was his 'child', Yiddish theatre had indeed had a very brief history. It was an 'undeveloped' child at that, particularly when compared to the theatrical traditions of Europe, whether they could be seen as extending as far back as ancient Greece or, within the narrower framework of Enlightenment theatre and the development of national theatres, to the eighteenth century.

By granting Goldfaden fatherhood of Yiddish theatre—that is, literary theatre in the Enlightenment tradition—turn-of-the-century intellectuals denied cultural legitimacy to the old Jewish folk performances such as *purim-shpiln* (Purim plays) and *batkhones* (wedding entertainments). Nor did they acknowledge the Haskalah comedies of the first half of the nineteenth century, whose authors had not been interested in creating a Yiddish stage, nor the Broder singers, who were acting out songs, monologues, and sketches in wine cellars and other makeshift theatres for some two decades before Goldfaden's involvement. While agreeing that these traditions provided the grounds on which Goldfaden created modern Yiddish theatre, they relegated them, in the words of one critic, to a cultural 'prehistory' from which modern theatre had to extricate itself.[6]

This division between a modern, literary stage and folk theatre mirrored the discourse of the bourgeois European theatre practitioners and critics of the Enlightenment period. They had declared theatre to be the handmaiden of literature and, by extension, of the Enlightenment, education, and nation-building. Their opposition to non-literary, improvisational entertainment was due to folk theatre's lower-class origins, its often inimical relationship to high culture, its lack of educational purpose, and its unruly environment. The

---

[6] Joel Entin, 'Di forgeshikhte funem yidishn teater' [The Prehistory of Yiddish Theatre], in *Suvenir tsu yakob gordins tsen-yerikn yubileyum* [Souvenir for Jacob Gordin's Tenth Anniversary] (New York: no publisher given, 1901), 15–22.

Yiddish critics' rejection of folk performances fits squarely into the legacy of the Enlighteners' condemnation of improvisational folk traditions: for example, Johann Christoph Gottsched's theatrical reforms, Joseph von Sonnenfels's feud with the Viennese folk theatre in the eighteenth century, and Russian intellectuals' attacks on *balagan* (Russian fairground entertainment) in the nineteenth century.[7]

Despite his position as the father of Yiddish theatre, Goldfaden was deeply disturbed and frustrated by his powerlessness against the forces—particularly the actors and competing ideas about the identity of modern Yiddish theatre—that undermined his efforts to raise the child into a mature, upstanding adult. He did not only see himself as the father of some abstract notion of theatre, or the creator of the first Yiddish plays; particularly in the early years his responsibilities extended to a paternal (and paternalistic) relationship with his actors, many of whom were young men and women who had run away from home to join the early wandering theatre troupes in Russia and Romania. But not only was he almost a generation older than many of his actors; he was also far better educated. Most of the early actors had little schooling, and some could barely read, which added to their supposed childlike dependence. In eastern Europe Goldfaden therefore exerted considerable power over his performers, teaching them how to act and to adhere to his vision of the theatre. But he lost his hold over them when these stage-struck teenagers emigrated, matured, and became stars.

Having moved to America in 1888, several years after some of his actors had established themselves in New York, Goldfaden tried to assume directorial control over the Romanian Opera House, but the performers, apparently fearing his dictatorial style, ousted him through a strike and he was forced to return to Europe. He fared no better when he went back in 1903. While in eastern Europe his plays continued to hold a central place in the repertoire during the early 1900s, in New York his works were shown only intermittently, to fill an evening between two feature productions or for benefit performances. Goldfaden, who had not produced a new play since the mid-1890s, simply could not compete with the plethora of local playwrights. In a letter to his friend and fellow Yiddish writer Yankev Dinezon (1856?–1919), Goldfaden expressed his sense of defeat:

I have no complaints that the American Yiddish theatre did not recognize its father and does not want to have anything to do with me. . . . But I have a complaint, although I don't know against whom, that my dear child is growing up a *sheygets*

---

[7] See Roland Dressler, *Von der Schaubühne zur Sittenschule. Das Theaterpublikum vor der vierten Wand* (Berlin: Henschel Verlag, 1993) and Catriona Kelly, *Petrushka: The Russian Carnival Puppet Theatre* (Cambridge: Cambridge University Press, 1990).

[non-Jewish male], an impertinent child, and I should prepare myself that some day they will curse me for this precious brat that I brought into the world.

As he explained further, for Goldfaden this loss of parental control was directly related to the experience of migration: 'Among a people whose children and parents are forced to migrate at different times and often on different paths, it is common for children not to recognize their parents and even for parents not to find the way to their children.'[8] Although, from a comfortable distance, New York actors—or his 'children', as he called them—still revered Goldfaden as the man who had fathered Yiddish theatre, they no longer felt a filial duty towards him.[9] They had outgrown the patriarchal Old World model, and Goldfaden's expectations of gratitude for having saved them from their lowly and shady, if not criminal, past no longer fitted their self-image as stars and professionals in a modern, American theatrical world.[10]

But the father was also rejected on ideological grounds by the group of young radical intellectuals who became the cultural arbiters of the immigrant community. From the late 1880s onwards these men battled against what they considered the legacy of folk performance traditions, which they located in Goldfaden's early comedies. They also fought against the commercial nature of the plays by Moyshe Hurwitz (1844–1910), Joseph Lateiner (1853–1935), and others, the themes and messages of whose historical operas were reminiscent of *purimshpiln*. Attempting to demarcate the line between the 'primitive' and the more 'developed' state of Yiddish theatre, they criticized any actor or play they did not approve of as *purimshpiler*, *purimshpil*, *batkhn* (wedding jester), *balagan*, or Shmendrik and Kuni Leml, the foolish and backward title characters of two of Goldfaden's early comedies.[11] Committed to cosmopolitan ideals of art, these intellectuals asserted that with his early slapstick comedies and musical plays steeped in nationalist sentiment, Goldfaden had put the theatre on the wrong track, thereby laying the foundation for *shund*, or cheap commercial entertainment. Instead of uplifting the theatre, they charged, he had given in to the demands of the masses, and instead of leading them

---

[8] Zylbercweig (ed.), *Leksikon*, i. 330.

[9] On Goldfaden's complaints about his 'children' no longer recognizing their 'father', see Leon Kobrin, *Erinerungen fun a yidishn dramaturg* [Recollections of a Yiddish Playwright], 2 vols. (New York: Komitet far Kobrins Shriftn, 1925), ii. 159.

[10] Ibid. Goldfaden noted that several of his early actors were pimps and pickpockets when he invited them to join his troupe.

[11] In his compelling article 'Fear of Purim' Michael C. Steinlauf uses Bakhtin's concept of the 'carnivalesque' to unravel the roots of Y. L. Peretz's distaste for popular Yiddish theatre, which he locates in Peretz's hatred of Purim and the *purimshpil*. See Michael C. Steinlauf, 'Fear of Purim: Y. L. Peretz and the Canonization of Yiddish Theater', *Jewish Social Studies*, 1/3 (Spring 1993), 44–65.

closer to European contemporary art, he had offered them parochial fantasies.

For Goldfaden, however, it was precisely the reforming efforts of these
intellectuals, and of Gordin in particular, that signified the worst form of
betrayal and corruption. In response to Gordin's *Di shkhite* (The Slaughter),
which explored the humiliating life of a poor young woman at the hands of
her husband and ends with her murdering him, Goldfaden charged bitterly:
'He took my beloved child, my Jewish child, my Benjamin, and converted
it.'[12] By referring to the Yiddish theatre as his 'Benjamin', Goldfaden not only
emphasized his paternal link but, more significantly, equated himself with the
biblical Jacob, from whom the Jewish people descend. Thus he reasserted for
himself the rightful position of the patriarch of a theatre in the Jewish tradition while attacking Gordin for turning it into a non-Jewish art form.

Gordin, the Russified intellectual, came to the 'Romanian-born' Yiddish
stage as a stranger. He was a member of the Russian intelligentsia, his prior
connection to theatre being his position as a Russian theatre critic with the
weekly paper *Nedelya* (Week), but he had no contact with the cultural world
of Yiddish until he turned to Yiddish journalism and theatre when he arrived
in New York in 1891. Partly out of financial need and partly out of a zealous
desire to educate the 'undeveloped' masses, he embarked on a career as a Yiddish playwright. He too claimed paternal feelings towards the stage, but, as
one who became involved after Goldfaden's theatre had been in existence for
fifteen years and whose mission it was to reform what Goldfaden had created,
he presented himself in terms of a loving and devoted foster-parent trying
to save an abandoned child. By describing the Yiddish stage as fatherless,
Gordin in effect denied Goldfaden's position; even if the latter was its pro-
genitor, he was no more than an absent and negligent father. Yet Gordin held
the Jewish masses equally responsible for the poor state of the theatre, describing in his feuilleton, 'Judith', a mother (the masses) who obstinately tries
to prevent his efforts to help her daughter (the theatre):

Judith had a sickly undeveloped little daughter. The child grew up uncared for,
wandered in the rubbish, wore gypsy rags. I raised her up from the rubbish heap,
took off her rags and dressed her in the clothes that children from decent families
wear, washed her dirty little face and showed the world her charm and intelligence.
I gave her presents. . . . The presents maybe aren't worth much, but nobody was
giving her any that were more valuable, better, more costly. Instead of gratitude I
often hear from the mother insults and curses, and she often perversely permits me
to put the child back in her old rags. But [the child] remains my beloved. . . . She
and I seem to have nothing in common; however, we are one body and one soul.

[12] Kobrin, *Erinerungen*, 158.

She doesn't care about me. . . . I know: when I fall, her bought-for-money friends will dance on my body and she'll remain indifferent. If I died today, she'd forget me tomorrow.[13]

Like Goldfaden, Gordin expressed an intense emotional relationship that was not reciprocated by the object of his love. While he did not share Goldfaden's sense of frustrated paternal entitlement, he resented being spurned by the audience on whose behalf he professed to work.

Although for the purposes of this vignette Gordin presented the Jewish mass audience as a mother figure, the intellectuals usually depicted spectators as children. These descriptions, however, varied according to whether they were portraying an individual theatregoer or the audience as a whole. Several sketches focused on the spectator who visits the theatre for the first time and, overwhelmed by the entire experience, fails to comprehend the significance and meaning of the performance. Such portrayals were usually affectionate, if condescending towards the newcomer, who does not understand that he has to remove his hat, or that the play does not end at the intermission. Such spectators, the intellectuals seemed to say, were pure, unspoiled, undeveloped children whose reactions, even if inappropriate for the circumstances, were entirely genuine. Similarly, anecdotes circulated, particularly in response to Gordin's plays, in which spectators could not distinguish between reality and the fictional nature of performance. Most famous is the story of the old man who invited Jacob Adler for dinner as he performed Dovid Moysheles in *Der yidisher kenig lir* (The Jewish King Lear, 1892) because Dovid was being starved by his daughters. This anecdote has become emblematic of the early Yiddish theatre audience and of Yiddish theatre in general. Repeated by almost every critic and scholar discussing the nature of Yiddish theatre, the 'childlike' character of the audience has, by default, become a historical 'fact'. While audience responses such as this certainly occurred, and each performance had its share of newcomers who discovered for the first time the splendours and wonders of the theatre, the majority of spectators on any given night were regular theatregoers, well aware of theatrical conventions, and quite able to discern for themselves whether they were watching a good or bad performance. By and large they used different criteria from the critics: literary quality and realist representation were of secondary importance, for Yiddish audiences placed a higher premium on theatrical aspects such as acting or singing, and on a setting or message to which they could relate emotionally. In stark contrast to their image of the pure and naive greenhorn visiting the theatre, intellectuals used very different rhetoric to describe the

---

[13] Quoted in Nahma Sandrow, *Vagabond Stars: A World History of Yiddish Theater* (New York: Harper & Row, 1977), 160.

audience as a whole. Taken collectively, these seemingly impressionable children were depicted as having been duped and corrupted by *shund*, and as now clinging obstinately to their misguided tastes. A greenhorn could potentially still be moulded into appreciating art, but the audience, as an entity raised on commercial entertainment, seemed to stand in the way of the critics' efforts to create a highbrow theatre.

Despite this audience resistance, the radical intellectuals generally believed that Gordin and others writing realist drama were moving Yiddish theatre forward. The 'improvements', such as stories seemingly taken from life, logical plot development, natural speech instead of the conventional *daytshmerish* (Germanized Yiddish), the actors' closer attention to the text, a more natural acting style, and the introduction of the 'fourth wall', which encroached on the direct contact between actors and audiences, were seen as welcome steps away from *shund* towards a 'higher' art form. Despite Gordin's own misgivings about his impact, others had high hopes that he would single-handedly take Yiddish theatre from its primitive state to the heights of contemporary European theatre, thereby forcing an artistic development within one generation which, as critics pointed out, had taken world theatre hundreds of years. As the lexicographer Alexander Harkavy (1863–1939) explained, theatre developed from the 'primitivism' of ancient Chinese and Indian performances and the *farbeserte* (improved) Greek and Roman plays to the heights of contemporary drama: 'Theatre art has become more beautiful and refined over the centuries. Today theatre is at a very fine level. . . . Now truth is the major concern. Today's critics consider a play good if it presents something real and is played naturalistically, and condemn a play whose content is nonsensical no matter how well it is performed.'[14] In other words, according to these critics, early twentieth-century realism represented the pinnacle of cultural development.

Those who wanted to defend Yiddish theatre's position as popular or 'low' culture would point to the fact that such a young theatre could not produce writers like Ibsen or Hauptmann; modern Yiddish culture was still too undeveloped to produce such genius. Others, however, proudly pointed out that this 'child' was making great strides, and that despite its short history Yiddish theatre could already boast writers such as Gordin who, even if he was not Ibsen, was, after all, writing in the same vein. Yiddish theatre, they asserted, had travelled an enormous cultural distance during its brief existence. Its accelerated development from its primitive beginnings to realism allowed it almost to catch up with the slower-paced European theatre. 'When Gold-faden began to build the Yiddish theatre, the non-Jewish theatre was almost

---

[14] Alexander Harkavy, 'Teater' [Theatre], in Minikes (ed.), *Di idishe bine*, unpaginated.

on the same level as it is today. . . . Realist drama was already in bloom.'[15] Being the product of a specific historical moment, Yiddish theatre, of course, reflected the dominant artistic trends of the time; it could not follow the historical process of European drama.

After 1900 American Yiddish theatre had indeed become, even if in a limited form, a forum for playwrights belonging to the intelligentsia, such as Gordin, Leon Kobrin (1872–1946), and Moyshe Katz (1864–1941), who professed to write in a realist manner. Critics were also encouraged by the increased cultural interaction between Yiddish theatre and the European contemporary art scene: through translations of plays by Hauptmann, Chirikov, Strindberg, and Gorky, audiences were given the opportunity to see the latest international literary products. Likewise, a few Yiddish plays were for the first time produced on American and European stages, among them Gordin's *Kreutzer sonata* (in English and Russian), Dovid Pinski's *Yankl der shmid* (Yankl the Blacksmith) (in German), and Sholem Asch's *Got fun nekome* (God of Vengeance), which was the first Yiddish play to be staged at Max Reinhardt's Deutsches Theater in Berlin in 1907, and was shortly thereafter performed successfully in Russian.

For some Yiddish intellectuals, this discovery of Yiddish drama by well-known European and American directors and actors seemed to be a sign that Yiddish theatre was reaching cultural maturity and was recognized as an equal player in the field of contemporary theatre. Forty years later, however, the actor, director, and critic Jacob Mestel (1884–1958) considered the view that Yiddish theatre would soon 'stand right in the middle of world theatre' a naive illusion: 'while Stanislavsky had already gathered the sheaves of [the German director Otto] Brahm's realism and Reinhardt had spread Gordon Craig and [Adolphe] Appia's early stage visions, Mishurat–Gimpl mediocrities [both directors of Yiddish troupes in eastern Europe] still dressed in rags and treated naive gapers to buffoonery'.[16] Despite Yiddish drama's occasional forays into the European theatre scene, he claimed, Yiddish theatre was still firmly rooted in and characterized by shabby troupes for which the artistic experiments of Brahm and Reinhardt in Berlin and Stanislavsky in Moscow were unimaginable. Moreover, even those intellectuals who believed themselves to be on a par with the latest European trends still advocated realism when stage designers such as Craig and Appia were already transcending it by creating their impressionistic stage visions.

The state of the theatre served as one of the primary yardsticks for the cultural maturity of the Jewish immigrants, and intellectuals became almost

---

[15] Hillel Zolotarov, 'Der onfang fun der yidisher drame in rusland' [The Beginnings of Yiddish Drama in Russia], in *Suvenir*, 24, 26.   [16] Mestel, *Undzer teater*, 67.

obsessed with analysing it, monitoring its development like that of a child whose moral and intellectual welfare was under permanent threat, and needed constant close supervision. In an article summarizing the 1906–7 season the critic, playwright, and future chronicler of the Yiddish stage Bernard Gorin (1868–1925), for example, framed his discussion with the question of whether or not the theatre had 'progressed' that year, comparing the number of staged realist plays and their success or failure with those of the previous season.

The playwright Dovid Pinski (1872–1959), whose own early plays had received attention in translation but were rarely performed on the professional Yiddish stage, was convinced that Yiddish drama had indeed reached a truly artistic level. In his 1909 essay *Dos idishe drama* (The Yiddish Drama),[17] he divided the history of Yiddish drama into three discrete periods of development, a model to which scholars and critics refer implicitly or explicitly to this day: the primitive beginnings under Goldfaden; the intermediary phase under Gordin, who combined primitive elements with some artistic expression; and a last and highest state which was the first to produce real art and which represented his own ideals. He criticized both Goldfaden and Gordin for having made compromises in their writings in order to have their plays performed, and he was not the only one to attack Gordin and other realist playwrights on these grounds. In fact, Abraham Cahan (1860–1951), the editor of the *Arbeter tsaytung* (Workman's Paper) and later of the *Forverts* (Jewish Daily Forward), was the first to characterize Gordin's dramas not as 'good' plays in league with the European realist models, but as plays which were merely 'better' than the 'bad' ones in the tradition of Lateiner and Hurwitz.[18] Critics often scrutinized these 'better' plays, as dramas by intellectuals were generally called, finding fault with such things as plot development and character motivation, ostensibly in an attempt to teach the laws of dramatic art not only to the general public, but also to the author.

Bernard Gorin, however, held that the harshness of the criticism, and the severity with which critics judged the theatre and demanded supposedly universal artistic standards, revealed their failure to understand the particular situation of the Yiddish stage. Their attempt to catapult Yiddish theatre to the heights of contemporary drama and their insistence on unreasonable (albeit, as Gorin agreed, objectively correct) artistic standards was misguided. Ever the cultural evolutionist, he argued that using criteria developed by Aristotle was appropriate only for drama whose tradition was as old as the Greek philosopher, but not for a theatre still at the beginning of its develop-

---

[17] New York: Drukerman, 1909.

[18] A. Cahan, 'Di yidishe bine: *Sibirye* in yunyon teater' [The Yiddish Stage: *Siberia* in the Union Theatre], *Arbeter tsaytung*, 20 Nov. 1891.

ment: 'Donning the heavy armoury of classical and modern art to fight a baby who has just been born', argued Gorin, was simply counter-productive.[19] While he agreed that every intellectual would want to see Yiddish drama on a par with drama of other cultures that had 'already risen to the highest point of perfection', he condemned this expectation as elitist, arguing that a theatre at this state of development could flourish only if 'it can satisfy the coarse taste of an uneducated man as well as the fine taste of the expert'.[20] In other words, the Yiddish theatre still needed to display its childlike, or *shund*, qualities if it was to succeed. Only if writers and critics accepted this reality, he argued, could the Yiddish theatre 'be restored, and . . . a national drama be created'.[21] While he was firmly and unambiguously wedded to the ideal that intellectuals should support the people's cultural development, he regarded this as a long-term process which demanded of writers and critics that they meet the people halfway instead of expecting them to rise to their level without sufficient preparation.

The literary critic Bal Makhshoves (Isidor Eliashev, 1873–1924), responding from Riga to the ongoing debates in New York, also criticized the idea of lifting the masses to the cultural heights of the elite. But while Gorin still believed that this was ultimately a possibility, Bal Makhshoves went further, challenging the New York intellectuals' central premiss of linear cultural evolution. In an article in *Tsukunft* (Future), he attacked them directly for having 'the naive opinion that their taste, their opinion is the only correct one. . . . They believe in their own taste like an idol . . .'. Their concept of realism as the pinnacle of artistic achievement, he implied, was not an objective standard of art but a matter of taste. Unlike most of his colleagues across the ocean, Bal Makhshoves accepted that there was a stratification in art and taste along class lines. Culture and society, he implied, did not develop in a single trajectory to ever higher levels, but were divided by class and moved along different paths. Although the New York critics also acknowledged that taste varied according to class, Bal Makhshoves was the only one who believed that the lower classes had a right to their preference in entertainment. Because social groups had different tastes, he declared, they usually frequented different theatres. And he reminded his readers that, among the Jews, only the workers and petite bourgeoisie had created their own theatre; all other classes frequented plays performed in other languages. Instead of comparing Yiddish theatre to the theatre of the European elite—sponsored by the state and supported by a

---

[19] B. Gorin, 'Der yidisher teater' [The Yiddish Theatre], *Tsukunft*, 16 (Jan. 1911), 70.
[20] B. Gorin, 'What Do We Expect of Yiddish Drama?', in Steven Cassedy (ed.), *Building the Future: Jewish Immigrant Intellectuals and the Making of* Tsukunft (New York: Holmes & Meier, 1999), 121, 118. The article originally appeared in *Tsukunft*, 18 (Jan. 1913).   [21] Ibid. 123.

large intelligentsia—Bal Makhshoves argued, critics needed to accept it for what it was—a theatre of the masses. As such it was no different from those in other countries:

It is naive to expect from the Jewish masses what none of the European masses have: a taste for modern drama. It is naive to speak of a crisis in Yiddish theatre when in reality Yiddish theatre is no lower than other theatres with regard to the artistic taste of the masses. . . . And thirdly, it is naive to speak of the Yiddish theatre in the sense that one speaks of the Deutsches Theater in Berlin.[22]

If Yiddish theatre were to be changed, Bal Makhshoves suggested, the intellectuals should not try to alter the repertoire in the existing, lower-class, commercial playhouses, but create a stage of their own modelled on the Théâtre Libre in Paris or the Freie Bühne in Berlin. Only a separate theatre not ruled by the commercial pressures and theatrical conventions of the existing institutions could possibly set different artistic standards. In 1913, shortly after the Little Theatre movement inspired by the European Free Theatres was launched in the United States, the critic Shoel-Yosef Yanovsky (1864–1939) followed Bal Makhshoves's lead and suggested that creating a Yiddish Little Theatre would counter the lack of a forum for literary plays. But creating a separate professional theatre, of course, would have undermined the intellectuals' principles of uniting the classes through theatre and raising the intellectual level of the masses. And indeed the critics, who dominated the scene at the turn of the century, made no attempt to found such a stage.[23]

With the waning of Gordin's influence and his death in 1909, critics began to realize the limits of their power to force a rapid artistic evolution on the Yiddish theatre. No matter how intensively they worked on teaching audiences to appreciate realist art, the child had not moved as far along the trajectory as its collective fathers had hoped. While the intellectuals attributed this to the slow development of the people and their cultural institutions, the problem was, as Bal Makhshoves asserted, their paradigm of theatre as a monolithic entity moving to an ever higher status. These battles to turn the child into a mature, valuable adult—that is, to turn an institution for popular entertainment into one for literary, artistic productions—continued for decades.

---

[22] Bal Makhshoves [Isidor Eliashev], 'Tsi iz faran a krizis in yidishn teater?' [Is there a Crisis in Yiddish Theatre?], *Tsukunft*, 15 (June 1910), 343–4; repr. as 'Tsu der yidisher teater-frage' [Concerning the Yiddish Theatre Question], in id., *Geklibene shriftn* [Collected Writings], 5 vols. (Warsaw: Kooperativ 'Bikher', 1929), iii. 71–8.

[23] Some of them, however, most notably Entin, did support amateur theatre clubs founded to create a forum for literary plays. The intellectuals' discussion concerning the state of the Yiddish stage is more fully explored in Nina Warnke, 'Reforming the New York Yiddish Theater: The Cultural Politics of Immigrant Intellectuals and the Yiddish Press, 1887–1910', Ph.D. thesis, Columbia University, 2001, 248–77.

Although aesthetic sensibilities changed over time, the basic dialectic between non-literary and literary, between *shund* and art, between the naive child and the sophisticated adult, remained.

During the 1910s and early 1920s the number of Yiddish theatres grew substantially to accommodate the increasing and dispersing immigrant community, which allowed for a wider variety of companies with regard to style and artistic expression. While the vast majority of these troupes continued to produce comedies, operettas, and melodramas aimed at entertainment-seeking, lower-class audiences, from the late 1910s onwards a new generation of actors, directors, designers, and critics took the lead to create a *kunst teater* (art theatre) movement with literary and avant-garde productions. The ability to create and sustain art theatre companies was closely linked to a shift in the politics of Jewish identity in eastern Europe. It had helped to create the broader base of an intellectually minded population that was deeply committed to Yiddish as its language and culture, a commitment many immigrants brought with them to America.

In the 1920s modernism made it possible to revisit the previously despised 'primitive' from the vantage point of sophisticated art and present it in a highly stylized form. When actor-manager Maurice Schwartz (1888–1960) staged three modernist productions of plays by Goldfaden, critics, as Joel Berkowitz has shown, had a chance to reassess the works of 'the father of Yiddish theatre' and their relationship to him.[24] Not surprisingly, the 'child' as the metaphor of choice for early theatre dominated the reviews. By separating the father (as author) from his child (early Yiddish theatre and its performance traditions), most critics recognized Goldfaden's genius as a writer and affirmed his position in the canon of Yiddish dramatic literature. The father, one critic argued, was 'perhaps too great and too brilliant for our first theatre children'.[25] For most critics, a traditional performance of a Goldfaden play was aesthetically unthinkable because it was too 'primitive' and crude: 'we look upon Goldfaden's theatre as a curiosity, as something primitive, as a childhood photograph of ourselves'.[26] Echoing this sentiment, another reviewer remarked that a Goldfaden production served as a 'reminder of those years when we ourselves were young and the Yiddish theatre still in its swaddling clothes'.[27]

[24] Joel Berkowitz, 'The Tallis or the Cross? Reviving Goldfaden at the Yiddish Art Theatre, 1924–26', *Journal of Jewish Studies*, 50 (Spring 1999), 120–38.
[25] A. Mukdoyni [Alexander Kapel], 'Di kishefmakherin' [The Sorceress], *Morgen zhurnal*, 20 Mar. 1925; quoted in Berkowitz, 'The Tallis or the Cross?', 127.
[26] Nokhem Buchvald, 'Goldfaden's a shpil modernizirt' [A Play by Goldfaden Modernized], *Frayhayt*, 1 Feb. 1924; quoted in Berkowitz, 'The Tallis or the Cross?', 125.
[27] Moyshe Dines, 'Teater notitsn' [Theatre Notes], *Yidishe velt*, 15 May 1925; quoted in Berkowitz, 'The Tallis or the Cross?', 127.

While Goldfaden's plays were reminders of the theatrical childhood, Schwartz's modernist renditions of them ensured that the spectators did not have to relive its poverty and the embarrassment associated with it. On the contrary, such productions consciously celebrated and asserted how far Yiddish theatre had developed artistically.

As Goldfaden was lifted into the pantheon of canonical writers, the early days of Yiddish theatre receded into a past no one wanted to revisit, serving only as a convenient foil to highlight the theatre's achievements since its 'naive', 'poor', and 'crude' beginnings. Since most Yiddish critics who created the historical record of Yiddish theatre were not disinterested reviewers but regarded it as their personal mission to create and support art theatre—many being directly involved as playwrights and directors—the tendency to insist on the 'progress' of Yiddish theatre and to refer disparagingly to forms they did not consider 'art' was particularly pronounced. As quoted above, the critic and director Jacob Mestel, whose book *Undzer teater* (Our Theatre) stressed this constant aspiration to build a better theatre, could make only disdainful remarks about the theatre of directors such as Meyer Mishurat (1866?–1922) and Yankev-Ber Gimpl (1840–1906). Zylbercweig's *Leksikon* betrays a similar attitude: both Mishurat, who headed a troupe that toured the smaller towns of the Pale, and Gimpl, who was the well-known director of the Yiddish theatre in Lviv for seventeen years, received entries of no more than one column.[28]

These writings have influenced subsequent historians of Yiddish theatre who, although no longer involved in the past cultural battles, accepted many of the established paradigms. Taking his cue from Mestel, David S. Lifson, in his book *The Yiddish Theatre in America*,[29] focused on the art theatre movement of the 1920s and 1930s, discussing the preceding forty years of Yiddish theatre in America only in a cursory manner. Irving Howe's influential work *World of our Fathers*[30] also reveals attitudinal traces from previous critics. Although critical of the turn-of-the-century intellectuals for their harsh judgement of *shund* and their unwillingness to understand its significance, he betrays his own condescension towards early theatre by depicting it as child-like, 'naive', and full of 'raw emotion' and 'innocence'. Anecdotes such as the one mentioned above about the spectator's response to the starving Kenig Lir only served to bolster this image. Given the relatively small number of art

[28] Gimpl was, in fact, a significant figure in Yiddish theatre. Living outside Russia, where Yiddish theatre was hampered by its official ban, Gimpl could build a permanent troupe in Lviv, which attracted many actors from other regions. Over and over again, however, he lost performers who received invitations from American Yiddish companies. Among them were such prominent actors as Berta Kalish and Regina Prager, who began their careers under his tutelage.

[29] New York: Thomas Yoseloff, 1965.   [30] New York: Harcourt Brace Jovanovich, 1976.

theatre troupes compared to those of the popular genre, they have received a disproportionate amount of scholarly attention, skewing the image and our understanding of Yiddish theatre as a whole. Charting new trends in artistic highbrow achievements is, of course, not limited to critics and historians of Yiddish theatre; it has been the goal of most traditional theatre history. Given Western culture's belief in the idea of progress, as Alan Woods has argued, theatre histories have tended to concentrate on avant-garde movements instead of more traditional and popular forms because 'stressing the new implies that history is synonymous with *progress*'.[31]

Many recent studies, including the chapters in this volume, indicate a widening of the field and welcome departures from the paradigms set by the Yiddish critics. While much research on art theatre troupes and individual artists associated with them still awaits scholars, we need to focus increasingly on theatrical creations not deemed literary or artistic, and on the function popular theatre had for its audiences. For example, exploring aspects of performance in the Yiddish theatre, including the musical component of the popular genre, may teach us much about its appeal to a mass audience. Most importantly, we need to question further and analyse the paradigms set by the early critics, particularly their concepts of the 'primitive' and 'naive' and of *shund*. In order to comprehend Yiddish theatre and its impact on the Yiddish-speaking population in both Europe and the worldwide centres of dispersion, we need to study the despised 'child', the Hurwitzes and Lateiners, and Gimpls and Mishurats, the methods and messages they used, and the audiences they entertained. We need to approach them not from the vantage point of their critics—as a cultural manifestation to be suppressed—but as a legitimate art form. Such an approach should help us to work towards a more balanced and nuanced understanding of the Yiddish theatre, its richness and variety of expression, and its social function.

---

[31] Alan Woods, 'Emphasizing the Avant-Garde: An Exploration in Theatre Historiography', in Thomas Postlewait and Bruce A. McConachie (eds.), *Interpreting the Theatrical Past: Essays in the Historiography of Performance* (Iowa City: University of Iowa Press, 1989), 167.

Notes on Contributors

AHUVA BELKIN is head of the Theoretical Concentration in the Theatre Studies Department at Tel Aviv University, where she specializes in iconography and theatre, mask and masquerade, fools and jesters, feminist theatre, and Jewish folk theatre, in particular the *purimshpil* and the work of Avrom Goldfaden. Her books include *Between Two Cities: The Hebrew Play 'Simchat purim'* (Heb.) (Łódź, 1997) and *Leone de' Sommi and the Performing Arts* (Tel Aviv, 1997). Her many articles focus on Jewish theatre, the *purimshpil*, ritual and carnival, and art and iconography in Baroque and Renaissance theatre.

JOEL BERKOWITZ is Assistant Professor of Modern Jewish Studies at the State University of New York at Albany. He has taught Yiddish literature at Oxford University, and English and theatre in the City University of New York system. He is the author of *Shakespeare on the American Yiddish Stage* (Iowa City, 2002), and has published articles on Yiddish theatre and drama in *Theatre Survey*, *Assaph*, *The Journal of Jewish Studies*, and *Jewish Social Studies*.

PAOLA BERTOLONE holds a Ph.D. in performing arts from the University of Rome 'La Sapienza', where she currently teaches in the Department of Theatre. She is the author of many essays and two books: *L'esilio del teatro: Goldfaden e il moderno teatro yiddish* (Rome, 1994) and *I copioni di Eleonora Duse* (Pisa, 2000). She is currently working at the private archives of the Polish Italian director Alessandro Fersen.

MIROSŁAWA M. BUŁAT holds a Ph.D. in theatre studies from the Jagiellonian University in Cracow, where she currently teaches the history of Polish and European theatre. Her thesis, 'Krokewer Jidisz Teater (Krakowski teatr żydowski): miedzy "szundem" a sztuka' [Yiddish Theatre in Cracow: Between "Shund" [Trash] and Art'] (2001), examines the history of Cracow's Yiddish theatre in the inter-war period (1918–39). She has published several articles dealing with the Yiddish theatre in Poland and Polish–Jewish cultural contacts in the realm of theatre.

BRIGITTE DALINGER is currently working on a study of Jewish drama in Vienna (in Yiddish and German), supported by a scholarship from the Austrian Academy of Sciences. She is the author of *'Verloschene Sterne'. Geschichte des jüdischen Theaters in Wien* ['Extinguished Stars': The History of the Jewish Theatre in Vienna] (Vienna, 1998), and co-editor, with Thomas Soxberger, of Abish Meisels's review *Fun sechisstow bis amerika* (Vienna, 2000), a bilingual Yiddish–German edition. She lectures on Yiddish theatre and drama at the University of Vienna.

BARBARA HENRY is Mellon Fellow in Slavic Literatures at Northwestern University, and former Max Hayward Fellow in Russian at St Antony's College, Oxford. She is the author of *The Crooked Mirror: Parody and the Russian Theatre*, forthcoming from Oxford University Press.

JOHN D. KLIER is Corob Professor of Modern Jewish History in the Department of Hebrew and Jewish Studies at University College London. He is the author of *Russia Gathers her Jews: The Origins of the Jewish Question in Russia, 1772–1825* (DeKalb, Ill., 1986), of which there is a considerably expanded Russian edition: *Rossiia sobiraet svoikh evreev* (Moscow, 2000), and, with S. Lambroza, the editor of *Pogroms: Anti-Jewish Violence in Modern Russian History* (Cambridge, 1992). He is co-editor of *East European Jewish Affairs*.

DAVID MAZOWER is a journalist with BBC World Service. He is the author of *Yiddish Theatre in London* (2nd edn. London, 1996), and has published a number of articles on Anglo-Yiddish culture, the Jewish East End, and his great-grandfather, Sholem Asch.

LEONARD PRAGER is Emeritus Professor of English at the University of Haifa, whose Yiddish Studies programme he founded and taught for many years. He has written widely on Yiddish language and literature in journals and encyclopedias, and has compiled the pioneering bibliographies *Yiddish Literary and Linguistic Periodicals and Miscellanies: A Selected Annotated Bibliography*, with A. A. Greenbaum (Darby, Pa., 1982), and *Yiddish Culture in Britain: A Guide* (Frankfurt am Main, 1990). He is co-editor of Project Onkelos, an internet archive of Yiddish texts, and editor of the website The World of Yiddish/Di velt fun yidish and of the electronic journal *The Mendele Review*.

NAHMA SANDROW is Professor of English at Bronx Community College, CUNY, and the author of *Surrealism: Theater, Arts, Ideas* (New York, 1972), *Vagabond Stars: A World History of Yiddish Theater* (New York, 1977), and *God, Man, and Devil: Yiddish Plays in Translation* (Syracuse, 1999), and has written articles about ethnic and other theatres. She wrote the books for two award-winning off-Broadway musicals based on Yiddish theatre material: *Kuni-Leml* and *Vagabond Stars*.

NINA WARNKE is Assistant Professor of Yiddish at the University of Texas at Austin. Her doctoral dissertation, 'Reforming the New York Yiddish Theater: The Cultural Politics of Immigrant Intellectuals and the Yiddish Press, 1887–1910' (Columbia University, 2001), examines critics' responses to American Yiddish theatre at the turn of the century. Her work on Yiddish theatre has appeared in the *YIVO Annual* and *Theatre Journal*.

SETH L. WOLITZ holds the Gale Chair of Jewish Studies at the University of Texas at Austin, where he is also Professor of French, Slavic, and Comparative Literature. His many publications include a critical edition of the work of

Bernart de Ventadorn, and he is the author of *The Proustian Community* (New York, 1971) and *The Renaissance of Kosher Cuisine: From Ethnicity to Universality* (Jerusalem, 1999), and editor of *The Hidden Isaac Bashevis Singer* (Austin, Tex., 2001). He has also written many articles, including 'The Jewish Art Renaissance in Russia' for the first Modern Jewish Art Exhibition in Jerusalem and, most recently, on Peretz's short story 'Venus and Shulamis'. He is a specialist in Yiddish literature and has published on Yiddish novels and theatre.

Bibliography

❧

Compiled by
JOEL BERKOWITZ

ABEND, DROR, '"Scorned my nation": A Comparison of Translations of *The Merchant of Venice* into German, Hebrew and Yiddish', Ph.D. thesis, New York University, 2001.

ABRAMOVITSH, S. Y., *Ale verk fun mendele moykher sforim* [Complete Works of Mendele Moykher Sforim] (Warsaw: Farlag Mendele, 1913).

ABRAMSKY, G., *Bamot-yiskhak o gey-khizayon* [The High Places of Laughter or the Valley of Vision]. (No place or date given: Salon 'Pomo Verde').

ADLER, JACOB, *A Life on the Stage*, ed. and trans. Lulla Rosenfeld (New York: Knopf, 1999).

ADLER, TSILI, with YAKOV TIKMAN, *Tsili adler dertseylt* [Celia Adler Relates], 2 vols. (New York: Tsili Adler Foundation un Bukh-Komitet, 1959).

ADLER ROSENFELD, LULLA, *Bright Star of Exile: Jacob Adler and the Yiddish Theatre* (New York: Thomas Y. Crowell, 1977).

Akhtsik yor yidish teater in rumenye 1876–1956 [Eighty Years of Yiddish Theatre in Romania 1876–1956] (Bucharest: no publisher given, 1956).

ALTSHULER, MORDECHAI, *Hate'atron hayehudi bevrit hamo'atsot* [The Jewish Theatre in the Soviet Union] (Jerusalem: Hebrew University, 1996).

APTER-GABRIEL, RUTH (ed.), *Tradition and Revolution: The Jewish Renaissance in Russian Avant-Garde Art, 1912–1928* (Jerusalem: Israel Museum, 1988).

ASCH, SHOLEM, *Dramatishe shriftn* [Dramatic Works], 3 vols. (Vilna: Sholem Ash Komitet, 1922).

—— *Fun shtetl tsu der groyser velt* [From Small Town to the Great World] (Buenos Aires: Yosef Liftshits Fond, 1972).

—— *Got fun nekome* [God of Vengeance] (Warsaw: Tsentral, 1913); in Asch, *Dramatishe shriftn* [Dramatic Works], 3 vols. (Vilna: Sholem Ash Komitet, 1922), iii. 1–96; *God of Vengeance*, in Joseph C. Landis (ed. and trans.), *The Dybbuk and Other Great Yiddish Plays* (New York: Bantam Books, 1966), 69–114.

AVISHAR, SHMUEL, *Hamaḥazeh vehate'atron ha'ivri vehayidi* [Hebrew and Yiddish Drama and Theatre] (Jerusalem: Reuven Mas, 1996).

BAKER, ZACHARY, 'The Lawrence Marwick Collection of Copyrighted Yiddish Plays at the Library of Congress', *Association of Jewish Libraries: Annual Convention*, 35 (2000), 116–20.

—— 'Yiddish in Form and Socialist in Content: The Observance of Sholem Aleichem's Eightieth Birthday in the Soviet Union', *YIVO Annual*, 23 (1996), 209–31.

BAKHTIN, MIKHAIL, *Rabelais and his World*, trans. Helene Iswolsky (Bloomington: Indiana University Press, 1984).

BAL MAKHSHOVES [Isidor Eliashev], 'Tsi iz faran a krizis in yidishn teater?' [Is there a Crisis in the Yiddish Theatre?], *Tsukunft*, 15 (June 1910), 341–5; repr. as 'Tsu der yidisher teater-frage' [Concerning the Yiddish Theatre Question], in id., *Geklibene shriftn* [Collected Writings], 5 vols. (Warsaw: Kooperativ 'Bikher', 1929), iii. 71–8.

BAR-DAYAN, H., *Lereshito shel maḥazeh hahaskalah—al operah komit beyidish* [The Beginnings of the Haskalah Play: On a Comic Opera in Yiddish] (Jerusalem: Second World Congress of Jewish Studies, 1957).

BARISH, JONAS, *The Anti-Theatrical Prejudice* (Berkeley: University of California Press, 1981).

BAUMGARTEN, JEAN, 'Le "Purim shpil" et la tradition carnavalesque juive' [The *Purimshpil* and the Jewish Carnivalesque Tradition], in id., *Introduction à la littérature yiddish ancienne* [Introduction to Old Yiddish Literature] (Paris: Cerf, 1993), 443–73.

—— *Le Yiddish* (Paris: Presses Universitaires de France, 1990).

BAYERDÖRFER, HANS-PETER, '"Geborene Schauspieler". Das jüdische Theater des Ostens und die Theaterdebatte im deutschen Judentum' ['Born Performers': The Jewish Theatre from the East and the Theatre Debate within German Jewry], in Otto Horch and Charlotte Wardi (eds.), *Jüdische Selbstwahrnemung* [Jewish Self-Perception] (Tübingen: Max Niemeyer Verlag, 1997), 195–215.

BEAM, PATRICIA S., 'Aesthetic Movements in the Yiddish Theatre', MA thesis, University of North Carolina at Chapel Hill, 1971.

BECK, EVELYN TORTON, *Kafka and the Yiddish Theater* (Madison: University of Wisconsin Press, 1971).

BECKERMAN, AARON, *F. Bimko: der dramaturg un realist* [F[ishl] Bimko: The Playwright and Realist] (New York: no publisher given, 1944).

BECKERMANN, RUTH (ed.), *Die Mazzesinsel. Juden in der Wiener Leopoldstadt 1918–1938* [The Island of Matzah: Jews in Vienna's Leopoldstadt, 1918–1938] (Vienna: Löcker Verlag, 1984).

BEIZER, MIKHAIL, *The Jews of St Petersburg: Excursions through a Noble Past* (Philadelphia: Jewish Publication Society, 1989).

—— 'The Petrograd Jewish Obshchina (Kehillah) in 1917', *Jews and Jewish Topics in the Soviet Union and Eastern Europe*, 3 (Winter 1989), 5–29.

BELKIN, AHUVA, 'Citing Scripture for a Purpose: The Jewish *Purimspiel* as a Parody', *Assaph*, C12 (1997), 45–59.

—— 'Kapoyerdiker kapoyer: der yidisher karnaval-teater' [Inverted Inversion: Yiddish Carnival Theatre], *Oksforder yidish*, 3 (1995), 449–72.

BELLING, VERONICA, 'The Golden Years of Yiddish Theatre in South Africa, 1902–1910', *Jewish Affairs*, 55 (2000), 7–14.

BEN-ARI, R., *Habimah* (Chicago: L. M. Shteyn, 1937).

BEN-ISRAEL, HEDVA, 'From Ethnicity to Nationalism', *Contention*, 5/13 (Spring 1996), 51–68.

BEN-SCHACH, JANE RESPITZ, 'The False Messiah in Yiddish Literature: A Comparison between Two Dramatic Works', MA thesis, McGill University, 1990.

BEN-SION, E., *Evrei reformatory* (St Petersburg: no publisher given, 1882).

BEREGOVSKY, M., *Arfy na verbakh: Prizvanie i sud'ba Moiseia Beregovskogo* [Lyres in the Willows: The Calling and Destiny of Moyshe Beregovski] (Moscow: Evreiskii universitet v Moskve and Gesharim, 1994).

BERG, HETTY, 'Jiddisch theater in Amsterdam in de achttiende eeuw' [Yiddish Theatre in Amsterdam in the Eighteenth Century], *Studia Rosenthaliana*, 26 (1992), 10–37.

—— 'Thalia and Amsterdam's Ashkenazi Jews in the Late 18th and Early 19th Centuries', in Jonathan Israel and Reinier Salverda (eds.), *Dutch Jewry: Its History and Secular Culture (1500–2000)* (Leiden: Brill, 2002).

BERGER, SIDNEY L., 'The Theme of Persecution in Selected Dramas of the Yiddish Art Theatre', Ph.D. thesis, University of Kansas, 1964.

BERKOVITSH, YISROEL, *Hundert yor yidish teater in rumenye* [A Hundred Years of Yiddish Theatre in Romania] (Bucharest: Criterion, 1976).

BERKOWITZ, JOEL, 'The "Mendel Beilis Epidemic" on the Yiddish Stage', *Jewish Social Studies*, 8 (Fall 2001), 199–225.

—— *Shakespeare on the American Yiddish Stage* (Iowa City: University of Iowa Press, 2002).

—— 'The Tallis or the Cross? Reviving Goldfaden at the Yiddish Art Theatre, 1924–26', *Journal of Jewish Studies*, 50 (Spring 1999), 120–38.

—— 'A True Jewish Jew: Three Yiddish Shylocks', *Theatre Survey*, 37 (May 1996), 75–98.

BERKOWITZ, JOEL, 'Wicked Daughters, Wilting Sons: Jacob Gordin's King and Queen Lear', *Assaph*, C12 (June 1997), 125–48.

—— and JEREMY DAUBER, 'Translating Yiddish Comedies of the Jewish Enlightenment', *Metamorphoses*, 9 (Spring 2001), 90–112.

BERMAN, L., *In loyf fun di yorn: zikhroynes fun a yidishn arbeter* [As the Years Go By: Memoirs of a Jewish Worker], 2nd edn. (New York: Farlag Unzer Tsayt, 1945).

BERNARDI, JACK, *My Father the Actor* (New York: W. W. Norton, 1971).

BERTOLONE, PAOLA, *L'esilio del teatro: Goldfaden e il moderno teatro yiddish* [The Exile of Theatre: Goldfaden and the Modern Yiddish Theatre] (Rome: Bulzoni, 1994).

BIALIK, ILANA, 'Audience Response in the Yiddish Shund Theatre', *Theatre Research International*, 13 (Summer 1988), 97–105.

BIALIN, A. H., *Moris shvarts un der yidisher kunst teater* [Maurice Schwartz and the Yiddish Art Theatre] (New York: Itshe Biderman, 1934).

BILOV, S., and A. VELEDNITSKY, Introduction to Avrom Goldfaden, *Geklibene dramatishe verk* [Selected Dramatic Works] (Kiev: Melukhe-farlag, 1940), 3–64.

BINEVICH, EVGENY, 'Gastrolery v peterburge' [Touring Performers in St Petersburg], Preprint 9 of the Obshchestvo 'evreiskoe nasledie' [Jewish Heritage Society], <http://www.jewish-heritage.org>.

—— *Nachalo evreiskogo teatra v Rossii* [The Origin of Jewish Theatre in Russia] (Moscow: Jewish Heritage Society, 1994).

—— '"Svoi" teatr v peterburge' ['Our Own' Petersburg Theatre], Preprint 39 of the Obshchestvo 'evreiskoe nasledie' [Jewish Heritage Society], <http://www.jewish-heritage.org>.

BLIAKHER, SHABTSE, *Eyn un tsvantsik un—eyner* [Twenty-one Plus—One] (New York: Vilner Farlag, 1962).

BOAL, AUGUSTO, *The Theater of the Oppressed*, trans. Charles A. and Maria-Odilia Leal McBride (New York: Urizen Books, 1979; repr. New York: Theater Communications Group, 1985).

BOLLE, KEES, 'Secularization as a Problem for the History of Religions', *Comparative Studies in Society and History*, 12 (1970), 242–59.

BOROVOY, S. (ed.), *Mendele un zayn tsayt: materyaln tsu der geshikhte fun der yidisher literatur in XIXtn yorhundert* [Mendele and his Era: Materials towards the History of Nineteenth-Century Yiddish Literature] (Moscow: Emes, 1940).

BOTOSHANSKI, JACOB, *Nokh der forshtelung: groteskn un bilder funem idishn aktyorn-lebn* [After the Performance: Grotesques and Images from the Lives of Yiddish Actors] (Buenos Aires: Farlag Shlayfer, 1926).

BRECHT, BERTOLT, 'Notes on the Folk Play' (1957), in id., *Brecht on Theatre*, ed. and trans. John Willett (New York: Hill & Wang, 1964), 153–6.

BRENNER, DAVID A., '"Making Jargon Respectable": Leo Winz, *Ost und West* and the Reception of Yiddish Theatre in Pre-Hitler Germany', *Leo Baeck Institute Year Book*, 42 (1997), 51–66.

BROOKS, PETER, *The Melodramatic Imagination* (New Haven: Yale University Press, 1984).

BUCKALSKI, SIMAO, *Memorias da minha juventude e do teatro idiche no Brasil* [Memories of My Youth and of the Yiddish Theatre in Brazil] (São Paulo: Editora Perspectiva, 1995).

BUKHVALD, NOKHEM, *Teater* [Theatre] (New York: Farlag-Komitet Teater, 1943).

BUŁAT, MIROSŁAWA, '"Jung Teater" i "Naj Teater" w Krakowie' ['Young Theatre' and 'New Theatre' in Cracow], *Pamiętnik Teatralny*, 3–4 (1996), 511–39.

—— 'Kraków—żydowska mozaika teatralna' [Cracow—Jewish Theatre Mosaic], in Jan Michalik and Eugenia Prokop-Janiec (eds.), *Teatr żydowski w Krakowie: Studia y materiały* [Jewish Theatre in Cracow: Studies and Materials], trans. Anna Ciałowicz (Cracow: Universytet Jagielloński, 1995), 30–8.

—— 'Krokewer Jidisz Teater (Krakowski teatr żydowski): miedzy "szundem" a sztuka' [Cracow Yiddish Theatre: Between "Shund" [Trash] and Art', Ph.D. thesis, Jagiellonian University, 2001.

BURKO, FAINA, 'The Soviet Yiddish Theatre in the Twenties', Ph.D. thesis, Southern Illinois University at Carbondale, 1978.

BURSHTEYN, PEYSEKHKE, *Geshpilt a lebn* [A Life Performed] (Tel Aviv: no publisher given, 1980).

BUZGAN, KHEVEL, *Hantbukh far aktyorn* [Handbook for Actors] (Warsaw: M. Karpinovitsh, 1937).

CAHAN, ABRAHAM, *Bleter fun mayn lebn* [Pages from My Life], 5 vols. (New York: Forverts, 1926–31).

CASSEDY, STEVEN, *To the Other Shore: The Russian Jewish Intellectuals who Came to America* (Princeton: Princeton University Press, 1997).

—— (ed.), *Building the Future: Jewish Immigrant Intellectuals and the Making of 'Tsukunft'* (New York: Holmes & Meier, 1999).

CHEMERINSKY, CHAIM, 'Ayarati motili' [My Town Motayali], *Rashumot*, 2 (1927), 5–124.

CLARK, BARRETT H. (ed.), *European Theories of the Drama* (New York: Crown, 1947).

CYPKIN, DIANE, 'Second Avenue: The Yiddish Broadway', Ph.D. thesis, New York University, 1986.

DALINGER, BRIGITTE, 'Begegnungen mit dibbukim. Chassidische Mystik im modernen Wiener Theater zwischen 1880 und 1938' [Encounters with Dybbuks: Hasidic Mysticism in the Modern Viennese Theatre between 1880 and 1938], *Menora*, 11 (2000), 229–50.

—— '"Jüdaly mit dem Wandersack" bricht "auf nach Tel Aviv". Zionismus und populäres jiddisches Theater' ['Jüdaly and his Travelling Bag' Goes 'to Tel Aviv': Zionism and Popular Yiddish Theatre], *Das Jüdische Echo. Zeitschrift für Kultur und Politik*, 47 (Oct. 1998), 250–6.

—— 'Jüdisches Theater in Wien' [Jewish Theatre in Vienna], MA thesis, University of Vienna, 1991.

—— 'Poczatki teatru żydowskiego w Wiedniu' [Beginnings of the Yiddish Theatre in Vienna], in Anna Kuligowska-Korzeniewska and Małgorzata Leyko (eds.), *Teatr żydowski w Polsce* [Jewish Theatre in Poland] (Łódź: Wydawnictwo Uniwersytetu Łódzkiego, 1998), 332–41.

—— *'Verloschene Sterne'. Geschichte des jüdischen Theaters in Vienna* ['Extinguished Stars': The History of the Jewish Theatre in Vienna] (Vienna: Picus Verlag, 1998).

DAUBER, JEREMY ASHER, 'The Usage of Classical Religious Texts by Early Modern Hebrew and Yiddish Writers of the Enlightenment', D.Phil. thesis, University of Oxford, 1999.

DAVIS, JIM, 'The East End', in Michael R. Booth and Joel H. Kaplan (eds.), *The Edwardian Theatre: Essays on Performance and the Stage* (Cambridge: Cambridge University Press, 1996), 201–19.

DELL, HARRY, *Impresario* (New York: no publisher given, 1967).

DENK, DOVID, *Hinter di kulisn* [Behind the Scenes] (New York: Farlag Vokhnblat, 1959).

—— *Shvarts af vays* [Black on White] (New York: no publisher given, 1963).

DIAMANT, ZAYNVL, *Leksikon fun der nayer yidisher literatur* [Lexicon of the New Yiddish Literature] (New York: Congress for Jewish Culture, 1958).

DIMOV, OSIP, *Vos ikh gedenk* [What I Remember], 2 vols. (New York: CYCO, 1943).

DINEZON, YANKEV, *Zikhroynes un bilder: shtetl, kinderyorn, shrayber* [Memories and Scenes: *Shtetl*, Childhood, Writers] (Warsaw: Farlag Akhiseyfer, no date given).

DOBRUSHIN, YEKHEZKEL, *Binyomin zuskin* [Benjamin Zuskin] (Moscow: Melukhe-farlag, 1939).

—— *Di dramaturgye fun di klasiker* [The Dramaturgy of the Classic Writers] (Moscow: Emes, 1948).

—— *Mikhoels der aktyor* [Mikhoels the Actor] (Moscow: Emes, 1940).

—— 'Moskovskii Evreiskii Teatr' [Moscow Jewish Theatre], in *Teatral'naya entsiklopediya*, ed. S. S. Morkul'sky, 6 vols. (Moscow: Gos. nauch. izd-vo 'Sov. entsiklopediya', 1961–7), iii. 936.

Drama Review, 24: *Jewish Theatre* (1980).

DREGEL, G., *Khorosho sshityi frak: Komediya v 4-kh deistviyakh. Perevod S. S. Parfenova* [The Well-Tailored Frock-Coat: A Comedy in Four Acts. Trans. S. S. Parfenov] (n.d.), St Petersburg Theatrical Library, Tsarist Censor's Collection, *fond* 12745.

DRESSLER, ROLAND, *Von der Schaubühne zur Sittenschule. Das Theaterpublikum vor der vierten Wand* [From Entertainment Stage to School of Manners: The Theatre Audience before the Fourth Wall] (Berlin: Henschel Verlag, 1993).

DRUXMAN, MICHAEL B., *Paul Muni: His Life and his Films* (South Brunswick: A. S. Barnes, 1974).

DVORZHETSKI, M., M. TSANIN, and RUVN RUBINSHTEYN (eds.), *Yankev mansdorf in zayn dor* [Jacob Mansdorf in his Generation] (no place given: Culture Federation of Histadrut Ivrit and Jacob Mansdorf Fund, n.d.).

DZIGAN, SHMUEL, *Dzhigan: der koyekh fun yidishn humor* [Dzigan: The Power of Jewish Humour] (Tel Aviv: no publisher given, 1974).

EGO, BEATE (ed.), *Targum Scheni zu Ester. Übersetzung, Kommentar und theologische Deutung* [Second Targum of Esther: Translation, Commentary, and Theological Interpretation] (Tübingen: Mohr, 1996).

EHRENREICH, CHAIM, *Figurn un profiln af der yidisher bine* [Figures and Profiles on the Yiddish Stage] (Tel Aviv: Khaim Erenraykh Bukh-Komitet, 1976).

EIDHERR, ARMIN, '"Auf stillem Pfad . . .". Jiddische Schriftsteller in Wien' ['On a Silent Path . . .': Yiddish Authors in Vienna], *Literatur und Kritik*, 273–4 (1993), 47–55.

ELGE, ANBA, and S. D.-SKY (pseuds.), *Schastlivye dni Potasha i Perlmutra (iz zhizni amerikanskikh evreev)* [Potash and Perlmuter's Happiest Days (from the Lives of American Jews)] (Moscow: Izdanie *Teatral'noi Gazety*, 1916).

ELYASHEVICH, D. A., *Pravitel'stvennaya politika i evreiskaya pechat' v Rossii, 1797–1917* [Government Policy and Jewish Printing in Russia, 1797–1917] (St Petersburg: Mosty Kul'tury; Jerusalem: Gesharim, 1999).

ENTIN, JOEL, 'Di forgeshikhte funem yidishn teater' [The Prehistory of Yiddish Theatre], in *Suvenir tsu yankev gordins tsen-yerikn yubileyum* [Souvenir for Jacob Gordin's Tenth Anniversary] (New York: no publisher given, 1901), 15–22.

EPSTEIN, SHIFRA, *'Danielshpil' bahasidut bobov* [The 'Daniel Play' of the Bobover Hasidim] (Jerusalem: Magnes Press, 1998).

ERDMAN, HARLEY, 'Jewish Anxiety in "Days of Judgement": Community Conflict, Antisemitism, and the *God of Vengeance* Obscenity Case', *Theatre Survey*, 40 (May 1999), 51–74.

ERIK, MAX, *Etyudn tsu der geshikhte fun der haskole* [Studies on the History of the Haskalah] (Minsk: Melukhe-farlag far vaysruslendisher Kultur, 1934).

—— *Di geshikhte fun der yidisher literatur fun di eltste tsaytn biz der haskole tkufe* [The History of Yiddish Literature from Olden Times to the Haskalah Period] (Warsaw: Kultur-lige, 1928).

ERLICH, VICTOR, 'Vispianskis hashpoe af *Baynakht afn altn mark*' [Wyspiański's Influence on *A Night in the Old Marketplace*], *Yivo bleter*, 28 (Autumn 1946), 81–99.

Evreiskaya entsiklopediya: Svod znanii o evreistve i ego kul'ture v proshlom i nastoyashchem [The Jewish Encyclopaedia: Collected Learning on the Jews and their Culture in the Past and Present], ed. L. Katsenelson, 16 vols. (St Petersburg: Izdanie Obshchestva dlya Nauchnykh Evreiskikh Izdanii i Izdatel'stva Brokgauz-Efron, 1906–13).

EYNES, AVROM, *Fun lublin biz rige: goles-oprikhtn fun idishn aktyor* [From Lublin to Riga: Wanderings of a Yiddish Actor] (Riga: self-published, 1940).

FASS, MOSHE, 'Theatrical Activities in the Polish Ghettos during the Years 1939–1942', *Jewish Social Studies*, 38 (Winter 1976), 54–72.

FEDER, SAMY, 'The Yiddish Theatre of Belsen', in Rebecca Rovit and Alvin Goldfarb (eds.), *Theatrical Performance during the Holocaust: Texts, Documents, Memoirs* (Baltimore: Johns Hopkins University Press, 1999), 156–8.

FINKELSHTEYN, LEO, *Dortn un do: vegn dem dertseyler un dramatiker f. bimko* [There and Here: About the Novelist and Dramatist F[ishl] Bimko] (Toronto: Farlag Gershon Pomerants Esey-biblyotek, 1950).

FISCH, HAROLD, 'Reading and Carnival: On the Semiotics of Purim', *Poetics Today*, 15 (1994), 55–74.

FISHER, KRYSIA, MICHAEL C. STEINLAUF, and HENRYK GREENBERG (eds.), *Ida Kaminska: Grande Dame of the Yiddish Theater* (New York: YIVO Institute for Jewish Research, 2001).

FISHMAN, JACOB, B. LEVIN, and B. STABINOVITSH (eds.), *Finf un tsvantsik yor folks-bine* [Twenty-Five Years of the Folksbiene] (New York: Posy-Shoulson Press, n.d.).

—— LOUIS MANN, and BEYNUSH STEYVIN (eds.), *Fertsik yor folksbine* [Forty Years of the Folksbiene] (New York: no publisher given, 1955).

FISHZON, A., 'Zapiski evreiskogo antreprenera' [Notes of a Jewish Entrepreneur], *Biblioteka 'Teatra i Iskusstva'*, 12 (1913), 18.

FITZPATRICK, SHEILA, *The Cultural Front: Power and Culture in Revolutionary Russia* (Ithaca, NY: Cornell University Press, 1992).

FOOTE, I. P., 'The St Petersburg Censorship Committee, 1828–1905', *Oxford Slavonic Papers*, NS 24 (1991).

FOREMAN, MARLENE PHYLLIS, 'Remembrances of Cincinnati's Yiddish Theatre', MA thesis, University of Cincinnati, 1972.

FREEDEN, HERBERT, *Jüdisches Theater in Nazideutschland* [Jewish Theatre in Nazi Germany] (Tübingen: Mohr, 1964).

FREEMAN, MOSES, *Fuftsik yor geshikhte fun idishn lebn in filadelfye* [Fifty Years of the History of Jewish Life in Philadelphia], 2 vols. (Philadelphia: Kultur, 1934).

Freie Jüdische Volksbühne. Pressestimmen [Free Jewish People's Theatre Organization: Press Commentaries] (Vienna: Gründungskomitee der Jüdischen Künstlerbühnen, 1921).

FROST, MATTHEW, 'Marc Chagall and the Jewish State Chamber Theatre', *Russian History*, 8 (1981), 90–107.

Fuftsn yor 'vilner trupe' [Fifteen Years of the Vilna Troupe] (Łódź: Lodzher Teater-Komitet, 1931).

FUKS-MANSFELD, RENATE G., 'West- en Oost-Jiddisch op het toneel in Amsterdam aan het einde van de achttiende eew' [Western and Eastern Yiddish Theatre in Amsterdam at the End of the Eighteenth Century], *Studia Rosenthaliana*, 26 (1992), 91–6.

—— 'West- und Ostjiddisch auf Amsterdamer Bühnen gegen Ende des achtzehnten Jahrhunderts' [Western and Eastern Yiddish on the Amsterdam Stage at the End of the Eighteenth Century], in Astrid Starck (ed.), *Westjiddisch. Mündlichkeit und Schriftlichkeit/Le Yiddish occidental: Actes du Colloque de Mulhouse* [Western Yiddish, Oral and Written: Proceedings of the Mulhouse Colloquium] (Aarau: Sauerländer, 1994), 112–18.

FURNISH, BENJAMIN ALAN, 'If You Stop Remembering, You Forget: Nostalgia in Jewish-American Theatre and Film, 1979–1999', Ph.D. thesis, University of Kansas, 2000.

GADBERRY, GLEN W., 'Nazi Germany's Jewish Theatre', *Theatre Survey*, 21 (1980), 15–32.

GAINES, FREDERICK EUGENE, 'The Effect of Collective Theatre Practices on the American Playwright', Ph.D. thesis, University of Minnesota, 1982.

GASSNER, JOHN, and RALPH G. ALLEN (eds.), *Theatre and Drama in the Making* (Boston: Houghton Mifflin, 1964).

GERSHTEIN, ANNA, 'Notes on the Jewish State Theater of Belorussia', *Jews in Eastern Europe*, 27 (1995), 27–42.

GESSEN, YU. I., 'Smena obshchestvennykh techenii. II. "Pervyi russko-evreiskii organ"' [The Shift of Social Trends, II: The First Russian Jewish Periodical], *Perezhitoe*, 3 (1911).

GLASS, MONTAGUE, and CHARLES KLEIN, *Potash i Perlmutr: komediya v 3-kh deistviyakh (iz zhizni Evreev v Amerike) Soch. Montag'yu Glass i Charlz Klein, per. Boyarinova (Apollonova)* [Potash and Perlmuter: A Comedy in Three Acts (from the Lives of Jews in America), by Montague Glass and Charles Klein, trans. Boyarinov (Apollonov)] (Petrograd: Izdanie zhurnala *Teatr i Iskusstvo*, no date given).

GLATSHTEYN, JACOB, *In tokh genumen: eseyen 1948–1956* [Sum and Substance: Essays, 1948–1956] (New York: Farlag fun Idish Natsyonaln Arbeter Farband, 1956).

GLIKSON, YOSEF, 'Yung-teater', in Itsik Manger, Moyshe Perenson, and Jonas Turkow (eds.), *Yidisher teater in eyrope tsvishn beyde velt-milkhomes* [Yiddish Theatre in Europe between the Two World Wars], 2 vols. (New York: Congress for Jewish Culture, 1968), i: *Poyln* [Poland], 127–47.

GOETHE, JOHANN WOLFGANG VON, 'Shakespeare ad Infinitum', trans. Randolph S. Bourne, in John Gassner and Ralph G. Allen (eds.), *Theatre and Drama in the Making* (Boston: Houghton Mifflin, 1964).

GOLDBERG, ISAAC, *The Drama of Transition: Native and Exotic Playcraft* (Cincinnati: Stewart Kidd, 1922).

GOLDBERG, JUDITH N., *Laughter through Tears: The Yiddish Cinema* (Rutherford, NJ: Fairleigh Dickinson University Press, 1983).

GOLDBERG, RUVN, 'Yidish teater' [Yiddish Theatre], *Yivo bleter*, 44 (1973), 304–10.

GOLDBERG, Y. (ed.), *Unzer dramaturgye* [Our Dramaturgy] (New York: YKUF and Yekhiel Levenstein Bukh-Komitet, 1961).

GOLDENBERG, MIKHAIL, *Zhizn' i sudba Solomona Mikhoelsa* [The Life and Fate of Solomon Mikhoels] (Baltimore: Vestnik, 1995).

GOLDFADEN, AVROM, 'Czarownica' [The Sorceress], typescript in Yiddish, Archiwum Ringelbluma, Archiwum, Żydowski Instytut Historyczny, Warsaw, folder I/613.

—— *Di kishefmakherin* [The Sorceress] (Warsaw, 1887; repr. Warsaw: P. Kantorowicz, 1930).

—— *Oysgeklibene shriftn: Shulamis un Bar kokhba* [Selected Writings: *Shulamis* and *Bar Kokhba*], ed. Shmuel Rozhansky (Buenos Aires: YIVO, 1963).

GOLDMAN, ERIC A., *Visions, Images, and Dreams: Yiddish Film Past and Present* (Ann Arbor: UMI Research Press, 1979).

GOODMAN, PHILIP, *The Purim Anthology* (Philadelphia: Jewish Publication Society, 1949).

GORDIN, JACOB, *Ale shriftn*, 4 vols. (New York: Hebrew Publishing Company, 1910).

GORDON, MEL, 'Granovsky's Tragic Carnival: Night in the Old Market', *Drama Review*, 29 (Winter 1985), 91–4.

GORIN, B., *Di geshikhte fun idishn teater* [The History of the Yiddish Theatre], 2 vols. (New York: Literarisher Farlag, 1918; rev. New York: Max N. Mayzel, 1923).

—— 'Der yidisher teater' [The Yiddish Theatre], *Tsukunft*, 16 (Jan. 1911), 70–5.

—— 'What Do We Expect of Yiddish Drama?', *Tsukunft*, 18 (Jan. 1913); repr. in Steven Cassedy (ed.), *Building the Future: Jewish Immigrant Intellectuals and the Making of* Tsukunft (New York: Holmes & Meier, 1999).

GOT, JERZY, 'Aus dem Theaterleben in der Provinz von Galizien im 18. und 19. Jahrhundert' [From the Theatrical Life in the Province of Galicia in the Eighteenth and Nineteenth Centuries], *Studia Austro-Polonica*, 5 (1996), 439–57.

GOTESFELD, KHONE, *Brodvey un tel-aviv* [Broadway and Tel Aviv] (New York: Khone Gotesfeld Bukh-komitet, 1951).

—— *Vos ikh gedenk fun mayn lebn* [What I Remember from My Life] (New York: Fareynikte Galitsyaner in Amerike, 1960).

GOTLIB, YANKEV, *H. leyvik, zayn lid un drame* [H. Leivick: His Poetry and Drama] (Kaunas: Pasaulis, 1939).

GOULD, LEA SHAMPANIER, 'Artef Players Collective: A History', MA thesis, Cornell University, 1953.

GOURFINKEL, NINA, 'Les Théâtres hébraïques et yiddish à Moscou' [The Hebrew and Jewish Theatres in Moscow], in Denis Bablet and Jean Jacquot (eds.), *L'Expressionisme dans le théâtre européen* [Expressionism in the European Theatre] (Paris: CNRS, 1984).

GRACE-POLLAK, SOPHIE, 'Shomer in the Light of "Shomer's Mishpet"', *Ḥuliyot*, 5 (Winter 1999), 109–60.

GRANOVSKY, ALEXANDER, *Ot geyt a mentsh* [There Goes a Man], trans. Jacob Mestel (New York: YKUF, 1948).

GREENBAUM, ALFRED ABRAHAM, 'The Belorussian State Jewish Theater in the Interwar Period', *Jews in Eastern Europe*, 2 (2000), 56–75.

GRIS, NOAH, 'A yidisher teater-trupe in pariz in yor 1896' [A Yiddish Theatre Troupe in Paris in 1896], *Yivo bleter*, 44 (1973), 261–5.

GROBER, KHAYELE, *Mayn veg aleyn* [My Own Way] (Tel Aviv: Farlag Y. L. Peretz, 1968).

GUINSBERG, J., *Aventuras de uma língua errante: Ensaios de literatura e teatro ídiche* [Adventures of a Wandering Tongue: Essays on Yiddish Literature and Theatre] (São Paulo: Perspectiva, 1996).

HAENNI, SABINE, 'The Immigrant Scene: The Commercialization of Ethnicity and the Production of Publics in Fiction, Theater, and the Cinema, 1890–1915', Ph.D. thesis, University of Chicago, 1998.

HALKIN, SHMUEL, *Bar-kokhba* (Moscow: Melukhe-farlag 'Der Emes', 1939).

—— *Shulamis* (Moscow: Emes, 1940).

HALPERN, DINA, 'Mayne bagegenishn mit itsik manger'n' [My Encounters with Itsik Manger], *Folks-sztyme*, 23–30 Dec. 1988.

HAMM, MICHAEL F., 'Kishinev: The Character and Development of a Tsarist Frontier Town', *Nationalities Papers*, 26/1 (1998), 25.

HANNOWA, ANNA, *Jakub Rotbaum: Świat zaginiony. Malarstwo, rysunki* [Yankev Rotboym: The World that has Perished. Paintings, Drawings] (Wrocław: Ośrodek Badań Twórczości Jerzego Grotowskiego i Poszukiwań Teatralno-Kulturowych, 1995).

HAPGOOD, HUTCHINS, *The Spirit of the Ghetto* (1902; repr. Cambridge, Mass.: Harvard University Press, 1967).

HARASZTI-TAKÁCS, MARIANNE, 'Fifteenth-Century Painted Furniture with Scenes from the Esther Story', *Jewish Art*, 15 (1989), 14–25.

HARENDORF, S. Y., *Teater karavanen* [Theatre Caravans] (London: Fraynt fun Yidish Loshn, 1955).

—— *Yidish teater in england* [Yiddish Theatre in England], *Yivo bleter*, 43 (1966), 225–48.

HARKAVY, ALEXANDER, 'Teater' [Theatre], in Khonen Y. Minikes (ed.), *Di idishe bine* [The Yiddish Stage] (New York: Katzenelenbogen, 1897), unpaginated.

HECK, T. F., *Commedia dell'arte: A Guide to the Primary and Secondary Literature* (New York: Garland, 1988).

HEILMAN, ROBERT B., *Tragedy and Melodrama* (Seattle: University of Washington Press, 1968).

HENRIQUES, BASIL L. Q., *Club Leadership* (London: Oxford University Press, 1933).

—— *The Indiscretions of a Magistrate: Thoughts on the Work of the Juvenile Court* (London: Harrap, 1951).

HESKES, IRENE, 'Music as Social History: American Yiddish Theater Music, 1882–1920', *American Music*, 2 (1984), 73–87.

HIRSCHBEIN, PERETZ, *Grine felder: komedye in 3 aktn (a mayse fun idish dorfishn leben)* [Green Fields: A Comedy in Three Acts (A Story of Jewish Village Life)], in *Gezamlte dramen* (New York: Literarishe-dramatishe Faraynen in amerike, 1916), v. 255–318.

—— *Mayne kinder-yorn* [My Childhood Years] (Warsaw: Literarishe Bleter, 1932).

HIRSHHOYT, Y., 'Di historiker funem yidishn teater' [The Historians of the Yiddish Theatre], in Itsik Manger, Jonas Turkow, and Moyshe Perenson (eds.), *Yidisher teater in eyrope tsvishn beyde velt-milkhomes* [Yiddish Theatre in Europe between the World Wars] (New York: Congress for Jewish Culture, 1971), 7–38.

HOBERMAN, J., *Bridge of Light: Yiddish Film between Two Worlds* (New York: Museum of Modern Art and Schocken Books, 1991).

HOLCER, RACHELA, 'Teatr żydowski w Krakowie' [Jewish Theatre in Cracow], in Jan Michalik and Eugenia Prokop-Janiec (eds.), *Teatr żydowski w Krakowie: Studia i materiały* [Jewish Theatre in Cracow: Studies and Materials], trans. Anna Ciałowicz (Cracow: Księgarnia Akademicka, 1995).

HOROVITS, NORBERT, 'Yidish teater fun der sheyres-hapleyte' [The Yiddish Theatre of Holocaust Survivors], in *Fun noentn over* (New York: Congress for Jewish Culture, 1955), 113–82.

HOROWITZ, ELLIOTT, 'The Rite to be Reckless: On the Perpetration and Interpretation of Purim Violence', *Poetics Today*, 15 (1994), 9–54.

HOROWITZ, MAYER, 'Bibliography of Yiddish Translations of English Literature', *Jewish Book Annual*, 11 (1952–3), 136–53.

HOWE, IRVING, *World of our Fathers* (New York: Harcourt Brace Jovanovich, 1976).

—— and ELIEZER GREENBERG (eds.), *Voices from the Yiddish* (Ann Arbor: University of Michigan Press, 1972).

HUGO, VICTOR, 'Préface à *Cromwell*', in Barrett H. Clark (ed.), *European Theories of the Drama* (New York: Crown, 1947); repr. from *Dramatic Works of Victor Hugo* (Boston, 1909), vol. iii.

IDELSOHN, ABRAHAM Z., *Jewish Music: Its Historical Development* (New York: Henry Holt, 1929; repr. New York: Dover, 1992).

IRIS, SHMUEL, *Ot azoy hot men geshpilt teater* [That's how Theatre was Performed] (Buenos Aires: A Gezelshaftlekher Komitet, 1956).

IVANOV, VLADISLAV, 'Petrogradskie sezony evreiskogo kamernogo teatra' [The Petrograd Seasons of the Jewish Chamber Theatre], *Moskva*, 2 (1998), 571–97.

IVANOV, VLADISLAV, *Russkie sezony teatra Gabima* [Habimah's Russian Seasons] (Moscow: Artist. Rezhisser. Teatr, 1999).

JAHN, HUBERTUS F., *Patriotic Culture in Russia during World War I* (Ithaca, NY: Cornell University Press, 1995).

JOHN, MICHAEL, and ALBERT LICHTBLAU, *Schmelztiegel Wien—Einst und Jetzt. Zur Geschichte und Gegenwart von Zuwanderung und Minderheiten* [Melting-Pot Vienna—In Former Times and Now: Immigration and Minorities in History and Today] (Vienna: Böhlau Verlag, 1993).

JOHNSTON, JOHN, *The Lord Chamberlain's Blue Pencil* (London: Hodder & Stoughton, 1990).

KADISON, LUBA, and JOSEPH BULOFF, *On Stage, Off Stage* (Cambridge, Mass.: Harvard University Press, 1992).

KAGAN, BERL, *Leksikon fun yidish-shraybers* [Lexicon of Yiddish Writers] (New York: R. Ilman-Kohen, 1986).

KAGANOFF, NATHAN M., SUSAN LANDY, and BRUCE ROSEN, *Catalog of the Abram and Frances Pascher Kanof Collection of Yiddish Theatre and Motion Picture Posters Found in the Library of the American Jewish Historical Society* (Waltham, Mass.: The Library, 1972).

KAMINSKA, ESTHER-ROKHL, *Briv* [Letters], ed. Mark Turkow (Vilna: B. Kletskin, 1927).

KAMINSKA, IDA, *My Life, My Theater*, trans. Curt Leviant (New York: Macmillan, 1973).

KAPPER, SIGFRIED, 'Ahasverus—Ein jüdisches Fastnachtspiel' [Ahasuerus: A Jewish *Fastnachtspiel*], in *Zeitschrift für Literatur, Kunst und öffentliches Leben*, vol. iv (Leipzig: Deutsches Museum, 1854), 490–7, 529–43.

KARPINOVITSH, AVROM, 'Zikhroynes fun a farshnitener teater heym' [Memoirs of an Annihilated Home of Theatre], *Oksforder yidish*, 2 (1991), 241–54.

KAUFMAN, DAHLIA, 'The First Yiddish Translation of Julius Caesar', in David Goldberg (ed.),*The Field of Yiddish*, 5th collection (New York: YIVO and Northwestern University Press, 1993), 219–42.

—— 'Targumei maḥazot le'ivrit uleyidish misof hame'ah ha-18 ve'ad lishenat 1883' [Hebrew and Yiddish Drama Translations from the Late Eighteenth Century to 1883], Ph.D. thesis, Hebrew University, 1983.

KAUFMAN, RHODA HELFMAN, 'The Yiddish Theatre in New York and the Immigrant Community: Theatre as Secular Ritual', Ph.D. thesis, University of California, Berkeley, 1986.

KELLY, CATRIONA, *Petrushka: The Russian Carnival Puppet Theatre* (Cambridge: Cambridge University Press, 1990).

KERLER, DOV-BER (ed.), *The Politics of Yiddish*, vol. iv of *Winter Studies in Yiddish* (Walnut Creek, Calif.: AltaMira Press, 1998).

KLIER, JOHN D., 'The Polish Revolt of 1863 and the Birth of Russification: Bad for the Jews?', *Polin*, 1 (1986), 91–106.

KLINGER, Y. H. (ed.), *Hundert yor yidish teater, 1862–1962* [A Hundred Years of Yiddish Theatre, 1862–1962] (London: Yidishe kultur-gezelshaft, 1962).

KLOS, MAX, *Baym shayn fun rampe-likht* [By the Glow of the Footlights] (Buenos Aires: Stilos, 1972).

KOBRIN, LEON, *Erinerungen fun a yidishn dramaturg* [Recollections of a Yiddish Playwright], 2 vols. (New York: Komitet far Kobrins Shriftn, 1925).

—— *Mayne fuftsik yor in amerike* [My Fifty Years in America] (Buenos Aires: Farlag Yidbukh, 1955).

KOHLBAUER-FRITZ, GABRIELE, 'Jiddische Subkultur in Wien' [Yiddish Subculture in Vienna], in Peter Bettelheim and Michael Ley (eds.), *Ist jetzt hier die 'wahre Heimat'? Ostjüdische Einwanderung nach Wien* [Is this the 'True Homeland'? East European Immigration to Vienna] (Vienna: Picus Verlag, 1993), 89–115.

—— (ed.), *In a Schtodt woss schtarbt — In einer Stadt, die stirbt. Jiddische Lyrik aus Wien* [In a Dying City: Yiddish Poems from Vienna] (Vienna: Picus Verlag, 1995).

KONIGSBERG, IRA, '"The Only 'I' in the World": Religion, Psychoanalysis, and *The Dybbuk*', *Cinema Journal*, 36 (Summer 1997), 22–42.

KORN, YITSKHOK, *Yidish in rumenye: eseyen* [Yiddish in Romania: Essays] (Tel Aviv: Farlag Abukah, 1989).

KORNBLITH, Z., *Di dramatishe kunst* [The Dramatic Art] (New York: Itshe Biderman, 1928).

KORZENIEWSKI, BOHDAN, and ZBIGNIEW RASZEWSKI, *Teatr żydowski w Polsce do 1939* [Yiddish Theatre in Poland to 1939], special issue of *Pamiętnik Teatralny* (Warsaw: Polska Akademia Nauk/Institut Sztuki, 1992).

KOTLERMAN, BORIS, 'The Prewar Period of the Birobidzhan State Jewish Theater, 1934–1941', *Jews in Eastern Europe*, 1 (2001), 29–59.

KOVARSKY, H., 'An-skis "dibek" in balaykhtung fun der psikologye' [Ansky's *Dybbuk* in the Light of Psychology], *Yivo bleter*, 4 (Oct. 1932), 209–22.

KRASNEY, ARIELA, *Habadḥan* [The Wedding Jester] (Ramat Gan: Bar-Ilan University Press, 1998).

KUGEL, ALEKSANDR, 'M. S. Rivesman', *Zhizn' Iskusstva*, 26 (1924), 4.

—— 'Zametki' [Notes], *Teatr i Iskusstvo*, 43 (1916), 866–9.

KULIGOWSKA-KORZENIEWSKA, ANNA, and MAŁGORZATA LEYKO (eds.), *Teatr żydowski w Polsce* [Yiddish Theatre in Poland] (Łódź: Wydawnictwo Uniwersytetu Łódzkiego, 1998).

LAGARDE, PAULUS DE (ed.), *Hagiographa Chaldaice* (1873; repr. Osnabrück: Otto Zeller, 1967).

LAHAD, EZRA, *Hamaḥazot beyidish bamakor uvetirgum: bibliografiyah/Dramatishe verk af yidish, originele un iberzetste: a bibliografye* [Original and Translated Yiddish Plays: A Bibliography] (Haifa: no publisher given [2001]).

—— *Maḥazot amami'im beyidish: maḥazot avraham goldfaden* [Yiddish Folk Plays: The Plays of Avrom Goldfaden], Amli—meḥkarim bibliografi'im bemusikah [AMLI Studies in Music Bibliography], ed. Moshe Gorali, 4 (Haifa: Haifa Music Museum and Library, 1970).

LANDIS, JOSEPH C. (ed.), *Memoirs of the Yiddish Stage* (Flushing, NY: Queens College Press, 1984).

LARESKU, S., ' "Jüdaly mit dem Wandersack": Realistisches Bild mit Tanz und Gesang in 3 Szenen' ['Yudele with his Travel Bag': Realistic Portrait with Dances and Songs in Three Scenes], Niederösterreichisches Landesarchiv St Pölten, Theaterzensursammlung, Volkssänger box 14, Edelhofer 1904, Z 22/13 P.B., 24 Nov. 1904.

LARRUE, JEAN-MARC, *Le Théâtre yiddish à Montréal* (Montreal: Éditions Jeu, 1996).

LAWRENCE, JEROME, *Actor: The Life and Times of Paul Muni* (New York: Putnam, 1974).

LE GOFF, JACQUES, 'The Learned and Popular Dimensions of Journeys in the Otherworld in the Middle Ages', in Steven L. Kaplan (ed.), *Understanding Popular Culture* (Amsterdam: Mouton, 1984), 19–39.

LEA, K. M., *Italian Popular Comedy: A Study in the Commedia dell'arte, 1560–1620* (Oxford: Clarendon Press, 1934; repr. New York: Russel & Russel, 1962).

LEBEDIKER, DER [Chaim Gutman], *Di ferte vant* [The Fourth Wall] (Warsaw: Farlag Akhiseyfer, n.d.).

Leksikon far der nayer yidisher literatur [Lexicon of New Yiddish Literature], 8 vols. (New York: CYCO, 1956–81).

LERNER, WARREN ZOLLERY, 'The Yiddish Theatre and Drama', MA thesis, University of Nebraska, 1933.

LEVINE, LAWRENCE W., *Highbrow/Lowbrow: The Emergence of Cultural Hierarchy in America* (Cambridge, Mass.: Harvard University Press, 1988).

LIFSHITS, Y., 'Batkhonim un leytsim bay yidn' [Jewish Wedding Entertainers and Jesters], in Jacob Shatzky (ed.), *Arkhiv far der geshikhte fun yidishn teater un drame* [Archive for the History of Yiddish Theatre and Drama] (Vilna: YIVO, 1930), 38–74.

LIFSON, DAVID S., *The Yiddish Theatre in America* (New York: Thomas Yoseloff, 1965).

LIPSKY, LOUIS, *Tales of the Yiddish Rialto: Reminiscences of Playwrights and Players in New York's Jewish Theatre in the Early 1900s* (New York: Thomas Yoseloff, 1962).

LIPTZIN, SOL, *Eliakum Zunser: Poet of his People* (New York: Berhman House, 1950).

——*A History of Yiddish Literature* (Middle Village, NY: Jonathan David, 1972).

LITVAKOV, MOYSHE, *Finf yor melukhisher idisher kamer-teater* [Five Years of the State Yiddish Chamber Theatre] (Moscow: Farlag Shul un Bukh, 1924).

LOEWE, L. L., *Basil Henriques: A Portrait* (London: Routledge & Kegan Paul, 1976).

LOTTES, GUNTER, 'Popular Culture and the Early Modern State in Sixteenth-Century Germany', in Steven L. Kaplan (ed.), *Understanding Popular Culture* (Amsterdam: Mouton, 1948).

LYUBOMIRSKI, Y., *Af di lebnsvegn* [On Life's Journey] (Moscow: Farlag Sovetski Pisatel, 1976).

——*Melukhisher yidisher teater in ukraine* [State Yiddish Theatre in Ukraine] (Kharkov: Literatur un Kunst, 1931).

——*Mikhoels* (Moscow: Izdat. Iskusstvo, 1938).

MALTER, HENRY, 'Purim Plays', in Isidore Singer (ed.),*The Jewish Encyclopedia*, 12 vols. (New York: Funk & Wagnall's, 1901–12), x. 279–80.

MAMANA, JUNE, 'From the Pale of Settlement to "Pacific Overtures": The Evolution of Boris Aronson's Visual Aesthetic', Ph.D. thesis, Tufts University, 1997.

MANGER, ITSIK, JONAS TURKOW, and MOYSHE PERENSON (eds.), *Yidisher teater in eyrope tsvishn beyde velt-milkhomes* [Yiddish Theatre in Europe between the World Wars], 2 vols. (New York: Congress for Jewish Culture, 1968).

Marc Chagall and the Jewish Theater (New York: Guggenheim Museum, 1992).

MARKOVITSH, JOSEPH, 'Fun mayne fuftsik yor in england' [About my Fifty Years in England], *Di idishe shtime* [The Jewish Voice] (London), 13 Nov. 1953–9 Apr. 1954.

MARKS, RICHARD, G., *The Image of Bar Kokhba in Traditional Jewish Literature: False Messiah and National Hero* (University Park: Pennsylvania State University Press, 1994).

MARMOR, KALMEN, *Yankev gordin* [Jacob Gordin] (New York: YKUF, 1953).

MASSINO, GUIDO, 'Jizchak Löwy, "l'amico russo" di Franz Kafka' [Isaac Löwy, Franz Kafka's 'Russian Friend'], *Rassegna Mensile di Israel*, 62 (1996), 279–300.

MAZO, JOSEPH H., 'The Rise of the Yiddish Theatre', MA thesis, University of Washington, 1963.

MAZOWER, DAVID, *Yiddish Theatre in London*, 2nd edn. (London: Jewish Museum, 1996).

MEDOVOY, GEORGE, 'The Federal Theatre Project Yiddish Troupes', Ph.D. thesis, University of California, Davis, 1975.

MEISEL, NACHMAN, *Avrom goldfaden: der foter fun yidishn teater* [Avrom Goldfaden: The Father of the Yiddish Theatre] (Warsaw: Farlag Groshn Bibliotek, 1935).

—— *Geven a mol a lebn: dos yidishe kultur-lebn in poyln tsvishn beyde velt-milkhomes* [Once Upon a Life: Yiddish Cultural Life in Poland between the World Wars] (Buenos Aires: Tsentral-farband fun Poylishe Yidn in Argentine, 1951).

MEISELS, ABISH, 'Die jüdische Heldin oder Herz und Hand fürs Vaterland', Komödie in vier Aufzügen [The Jewish Heroine; or, Heart and Hand for the Fatherland, a Comedy in Four Acts], Niederösterreichisches Landesarchiv St Pölten, Theaterzensursammlung, box 729.

—— 'Der Traum des Reservisten', Märchen in vier Aufzügen[The Dream of a Reserve Officer, a Fairy-Tale in Four Acts], Niederösterreichisches Landesarchiv St Pölten, Theaterzensursammlung, box 729.

—— *Von Sechistow bis Amerika / Fun sechistow bis amerika. Eine Revue in 15 Bildern / A rewi in 15 bilder* [From Sechistow to America: A Review in Fifteen Tableaux], ed. and trans. Brigitte Dalinger and Thomas Soxberger (Vienna: Picus Verlag, 2000).

MELMAN, MARIAN, 'Teatr żydowski w Warszawie' [Jewish Theatre in Warsaw], in Emilia Borecka, Marian Drozdowski, and Halina Janowska (eds.), *Warszawa II Rzeczypospolitej*, 5 vols. (Warsaw: Panstwowe Wydawnictwo Naukowe, 1968–73), 381–400.

MENDELOVITCH, BERNARD, 'Memories of London Yiddish Theatre', Seventh Annual Avrom-Nokhem Stencl Lecture in Yiddish Studies (Oxford: Oxford Centre for Postgraduate Hebrew Studies, 1990).

MERKUR, VOLF, *Merkuriozn* [Mercurios] (Philadelphia: Nebekhaleyn, 1948).

MESTEL, JACOB, 'Goldfaden als traditsye af der bine' [Goldfaden as Tradition on the Stage], in Jacob Shatzky (ed.), *Goldfaden-bukh* [Goldfaden Book] (New York: Jewish Theatre Museum, 1926), 11–15.

—— *Literatur un teater* [Literature and Theatre] (New York: YKUF, 1943).

—— *70 yor teater repertuar* [Seventy Years of Theatre Repertoire] (New York: YKUF, 1954).

—— *Undzer teater* [Our Theatre] (New York: YKUF, 1943).

MICHALIK, JAN, and EUGENIA PROKOP-JANIEC (eds.), *Teatr żydowski w Krakowie: Studia y materiały* [Yiddish Theatre in Cracow: Studies and Materials], trans. Anna Ciałowicz (Cracow: Uniwersytet Jagielloński, 1995).

MIDE, A., *Epizodn fun yidishn teater* [Episodes from the Yiddish Theatre] (Buenos Aires: Asociación judeo argentina de estúdios históricos, 1954).

MIDELFORT, ERIK, 'Sin, Melancholy, Obsession: History and Culture in the Sixteenth Century', in Steven L. Kaplan (ed.), *Understanding Popular Culture* (Amsterdam: Mouton, 1984).

MILLER, JAMES, *The Detroit Yiddish Theater, 1920 to 1937* (Detroit: Wayne State University Press, 1967).

MINIKES, KHONEN Y. (ed.), *Di idishe bine* [The Yiddish Stage] (New York: Katzenelenbogen, 1897).

MIRON, DAN, 'Folklore and Antifolklore in the Yiddish Fiction of the Haskala', in Frank Talmage (ed.), *Studies in Jewish Folklore* (Cambridge, Mass.: Association for Jewish Studies, 1980), 214–49.

—— *A Traveler Disguised: The Rise of Modern Yiddish Fiction in the Nineteenth Century* (New York: Schocken, 1973).

MOREVSKI, AVROM, *Ahin un tsurik* [There and Back], 4 vols. (Warsaw: Farlag Yidish Bukh, 1960); abridged as *There and Back*, trans. Joseph Leftwich (St Louis: Warren H. Green, 1967).

—— 'Kulturlozikayt' [Culturelessness], *Literarishe bleter*, 14 (1937), 221–2.

MUKDOYNI, A. [Alexander Kapel], 'Avrom goldfaden', in Jacob Shatzky (ed.), *Goldfaden-bukh* (New York: Yiddish Theatre Museum, 1926), 6–8.

—— *In varshe un in lodzh (mayne bagegenishn)* [In Warsaw and in Łódź (My Encounters)] (Buenos Aires: Tsentral-farband fun Poylishe Yidn in Argentine, 1955).

—— *Teater* (New York: A. Mukdoyni Yubiley-Komitet, 1927).

—— *Yitskhok leybush perets un dos yidishe teater* [Yitskhok Leybush Peretz and the Yiddish Theatre] (New York: YKUF, 1949).

MURPHY, DANIEL J., 'Yiddish at the Abbey Theatre, Dublin', *Bulletin of Research in the Humanities*, 81 (Winter 1978), 431–5.

MYER, MORRIS, *Idish teater in london, 1902–1942* [Yiddish Theatre in London, 1902–1942] (London: M. Mayer [1943]).

NADIR, MOYSHE [Isaac Reiss], *Mayne hent hobn fargosn dos dozige blut* [My Hands Spilled that Blood] (New York: Farlag Verbe, 1919).

NAHSHON, EDNA, *Yiddish Proletarian Theatre: The Art and Politics of the Artef, 1925–1940* (Westport, Conn.: Greenwood Press, 1998).

NAUMANN, HANS, *Primitive Gemeinschaftskultur* [Primitive Shared Culture] (Jena: E. Diederichs, 1921).

NIGER, S. [Shmuel Charney], *Dertseylers un romanistn* [Short-Story Writers and Novelists] (New York: CYCO, 1946).

—— *Fun mayn togbukh* [From My Diary] (New York: Congress for Jewish Culture, 1973).

—— *H. leyvik, 1888–1948* [H. Leivick, 1888–1948] (Toronto: Leyvik Yoyvl-Komitet, 1951).

—— *Kritik un kritiker* [Criticism and Critics] (Buenos Aires: Argentina Division of the Congress for Jewish Culture, 1959).

—— 'Der novi fun der erd: Sholem ash', *Literarishe monatshriften*, 4 (1908), cols. 113–42; repr. in id., *Sholem ash, zayn lebn zayne verk* [Sholem Asch: His Life and Work] (New York: S. Niger Book Committee of the Congress for Jewish Culture, 1960).

—— *Sholem ash, zayn lebn zayne verk* [Sholem Asch: His Life and Work] (New York: S. Niger Book Committee of the Congress for Jewish Culture, 1960).

N.N. [N. Negorev (Aleksandr Kugel)], 'Khronika' [Chronicle], *Teatr i Iskusstvo*, 19 (1907), 309.

NOVERSHTERN, ABRAHAM, 'Between Dust and Dance: Peretz's Drama and the Rise of Yiddish Modernism', *Prooftexts*, 12 (1992), 71–90.

ODELL, G. C. D., *Annals of the New York Stage*, 15 vols. (New York: Columbia University Press, 1927–49).

ORSHANSKI, BER, *Teater-shlakhtn* [Theatre Battles] (Moscow: Tsentraler Felker-farlag fun FSSR, 1931).

OSHEROVITSH, M., *Dovid kesler un muni vayzenfraynd* [David Kessler and Muni Weisenfreund] (New York: no publisher given, 1930).

—— Z. H. RUBINSHTEYN, and ZALMEN ZYLBERCWEIG (eds.), *Dos rumshinski-bukh* [The Rumshinsky Book], 2 vols. (New York: Trio Press, 1931).

OTTE, MARLINE SYLTA, 'Jewish Identities in German Popular Entertainment, 1890–1930', Ph.D. thesis, University of Toronto, 1999.

OXAAL, IVAR, 'Die Juden im Wien des jungen Hitler. Historische und soziologische Aspekte' [Jews in Vienna when Hitler was Young: Historical and Sociological Aspects], in Gerhard Botz, Ivar Oxaal, and M. Pollak (eds.),

Eine zerstörte Kultur. Jüdisches Leben und Antisemitismus in Wien seit dem 19. Jahrhundert [A Devastated Culture: Jewish Life and Antisemitism in Vienna since the Nineteenth Century] (Buchloe: Obermayer Verlag, 1990), 29–60.

OYSLENDER, NOKHEM, *Yidisher teater, 1887–1917* [Yiddish Theatre, 1887–1917] (Moscow: Melukhe-farlag, 1940).

—— and URI FINKEL, *A. goldfadn: materyaln far a biografye* [A. Goldfaden: Materials towards a Biography] (Minsk: Institut far vaysruslendisher kultur, 1926).

PALEPADE, BENTSION, *Beyn hashmoshes* [At Dusk] (Buenos Aires: no publisher given, 1951).

—— *Zikhroynes fun a halbn yorhundert idish teater* [Memoirs of a Half-Century of Yiddish Theatre] (Buenos Aires: no publisher given, 1946).

PASKIN, SYLVIA (ed.), *When Joseph Met Molly: A Reader on Yiddish Film* (Nottingham: Five Leaves Publications, 1999).

PATT, SARAH, *Lebn un shafn: 60 yor arbet far yidisher kultur un kunst in amerike* [Life and Work: Sixty Years' Work for Yiddish Culture and Art in America] (Tel Aviv: Farlag Oyfkum, 1971).

PERETZ, Y. L., *Sholem ash, fun shtetl tsu der velt* [Sholem Asch: From the *Shtetl* to the World], ed. Shmuel Rozhansky (Buenos Aires: Yoysef Lifshits Fund, 1972), 350–54; 1st pub. in Peretz, *Di verk*, 13 vols. (New York: Farlag Idish, 1920), X. 191–5.

—— 'What our Literature Needs', in Irving Howe and Eliezer Greenberg (eds.), *Voices from the Yiddish* (Ann Arbor: University of Michigan Press, 1972).

PERKOF, YITSKHOK, *Avrom goldfadn: mayne memuarn un zayne brif* [Avrom Goldfaden: My Memoirs and his Letters] (London: Jouques Print Works, 1908).

PERLMUTER, H., *An aktyor in oyshvits* [An Actor in Auschwitz] (Tel Aviv: Farlag Hamenorah, 1972).

—— *Bine-maskes bay katsetler: yidish teater nokhn khurbn* [Stage Masks of the Concentration Camp Survivors: Yiddish Theatre after the Holocaust] (Tel Aviv: Farlag Hamenorah, 1974).

PERLMUTER, SHOLEM, *Yidishe dramaturgn un teater-kompozitors* [Yiddish Playwrights and Theatre Composers] (New York: YKUF, 1952).

PHILIPP, MICHAEL, *Nicht einmal einen Thespiskarren. Exiltheater in Shanghai, 1939–1947* [Not Even a Thespis Cart: Exile Theatre in Shanghai, 1939–1947] (Hamburg: Hamburger Arbeitstelle fur deutsche Exilliteratur, 1996).

PICON, MOLLY, and JEAN BERGANTINI GRILLO, *Molly!* (New York: Simon & Schuster, 1980).

PICON-VALLIN, BÉATRICE, *Le Théâtre juif soviétique pendant les années vingt* [Soviet Jewish Theatre during the 1920s] (Lausanne: La Cité-L'Âge d'Homme, 1973).

PINSKI, D., *Dos idishe drama* [Yiddish Drama] (New York: Drukerman, 1909).

PLADOTT, DINNAH, 'The Yiddish Theatre as a Species of Folk Art: Joseph Lateiner's *The Jewish Heart* (1908)', in Mark Gelber (ed.), *Identity and Ethos: Festschrift for Sol Liptzin on the Occasion of his 85th Birthday* (New York: Peter Lang, 1986), 69–87.

POLLAK, OLIVER B., 'The Yiddish Theater in Omaha, 1919–1969', in Leonard Jay Greenspoon (ed.), *Yiddish Language and Culture Then and Now* (Omaha, Nebr.: Creighton University Press, 1998), 127–63.

Polnoe Sobranie Zakonov Rossiiskoi Imperii: Sobranie tret'e i dopolneniya [Complete Legal Code of the Russian Empire: Third Collection with Addenda], 33 vols. (St Petersburg: V Gosudarstvennoi tip., 1885–1916), vol. ii.

PORTNOY, EDWARD, 'Modicut Puppet Theatre: Modernism, Satire, and Yiddish Culture', *TDR* 43 (Fall 1999), 115–34.

POSTLEWAIT, THOMAS, 'Autobiography and Theatre History', in Thomas Postlewait and Bruce A. McConachie (eds.), *Interpreting the Theatrical Past* (Iowa City: University of Iowa Press, 1989), 248–72.

PRAGER, LEONARD, 'Of Parents and Children: Jacob Gordin's *The Jewish King Lear*', *American Quarterly*, 18 (Autumn 1966), 506–16.

—— 'Shakespeare in Yiddish', *Shakespeare Quarterly*, 19 (Spring 1968), 149–58.

—— *Yiddish Culture in Britain: A Guide* (Frankfurt am Main: Peter Lang, 1990).

—— 'Yiddish Theater in Cairo', *Israeli Academic Center in Cairo: Bulletin*, 16 (1992), 24–30.

—— and BRAD SABIN HILL, 'Yiddish Manuscripts in the British Library', *British Library Journal*, 21/1 (Spring 1995), 81–108.

PRELOOKER, JAAKOFF, *Under the Czar and Queen Victoria* (London: no publisher given, 1895).

PRILUTSKI, NOAH, 'Farvos iz dos yidishe teater oyfgekumen azoy shpet?' [Why Did Yiddish Theatre Appear So Late?], *Yivo bleter*, 26 (Sept.–Oct. 1945), 96–104.

—— *Yidish teater* [Yiddish Theatre], 2 vols. (Białystok: A. Albek, 1921).

—— *Zamlbikher far yidishn folklor, filologye un kulturgeshikhte* [Anthologies of Yiddish Folklore, Philology and Cultural History] (Warsaw: Nayer Farlag, 1912).

PRINZ, JOACHIM, 'A Rabbi under the Hitler Regime', in H. A. Strauss and K. R. Grossmann (eds.), *Gegenwart im Rückblick* [The Present in Retrospect] (Heidelberg: Lothar Stiehm, 1970), 231–8.

PRIZAMENT, SHLOYME, *Broder zinger* [Broder Singers] (Buenos Aires: Tsentral-farband fun Poylishe Yidn in Argentine, 1960).

PRIZHANSKY, N. 'O vozrozhdenii evreiskogo teatra' [On the Renaissance of Jewish Theatre], *Nedel' naya Khronika Voskhoda*, 8 (24 Feb. 1905).

PULAVER, MOYSHE (ed.), *Ararat* (Tel Aviv: Farlag Y. L. Peretz, 1972).

QUINT, ALYSSA, 'Hamaḥazeh "bar kokhba" me'et avraham goldfaden' [The Play *Bar Kokhba* by Avrom Goldfaden], *Ḥuliyot*, 6 (Fall 2000), 79–90.

RAKOV, NOKHEM, 'Der Talmud-Chuchem. Lebensbild in 5 Acten von Rakow' [The Scholar: Portrait of Life in Five Acts by Rakov] (1909) (Yiddish, in German transliteration), St Petersburg Theatrical Library, Tsarist Censor's Collection, *fond* 1031.

RAVITSH, MELEKH, *Mayn leksikon* [My Lexicon], 4 vols. (vols. i–iii Montreal; vol. iv Tel Aviv, 1945–82).

REYZEN, ZALMEN, *Fun mendelson biz mendele* [From Mendelssohn to Mendele] (Warsaw: Farlag Kultur-lige, 1923).

—— *Leksikon fun der yidisher literatur, prese un filologye* [Lexicon of Yiddish Literature, Press, and Philology], 4 vols. (Vilna: B. Kletskin, 1926–9).

—— 'Zilbertsvaygs *Leksikon fun yidishn teater*' [Zylbercweig's *Lexicon of the Yiddish Theatre*], *Yivo bleter*, 2 (1931), 251–66.

RICH, FRANK, and LISA ARONSON, *The Theatre Art of Boris Aronson* (New York: Knopf, 1987).

RIVESMAN, M., 'The Past and the Future of Yiddish Theatre', trans. Benjamin and Barbara Harshav, in *Marc Chagall and the Jewish Theatre* (New York: Solomon Guggenheim Foundation, 1992).

RIVKIN, B. [Bernard Weinryb], *H. leyvik, zayne lider un dramatishe verk* [H. Leivick: His Poems and Dramas] (Buenos Aires: Farlag Yidbukh, 1955).

ROBACK, A. A., *The Story of Yiddish Literature* (New York: Yiddish Scientific Institute, 1940).

—— *Supplement to the Story of Yiddish Literature* (Cambridge, Mass.: Sci-Art Publishers, 1940).

ROME, DAVID (ed.), *The Yiddish Theatre: The Adler* (Montreal: National Archives, Canadian Jewish Congress, 1987).

ROSKIES, DAVID, *A Bridge of Longing: The Lost Art of Yiddish Storytelling* (Cambridge, Mass.: Harvard University Press, 1995).

ROTBOYM, YANKEV, 'Itsik mangers debyut als dramaturg (zikhroynes fun a rezhiser)' [Itsik Manger's Debut as a Dramatist (Director's Memoirs)], *Fołks-sztyme*, 18 Oct. 1991, 1 Nov. 1991.

ROTTE, JOANNA HELEN, 'The Principles of Acting According to Stella Adler', Ph.D. thesis, City University of New York, 1983.

ROZHANSKY, SHMUEL, *Gedrukte vort un teater in argentine* [The Printed Word and Theatre in Argentina] (Buenos Aires: no publisher given, 1941).

—— Introduction to Avrom Goldfaden, *Oysgeklibene shriftn* [Selected Writings] (Buenos Aires: YIVO, 1963).

ROZIER, GILLES, *Moyshe Broderzon: Un écrivain yiddish d'avant-garde* [Moyshe Broderzon: A Yiddish Avant-Garde Writer] (Saint-Denis: Presses Universitaires de Vincennes, 1999).

—— 'Les Paradoxes de l'engagement: Haïm Slovès (Białystok, 19 juin 1905– Paris, 8 septembre 1988)' [The Paradoxes of Engagement: Chaim Sloves], *Archives Juives*, 30 (1997), 71–84.

RUBEL, ELINOR, 'Lahakat hayung teater' [The Yung Theatre Troupe], MA thesis, Hebrew University, Jerusalem, 1990.

RUMSHINSKY, JOSEPH, *Klangen fun mayn lebn* [Echoes of My Life] (New York: Itshe Biderman, 1944).

SANDERS, RONALD, *Downtown Jews: Portraits of an Immigrant Generation* (New York: Harper & Row, 1969).

SANDROW, NAHMA, '"A Little Letter to Mama": Traditions in Yiddish Vaudeville', in Myron Matlaw and Ray B. Browne (eds.), *American Popular Entertainment* (Westport, Conn.: Greenwood Press, 1979), 87–95.

—— *Vagabond Stars: A World History of Yiddish Theatre* (New York: Harper & Row, 1977; repr. New York: Limelight Editions, 1986, and Syracuse, NY: Syracuse University Press, 1999).

SAUBER, MARIANA, 'Le Théâtre yiddish et sa langue' [Yiddish Theatre and its Language], *Temps Modernes*, 41 (1984), 557–67.

SAUNDERS, DAVID, 'Russia and Ukraine under Alexander II: The Valuev Edict of 1863', *International History Review*, 17/1 (1995), 23–50.

—— 'Russia's Ukrainian Policy (1847–1905): A Demographic Approach', *European History Quarterly*, 25 (1995), 181–208.

SAVCHENKO, FEDIR, *Zaborona ukrainstva 1876 r.* [The Suppression of Ukrainian Activities in 1876] (Kharkiv: Derzhavie vidavnitstvo Ukraini, 1930; repr. Munich: Wilhelm Funk Verlag, 1970).

SCHAFFER, CARL, 'Leivick's *The Golem* and the Golem Legend', in Patrick D. Murphy (ed.), *Staging the Impossible: The Fantastic Mode in Modern Drama* (Westport, Conn.: Greenwood Press, 1992), 137–49.

SCHEDRIN, VASSILI, 'Equation of GOSET: History of Yiddish Theatre in the USSR', in Leonard Jay Greenspoon (ed.), *Yiddish Language and Culture Then and Now* (Omaha, Nebr.: Creighton University Press, 1998), 93–108.

SCHEIN, JOSEPH, *see* SHAYN, YOSEF

SCHILDKRAUT, JOSEPH, *My Father and I* (New York: Viking, 1959).

SCHILLER, FRIEDRICH, 'Die Schaubuhne als eine moralische Anstalt betrachtet' [The Stage as a Moral Institution'], in John Gassner and Ralph G. Allen (eds.), *Theatre and Drama in the Making* (Boston: Houghton Mifflin, 1964).

SCHMUCK, HILMAR, *Jüdischer Biographischer Index* [Jewish Biographical Index], 4 vols. (Munich: K. G. Saur, 1998).

—— and PINCHAS LAPIDE (eds.), *Jüdischer Biographischer Archiv* [Jewish Biographical Archive] (Munich: K. G. Saur, 1995).

SCHNEIDER, DAVID, 'Critical Approaches to Modern Yiddish Drama', in Dov-Ber Kerler (ed.), *History of Yiddish Studies*, vol. iii of *Winter Studies in Yiddish* (Chur: Harwood Academic Publishers, 1991), 103–15.

SCHUDT, JOHANN J., *Jüdische Merckwürdigkeiten, vorstellende was sich Curieuses und Denckwürdiges in den neuen Zeiten* [Jewish Oddities: Presenting that which is Curious and Memorable in Recent Times], 4 vols. (Frankfurt: no publisher given, 1714–18).

SCHWARTZ, JULIAN, *Literarishe dermonungen* [Literary Recollections] (Bucharest: Criterion, 1975).

SECUNDA, VICTORIA, *Bei mir bist du schon: The Life of Sholom Secunda* (New York: Magic Circle Press, 1982).

SEIDMAN, AARON, 'The First Performance of Yiddish Theatre in America', *Jewish Social Studies*, 10 (1948), 67–70.

SEIGER, MARVIN, 'A History of the Yiddish Theatre in New York City to 1892', Ph.D. thesis, Indiana University, 1960.

SELLER, MAXINE SCHWARTZ, *Ethnic Theatre in the United States* (Westport, Conn.: Greenwood Press, 1983).

SHALIT, LEVI, *Meshiekh-troymen in leyviks dramatishe poemes* [Messianic Dreams in Leivick's Dramatic Poems] (Munich: Eynzam, 1947).

SHANDLER, JEFFREY, 'Ost und West, Old World and New: Nostalgia and Antinostalgia on the Silver Screen', in Sylvia Paskin (ed.), *When Joseph Met Molly: A Reader on Yiddish Film* (Nottingham: Five Leaves Publications, 1999), 69–101.

SHATZKY, JACOB, 'Di ershte geshikhte fun yidishn teater' [The First History of Yiddish Theatre], *Filologishe shriftn*, 2 (Vilna: B. Kletskin, 1928), 215–64.

—— 'Geshikhte fun yidishn teater' [The History of Yiddish Theater], in R. Abramovitch *et al.* (eds.), *Algemeyne entsiklopedye* [General Encyclopedia], 11 vols. (Paris: Dubnov-Fond, 1934–66), vol. ii, cols. 389–414.

SHATZKY, JACOB, 'Der kamf kegn purim-shpil in praysn in 18tn y[or]h[undert]' [The Struggle against the *Purimshpil* in Eighteenth-Century Prussia], *Yivo bleter*, 15 (Jan.-Feb. 1940), 28–38.

—— 'Purim-shpiln un leytsim in amsterdamer geto', [*Purimshpiln* and Jesters in the Amsterdam Ghetto], *Yivo bleter*, 19 (Mar.–Apr. 1942), 212–20.

—— 'Teater-farvaylungen bay di ashkenazim in holand' [Theatrical Entertainments of the Ashkenazim in Holland], *Yivo bleter*, 21 (May–June 1943), 302–22.

—— 'Yidisher teater in varshe in der ershter helft fun 19tn y[or]h[undert]' [Yiddish Theatre in Warsaw in the First Half of the Nineteenth Century], *Yivo bleter*, 14 (Jan.–Feb. 1939), 1–9.

—— (ed.), *Arkhiv far der geshikhte fun yidishn teater un drame* [Archive for the History of Yiddish Theatre and Drama] (New York: YIVO, 1930).

—— (ed.), *Goldfaden-bukh* [Goldfaden Book] (New York: Idisher Teater Muzey, 1926).

—— (ed.), *Hundert yor goldfadn* [A Hundred Years of Goldfaden] (New York: YIVO, 1940); 1st pub. in *Yivo bleter*, special Goldfaden issue, 15 (May–June 1940).

SHAYN, YOSEF [Joseph Schein], *Arum moskver yidishn teater* [Around the Moscow Yiddish Theatre] (Paris: Éditions Polyglottes, 1964).

—— 'Yidisher teater in sovetn-farband' [Yiddish Theatre in the Soviet Union], in Itsik Manger, Jonas Turkow, and Moyshe Perenson (eds.), *Yidisher teater in eyrope tsvishn beyde velt-milkhomes: sovetn-farband, mayrev-eyrope, baltishe lender* [Yiddish Theatre in Europe between the World Wars: The Soviet Union, Western Europe, and the Baltic Countries], 2 vols. (New York: Congress for Jewish Culture, 1971), 39–164.

SHIPER, YITSKHOK, *Geshikhte fun yidisher teater-kunst un drame* [The History of Yiddish Theatre Art and Drama], 3 vols. (Warsaw: Kultur-lige, 1923–8).

SHMERUK, KHONE, 'Hashem hamashma'uti mordkheh-markus: gilgulo hasifruti shel ide'al ḥevrati' [The Significant Name Mordkhe-Markus: The Literary Reincarnation of a Social Ideal], *Tarbiz*, 29 (1959–60), 76–98.

—— *Maḥazot mikra'im beyidish, 1697–1750* [Yiddish Biblical Plays, 1697–1750] (Jerusalem: Israel Academy of Sciences and Humanities, 1979).

—— 'Di moyshe rabeynu bashraybung: an umbavuste drame fun 18tn yorhundert' [The Moses Story: An Unknown Drama from the Eighteenth Century], *Di goldene keyt*, 14 (1964), 296–320.

—— *Peretses yiesh-viziye: interpretatsye fun y.l. peretses baynakht afn altn mark un kritishe oysgabe fun der drame* [Peretz's Vision of Despair: An Interpretation of Y. L. Peretz's *A Night in the Old Marketplace* and a Critical Edition of the Drama] (New York: YIVO, 1971).

—— 'The Stage-Design of Peretz' *Baynakht oyfn altn mark* ', *Scripta Hierosolymitana*, 19 (1967), 39–57.

—— ' "Tsezeyt un tseshpreyt" lesholem aleykhem vehahatsagot shel hamaḥazeh besafah hapolanit bevarshe beshanim 1905–1910' [Sholem Aleykhem's Comedy *Tsezeyt un tseshpreyt* and its Performance in Polish in Warsaw from 1905 to 1910], in Ezra Mendelsohn and Khone Shmeruk (eds.), *Kovets mekharim al yehudei polin: sefer lezikhro shel paul glikson* [Studies on Polish Jewry: Paul Glikson Memorial Volume] (Jerusalem: Hebrew University, 1987), 79–95.

SHMUELEVITSH-HOFFMAN, MIRIAM, 'Di khavley leyde funem yoysef pap yidishn teater' [The Birth Pangs of the Joseph Papp Yiddish Theatre], *Oksforder yidish*, 3 (1995), 809–32.

SHNEYER, Z., '*Bar kokhba*, a retsenzye' [*Bar Kokhba*: A Review], *Shtern*, 22 June 1939.

SHOMER-BACHELIS, ROSE, *Vi ikh hob zey gekent: portretn fun bavuste idishe perzenlekhkaytn* [As I Knew Them: Portraits of Renowned Jewish Personalities] (Los Angeles: no publisher given, 1955).

—— and MIRIAM SHOMER-TSUNZER, *Unzer foter shomer* [Our Father Shomer] (New York: YKUF, 1950).

SHTENTSL, A. N. [A. N. Stencl] (ed.), *Yoyvl almanakh, loshn un lebn 1956* [Jubilee Almanac of the Loshn un Lebn (Language and Life) Society 1956] (London, 1956).

SHTERNBERG, JACOB, *Vegn literatur un teater* [On Literature and Theatre] (Tel Aviv: H. Leivick-farlag, 1987).

SHTERNSHIS, ANNA, 'Soviet and Kosher: Soviet Jewish Cultural Identity, 1917–41', D.Phil. thesis, University of Oxford, 2001.

SHULMAN, ELAZAR, *Sefat-yehudit ashkenazit vesifrutah: mikets hame'ah ha-15 ad kets shenot hame'ah ha-18* [The Jewish Ashkenazi Language and its Literature: From the End of the Fifteenth Century to the End of the Eighteenth Century] (Riga: Eli Levin Press, 1913).

SHULMAN, ELIYOHU, 'Sholem-aleykhems debyut in amerike' [Sholem Aleykhem's American Debut], *Yivo bleter*, 4 (Dec. 1932), 419–31.

SHUNAMI, SHLOMO, *Bibliography of Jewish Bibliographies*, 2nd edn. (Jerusalem: Magnes Press, 1965).

SIEGEL, BEN, *The Controversial Sholem Asch* (Bowling Green, Ohio: Bowling Green University Popular Press, 1978).

SIMON, SHLOYME, *H. leyviks goylem* [H. Leivick's Golem] (New York: Idish lebn, 1927).

SLOBIN, MARK, 'The Music of the Yiddish Theatre: Manuscript Sources at YIVO', *YIVO Annual*, 18 (1983), 372–90.

—— *Tenement Songs: The Popular Music of the Jewish Immigrants* (Urbana: University of Illinois Press, 1982).

SLOTNITZKY, JACOB, 'Der Talmud Chuchem. Lebensbild in 5 Akten von Jakobi. Bearbaitet Jacob Slotnitzky' [The Learned Student: A Portrait from Life in Five Acts by Jakobi, adapted by Jacob Slotnitzky] (1908) (Yiddish, in German transliteration), St Petersburg Theatrical Library, Tsarist Censor's Collection, *fond* 1474.

SLOVES, H., *In un arum: eseyen* [In and Around: Essays] (New York: YKUF, 1970).

SOLOMON, ALISA, *Re-Dressing the Canon: Essays on Theatre and Gender* (London: Routledge, 1997).

SOXBERGER, THOMAS, 'Jiddische Literatur und Publizistik in Wien' [Yiddish Literature and Publishers in Vienna], MA thesis, University of Vienna, 1994.

—— 'Strukturen des jiddischen Kulturlebens in Wien. Verlage und Druckereien, Vereinswesen' [Structures of Yiddish Cultural Life in Vienna: Publishing Houses and Presses, Associations], unpublished manuscript.

SPEKTOR, M., 'Velvel der shiber' [Velvel the Baker's Assistant], *Der Tog*, 63 (1904).

SPRENGEL, PETER, 'Kafka und der "wilde Mensch". Neues von Jizchak Löwy und dem jiddischen Theater' [Kafka and the 'Wild Man': The Latest on Isaac Löwy and the Yiddish Theatre], *Jahrbuch der Deutschen Schiller-Gesellschaft*, 39 (1995), 305–23.

—— *Populäres jüdisches Theater in Berlin von 1877 bis 1933* [Popular Jewish Theatre in Berlin from 1877 to 1933] (Berlin: Haude & Spener, 1997).

—— *Scheunenviertel-Theater. Jüdische Schauspieltruppen und jiddische Dramatik in Berlin (1900–1918)* [*Scheunenviertel* Theatre: Jewish Theatre Troupes and Yiddish Dramatic Art in Berlin (1900–1918)] (Berlin: Fannei & Walz, 1995).

STAERK, W., 'Die Purim-Komödie *Mekhires yoysef* ' [The Purim Comedy *The Sale of Joseph*], *Monatsschrift für Geschichte und Wissenschaft des Judentums*, NS 30 (1922), 294–9.

STARCK, ASTRID, 'Alsatian Yiddish Theater at the Turn of the Century', in Dagmar C. G. Lorenz and Gabriele Weinberger (eds.), *Insiders and Outsiders: Jewish and Gentile Culture in Germany and Austria* (Detroit: Wayne State University Press, 1994), 100–8.

STARCK-ADLER, ASTRID, 'Introduction au théâtre yiddisch alsacien au XIXe siècle' [Introduction to Nineteenth-Century Alsatian Yiddish Theatre], *Yod*, 31–2 (1992), 145–57.

STAVISH, CORINNE B., 'There's Nothing Like That Now: The Yiddish Theatre in Chicago—Personal Perspectives', MA thesis, Northeastern Illinois University, 1979.

STEINLAUF, MICHAEL C., 'Fear of Purim: Y. L. Peretz and the Canonization of Yiddish Theater', *Jewish Social Studies*, 1/3 (Spring 1993), 44–65.

—— 'Jews and Polish Theater in Nineteenth Century Warsaw', *Polish Review*, 32 (1987), 439–58.

—— 'Polish-Jewish Theater: The Case of Mark Arnshteyn', Ph.D. thesis, Brandeis University, 1988.

—— 'Sources for the History of Jewish Theatre in Poland', *Gal-Ed: On the History of the Jews in Poland*, 15–16 (1997), 83–103.

STRAUSS, JUTTA, 'Aaron Halle-Wolfssohn: A Trilingual Life', D.Phil. thesis, University of Oxford, 1994.

—— 'Aaron Halle-Wolfssohn. Ein Leben in drei Sprachen' [Aaron-Halle Wolfssohn: A Life in Three Languages], in Anselm Gerhard (ed.), *Musik und Ästhetik im Berlin Moses Mendelssohns* [Music and Aesthetics in Moses Mendelssohn's Berlin] (Tübingen: Max Niemeyer, 1999), 57–75.

Svod Zakonov Rossiiskoi Imperii [Legal Code of the Russian Empire], book 4, vols. xiii–xvi, ed. M. Nyurenberg (Moscow: Tovarishchestvo Skoropechatni A. A. Levenson, 1910); book 5, vols. xiii–xvi, ed. I. D. Mordukhai-Boltovsky (St Petersburg: Russkoe Knizhnoe Tovarishchestvo 'Deyatel′', 1914).

SWIFT, E. ANTHONY, 'Fighting the Germs of Disorder: The Censorship of Russian Popular Theatre, 1888–1917', *Russian History*, 18 (Spring 1991).

TAUB, MICHAEL, 'Social Issues in Peretz's Short Dramas', *Yiddish*, 10 (1995), 18–24.

—— 'Yiddish Theatre in Romania: Profile of a Repertoire', *Yiddish*, 8 (1991), 59–68.

TAYTLBOYM, AVROM, *Teatralia* (Warsaw: Yatshkovskis Bibliotek, 1929).

Teater-almanakh: london 1939–1943 [Theatre Almanac: London, 1939–43] (London: M. Markov, 1943).

Teater-bukh [Theatre Book] (Kiev: Kultur-lige, 1927).

THISSEN, JUDITH, 'Jewish Immigrant Audiences in New York City, 1905–14', in Melvyn Stokes and Richard Maltby (eds.), *American Movie Audiences: From the Turn of the Century to the Early Sound Era* (London: BFI Publishing, 1999), 15–28.

THISSEN, JUDITH, 'Moyshe Goes to the Movies: Jewish Immigrants, Popular Entertainment, and Ethnic Identity in New York City (1880–1914)', Ph.D. thesis, Utrecht University, 2001.

THOMASHEFSKY, BESSIE, *Mayn lebns-geshikhte* [My Life Story] (New York: Varhayt, 1916).

THOMASHEFSKY, BORIS, *Mayn lebns-geshikhte* [My Life Story] (New York: Trio Press, 1937).

—— *Tomashevski's teater shriftn* [Thomashefsky's Theatre Writings] (New York: Lipshits Press, 1908).

TIRKEL, DOVID BER, *Di yugntlekhe bine: geshikhte fun di idish-hebreyishe dramatishe gezelshaftn* [The Juvenile Stage: The History of Yiddish-Hebrew Dramatic Societies] (Philadelphia: Hebrew Literature Society, 1940).

TRETSEK, L. O. 'O vozrozhdenii evreiskogo teatra' [The Resurrection of the Jewish Theatre], *Nedel' naya Khronika Voskhoda*, 12 (24 Mar. 1905), 45.

TROY, SHARI S., 'On the Play and the Playing: Theatricality as Leitmotif in the Purim Play of the Bobover Hasidim', Ph.D. thesis, City University of New York, 2001.

TSANIN, M. (ed.), *Briv fun sholem ash* [Letters of Sholem Asch] (Bat-Yam: Beyt Sholem Ash, 1980).

Tsen yor artef [Ten Years of Artef] (New York: Tsenyorikn yuviley, 1937).

TSEYTLIN, ELKHONEN, *Bukh un bine: notitsn un refleksn iber literatur un teater* [Book and Stage: Notes and Reflections on Literature and Theatre] (Warsaw: E. Tsaytlin, 1939).

TSINBERG, YISROEL, *Di geshikhte fun der literatur bay yidn* [The History of Jewish Literature], 10 vols. (Vilna: Tomor, 1929–66).

TSUKER, NEKHEMYE, *Fir doyres idish teater: di lebns-geshikhte fun zina rapel* [Four Generations of Yiddish Theatre: The Biography of Zina Rapel], 2 vols. (Buenos Aires: Nekhemye Tsuker, 1944).

—— (ed.), *Zeks yor beser idish teater* [Six Years of Better Yiddish Theatre] (Buenos Aires: no publisher given, 1951).

TURKOW, JONAS, *Farloshene shtern* [Extinguished Stars] (Buenos Aires: Tsentral-farband far Poylishe Yidn in Argentine, 1953).

—— *Vegvayzer far dramatishe krayzn* [Guide for Drama Clubs] (Warsaw: Rekord, 1924).

TURKOW, ZYGMUNT, *Fragmentn fun mayn lebn* [Fragments from My Life] (Buenos Aires: Tsentral-farband far Poylishe Yidn in Argentine, 1951).

—— *Di ibergerisene tkufe* [The Interrupted Era] (Buenos Aires: Tsentral-farband far Poylishe Yidn in Argentine, 1961).

—— *Shmuesn vegn teater* [Conversations on the Theatre] (Buenos Aires: Farlag Unzer Bukh, 1950).

—— *Teater-zikhroynes fun a shturmisher tsayt* [Theatre Memoirs from a Tempestuous Time] (Buenos Aires: Tsentral-farband far Poylishe Yidn in Argentine, 1956).

TURKOW-GRUDBERG, YITSKHOK, *Af mayn veg (shrayber un kinstler)* [On My Way (Writers and Actors)] (Buenos Aires: Tsentral-farband fun Poylishe Yidn in Argentine, 1964).

—— *Geven a yidish teater: dos yidishe teater in poyln tsvishn beyde velt-milkhomes* [There was a Yiddish Theatre: Yiddish Theatre in Poland between the World Wars] (Tel Aviv: I. Turkow, 1968).

—— *Goldfaden un gordin* [Goldfaden and Gordin] (Tel Aviv: S. Grinhoyz, 1969).

—— *Di mame ester rokhl* [My Mother, Esther Rokhl] (Warsaw: Yidish Bukh, 1951).

—— *Sholem ashes derekh in der yidisher eybikayt* [Sholem Asch's Path in Jewish Eternity] (Bat-Yam: Bet Shalom Ash, 1967).

—— *Sovyetishe dramaturgye* [Soviet Dramaturgy] (Warsaw: Yidish Bukh, 1955).

—— *Varshe: dos vigele fun yidishn teater* [Warsaw: The Cradle of Yiddish Theatre] (Warsaw: Yidish Bukh, 1956).

—— *Yidish teater in poyln* [Yiddish Theatre in Poland] (Warsaw: Yidish Bukh, 1951).

—— *Zigmunt turkov* (Tel Aviv: Dfus Orli, 1970).

TURNER, VICTOR, *From Ritual to Theatre: The Human Seriousness of Play* (New York: PAJ Publications, 1982).

USOV, P. S., 'Iz moikh vospominanii', *Istoricheskii Vestnik*, II (Jan.–Mar. 1883), 342–3.

VAN GENNEP, ARNOLD, *The Rites of Passage*, trans. M. Vizedom and G. Caffee (Chicago: University of Chicago Press, 1960).

VANVILD, M. (pseud.), *Pseydo-kunst un pseydo-kritik* [Pseudo-Art and Pseudo-Criticism] (Łódź: no publisher given, 1921).

VASERMAN, YANKEV, *Dos teater un der sotsyalizm* [Theatre and Socialism] (Warsaw: Y. Vaserman, 1921).

VAYNRIB, B., 'An umbakante yidishe komedye fun poyzner gegnt' [An Unknown Yiddish Comedy from the Posen District], *Yivo bleter*, 2 (1931), 358–66.

VAYNSHTEYN, B., 'Di ershte yorn fun yidishn teater in odes un in nyu-york' [The First Years of the Yiddish Theatre in Odessa and New York], in Jacob Shatzky (ed.), *Arkhiv far der geshikhte fun yidishn teater un drame* (New York: YIVO, 1930), 243–54.

VEIDLINGER, JEFFREY, 'Let's Perform a Miracle: The Soviet Yiddish State Theater in the 1920s', *Slavic Review*, 57 (Summer 1998), 372–97.

—— *The Moscow State Yiddish Theater* (Bloomington: Indiana University Press, 2000).

VINER, MEIR, *Tsu der geshikhte fun der yidisher literature in 19-tn yorhundert* [Towards the History of Yiddish Literature in the Nineteenth Century], 2 vols. (New York: YKUF, 1945).

VINTSHEVSKI, MORRIS, *A tog mit yankev gordin* [A Day with Jacob Gordin] (New York: Farlag M. Mayzel, 1909).

VOVSI-MIKHOELS, NATALIA, *Avi shelomo mikhoels* [My Father Shloyme Mikhoels] (Tel Aviv: Hakibbutz Hameuchad, 1982).

—— *Moi otets solomon mikhoels* [My Father Solomon Mikhoels] (Tel Aviv: Iakov Press, 1984).

WALDINGER, ALBERT, 'Jacob Gordin and the Liberation of the American Yiddish Theater', *Yiddish*, 11 (1998), 72–80.

WALLAS, ARMIN A., 'Jiddisches Theater. Das Gastspiel der Wilnaer Truppe in Wien 1922/23' [Yiddish Theatre: The Vilna Troupe's Vienna Tour, 1922–3], *Das Jüdische Echo*, 44 (1995), 179–92.

WARNKE, NINA, 'Of Plays and Politics: Sholem Aleichem's First Visit to America', *YIVO Annual*, 20 (1991), 239–76.

—— 'Reforming the New York Yiddish Theater: The Cultural Politics of Immigrant Intellectuals and the Yiddish Press, 1887–1910', Ph.D. thesis, Columbia University, 2001.

WEICHERT, MIKHL, *Teater un drame* [Theatre and Drama], 2 vols. (Warsaw: B. Kletskin, 1922–6).

—— *Trupe tanentsap: a goldfaden-shpil in a galitsish shtetl* [*The Tanentsap Troupe*: A Goldfaden Play in a Galician *Shtetl*] (Tel Aviv: Hamenorah, 1966).

—— *Zikhroynes* [Memoirs] (Tel Aviv: Hamenorah, 1960).

WEINER, BINYOMIN, 'Judging Vengeance', *Pakn-Treger*, 23 (Winter 1996), 10–15.

WEINREICH, BEATRICE, and URIEL WEINREICH, *Yiddish Language and Folklore* (Amsterdam: Mouton, 1959).

WEINREICH, MAX, *Bilder fun der yidisher literatur-geshikhte fun di onheybn biz mendele moykher sforim* [Scenes from Yiddish Literary History from the Beginning to Mendele Moykher Sforim] (Vilna: Farlag Tomor, 1928).

—— *Geshikhte fun der yidisher shprakh* [History of the Yiddish Language] (New York: YIVO, 1973).

—— 'Tsu der geshikhte fun der elterer akhashveyresh-shpil' [Towards the History of the Older Ahasuerus Play], *Filologishe shriftn*, 2 (Vilna: B. Kletskin, 1928), 425–52.

WEINRYB, DOV, 'Gormim kalkalim vesotsialim bahaskalah hayehudit begermaniyah' [Economic and Social Factors in the Jewish Enlightenment in Germany], in *Keneset lezekher ḥaim naḥman bialik* [Conference in Memory of Chaim Nakhman Bialik] (Tel Aviv: Dvir, 1938), 432 ff.

WEISSENBERG, SAMUEL, 'Das Purimspiel von Ahasverus und Esther' [The Purim Play of Ahasuerus and Esther], *Mitteilungen der Gesellschaft für jüdische Volkskunde*, 13 (1904), 1–27.

WEITZNER, JACOB, *Meḥirat yosef bate'atron hayehudi ha'amami* [The Sale of Joseph in the Jewish Folk Theatre] (Tel Aviv: Farlag Y. L. Peretz, 1999).

—— *Sholem Aleichem in the Theater* (Northwood: Symposium Press, 1994).

WIENER, LEO, *The History of Yiddish Literature in the Nineteenth Century* (New York: C. Scribner's Sons, 1899).

WISHNIA, KENNETH, '"A Different Kind of Hell": Orality, Multilingualism, and American Yiddish in the Translation of Sholem Aleichem's *Mister Boym in Klozet*', *AJS Review*, 20 (1995), 333–58.

—— 'Yiddish in "Amerike": Problems of Translating Multilingual Immigrant Texts—Morris Rosenfeld's "Rent Strike" (1908)', *Yiddish*, 10 (1996), 140–60.

WITTKE, CARL, 'The Immigrant Theme on the American Stage', *Mississippi Valley Historical Review*, 39 (Sept. 1952), 211–32.

WOLITZ, SETH L., 'The Americanization of Tevye, or Boarding the Jewish *Mayflower*', *American Quarterly*, 40 (Dec. 1988), 514–36.

—— 'Forging a Hero for a Jewish Stage: Goldfadn's *Bar Kokhba*', *Shofar*, 20 (2002), 53–65.

—— 'Performing a Holocaust Play in Warsaw in 1963', in Claude Schumacher (ed.), *Staging the Holocaust: The Shoah in Drama and Performance* (Cambridge: Cambridge University Press, 1998), 130–46.

WOODS, ALAN, 'Emphasizing the Avant-Garde: An Exploration in Theatre Historiography', in Thomas Postlewait and Bruce McConachie (eds.), *Interpreting the Theatrical Past: Essays in the Historiography of Performance* (Iowa City: University of Iowa Press, 1989), 166–76.

YABLOKOFF, HERMAN, *Arum der velt mit yidish teater* [Around the World with Yiddish Theatre], 2 vols. (New York: no publisher given, 1968–9);

abridged as *Der payatz*, trans. Bella Mysell Yablokoff (Silver Spring, Md.:
Bartleby Press, 1995).

YESHURIN, YEFIM, *100 yor moderne yidishe literatur: bibliografishe tsushtayer*
[A Hundred Years of Modern Yiddish Literature: Bibliography] (New
York: Workmen's Circle Book Committee, 1965).

YO, MIKHAIL [Meir Yaffe], *Teater pesimizmen* [Theatre Pessimisms] (Riga:
Bilike Bikher, 1938).

YOUNG, BOAZ, *Mayn lebn in teater* [My Life in the Theatre] (New York:
YKUF, 1950).

ZABLE, ARNOLD, *Wanderers and Dreamers: Tales of the David Herman
Theatre* (South Melbourne: Hyland House, 1998).

ZAKIN, M., G. GELMAN, and VICTOR KOHN (eds.), *30 yor 'ift'* [Thirty
Years of IFT] (Buenos Aires: IFT [Argentinian Yiddish People's Theatre
and Art Society], 1962).

Zalmen zilbertsvayg yoyvl-bukh [Zalmen Zylbercweig Jubilee Book] (New York:
Yubiley-Komitet, 1941).

ZATZMAN, BELARIE, 'Yiddish Theatre in Montreal', *Canadian Jewish
Studies*, 6 (1998), 89–97.

ZEIFERT, MOYSHE, 'Di geshikhte fun idishn teater' [The History of the Yiddish Theatre], in Khonen Y. Minikes (ed.), *Di idishe bine* [The Yiddish
Stage] (New York: no publisher given, 1897).

ZOHN, HERSHEL, *The Story of the Yiddish Theatre* (Las Cruces, NM: Zohn,
1979).

ZOLOTAROV, HILLEL (Hillel Solotaroff), 'Di idishe bine' [The Yiddish
Stage] and 'Fun nayem idishen teater' [From the New Yiddish Theatre], in
Geklibene shriften [Collected Writings], ed. Joel Entin, 3 vols. (New York:
Dr. H. Solotaroff Publication Committee, 1924), ii. 161–201.

—— 'Der onfang fun der yidisher drame in rusland' [The Beginnings of Yiddish
Drama in Russia], in *Suvenir tsu yankev gordins tsen-yerikn yubileyum*
[Souvenir for Jacob Gordin's Tenth Anniversary] (New York, 1901), 23–30.

ZUCKER, NEKHEMYE, *Zeks yor beser yidish teater* [Six Years of Better Yiddish
Theatre] (Buenos Aires: no publisher given, 1951).

ZYLBERCWEIG, ZALMEN, *Hantbukh fun yidishn teater* [Handbook of the
Yiddish Theatre] (Mexico City: Zalmen Zylbercweig Yoyvl-Komitet baym
Yivo in Los Angeles, 1970).

—— *Hintern forhang* [Behind the Curtain] (Vilna: B. Kletskin, 1928).

—— *Teater-figurn* [Theatre People] (Buenos Aires: Elisheva, 1936).

—— *Teater mozayik* [Theatre Mosaics] (New York: Itshe Biderman, 1941).

—— *Di velt fun ester-rokhl kaminska* [The World of Esther-Rokhl Kaminska] (Mexico: no publisher given, 1969).

—— *Di velt fun yankev gordin* [The World of Jacob Gordin] (Tel Aviv: Elisheva, 1964).

—— *Vos der yidisher aktyor dertseylt* [What the Yiddish Actor has to Say] (Vilna: B. Kletskin, 1928).

—— (ed.), *Avrom goldfaden un zigmunt mogulesco* (Buenos Aires: Elisheva, 1936).

—— (ed.), *Leksikon fun yidishn teater* [Lexicon of Yiddish Theatre], 6 vols. (New York: Elisheva, 1931–70).

—— HARRY LANG, and A. BABITSH (eds.), *Eliyohu tenenholts yoyvl-bukh* [Elia Tenenholtz Jubilee Book] (Los Angeles: Eliyohu Tenenholts Yoyvl Komitet, 1955).

Index

🪶

A

A goldfaden kholem (by Yankev Rotboym) 191, 197; pl. 16
Abeles, Otto 108, 113
Aberbakh, Asher 169
Abramovitsh, Sholem Yankev:
  Masoes binyomim hashlishi (The Travels of Benjamin III) 52
  Priziv, Der (The Conscript) 40
actors 13, 53–4, 141
Adler, Celia (Tsili) 13, 119, 120
Adler, Jacob P. 15, 122, 124, 187, 208; pl. 5
Adler, Julius 124
Adler, Sam:
  director 170, 171
  Sore-sheyndl 170
advertisements 70, 165 n.; pl. 16
Akeydes yitskhok (by Avrom Goldfaden) 140, 141, 142–3
Alexander II, Tsar 5, 89
Alexander III, Tsar 5
Aleykhem, Sholem, *see* Sholem Aleykhem
Altshuler, Mordechai 17–18
Amerikanerin, Di (by Boris Thomashefsky) 72
Andreev, Leonid 66
Anglo-American Commission of Inquiry on European Jewry and Palestine 176
Ansky, S. (Solomon Rappoport):
  Dibek, Der (The Dybbuk) 49, 54, 57, 59, 94, 112, 188, 195, 196; pl. 8
  on Jewish theatre 73
antisemitism 23, 112, 116, 166, 178
  see also newspapers; pogroms
Antsipovich, V. 168
Apikoyres, Der (by Joseph Markovitsh) 124
Appia, Adolphe 210
Ariel, Harry 135 n.
Aristophanes 42
Aristotle 8, 54, 211
Arnshteyn, Mark:
  as director 172 n.
  Eybike lid, Dos (The Eternal Song) 67 n.
  Jewish theatre plan 167
  Vilner balebesl, Der (The Petty Householder of Vilna) 67 n.

Artef (Arbeter Teater Farband) 15–16
Artomovsky, *Zaporozhets za Dunayem* (Cossacks on the Danube) 91
Asch, Sholem:
  Got fun nekome (God of Vengeance) 19, 52, 66, 71, 113, 175–85, 188, 196, 210
  Meshiekhs tsaytn (The Messianic Era) 57
Ashendorf, Yisroel 152–4
audiences:
  Bucharest 166 n.
  Cracow 143, 151, 154–5
  London 126, 136, 175
  Moscow 91
  New York 17, 136, 208–9
  purimshpil performances 40
  St Petersburg 64, 65–6, 69, 166 n.
  Vienna 109, 116–17
  Yiddish pls. 4, 5
Auf nach Tel Aviv (by Abish Meisels) 115, 116
Averchenko, Arkady:
  Odessity (The Odessans) 71 n.
  performances 66

B

Baba Yaga 80
Baker, Zachary 96
Bakhtin, Mikhail 34, 206 n.
Bal Makhshoves (Isidor Eliashev) 212–13
balagan 205, 206
Bar kokhba (by Avrom Goldfaden) 20, 24, 56, 58, 64, 72 n., 81, 87, 89–90, 92, 95, 100–4, 140, 141, 142, 151–3, 169, 170, 189, 193
  adapted by Shmuel Halkin 20, 24, 87, 100–1, 103–4
Baratoff, Paul 113, 115, 116; pl. 9
Bardakh, Yu. M. 162
Barish, Jonas 7
batkhn (wedding jester) 1–2, 204, 206
Baumritter & Gonsher 82
Baynakht afn altn mark (by Yitskhok Leyb Peretz) 49, 55, 56, 58, 116; pl. 13
Beethoven, Ludwig van, *Fidelio* 91
Beilis, Mendel 71
Beitler, Nathan 176, 180, 183, 185

Belarus 18
Belkin, Ahuva 6, 20, 24
Bellini, Vincenzo, *Norma* 92
Belzer, Nisn (Nusn Spivak) 121
Ben ami (by Avrom Goldfaden) 56, 140
Ben-Israel, Hedva 89
Ben-Tsion, Emmanuel (Ben Sion, Ya. M.
     Priluker) 161, 162
Berkowitz, Joel 214
Berman, I. R. 83
Berman-Dvinsky 69
Bertolone, Paola 20, 24
Bessarabia 159
Bialik, Chaim Nachman 70 n.
Bible, translation into German 2, 30
Bilov, S. 90
Binevich, Evgeny 165 n.
Birnbaum, Nathan 108
Bleich, Yude 113
Blimele (by Joseph Lateiner) 123, 190, 193
Boal, Augusto 88, 89
Bobe mitn eynikl, Di (by Avrom Goldfaden)
     83, 169
Brahm, Otto 210
Branitsky, K. 168
Brecher, Egon 112, 114; pl. 9
Brecht, Bertolt 32, 81
Breytman, Paul 115
Brider lurye, Di (by Jacob Gordin) 72 n.
British Arts Council 185
Broder singers 78, 79, 110, 111, 142, 204
Broderzon, Moyshe 15
Brodyaga, Der (by Joseph Markovitsh) 124
Bronks ekspres (by Osip Dimov) 57
Bucharest:
     audiences 166 n.
     Jewish Company 162
Buenos Aires 5, 17 n.
Bukhvald, Nokhem (Nathaniel Buchwald)
     1, 8
Bułat, Mirosława 18–19, 24
Burshteyn, Peysekhke 13
Byron, Lord 55
     Manfred 58

C

Cahan, Abraham 202 n., 211
Canada 17
carnival 34, 42, 206 n.
censorship:
     American 183–4
     Austro-Hungarian 109
     British 177–85
     Russian 62–3, 162–6

Chagall, Marc 84, 86 n.
Chassene im Städtel (by Abish Meisels) 116
Chemerinsky, Mordkhe 36
Chicago 5
Chirikov, Evgeny, *Evrei* (The Jews) 66
Christianity 37, 78, 165, 173
Ciabatti, Giulio 85
Coleridge, Samuel Taylor 53, 58
Communist Party 96, 126
Company of Russian-German Operetta
     Artists 168
Copeau, Jacques 86
costume 40, 148–9, 153
Cracow:
     audiences 143, 151, 154–5
     Goldfaden performances 19, 140–4,
          147–54
     Jewish population 139, 147, 154–5
     Jewish Theatre 140–1, 144
     performances in Yiddish 19, 140, 145–9
Craig, Gordon 210
critics:
     New York 24, 201–2, 211–14
     St Petersburg (Petrograd) 64–6, 68, 72
     Vienna 23, 113
Csárdásfürstin (by Emerich Kalman) 112,
     190, 193, 196
Cypkin, Diane 16

D

Dalinger, Brigitte 19, 23
daytshmerish 50, 51, 209
Detroit 17
Deutsch, Isaac 112, 114, 115; pl. 9
Deutsch, Mina 115
Diamant, Dora 175, 185
Diamant, Zaynvl 78
Dibek, Der (by S. Ansky) 49, 54, 57, 59, 94,
     112, 188, 195, 196; pl. 8
Dibick, Der (by Moyshe Hurwitz) 109
Dimov, Osip:
     autobiography 13
     Bronks ekspres (Bronx Express) 57
     Eybiker vanderer, Der (The Eternal
          Wanderer) 50, 57
     Slushai, izrail! (Shma yisroel!; Hear, O
          Israel!) 66, 113, 117
     *Yoshke muzikant (Der zinger fun zayn
          troyer)* (Yoshke the Musician (The
          Singer of his Sorrow)) 116
Dinezon, Yankev 205
Dobrushin, Yekhezkel 12, 90, 95
Doktor almosado; oder, Di yidn in palermo
     (by Avrom Goldfaden) 83, 160, 168

Donizetti, Gaetano, *Lucia di Lammermoor* 92, 93
Dovid bemilkhome (by Avrom Goldfaden) 81
Dovids fidele (by Joseph Lateiner) 170
Dreiblatt, Paula 114, 115
Dukus, Der (by Alter Kacyzne) 57

E

East end vest (by Joseph Markovitsh) 124
Eisenstein, Sergei 101
Elyashevich, Dmitry 161, 162 n., 164 n.
emotionalism 52–6
Enlightenment 204–5
    see also Haskalah
Entin, Joel 213 n.
Ershte patsyentn, Di (by Mark Semyonovich Rivesman) 70
expressionism 56
Eybike lid, Dos (by Mark Arnshteyn) 67 n.
Eybiker vanderer, Der (by Osip Dimov) 50, 57
Eybiker yid, Der (by Dovid Pinski) 57

F

Familye tsvi, Di (*Der letster yid*) (by Dovid Pinski) 57
Farshidene glikn (by Joseph Markovitsh) 124; pl. 6
Feinman, Lilly pl. 6
Feinman, Sigmund:
    career 123
    Shabes koydesh (The Holy Sabbath) 123
Feldman, Ilia 170
Fenigshtayn, Herman 135
Feokistov, E. M. 163
Finkel, Uri 12, 81
Fishzon, Avrom 74, 165 n., 167, 168, 169, 170
Fitzpatrick, Sheila 96
Folksteater un Teater far Yugnt 147
Frankfurt, *purimshpil* destruction 32
Franz Joseph, Emperor 112, 146
Free Jewish Theatre 74 n.
Freie Jüdische Volksbühne 112–14, 116; pl. 9
Fremder, Der (by Jacob Gordin) 66 n., 113
Freud, Sigmund 19, 107
Friedmann, Desider 116
Fun sekhistov biz amerike (by Abish Meisels) 114–15

G

Game, H. C. 178, 180 n.
Gartenshteyn, L. S. 168

Gembler, Der (by Joseph Markovitsh) 124
German Dramatic-Operetta Troupe 169
German Jewish Troupe 164, 168, 169, 170, 172
German language 2, 30, 117, 166–7
German Operetta Artists 168
German Theatre Troupe 170
German Troupe of Kompaneyets 169
Gerro, Henry 135
Gimpl, Yankev-Ber 210, 215
Glass, Montague, *Potash and Perlmutter* 72 n.
Glickman, Renye 135
Glik, Dos (by Stanisław Przybyszewski) 67 n.
Goethe, Johann Wolfgang von:
    Faust 48, 58
    Goetz von Berlichingen 47, 58
    'Shakespeare ad Infinitum' 52
Goldberg, Yidl 128 n.
Goldenburg, Samuel 135
Goldene keyt, Di (by Yitskhok Leyb Peretz) 52, 57, 59, 117
Goldener shlisl, Der (by Joseph Markovitsh) 124
Goldfaden, Avrom:
    adaptations of plays 24, 85–6, 95–103, 143–9, 151–4
    Akeydes yitskhok (The Sacrifice of Isaac) 140, 141, 142–3
    autobiography 78–9
    ban stories 160, 161
    Bar kokhba 20, 24, 56, 58, 64, 72 n., 81, 87, 89–90, 92, 95, 100–4, 140, 141, 142, 151–3, 169, 170, 189, 193
    Ben ami 56, 140
    Bobe mitn eynikl, Di (The Grandmother and her Granddaughter) 83, 169
    company 5, 10, 79, 89, 162
    Cracow performances 19, 139, 140–4, 147–54
    Doktor almosado; oder, Di yidn in palermo (Doctor Almosado; or, The Jews in Palermo) 83, 160, 168
    Dovid bemilkhome (David at War) 81
    influence 4–5, 11, 78, 203, 204–8, 211
    Jewish role models 87, 89–90, 93–5, 99, 102–3
    Kaprizne tokhter, Di; oder, Kaptsnzon et hungerman (The Capricious Daughter; or, Pauperson and Hungerman) 69, 82–3, 140, 168, 169
    Kenig akhashveyresh (King Ahasuerus) 140, 169, 189, 193

Goldfaden, Avrom (*cont.*):
  Kishefmakherin, Di (The Sorceress) 20,
    24, 49, 52, 69, 77, 79–86, 87, 95, 143,
    147–9, 168, 189; pls. 2, 10, 12
  Meshiekhs tsaytn (The Messianic Age)
    140, 189, 196
  music 83, 90–1, 97, 127, 134, 144, 151
  productions 84–5, 95, 214–15
  Shmendrik 87, 91, 206
  Shulamis 20, 24, 48–9, 63–4, 69, 72 n., 83,
    87, 89, 92–100, 103–4, 109, 139, 140,
    141, 142, 150–1, 153–4, 168, 169, 189, 193;
    pl. 15
  studies of 14–15, 78
  Tsente gebot, Dos; oder, Loy sakhmoyd (The
    Tenth Commandment) 140, 143, 189,
    193
  Tsvey kuni leml, Di (The Two Kuni Lemls)
    81, 83, 141, 142, 143–6, 168, 169, 189, 195,
    206
  works 81, 82–3, 87
Goldfaden, Naftule 5
Goldmark, Carl, *Die Königin von Saba* 92
Goldshteyn, Rebecca 121 n., 125–7, 137
Goltsman, Yankl 169
Gordin, Jacob:
  attitude to audiences 207–8
  Brider lurye, Di (The Luria Brothers) 72 n.
  career 53, 161, 207
  criticisms of 67, 202 n., 207, 211
  Fremder, Der (The Stranger) 66 n.,
    113
  Got, mentsh, un tayvl (God, Man, and
    Devil) 49, 50, 51, 178 n., 189, 194, 195,
    196; pl. 7
  influence 201, 207, 209–10
  Kreutzer Sonata 189, 193, 194, 196, 210
  Mirele efros 66 n., 124, 175, 189, 193, 195,
    197
  Sappho 54, 59
  Shkhite, Di (The Slaughter) 65, 66 n.
  Sibirye (Siberia) 52
  studies of 15
  translations and adaptations 202–3
  Vienna performances 112
  Yidisher kenig lir, Der (The Jewish King
    Lear) 66 n., 189, 193, 208
Gorin, Bernard 12, 78, 90, 211–12
GOSET (Moscow State Yiddish Theatre):
  origins 75
  political status 95, 103–4
  productions 80, 84, 95
  studies of 16, 17
  Vienna performances 116

Got fun nekome (by Sholem Asch) 19, 52, 66,
    71, 113, 175–85, 188, 196, 210
  banned by Lord Chamberlain's Office
    175, 178–85
Got, mentsh, un tayvl (by Jacob Gordin) 49,
    50, 51, 178 n., 189, 194, 195, 196; pl. 7
  adapted by Maurice Schwartz as *God,
    Man, and Devil* 178 n.
Gottsched, Johann Christoph 205
goylem (*golem*) 9
Goylem, Der (by H. Leivick) 52, 54, 57, 58,
    59, 190, 196; pl. 11
Grand Palais, Commercial Road 125, 126,
    176, 185
Granovsky, Alexander:
  adaptations 56, 58, 84–5, 95, 96, 143
  Jewish Theatrical Society 73, 74
  Moscow State Yiddish Theatre 75, 116
  Yiddish Chamber Theatre 61, 75
Grazhdanin (by Joseph Markovitsh) 124
Grefin pototski (by Joseph Markovitsh) 124
Gresser, General P. A. 160
Grillparzer, Franz, *Medea* 66 n.
Grine felder (by Peretz Hischbein) 52, 116,
    176, 189, 195
Gusinov, S. M. 71
Gutzkow, Karl, *Uriel acosta* 66, 169, 189, 193
Gwatkin, Sir Norman 179 n., 180

H

Habimah 116
Haiden, Gisa 115
Halkin, Shmuel:
  adaptation of *Bar Kokhba* 20, 24, 87,
    100–1, 103–4
  adaptation of *Shulamis* 20, 24, 87,
    96–100, 103–4
Hallo! Hallo! Hier Radio Jerusalem (by
    Abish Meisels) 115–16
Halpern, Dina 124, 149, 175
Hapgood, Hutchins 16, 53, 55
Harendorf, Shmuel Yankev, *Kenig fun
    lampedusa, Der* (The King of
    Lampedusa) 175, 189, 196
Harkavy, Alexander 11, 209
Haskalah (Jewish Enlightenment) 2–3, 5,
    47, 79, 84, 90, 202
  see also Enlightenment
Hebrew language 34, 50–1, 73, 79, 116, 164
Hellin, David 3–4
Henriques, Basil 180–2, 183
Henry, Barbara 18, 24
Herbst, Leon 141
Herder, Johann Gottfried 51, 56

Herman, David 58
Hertsele meyukhes (by Moshe Rikhter) 69
Herzl, Theodor 103, 111
Hill, Brad Sabin 185
Hirschbein, Peretz:
  autobiography 13
  Grine felder (Green Fields) 52, 116, 176,
    189, 195
  Miryam (Miriam) 52
  performances 69
  Puste kretshme, Di (The Idle Inn) 49, 189,
    195
  Tkies-kaf (The Vow) 113
  Tsvishn tog un nakht (Between Day and
    Night) 52
Hirsh lekert (by H. Leivick) 58
Hirshhoyt, Yekhiel 25
Houdini, Harry 22
Howe, Irving 16, 215
Hugo, Victor:
  on copying 52
  Cromwell 48
  Hernani 55, 58
  Kean's influence 53
  on Romanticism 49, 54
  on Shakespeare 51
Hurwitz, Moyshe:
  company 5, 109
  criticisms of work 206, 211
  Dibick, Der (The Dybbuk) 109
  New York performances 79
  Vienna performances 112

I

Ibsen, Henrik 209
Idishe bine, Di (The Yiddish Stage) 10–11,
  203
Idishe drama, Dos (by Dovid Pinski) 211
Ignatiev, N. P. 161
Importirte dinst, Di; oder, Domestik servis (by
  Joseph Markovitsh) 124
In di keytn fun libe (by Joseph Markovitsh)
  124
In vald (by Joseph Markovitsh) 124
internet 22–3
Iris, Shmuel 116
Isaac sheftl (by Dovid Pinski) 54, 113
Israelitische Kultusgemeinde 109, 116
Itsik the Fiddler 36
Ivanov, Vladislav 74

J

Jakubowicz, Beno 142
Jewish Drama Circle, St Petersburg 69

Jewish Drama Troupe 71 n.
Jewish Heritage Society 61 n.
Jewish Literary-Dramatic Troupe 70
Jewish Theatrical Society, Petrograd 73, 74,
  75
Jewish Theatrical Troupe 169
Johannesburg 5
Jüdaly mit dem Wandersack (by S. Larescu)
  111
Jüdische Bühne 111, 112, 114, 115, 117; pl. 14
Jüdische Heldin, Die (by Abish Meisels) 112
Jüdische Kammerspiele 113
Jüdische Künstlerspiele 115–17; pl. 14
Jüdisches Kulturtheater 117
Jüdisches Künstlerkabarett 114, 115
Juive, La (by Eugène Scribe) 169

K

Kacyzne, Alter, *Der dukus* (The Duke) 57
Kafka, Franz 86 n., 175, 185
Kaganovich, Lazar 95, 100
Kaiser, Jenny 122
Kalich, Jacob 116
Kalish, Berta 215 n.
Kalman, Emerich, *Csárdásfürstin* (The
  Gypsy Princess) 112, 190, 193, 196
Kaminska, Esther-Rokhl 15, 68–9
Kaminsky, Avrom:
  company 64, 66, 67, 168
  St Petersburg performances 64, 66, 67
  Yidishe aktyorn af der rayze (Yiddish
    Actors on the Road) 67 n.
Kanfer, Mojżesz 139, 143, 144, 146
Kaniewska, Vera 115
Kapper, Sigfried 36
*Kaprizne tokhter, Di; oder, Kaptsnzon et
  hungerman* (by Avrom Goldfaden) 69,
  82–3, 140, 168, 169
Kats, Bella 151
Katz, Moyshe 210
Kazansky, Mikhail 168
Kean (by Shomer) 187
Kean, Edmund 53, 55
Kenig akhashveyresh (by Avrom Goldfaden)
  140, 169, 189, 193
Kenig far a nakht (by Shomer) 186–7, 192,
  193
Kenig fun lampedusa, Der (by Shmuel
  Yankev Harendorf) 175, 189, 196
Kessler, David 15
Kessler, Joseph pl. 16
Khantshe in amerike (by Nokhem Rakov)
  72
Khaveyrim (by Joseph Markovitsh) 124

Kishefmakherin, Di (by Avrom Goldfaden) 20, 24, 49, 52, 69, 77, 79–86, 87, 95, 143, 147–9, 168, 189; pls. 2, 10, 12
  adapted by Itsik Manger 86, 147, 148–9
  adapted by Yankev Rotboym 147, 149
Kivshenko, Elizaveta Vasilevna 167
Kleinman, Fryc 151, 153
Kleist, Heinrich von 58
Klier, John 18, 21, 23
Kobrin, Leon:
  autobiography 13
  Riversayd drayv (Riverside Drive) 51
  style 210
  Yankl boyle 50
Kohn, Henekh 149
Kol Nidre im Galuth (by Abish Meisels) 116
Kompaneyets, Avrom 141–2
Konvenshon (by Joseph Markovitsh) 124
Koralova, Miriam 142
Kornblith, Zishe 7–8
Kosiński, Jan 148
Kozlov, A. A. 165
Krelman, Isaac 135
Kreutzer Sonata (by Jacob Gordin) 189, 193, 194, 196, 210
Kugel, Alexander 64, 68, 73 n.
Kuni Leml, role of 142
Kval, Der 114

L
Lacosegliaz, Alfredo 85
language 34, 50–1, 59, 65 n., 159
Larescu, S., *Jüdaly mit dem Wandersack* (Jüdaly and his Travelling Bag) 111
Lateiner, Joseph:
  Blimele 123, 190, 193
  company 5
  Dovids fidele (David's Violin) 170
  influence 5, 64, 79, 206, 211
  Seyder nakht, Di (The Seder Night) pl. 16
  Vienna performances 112
Laykhtzin und fremelay (by Aaron Halle Wolfssohn) 3
Lazarus, Harris M. 179–81, 182, 183
le Goff, Jacques 35
Leivick, H.:
  Goylem, Der (The Golem) 52, 54, 57, 58, 59, 190, 196; pl. 11
  Hirsh lekert 58
  Shmates (Rags) 52, 59, 190, 195
  Shop 49
Leksikon far der nayer yidisher literatur 21

Lerner, Khane 142
Lessing, Gotthold Ephraim, *Nathan the Wise* 66
Levdiev, Aaron 36
Levidov, Lev 73
Levine, Lawrence 8
Libgold, Leon 142
Libgold, Zalmen 141, 142
Lifshits, Dovid 128 n.
Lifson, David 12, 215
lighting 149
Limburg, Berman, *Mekhires yoysef* (The Selling of Joseph) 37
liminal phenomena 33
Liptzin, Sol 177
literacy 35
Litman, Pepi 110
Little Theatre movement 213
Litvakov, Moyshe 17, 90
Łódź 141
London:
  Adler Street Folk House 185
  Grand Palais 125, 126, 176, 185
  Lord Chamberlain's Office 21–2, 175, 177–85, 186–7
  Markovitsh's career 122–7
  Missionary Society 161
  Museum of the Jewish East End 137
  Pavilion Theatre 119, 120, 123, 124, 125, 178 n.
  Princes Street Club 122
  Standard Theatre 123, 186
  Yiddish theatre 5, 19, 23, 175
London Hebrew Operatic and Dramatic Company 186, 187
London Yiddish Theatre 184, 185
Lord Chamberlain's Office:
  applications for licences to perform Yiddish plays 21–2, 177–8, 188–92 (Table 10.1)
  banning of *Got fun nekome* 175, 178–85
  licences to perform Yiddish plays 21–2, 185–7, 193–7 (Table 10.2)
Loshn un lebn (by Avrom-Nokhem Shtentsl) 175, 184, 185
Lovers of the Dramatic Arts of the *Shtetl* of Dunaevich 169
Lviv (Lemberg, Lwów) 139, 150, 151, 152, 215

M
Mahler, Gustav 19
Maksimovich (governor-general of Warsaw) 171, 172

Manger, Itsik:
  adaptation of *Di kishefmakherin* 86, 147, 148–9
  on *purimshpil* 35
Mapu, Abraham 89
Markov, Mark 135, 184
Markov, N. 64
Markovitsh, Joseph:
  Apikoyres, Der (The Heretic) 124
  'Berke goylem' ('Berke the Fool') 131–2
  Brodyaga, Der (The Vagabond) 124
  East end vest (East End West [End]) 124
  Farshidene glikn (Assorted Luck) 124; pl. 6
  Gembler, Der (The Gambler) 124
  Goldener shlisl, Der (The Golden Key) 124
  Grazhdanin (Citizen) 124
  Grefin pototski (Countess Pototski) 124
  Importirte dinst, Di; oder, Domestik servis (The Imported Servant; or, Domestic Service) 124
  In di keytn fun libe (In the Chains of Love) 124
  In vald (In the Forest) 124
  Khaveyrim (Comrades) 124
  'Kol Nidre' 128–30, 134
  Konvenshon (Convention) 124
  'Leybke' 133, 134
  life 120–7
  melo-deklamatsyes 19, 120, 127–37
  Mendl beylis (Mendel Beilis) 124, 190, 195
  Midber, Der (The Desert) 124
  Milyon far a yidn, A (A Million for a Jew) 124
  'Opgegebn broyt' ('Comeuppance') 133–4
  Pariz baynakht (Paris at Night) 124, 190, 195
  Revolutsyoner, Der (The Revolutionary) 124
  Selima 124
  Serkele di grefin (Sarah the Countess) 124
  Sheyne miryam, Di (Beautiful Miriam) 124
  'Shma yisroel' ('Hear, O Israel') 132–3, 134
  'Shtot meshugener, Der' ('The Village Idiot') 133
  'Tsu der khupe' ('Under the Wedding Canopy') 130–1
  Vaybershe melukhe, Di (The Women's Realm) 124
  works 24, 119–20, 124

Yisroel lebt un lakht (Israel Lives and Laughs) 124, 190, 196
Zapasner zoldat, Der (The Reserve Soldier) 124
Masoes binyomim hashlishi (by Sholem Yankev Abramovitsh) 52
Maximilian, Friedrich 47
Mazl-tov (by Sholem Aleykhem) 70
Mazower, David 19
Meisel, Nakhman 149
Meisels, Abish pl. 18
  Auf nach Tel Aviv (Let's Go to Tel Aviv) 115, 116
  Chassene im Städtel (A Wedding in the Shtetl) 116
  Fun sekhistov biz amerike (From Sechistow to America) 114–15
  Hallo! Hallo! Hier Radio Jerusalem (Hello! Hello! This is Radio Jerusalem) 115–16
  Jüdische Heldin, Die (The Jewish Heroine) 112
  Kol Nidre im Galuth (Kol Nidre in the Diaspora) 116
  New Yiddish Theatre 185
  Ohne Zertifikat nach Palästina (To Palestine without a Certificate) 115
  response to antisemitism 23
  Traum des Reservisten, Der (The Dream of a Reserve Officer) 112
  Wiener Rebbyzin, Die (The Viennese Rabbi's Wife) 115
Meisels, Clara 115
Mekhires yoysef (by Berman Limburg) 37
Melnikov, S. A. 69, 71, 72 n.
melo-deklamatsyes 19, 120, 127–37
melodrama 55, 90–2, 94
Meltser, Adolf 141, 142
Mendelssohn, Moses 2
Mendl beylis (by Joseph Markovitsh) 124, 190, 195
Mentshn (by Sholem Aleykhem) 70, 71
Meshiekhs tsaytn (by Avrom Goldfaden) 140, 189, 196
Meshiekhs tsaytn (by Sholem Asch) 57
messiah 57
Mestel, Jacob 78, 114, 210, 215
Meyer, Khayim 36
Midber, Der (by Joseph Markovitsh) 124
Mikhoels, Shloyme 15
Milyon far a yidn, A (by Joseph Markovitsh) 124
Minchovski, Pinchas 121
Minikes, Khonen 10–11, 203

Mirele efros (by Jacob Gordin) 66 n., 124,
   175, 189, 193, 195, 197
Miryam (by Peretz Hirschbein) 52
Mishurat, Meyer 210, 215
Mogilev, *purimshpil* 39
Mogulesco, Sigmund 15, 83, 142
Morevski, Avrom 13, 149
Moscow, Yiddish theatre 5, 16, 89, 144
   see also GOSET
Moscow Art Theatre 68
Moscow Jewish Dramatic and Opera
   Troupe 168
Moskovitsh, Maurice 124
Moyne, Lord 176
Mukdoyni, A. (Alexander Kapel) 90
Muni, Paul 122 n.
music:
   in Goldfaden's work 83, 90–1, 97, 144, 151
   in Markovitsh's work 24, 120
   in Yiddish drama 50, 55–6
Myer, Morris 182

N

Nahshon, Edna 16
Natan, Noemi 113
Natan, Simkhe 113, 115, 116, 139
nationalism 56–8, 95
Naumann, Hans 35
Nazism 116, 117, 150
New Yiddish Theatre (Nay Idish Teater)
   175, 176, 180, 184–5
New York:
   censorship 183–4
   Yiddish theatre 5, 11, 12, 16, 144, 201
newspapers:
   American 78, 201–2
   antisemitic 113, 161
   Jewish 160
   Russian 63, 160, 162, 165, 207
   St Petersburg 70
   Yiddish 14, 15 n., 78, 182
   Zionist 113
Neyman, Yekhezkel-Moyshe 149
Nicholas II, Tsar 63, 146
Niger, Shmuel 182–3
Nokhn tsholnt (by M. M. Yakhdov) 70

O

Obershneder (director) 162
Odessa:
   censorship 162–4
   performances 10, 162–3, 165
Ohne Zertifikat nach Palästina (by Abish
   Meisels) 115

Oppenheim, Rabbi David 31
Orleska, Miriam pl. 8
Orzhevsky, P. A. 166
Ostjuden 19, 108, 113, 117
Ostrovsky, Alexander, *The Storm* 55
Oyerbakh, Rokhl 149
Oyslender, Nokhem 12, 18, 81, 90
Oytser, Der (by Dovid Pinski) 49

P

Pale of Settlement:
   Beilis case 71
   censorship 62 n.
   Jewish way of life 82
   refugees from 72
   setting for drama 66–7
   Yiddish theatre 5, 64, 167, 171
Palestine 70 n., 111, 176
Pariz baynakht (by Joseph Markovitsh) 124,
   190, 195
Pastor, Sevilla 116
Pavilion Theatre 119, 120, 123, 124, 125
Peretz, Yitskhok Leyb:
   Baynakht afn altn mark (A Night in the
     Old Marketplace) 49, 55, 56, 58, 116;
     pl. 13
   Goldene keyt, Di (The Golden Chain) 52,
     57, 59, 117
   Shvester (Sisters) 52
   studies of 15
   on Yiddish theatre 206 n.
Perle, Yehoshua 149
Perlmuter, Sholem 78
Peterman, Irenee 121 n., 125
Petrograd, *see* St Petersburg
Philadelphia 5, 17
Picon, Molly 13, 116
Picon-Vallin, Béatrice 17, 80, 95
Pineles, Samuel 111
Pinski, Dovid:
   Eybiker yid, Der (The Eternal Jew) 57
   Familye tsvi, Di (*Der letster yid*) (The Tsvi
     Family (The Last Jew)) 57
   Idishe drama, Dos (Yiddish Drama) 211
   Isaac sheftl 54, 113
   Oytser, Der (The Treasure) 49
   performances 69, 211
   Shtumer meshiekh, Der (The Mute
     Messiah) 57
   Yankl der shmid (Yankl the Blacksmith)
     66 n., 175, 191, 194, 195, 197, 210
   Yeder mit zayn got (To Each his Own
     God) 57
Pleve, V. K. 163, 165 n.

Podzamcze, Schulim 111–12
pogroms 5, 89, 165, 173
Poland 18–19, 159
 see also Cracow; Lviv; Warsaw
police 166, 171, 173–4
Polish Jewish Theatre Company 140
Polish language 147, 159
Polnischen singers 110
Postlewait, Thomas 13
Potash and Perlmutter (by Montague Glass)
 72 n.
Prager, Leonard 19, 21, 136
Prager, Regina 215 n.
Prague 31, 36
prayers 50
Preiss, Michael 113
Priluker, Ya. M. 161–2, 164 n.
Prilutskaya (dramatist) 67 n.
Prizament, Moyshe 142
Prizament, Salo (Shloyme) 115, 127, 134,
 142, 151
Prizhansky, N. 161
Priziv, Der (by Sholem Yankev
 Abramovitsh) 40
Professor Brenner (by Aaron Tseytlin) 56–7
Przybyszewski, Stanisław, *Dos glik* (Luck;
 Polish: *Dla szczescia*) 67 n.
publishing, Yiddish 160, 162 n.
 see also newspapers
Pulver, Lev 97
puns 30–1
puppet theatre 19 n., 165
purimshpiln (Purim plays) pl. 1
 anachronisms 37–8
 influence 90, 204, 206
 language 29–32
 liminoid manifestation 33–4
 oral transmission 36–7
 origins 24
 performance tradition 2
 religious rules 32, 79
 subversive 23, 38–43, 59
 texts 7, 23, 29, 32, 36
 theatrical genre 29, 32–3, 34
Puste kretshme, Di (by Peretz Hischbein) 49,
 189, 195

R
Rabinovich, I. 72
Rabinovich, O. A. 164
Rakov, Nokhem:
 career 124
 Khantshe in amerike (Khantshe in
 America) 72

Talmid khokhem (The Learned Scholar)
 66 n., 67
Rapoport, N. D. 161, 162
Ravitsh, Melekh 21
Razvod (by Temorano) 169
Rebbe Yozelman (by Avrom Goldfaden) 169
rebellion 58–9
Reinhardt, Max 113, 183, 210
Reissmann, Jonah 112, 114
reviews:
 Cracow 146, 149, 154
 New York 17
 St Petersburg 64–6, 67–8
 Vienna 108–9
 Warsaw 149
 Yiddish periodicals 14
Revolutsyoner, Der (by Joseph Markovitsh)
 124
Reyzen, Zalmen 21
Rikhter, Moshe:
 Hertsele meyukhes (Hertsele the Aristocrat)
 69
 Sholem bayis (Domestic Harmony) 67 n.
Rimsky-Korsakoff, Nikolai, *Sadko* 97
Riversayd drayv (by Leon Kobrin) 51
Rivesman, Mark Semyonovich:
 company 69–70
 Ershte patsyentn, Di (The First Patients)
 70
 on Goldfaden 84–5
 Schastlivchik (The Lucky Man) 69, 70
Romania 18, 19 n.
Romanian Opera House 205
Rosenbaum, A. B. 167
Rosenblum, Nosn 169
Rotboym, Yankev:
 adaptation of *Di kishefmakherin* 147, 149
 A goldfaden kholem (A Goldfaden Dream)
 191, 197, pl. 16
Roth, Joseph 86 n.
Rousseau, Jean-Jacques 56
Rovner, Zaydl (Yankev Shmuel
 Morogowski) 121
Rozhansky, Shmuel 90
Rubin, Menakhem 144
Rumshinsky, Joseph 13
Russia:
 ban on performance of Yiddish plays
 160–2, 173–4
 Chief Office of Press Affairs (GUpDP)
 162–3, 167, 171–2, 174
 failure of 1883 ban 166–7, 170–3
 fairground entertainment 205
 February Revolution 74

Russia (*cont.*):
  language restrictions 159
  Ministry of Internal Affairs (MVD) 162,
    165, 167, 170, 172, 173
  October Revolution 74
  origins of 1883 ban 162–6
  performances of Yiddish theatre groups
    under 1883 ban 21, 168–70 (Table 9.1)
  Yiddish theatre 5, 17–18, 61–3, 74–5
  see also Moscow; St Petersburg; Soviet
    Union
Russian language 71
Russian Opera and Operetta Company 121
Russian Theatrical Society 74 n.
Russotto, H. A. 83

S
St Petersburg (Petrograd):
  audiences 64, 65–6, 69, 166 n.
  ban on Yiddish theatre 62, 160
  critics 64–6, 68, 72
  Ekaterinsky Theatre 71 n.
  Jewish Drama Circle 69–70
  Jewish societies 70–1, 73, 84
  Jewish Theatrical Society 73–4, 75
  Liteinyi Theatre 71 n.
  Nemetti Theatre 63
  Palm Theatre 69
  reviews of Yiddish theatre 64–6, 67–8
  Saburov Theatre 71 n., 72 n.
  Yiddish productions 62–7, 71–3
  Yiddish touring companies 62, 63–5, 67,
    89, 165–6, 167, 171
Salten, Felix 110
Samberg, Isaac 135
Sandrow, Nahma:
  on Goldfaden 82, 90
  on Gordin 66
  on GOSET 95
  on Romantic drama 20, 24
  on *shund* 8, 9
  works 12, 16
Sappho (by Jacob Gordin) 54, 59
Satz, Ludwig 124; pl. 6
scenery:
  Cracow productions 141, 148–9, 151, 153
  Goldfaden's work 78
  Kleinman's designs 151, 153
  Kosiński's designs 148–9
  Yiddish troupes 210
Schaffer, W. 186
Schastlivchik (by Mark Semyonovich
  Rivesman) 69, 70
Schein, Joseph 17

Schiller, Friedrich:
  Robbers, The 47, 55
  on theatre 52, 58
  Wilhelm Tell 56
Schlegel brothers 51
Schneider, David 19
Schnitzler, Arthur 19, 107, 108
Scholem, Gershom 176
Schudt, Johann 32, 36
Schwartz, Maurice pls. 7, 10
  adaptation of *God, Man, and Devil* 178 n.
  career 15
  productions 116, 143, 214–15
Scribe, Eugène, *Zhidovka* 169
Secunda, Sholem 22
Segalovitch, Clara 147
Seidman, Aaron 11 n.
Seiger, Marvin 16
Selima (by Joseph Markovitsh) 124
Sendung Semaels, Die (by Arnold Zweig) 115
Serkele di grefin (by Joseph Markovitsh) 124
sets, *see* scenery
Seyder nakht, Di (by Joseph Lateiner) pl. 16
Sforim, Mendele Moykher, *see* Abramovitsh,
  Sholem Yankev
Shabes koydesh (by Sigmund Feinman) 123
Shakespeare, William:
  All's Well That Ends Well 67 n.
  Hamlet 51
  King Lear 51
  language 50
  Merchant of Venice 185
  Richard III 101, 153
  Romanticism 51, 52, 56
  Yiddish productions 16
Shatzky, Jacob 14
Shaykevitsh, N. K. 168
Shaykevitsh, Nokhem Meyer, *see* Shomer
Shayn, Yosef 96
Shaynin (composer) 144
Shebuev, Nikolai 65
Sheyne miryam, Di (by Joseph Markovitsh)
  124
Shiper, Yitskhok 151 n.
Shkhite, Di (by Jacob Gordin) 65, 66 n.
Shmates (by H. Leivick) 52, 59, 190, 195
Shmendrik (by Avrom Goldfaden) 87, 91,
  206
Shmeruk, Khone 2 n., 172 n.
Sholem Aleykhem (Sholem Rabinovitsh):
  criticisms of 202 n.
  Mazl-tov (Congratulations) 70
  Mentshn (People) 70, 71
  on Shomer 187

Shver tsu zayn a yid (Hard to be a Jew) 50,
  57, 116, 192, 195, 196
status 96
Tevye der milkhiker (Tevye the Dairyman)
  192, 195, 197; pl. 17
Tsezeyt un tseshpreyt (Scattered and
  Dispersed) 57, 67 n., 72 n., 172 n.
Sholem bayis (by Moshe Rikhter) 67 n.
Shomer (Nokhem Meyer Shaykevitsh):
  Kean 187
  Kenig far a nakht (King for a Night)
    186–7, 192, 193
  novels 187
Shop (by H. Leivick) 49
Shoyshpiler, Isaac, *Moses* 4
Shriftzetser, Leyb 143
Shtentsl, Avrom-Nokhem:
  Loshn un lebn 175, 184, 185
  on Yiddish theatre 184–5
shtetls 40, 74, 120–1, 128–33, 169
Shtumer, Der (by A. Vayter) 113
Shtumer meshiekh, Der (by Dovid Pinski) 57
Shulamis (by Avrom Goldfaden) 20, 24,
  48–9, 63–4, 69, 72 n., 83, 87, 89,
  92–100, 103–4, 109, 139, 140, 141, 142,
  150–1, 153–4, 168, 169, 189, 193; pl. 15
  adapted by Shmuel Halkin 20, 24, 87,
  96–100, 103–4
Shulman, Elazar 29
shund 7–9, 201, 206, 209, 212, 214, 216;
  pl. 4
Shver tsu zayn a yid (by Sholem Aleykhem)
  50, 57, 116, 192, 195, 196
Shvester (by Yitskhok Leyb Peretz) 52
Sibirye (by Jacob Gordin) 52
Siegler, Maurice 111
Siegler–Pastor troupe 111, 115, 116
Sigall, Ben-Zion 115
Singer, I. J., *Yoshe kalb* 52, 192, 196
Slushai, izrail! (by Osip Dimov) 66, 113, 117
Smith, David 122
Society of Operetta Artists 168
Sokalsky, *Mazeppa* 91
songs 22, 50, 127–8
Sonnenfels, Joseph von 205
Sorokin, Aaron 128 n.
South America 17
Soviet Union 95–6, 154
  see also Russia
Spivakovsky, Yakov 63, 169, 170, 171
Stambulka, *Zhertvoprinoshenie Isaaka* (The
  Sacrifice of Isaac) 169
Standard Theatre 123, 186
Stanislavsky, Konstantin 210

State Yiddish Theatres 74–5
Stein, Alexander 116, pl. 8
Stewart, Potter 7
Street, G. S. 178
Streng, Max 114, 115
Strindberg, August, *The Father* 115
Swift, E. Anthony 163 n.
Szwejlich, Michal pl. 19

T
Talmid khokhem (by Nokhem Rakov) 66 n.,
  67
Tandler, Julius 107
Tantsman (director) 168
Temorano, *Razvod* (Divorce) 169
Tevye der milkhiker (by Sholem Aleykhem)
  192, 195, 197; pl. 17
Theatre Mirror 185
Thomashefsky, Bessie 13, 72
Thomashefsky, Boris:
  Amerikanerin, Di (The American Girl) 72
  autobiography 11, 13
  career 53, 121 n.
Tkies-kaf (by Peretz Hirshbein) 113
Toller, Ernst, *Hinkemann* 115, 116
Tolpud (director) 169
Tolstoy, D. A. 163–4, 166, 167
translations 2, 30, 71, 71 n., 117, 210
Traum des Reservisten, Der (by Abish
  Meisels) 112
Tretsek, L. O. 161
Treytler, Khayim-Binyomin (Charles)
  109–10, 140
Treytler, Malvina 140
Trupe tanentsap (by Mikhl Weichert) 145, 146
Tselniker, Meyer 115, 135, 175, 184
Tsente gebot, Dos; oder, Loy sakhmoyd (by
  Avrom Goldfaden) 140, 143, 189, 193
Tseytlin, Aaron:
  Professor Brenner 56–7
  Yankev frank (Jacob Frank) 57
Tsezeyt un tseshpreyt (by Sholem Aleykhem)
  57, 67 n., 72 n., 172 n.
Tsukerman, Lazar 167
Tsvey kuni leml, Di (by Avrom Goldfaden)
  81, 83, 141, 142, 143–6, 168, 169, 189, 195,
  206
Tsvishn tog un nakht (by Peretz Hischbein)
  52
Turkow, Jonas 13
Turkow, Zygmunt 13, 24, 139, 143, 150–4;
  pl. 14
Turner, Victor 33
Tzhizhik, Moyshe 121 n.

U

Ukraine 18, 89, 159
United States of America 5, 17, 154
    see also Chicago; Detroit; New York;
        Philadelphia
Urich, Sammy 141
Uriel acosta (by Karl Gutzkow) 66, 169, 189,
    193

V

Vakhnyanin, *Kupalo* (Pentecost) 91
Van Gennep, Arnold 33, 38
Vasilevsky, L. 69
Vasserman, Iakov 169
vaudeville, Yiddish 19 n.
Vaybershe melukhe, Di (by Joseph
    Markovitsh) 124
Vaysfeld, M. O. 169
Vayter, A., *Shtumer, Der* (The Mute) 113
Vayznfroynd, Fayvl and Saltshe 122 n.
Veidlinger, Jeffrey 16, 17
Velednitsky, A. 90
Verbl, Eiliyohu 89
Verdi, Giuseppe, *Nabucco* 92
Vienna:
    Anschluss 117
    audiences 109, 116–17
    critics 23, 113
    folk theatre 205
    Freie Jüdische Volksbühne 112–14, 116;
        pl. 9
    Israelitische Kultusgemeinde 109, 116
    Jewish community 108
    Jüdische Bühne 111, 112, 114, 115, 117;
        pl. 14
    Jüdische Kammerspiele 113
    Jüdische Künstlerspiele 115–17; pl. 14
    Jüdisches Kulturtheater 117
    Jüdisches Künstlerkabarett 114, 115
    reviews 108–9
    Theater in der Josefstadt 113, 116
    Yiddish theatre 19, 107–11, 117
Vilna Folks-teater 142
Vilna Troupe 58, 115, 116, 183 n.; pls. 8, 13
Vilner balebesl, Der (by Mark Arnshteyn)
    67 n.
Viner, Meir 12

W

Wagner, Richard 50
Warnke, Nina 7, 17, 24
Warsaw:
    censorship 164, 166
    publishing 82–3

Yiddish performances 3–4, 5, 145, 147,
    154, 164, 172
Warsaw German Dramatic-Operetta Troupe
    169
Warsaw Yiddish Arts Theatre (VYKT) 143,
    150, 151
weddings 1–2, 79, 204, 206
Weichert, Mikhl 13, 145–7
    Trupe tanentsap (The Tanentsap Troupe)
    145, 146
Weintraub-Graf, Lea 113, 115
Weissenberg, Samuel 38, 41
Wiener Rebbyzin, Die (by Abish Meisels)
    115
Wilson, John Dover 176
Witler, Ben-Zion 113, 115, 135
Wolfssohn, Aaron Halle, *Laykhtzin und
    fremelay* (Silliness and Sanctimony) 3
Wolitz, Seth 20, 24
Woods, Alan 216

Y

Yablokoff, Herman 13
Yakhdov, M. M., *Nokhn tsholnt* (After the
    Sabbath Meal) 70
Yakob, Moses 140–1
Yankev frank (by Aaron Tseytlin) 57
Yankl boyle (by Leon Kobrin) 50
Yankl der shmid (by Dovid Pinski) 66 n.,
    175, 191, 194, 195, 197, 210
Yanovsky, Shoel-Yosef 213
Yeder mit zayn got (by Dovid Pinski) 57
Yiddish Art Theatre, New York 12, 15, 116
Yiddish Chamber Theatre 61, 75
Yiddish language:
    attitudes towards 109, 116–17
    Goldfaden's career 79
    mixture of languages in Yiddish drama
        50–1
    Purim plays 34
    status 59
    varieties of 110
Yidishe aktyorn af der rayze (by Avrom
    Kaminsky) 67 n.
Yidisher kenig lir, Der (by Jacob Gordin) 66
    n., 189, 193, 208
'Yinglish' 51
Yisroel lebt un lakht (by Joseph Markovitsh)
    124, 190, 196
Yoshke muzikant (*Der zinger fun zayn troyer*)
    (by Osip Dimov) 116
Young, Boaz 13
Young, Clara 72–3; pl. 3
Yung Teater 145

Yushkevich, Semyon 66
Yuvelir, Kalmen 140

Z
Zapasner zoldat, Der (by Joseph Markovitsh)
124
Zaporozhets za Dunayem (by Artomovsky)
91
Zayderman, Dovid 135
Zeifert, Moyshe 11
Zeldovich, Mr 68–9
Zeyderman, Dovid 142
Zhertvoprinoshenie Isaaka (by Stambulka)
169
Zhitomirsky (director) 170, 172

Zionism:
Goldfaden's position 79, 81, 103, 160 n.
Jüdaly mit dem Wandersack 111
newspaper 113
Vienna productions 115
Zweig, Arnold, *Die Sendung Semaels*
(Semaels's Mission) 115
Zylbercweig, Zalmen:
acting 124
on Goldfaden 78, 90
Leksikon fun yidishn teater 6, 20–1, 128,
202, 215
on role of Kuni Leml 142 n.

Printed and bound by CPI Group (UK) Ltd, Croydon, CR0 4YY

09/06/2025

14685817-0003